PILGRIMAGE

PILGRI

PILGRIMAGE

A TRAVELLER'S GUIDE TO AUSTRALIA'S BATTLEFIELDS

GARRIE HUTCHINSON

Published by Black Inc.,
an imprint of Schwartz Publishing Pty Ltd

Level 5, 289 Flinders Lane
Melbourne Victoria 3000 Australia
email: enquiries@blackincbooks.com
http://www.blackincbooks.com

© Garrie Hutchinson 2006.
Reprinted 2006.

'Beach Burial' and 'An Inscription for Dog River' by Kenneth Slessor from his book *Selected Poems* (Angus & Robertson, 1957), reproduced with permission of HarperCollins Publishers, Australia.

Photographs on pages 25, 233, 255, 313, 360 with permission of the Australian War Memorial.

Every effort has been made to contact the copyright holders of material in this book. However, where an omission has occurred, the publisher will gladly include acknowledgement in any future edition.

ALL RIGHTS RESERVED
No part of this publication may be reproduced, stored in a retrieval system, or transmitted in any form by any means electronic, mechanical, photocopying, recording or otherwise without the prior consent of the publishers.

The National Library of Australia Cataloguing-in-Publication entry:

    Hutchinson, Garrie, 1949- .

    Pilgrimage: a traveller's guide to Australia's battlefields.

    Bibliography.
    Includes index.
    ISBN 1 86395 387 6.

    1. Battlefields - Guidebooks. I. Title.

    355.4

Maps by Jenny Sheehan
Index by John E. Simkin
Book design by Thomas Deverall
Printed in China by Imago

CONTENTS

Introduction: Travelling to War 1

1. GALLIPOLI 19
The Australians at Gallipoli, 1915 25 / *Gallipoli Today* 41 / *Travel Tool Kit* 79

2. PALESTINE 83
The Australians in Palestine, 1916–1918 87 / *Israel, Syria and Jordan Today* 96 / *Travel Tool Kit* 101

3. THE WESTERN FRONT 103
The Australians on the Western Front, 1916–1918 109 / *The Western Front Today* 129 / *Travel Tool Kit* 153

4. NORTH AFRICA & THE MEDITERRANEAN 157
The Australians in North Africa and the Mediterranean 165 / *North Africa and the Mediterranean Today* 186 / *Travel Tool Kits* 212

5. SOUTH-EAST ASIA 217
The Australians in South-East Asia 224 / *South-East Asia Today* 256 / *Travel Tool Kits* 295

6. NEW GUINEA 1942: THE BATTLE FOR AUSTRALIA 305
The Australians in New Guinea 313 / *Papua New Guinea Today* 343 / *Travel Tool Kit* 366

7. KOREA 371
The Australians in Korea 376 / *Korea Today* 383 / *Travel Tool Kit* 392

8. VIETNAM 395
The Australians in Vietnam 403 / *Vietnam Today* 408 / *Travel Tool Kit* 416

Index 419

LIST OF MAPS

Map of the Eastern Mediterranean. 23

Map of the Gallipoli Peninsula region. 24

Map of the Anzac Cove area. 50

Map of Cape Helles and Krithia. 68

Map of Suvla. 73

Map of First World War Palestine and Beersheva. 85

Map of the Western Front, 1916. 105

Map of Fromelles area. 111

Map of Villers Bretonneux and the Australian area of operation 1917–1918. 120

Map of Flanders Fields: the battlefields around Ypres. 133

Street map of Villers Bretonneux. 149

Map of Tobruk and North Africa. 167

Map of Crete. 172

Map of Syria and Lebanon. 176

Map of El Alamein. 181

Map of South-East Asia. 219

Map of Malaysia and Singapore. 226

Map of East Timor. 231

Map of Thai–Burma Railway and Hellfire Pass Walking Track. 244

Map of Borneo. 249

Map of Kanchanaburi. 284

Map of New Guinea and Northern Australia. 306

Map of the area of operations around Wau and Salamaua. 315

Maps of the Kokoda Track. 322

Map of Milne Bay. 331

Map of the Gona Buna area. 340

Map of the Australian and Commonwealth area of operations (Korea) 1951–1953. 373

Map of the Korean Peninsula. 373

Map of Vietnam and the Australian area of operations in Phuoc Tuy province. 405

Dedication

To: WX36620 E Battery Australian Heavy Artillery, VX50279 2/5th Independent Company, 118067 RAAF.

*

'We can truly say that the whole circuit of the earth is girdled with the graves of our dead ... and, in the course of my pilgrimage, I have many times asked myself whether there can be more potent advocates of peace on earth through the years to come, than this massed multitude of silent witnesses to the desolation of war.'
—King George V, Flanders, 1922.

INTRODUCTION
TRAVELLING TO WAR

In 1993 a midnight fax curled out of the machine. It was from an old 60s comrade who had wound up working in philanthropy in New York. He was looking for someone to cover the World Whitewater Rafting Championships in far eastern Turkey, an exercise in East–West fraternisation that had begun in Siberia a few years before. Teams from around the world were going to assemble on the river Çoruh, between Erzerum and Trabzon, for peaceful competition. It took about fifteen seconds to decide, and after a few weeks in a tent in eastern Turkey, I returned to Istanbul, and travelled around Aegean Turkey, then flew to Izmir, and spent two weeks getting back to Istanbul by bus. This is what changed my life.

I had not been in this part of the world before, and had not thoroughly taken to heart

p.1: The Sphinx, above Anzac Cove. (1996)

childhood stories of the Eastern Mediterranean. But Homer and the Bible, Achilles and St Paul, and war stories, thousands of years of war stories, suddenly made sense. My 'Pauline' flash of understanding occurred not on the road to Damascus but on the road to Troy. As you travel from Çanakkale around the coast towards the Big Wooden Horse, you skirt the Asian bank of the Dardanelles, aware that Gallipoli and Anzac are just a Byronic swim away. One of Australia's main 'foundation stories' took place just *there*, and Alexander the Great crossed just *here*, and, carrying a copy of the *Odyssey*, picked Achilles' shield from near *that* mound ...

So I made my first pilgrimage to Gallipoli and Anzac, and fell again under the spell of Australia's Homer, C E W Bean, another myth-maker and storyteller grounded in scrupulous detail. War stories. Perhaps more-learned Australians would not have been so affected, but I was. My life changed because I determined then and there to come back to this place, and the other places in the world where Australians had been, and find my way through the commingling of stories. Gallipoli and Troy are physically so close, as the seabird flies, that the narrative connection established itself, like pulling tight a knot.

That our new-world story is written in blood on those twisted European cliffs across the ditch from the classical story of an ancient invasion of Asia is, to me, what connects our new-world culture to the European tradition. That this connection is made in Turkey, the place which has been the interface between Asia and Europe for thousands of years seems entirely proper.

In the Lebanon, not far north of Beirut, is Nahr al Kalb, or Dog River, a steep-sided gorge where it enters the Mediterranean. Armies travelling north or south have to cross this river, and since the time of Rameses II in the 13th century BC, have carved memorials of their passing. Egyptians, Assyrians, Greeks, Romans, Mamelukes, British and French have carved their passage in the stone. So have Australians – twice. First in 1918, commemorating the capture of Damascus, Aleppo and Homs, and then one dated 20 December 1942 commemorating the liberation of Syria from the Vichy French, on the order of Australian commander Sir Thomas Blamey. The poet and journalist Kenneth Slessor, in the area as an official war correspondent, thought that Blamey comparing himself to Rameses and Nebuchadnezzar was a trifle hubristic, especially given the low regard many Australian soldiers had for him, and wrote a poem on behalf of the men.

Nahr al Kalb inscriptions: Napoleon III 1860–1861, Australia 1918 above a weathered 2500-year-old Assyrian king.

And we, though our identities have been lost,
Lacking the validity of stone or metal,
We, too, are part of this memorial,
Having put in for the cost.

Australia like Britain and other Commonwealth countries buries its military dead close to the place where they fell. There are more than 100,000 of us buried or remembered in more than 1800 cemeteries and memorials in 77 countries.

Our dead are everywhere but no place has the same resonance as Gallipoli. The unique location and terrain, the classical associations, the preservation of the battlefield, the Anzac myth-making of C E W Bean, but most of all because it has become the place where our history seems to begin. As it does for Turkey, because their modern nation was forged as well in the Çanakkale campaign, as they name it.

Australians are there at Gallipoli. Lester Lawrence, Reuters correspondent at Gallipoli, wrote a poem in 1915, published in the *ANZAC Book*.

Yet where the brave man lies who fell in fight
For his dear country, there his country is.

A conventional enough sentiment, perhaps. Bean and the Anzacs leaving in December 1915 were anguished at leaving their mates behind, wondering what would happen to the rough graves that had been invested as part of Australia in those eight awful months.

Lawrence continued :

Some flower that blooms beside the Southern foam
May blossom where our dead Australians lie,
And comfort them with whispers of their home;
And they will dream beneath alien sky,
Of the Pacific Sea.

Beside each of the graves, at Gallipoli and elsewhere, is a local flower tended by reverential gardeners.

Gallipoli is remarkable for many reasons, not least of which is that it must be one of the few battlefields where the wild geography has preserved its shape and form from the battles in 1915, until now. At other places you must divine events from stories, but at Gallipoli the hills and gullies still exist, and in some cases the trenches, too.

And then there are the 31 cemeteries on the Gallipoli Peninsula, 23, mostly around Anzac Cove, with Australians buried in them.

Bean reported, when he returned here in 1919, that the dead should remain buried where they fell, or as close to it as possible: 'I urged that the Australian government should as soon as possible express its wish as to whether graves should be retained in their present positions, and men's remains buried where they lay, or whether graves should be concentrated in a few large existing cemeteries. I had already recommended the former system and I now urged that this could well be carried out at Anzac provided that the whole of the area was vested in the Imperial War Graves Commission.'

Bean's 1919 report 'envisaged the whole Anzac area as one big graveyard, which would probably be visited by thousands of Australians and others yearly, and in which the dead, merely by being buried where they fell, or where their comrades had carried them, would commemorate their achievement better than any inscription.'

So instead of overwhelming ranks and files of white crosses, there are small, elegant and private cemeteries and memorials in occasionally inaccessible spots, glowing white in the afternoon sun, then glowing green. One, at Plugge's above the beach at Ari Burnu, has just twelve men buried in it.

The stone of which the cemeteries were constructed, Bean noted approvingly, quoting T J Pemberton, came from across the Dardanelles and was of the same class as that of which the Homeric walls of Troy were built.

Bean's great, simple idea is one of the main reasons why, as Major John North wrote in 1936, 'no battleground so easily lends itself to retrospective sentimentality' for those pilgrims who tread the ground. I take that to mean no other battlefield invokes the feelings in quite the same way as Gallipoli, which has had memorials and cemeteries and roads added to it, but which has essentially been left as it was in 1915. The spirit of place is moving because the place is where time, subject to the whim of temporary governments, has stood still.

For most Australians, Gallipoli represents a potent mixture of emotions: nationalism, sadness, nostalgia, anger, death, love and beauty. Hatred seems not to form much of the mix. Charles Bean was responsible for shaping our sensibilities in regard to Gallipoli. Whether we know it or not, so was Mustafa Kemal, who famously directed the defence of the tottering Ottoman Empire as a means towards the creation of modern Turkey eight years later, and became its first president.

His statement, made in 1934 and inscribed in white stone on the beach at Anzac Cove is the other reason why Gallipoli is a unique place: 'Those heroes that have shed their blood and lost their lives ... you are now lying in the soil of a friendly country. Therefore rest in peace. There is no difference between the Johnnies and the Mehmets

The 4th Battalion Parade Ground Cemetery viewed from Lone Pine. The ridge to the left is Plugge's Plateau, and Suvla Bay can be seen in the distance.

to us where they lie side by side here in this country of ours ... You, the mothers, who sent their sons from far away countries, wipe away your tears; your sons are now lying in our bosom and are in peace. And having lost their lives on this land they have become our sons as well.' No one, I think, could stand in front of this memorial, read the letters proud on the standing stone, and not cry.

During the Selarang Barracks Square incident in Singapore on 30 August 1942, some 15,000 prisoners, nearly all Australian, were concentrated into a small area of one of the old barracks at Changi by the Japanese for several days and nights with little water, food or sanitation. The aim was for each Australian to sign a document promising not to escape, which was against what the men saw as their duty, however quixotic the idea of escape from Singapore was at that time. Four men had been caught attempting to escape, and to concentrate the minds of the remaining POWs they were taken to Changi beach and executed on 2 September 1942. The men were then advised to sign 'under duress', and on 5 September, returned to their original barracks, and later many were sent to work as slave labour on the Thai–Burma Railway.

The beach where the four escapers were murdered is most likely the former 'officers beach' at Fairy Point, which is now a safe swimming beach at Changi Village. Two of the four were Australians. Corporal R E Breavington (a 38-year-old policeman from Fairfield in Melbourne) was the bravest man that the Australian commander at Changi, Lieutenant Colonel 'Black Jack' Galleghan had ever seen. Breavington had pleaded that his mate, Private V L Gale (23 years old, a fitter and turner from Balwyn) had only escaped on his orders, and should not be executed. The Japanese refused to listen, and the men saluted the Australian officers and were shot – by Sikhs. They did not die at once, Japanese soldiers had to administer the coup de grace. It was, as a poem of the day had it, an

Example, yes – of how to die,
And how to meet one's fate.
Example, true – of selfless love
A man has for his mate.

It is this sort of story that fed my childhood views of the Japanese, and the Australian experience in that war. We share the killing ground at Changi beach with some of the 50,000 Chinese Singaporeans killed in the *Sook Ching* massacres.

The Australians who died in Singapore are buried or commemorated at the Kranji War Memorial, a taxi ride up the Bukit Timah expressway to the north-west of the island.

Like every cemetery I have been to around the world administered by the Commonwealth War Graves Commission, it is peaceful, quiet, sombre and not much visited by the locals. Walking slowly, sweating, up the green grass between the ranks of graves, towards the memorial and the 24,000 names inscribed there, I looked at the markers on the stones, here a death from the battleship *Prince of Wales*, here a death from the 2/19th on the day of the attack, and here ... a Hutchinson. That really gave my heart a whack. You see your name written on a gravestone and it grabs your attention.

Private G A Hutchinson, VX 51041, 2/29th Infantry Battalion, buried near this spot, died on 20 January 1942, age seventeen.

Seventeen. He was no relation (but he has my name). My father was not much older, and on his way to Milne Bay in New Guinea by then. This Hutchinson must have lied about his age to enlist. I felt, what? Sad, and disturbed. It was like meeting an alternative history of me, and my father, because it could easily have been him (and me) buried here in Singapore, several lifetimes ago.

There are no Australian war graves in Vietnam. In 1966 Erroll Noack, the first conscript to be killed, fell to 'friendly fire' from his Australian comrades near Nui Dat. But Erroll's father, Wally, campaigned to make the authorities fly his body back to Australia.

I once drove to the place beneath Nui Dat (Mud Hill) where the Australian base had been. There is nothing there now. All that remains is a road that was once a piece of tarmac for helicopters; the place where the base buildings had been appeared to be a pig farm.

Long Tan, 1997.

Just months after it was abandoned, at the end of 1971, an Australian officer had visited and seen weeds and the 'empty husks of corrugated iron buildings already stripped by local scavengers ratting for timbers and iron'.

This was the destination for Australia's soldiers, volunteers and conscripts, this stretch of tarmac, this patch of weedy jungle. But there is no echo here, no purpose evident, except a couple of children playing with a ball on the road. Children annoyed at the interruption of the car. Mr Son, my guide, said, 'Australian veterans, they come, and go off in there,' past the pigs, 'looking for where their house was.' Do they ever find it? I asked. 'Oh yes, they find the place. They are very sad.'

The memorial at Long Tan was then a cement cross in the red soil, surrounded by four concrete posts and a bit of wire enclosing some straggly succulent plants. A circle of red bricks marks a dying white bush. A couple of cement posts indicate where a gate and a larger fence might once have been. (It has since been renewed.) I thought about the war there, and the Australians, and the Vietnamese who died here, one afternoon in 1966, when I was sitting in school, worrying about my year 12.

The Vietnamese point of view might perhaps be found in Bao Ninh's extraordinary novel *The Sorrow of War*. Bao Ninh was born in 1952 – making him a few years younger than me – and served in the Glorious 27th Youth Brigade, which went to war in 1969, the year that I did not. Five hundred served with him; Bao Ninh and nine others survived. At the end of the novel, in 1976 after 'Liberation', he writes of a fellow survivor: 'We also shared a common sorrow, the immense sorrow of war. It is a sublime sorrow, more sublime than happiness, and beyond suffering. It is thanks to our sorrow that we were able to escape the war, escape the continual killing and fighting ... It is also thanks to our mutual sorrow that we've been able to walk our respective roads again. Our lives may not be very happy, and they might well be sinful. But now we are living the most beautiful lives we could ever have hoped for, because it is a life in peace.'

Bao Ninh was an optimist. Nearly thirty years later, at the beginning of the 21st century, Australians are once again involved in various and different ways in the same places where our fathers and grandfathers and great-grandfathers fought. Mesopotamia (Iraq), Timor (Timor), Dutch East Indies (Indonesia) and New Guinea, and we are being bombed in New York and London, to name a few places.

I've gone to these sites (but not Iraq) looking for the Australian presence, to see what mark we have left and what stories we have told. It's surprising what you find – there are little corners of Libya and Vietnam, France and Korea, Papua New Guinea and Lebanon, Greece and Thailand that are forever Australian.

An apology needs to be made here. Not every battlefield or conflict has its story told here. In particular I apologise to those who served in the air and at sea – your battles are not marked by monuments in the sky or cemeteries in the ocean. I have not even visited every cemetery and every memorial on the land; for that I can only plead that I had to stop somewhere.

This book has been longer in the making than either world war, and has involved numerous adventures highlighted by getting hijacked by (luckily) amateurish terrorists in Egypt, and most miserably when suffering from malaria and dengue fever in New Guinea. Along the way I found that I had moved from taking photographs instead of writing notes to making notes about the photographs I was taking. Many of them are in the book, and I hope they convey something of the strange peace and beauty of landscapes and places that once were killing fields.

Garrie Hutchinson, January 2006

Pilgrimage Resources

There are many resources available to potential pilgrims in and around Australia, and on the internet. This is a guide to some of the basic research material and methods to consult before you travel.

Australian War Memorial
The Australian War Memorial was founded on an idea of C E W Bean's – that it should not only be a memorial, a shrine to Australia's war

The Roll of Honour at the Australian War Memorial in Canberra names all the men and women who have lost their lives in Australia's wars.

dead, but that it should also involve knowledge and understanding of war. Therefore it has a symbolic function embodied in the secular religion of the Anzac tradition in the Hall of Memory, the Roll of Honour and a museum, an archive and a library. And now, it must be added, surely the best website of any military museum in the world.

Bean's idea was brought to fruition by the memorial's first director, John Treloar, who was appointed to begin the collection in 1917 and

remained until 1952. The memorial did not open until 1941, and afterwards suffered periods of neglect, and perhaps a loss of focus. That changed in 1980 when the federal government increased its responsibilities to all wars, and began to increase funding. This coincided with a renewed interest by Australians in the Anzac tradition, and a few years later the arrival of the internet.

Above left: The Hall of Memory at the Australian War Memorial flanked by the arcades containing the Roll of Honour.

Above: Standing outside is Leslie Bowles' *The Man with the Donkey*, commissioned 1938, cast 1950.

Now the memorial is a wonder of the world, visited by more than two million people a year, and with new galleries hosting big objects such as the Second World War Lancaster bomber *G for George*, as well as the old and much-loved dioramas. And the internet has made the resources, especially of the vast collection of photographs, widely available.

Search functions are easy to use – if you are looking to track down a particular person and produce a record of service with enlistment and discharge. Other links will allow a search for honours, and links to the National Archive, where you may request a service record. www.naa.gov.au/the_collection/family_history/armed_services

The *Official History of the First World War*, edited by C E W Bean, is available online, at the AWM website, including the maps. Photographs, published in Volume XII, are all individually searchable.

The AWM website also contains the marvellous and growing online archive of Second World War and Korean War brigade and battalion war diaries. It also has a very good set of links to other related museums and other relevant websites. There is an encyclopedia.

The entire photographic archive is searchable – you can display virtually any picture in the collection on your computer, and order a print. This service is the envy of the world. **www.awm.gov.au**

If you can't visit the AWM then the internet is the next best thing.

The Commonwealth War Graves Commission
The Commonwealth War Graves Commission (CWGC) was established as the Imperial War Graves Commission in 1917, and changed its name in 1964. Its duty is to mark and maintain the graves of Commonwealth service men and women, and to maintain memorials to the dead whose graves are not known from the First and Second World Wars.

The CWGC website is another marvellous tool. Through it you can search for the location of any of the graves or memorial sites of any of

Mohammed Hamesh, chief gardener at the Knightsbridge Acroma War Cemetery at Tobruk. The Commonwealth War Graves Commission employs locals, who keep the cemeteries and memorials in immaculate condition everywhere in the world.

the 100,000 Australian servicemen and women who died in the First or Second World Wars. (The Korean and Vietnam wars are outside the organisation's remit.)

Go to **www.cwgc.org** and on the right of the screen is a box where you can search for a *casualty*, eg. Tom 'Diver' Derrick, or a *cemetery* eg. Tobruk.

Searching for Derrick will reveal that Lieutenant Thomas Currie Derrick, SX7964 was killed on 24/05/1945, aged 31. He was in the Australian Infantry and is buried in plot 24. A. 9 at the Labuan War Cemetery. Click on his highlighted name and you will see he won the

Victoria Cross with citation, the names of his parents and his unit – the famous 2/48th Battalion.

You might then be interested in looking at the 2/48th Battalion War Diary for 1945, to find out what they were up to at the time in Borneo.

Above left: Tom 'Diver' Derrick's grave in Labuan War Cemetery, Sabah, Malaysia.
Above: Albert Jacka lies in the St Kilda General Cemetery in Melbourne.

Search for Labuan or Tobruk, and you will find details of the War Cemetery – statistics, history, a plan and a photo. The plan will help guide you to the right grave if you visit. The 'cemetery reports' button at the bottom left will take you to an alphabetical list of all the burials in the cemetery.

Please note that those who died after a war, and not of directly war-related causes, will not be found. For example, the First World War hero Albert Jacka VC is not at the CWGC website – you will find the location of his and any other winner of the Victoria Cross at Iain Stewart's marvellous and comprehensive website at **www.victoriacross.org.uk**

Albert Jacka is buried in the St Kilda General Cemetery in Melbourne.

Australian War Cemeteries
The **Office of Australian War Graves,** part of the Department of Veterans' Affairs, maintains the 72 Commonwealth War Graves Commission Cemeteries on behalf of the CWGC in Australia. They are meticulously maintained, as they are throughout the world, with similar monuments.

The **Sydney War Cemetery** contains 734 war graves. The Memorial to the Missing commemorates 751 dead, and the Cremation memorial honours 199 men and women. The Stone of Remembrance is the only one in Australia, and was destined for Ambon in Indonesia, but trouble there meant it was never sent. The cemetery is located within the Rookwood Necropolis.

Springvale War Cemetery in the Springvale Necropolis in Melbourne contains 611 war graves. The Victorian Cremation memorial records the names of 72 service personnel.

The **Perth War Cemetery** contains 493 war graves, including six from the First World War. The Cremation memorial honours a further seven personnel. Adjoining the cemetery is the Perth War Cemetery Dutch Annexe where 25 people killed in February 1942 in Broome in a Japanese attack on their seaplanes are buried.

Other large war cemeteries include the **Centennial Park War Cemetery and Cremation Memorial** in South Australia (with 198 war graves, and nine cremations); the **Hobart War Cemetery and Tasmanian Cremation Memorial** (51 war graves and four cremations); and the **Atherton War Cemetery** with 164 graves; and the **Adelaide River War Cemetery** in the Northern Territory with 434 burials.

The **Cowra Australian War Cemetery** contains 27 war graves, including four killed during the Cowra Japanese POW breakout in 1944; adjacent is the **Japanese War Cemetery** with 523 graves, including those who died during the breakout. It is maintained by the CWGC but costs are recovered from the Japanese government.

The **German Military Cemetery** in Tatura in Victoria contains the graves of 250 German servicemen and civilian internees. A memorial commemorates others including 174 German missionaries. It is maintained on behalf of the German government.

Department of Veterans' Affairs Second World War website is one of the best introductions to the war in New Guinea available: **www.ww2australia.gov.au/index**

Shrine of Remembrance

Construction of Melbourne's Shrine of Remembrance commenced on Remembrance Day, 11 November 1927, and the first person to lay a wreath was Mrs Carrie Madden on behalf of her son, Private Les Fackerell of the 60th Battalion, who was killed at Fromelles in 1916 and whose body was never found. His name is inscribed on the memorial at VC Corner in France.

Since that day, and especially since the official opening in 1934, the Shrine has been the focus of remembrance in Victoria. In addition to its ceremonial function on Anzac Day, Remembrance Day and other notable anniversaries (including Fromelles Day on 19 July), and as a memorial, the shrine has had an increasing role in education and presentation of the Anzac tradition through art, military history and photographic exhibitions. A new visitor centre opened in 2003, and an education centre in 2006. **www.shrine.org.au**

The Shrine of Remembrance in Melbourne, with *Wipers* – a replica of the C. Sergeant Jagger bronze at the Royal Artillery memorial in London. On the reverse of the plinth is *The Driver*. Purchased 1937.

Australian Memorial Plaques

Since 1990, Ross Bastiaan has made and erected over 140 bronze plaques at Australian battlefields all over the world. One of the more sobering and reassuring feelings after you have struggled into some inaccessible corner of the world is that Ross has been there before you, and that there is an explanation of what took place there in the local language and English. This is one of Australia's truly great commemorative projects.

Find the complete list at **www.plaques.satlink.com.au/index**

Guide to Published References

A kind of companion volume to this book is *Eyewitness: Australians Write from the Front-Line* edited by Garrie Hutchinson (Black Inc., Melbourne, 2005) which contains some of the best writing about many of the places and battles included in this book – from C E W Bean on the Anzac Day Landing to the present day front-line in Iraq.

The best general reference to military matters is the *Oxford Companion to Australian Military History*, Peter Dennis, Jeffrey Grey, Ewan Morris and Robin Prior (Oxford University Press, South Melbourne, 1995).

The Department of Veterans' Affairs has published a wonderful (and inexpensive) series of short books on all Australia's major Second World War conflicts, to coincide with anniversaries. Mostly

One of Ross Bastiaan's Australian Memorial Plaques, outside the Mairie, Villers Bretonneux.

written by Richard Reid, they consist of an introductory essay, and a gallery of evocative pictures. Highly recommended. They may be ordered from the Australian War Memorial online shop at **www.awm.gov.au**

The **basic reference works** for Australian involvement in war are the Official Histories.

The Official History of Australia in the War of 1914–1918, edited by C E W Bean, and published by Angus and Robertson, Sydney, from 1921 onwards. There have been numerous reprints, but a complete set is now rare and expensive. Fortunately and wonderfully, the Australian War Memorial has published it on the internet, so we can all read it for free – including the maps, in colour at **www.awm.gov.au**

An on-going project is the publication of unit diaries – themselves a terrific resource.

Australia in the War of 1939–1945 comprises 22 volumes in five series – Army, Navy, Air, Civil and Medical – under the editorship of Gavin Long, published from 1952, by the Australian War Memorial. A reprint with new introductions but without the coloured maps of the Army, Navy and Air volumes was published by Collins, Sydney in 1986.

Australia in the Korean War 1950–53, by Robert O'Neill (Volume 1, 'Strategy and Diplomacy'; Volume II, 'Combat Operations'), was published by the Australian War Memorial, Canberra, in 1981.

The Official History of Australia's Involvement in Southeast Asian Conflicts 1948–75 is under the general editorship of Official Historian, Peter Edwards. Three volumes on Vietnam, two on the Malayan Emergency, one on the RAAF in Vietnam, one on the RAN throughout South-East Asia, and one on medical aspects, commenced in 1992 and are still being completed.

For **maps** of Australia's battlefields the great work is *An Atlas of Australia's Wars*, by John Coates (Oxford University Press, South Melbourne, 2001). The maps in the various volumes of the Official Histories are also excellent, but perhaps not so useful for walking the ground as those in the atlas.

For Australian **war memorials**, their history and role as a secular national religion and their place in the Australian psyche, the masterpiece is *Sacred Places: War Memorials in the Australian Landscape* by Ken Inglis (Melbourne University Press, Carlton South, 1998).

The best resource on the internet for Australian War Memorials is Michael Southwell-Keely's website at **www.skp.com.au/memorials/index** with more than 1000 memorials described.

For New Zealand, most of the basic documents are available on the internet, including the 50-volume official history of the Second World War. **www.nzetc.org**

Travel Risk Assessment

No one should need reminding that the world can change rapidly – bombs go off, wars break out, visa conditions change, hotels close. Anyone contemplating travel should always check the Australian government travel advisory website at **www.smartraveller.gov.au**

You must make your own risk assessment about travel, based on the advice given. You will also find on this website links to other countries' embassies and consulates. Many do not have websites and do not answer email inquiries – you will have to use the phone. Of course, if you have a good travel agent, they will give you good and up-to-date advice. If they are not 'good', they won't. I have experienced both.

I have made recommendations in this book about services I have used in some of the more out-of-the-way places – again, this is from my own experience, and things do change. From Australia I have found particular consultants at Flight Centre a tremendous help with airlines, and used them along with my own research on the internet. For organised travel in the Middle East, if you are using your own travel agent, I recommend you find arrangements in the Middle East packaged by Tempo Holidays.

Photographs

Garrie Hutchinson took all the photographs in the book between 1993 and 2005, using a variety of conventional and digital cameras. The exceptions are some First and Second World War photographs collected from dusty corners over the years, and some unique wartime images taken by Jack Hutchinson, and the late Michael Sheehan. Others – by Tony Clifton, Stephen Downes, Gavin Pinar and Mick Stone – are noted in the captions.

Thank You

This book has taken longer than both world wars to finish, and involved many adventures, some literally life-threatening along the way, on the ten or so journeys undertaken to these places. Thanks are due to hundreds of people. Not all of them knew they were helping me, and will not read this book to know that they did. The kindness of strangers literally saved my life in Aleppo, Balikpapan, Cairo, Hué, Jayapura, Lae, Rangoon, Tobruk and Vanimo.

Thanks to everyone at Black Inc for this and other projects – in particular to Morry Schwartz, Chris Feik, Sophy Williams, Caitlin Yates, Anna Lensky, Tom Deverall and Nadine Davidoff, for patience above and beyond the call of publishing duty; to intrepid Stephanie Holt for turning a mess into a ms; and to Jenny Sheehan for the marvellous maps. All remaining sins of commission and omission are my own.

In Australia, for essential conversation and services: James Clayden, Tony Clifton, Peter Cole-Adams, Ruth Dicker, Stephen Downes, Lambis Englezos, Cameron Forbes, Gary and Susan Hearst, Charles Jager, Silvia Kwon, Mark Madden, Shane Maloney, Jean McAuslan, Ross McMullin, Bruce Mildenhall, Cate O'Dwyer, John Phillips, Ian Robinson, Rosemary Sheehan, Myer Steinberg, Merita Tabain, Cynthia Tsao, Peter Weiniger.

On the road I thank in particular: in France, Martial Delebarre;

in Israel, Eli Galili, Leo Marks; in Korea, Annie Yu; in Lebanon, Ed Blanche, Mona Ziade; in Libya, Hassan Founi, Abdul and Idriess, Mansour el-Shuieb; in Papua New Guinea, Chris Abel in Milne Bay, Jesse Eloda, Ianna Levu, Steven Wanire, comrades of the Kokoda Track, Kelly and Donna Harvey-Hall in Wau; in Thailand, Rod Beattie (I thank Rod and the Thailand–Burma Railway Centre for the Kenchanaburi map); in Turkey, Gavin Pinar, Hanifi Araz and Captain Ali Efe.

And at home, as always: Alex, Esther, Isobel and Karen.

Some paragraphs, incidents, descriptions and events might have been seen in earlier incarnations in the *Age*, the *Sunday Age*, *Meanjin*, and in *Not Going to Vietnam: Journeys Through Two Wars* (Sceptre, Sydney, 1999) and *An Australian Odyssey: Giza to Gallipoli* (Sceptre, Sydney, 1997).

I.

GALLIPOLI

THE GALLIPOLI CAMPAIGN HAD ITS ORIGINS IN THE stalemate in France at the end of 1914. The initial German offensive had failed to encircle Paris, the French counter-attack had stalled, and the British had lost the cream of their professional army in Flanders. A 750-kilometre system of trenches had been established, running from the Belgian coast to France's border with Switzerland. No one on either side had any idea how to break this deadlock.

A plan, ambitious or foolhardy, was developed and promoted by Winston Churchill and others to use the Royal Navy to attempt a bold stroke in a new area. Using the navy to take Constantinople (today Istanbul) would help the Russians, and would bleed Germany by opening a new front and knocking its sympathiser, Turkey, out of the war.

p.19: Sunset Anzac Cove, 1996.

The Dardanelles is the narrow strait between the northern European coast and the southern Asian mainland of modern Turkey. It leads through the Sea of Marmara to Istanbul, and then to the Black Sea. The entrance to the Dardanelles was guarded by the Gallipoli peninsula, which at the town of Çanakkale is barely 500 metres wide; in 1914, it was guarded by well-protected artillery in fortresses on both shores. On 18 March 1915, after a month of shelling the forts and artillery positions, a British and French fleet of eighteen battleships attempted to force the Dardanelles but one third of the ships were sunk or damaged by mines and coastal artillery. (Turkey now celebrates 18 March as its victory day.) But although the purely naval action had failed, the idea would not disappear.

Instead, the Gallipoli peninsula was to be seized by simultaneous landings at Gabatepe by the Australians and New Zealanders, and at Cape Helles by the British. The fort at Kumkale on the Asian side of the Dardanelles was to be taken by the French. The invasion proceeded with the 70,000 men available to the British commander-in-chief, General Sir Ian Hamilton, about half the number considered necessary for success. The landings, on 25 April, were bloody and virtually everywhere unsuccessful, with little ground gained at great cost. The Australians and New Zealanders, who landed a few hundred metres north of their intended landing spot, were confronted by unknown wild country of cliffs and ravines.

Similarly, at the five landing beaches at Cape Helles, objectives were not gained and great casualties were inflicted. On the Aegean or western side of Cape Helles, the landings met less defence and were more successful because less defended, but the opportunity to reinforce success by quickly capturing the commanding height of Achi Baba and the village of Krithia was not taken. The French at Kumkale were defeated in a couple of days and withdrew.

British Lieutenant General Aylmer Hunter Weston advised the new commanders they should drive the men 'without any regard to the yelping of subordinate commanders for reinforcements or to their cry that their men are dead with fatigue', but that tactic was never going to succeed against the more tactically astute Turkish commanders, who had many more men to sacrifice in the defence of their homeland.

Fierce and costly fighting, especially in May in the Anzac area, and at Krithia, failed to gain any ground. By August the last throw of the dice was organised, with five new divisions to land at Suvla Bay,

The view across the Razor Back towards the Nek. The Turkish and Australian memorials are visible at the top of the ridge. The Sphinx is on the left. (1996)

fifteen kilometres north of Anzac Cove. British forces were to sweep up the relatively few defenders around the low hills and seize the heights behind Chunuk Bair and join up with a breakout attack along the northern ridges from Anzac Cove, while diversions were to be staged along the ridge line at the Nek, Quinn's Post and Lone Pine.

Beginning on 6 August, the offensive was a debacle; the diversions failed to fool the Turks, and incompetent leadership caused enormous casualties. Confusion reigned – about the plan for the troops at Suvla and the urgency with which action was to be taken.

Although the New Zealanders took the vital heights of Chunuk Bair, they were decimated in the process, and were therefore unable to support the suicidal Australian Light Horse charge at the Nek. Australians were able to gain ground at Lone Pine in one of the most close up and savage battles in modern history. Seven Australians were awarded the Victoria Cross. The British, meanwhile, spent 8 August at Suvla at leisure, swimming and drinking tea. When their attack on the hills finally began, on 9 August, the Turks were reinforced and ready.

The appalling cost for both sides of the August battles meant that nothing substantial could be achieved. There could be no massive reinforcement and evacuation was the only option. Anzac and Suvla were evacuated on 19 and 20 December without a single casualty (in the best planned operation of the whole campaign) and Helles in January.

More than 21,200 British, 10,000 French, 8700 Australians, 2700 New Zealanders, 1350 Indians and 49 Newfoundlanders were killed during the Gallipoli campaign. The Allied wounded totalled over 97,000, including 26,111 Australians and 7571 New Zealanders.

Gallipoli is as much about New Zealand, Britain and France as it is about Australia. Each country's servicemen suffered from poor leadership, and each grew in the bravery and fortitude of the survivors.

But 'Anzac' is something else. It is about the creation of Australia in sacrifice and suffering, and about the tradition of the Australian character. 'Anzac stood, and still stands, for reckless valour in a good cause, for enterprise, resourcefulness, fidelity, comradeship, and endurance that will never own defeat,' wrote Charles Bean, Australia's official war historian and the prime creator of the Anzac legend.

The Australian and New Zealand landing place is now called Anzac Cove. It was a tiny place, barely a kilometre from the beach to the frontline. The Diggers did the best they could in the thirsty heat of the summer, to the freezing cold of winter. There was nowhere safe from Turkish shelling, death was everywhere, but daily life seems to have taken on the camaraderie and routine of a long camping trip. Compared to what the survivors were destined for in France, one said it was a 'curiously happy time'.

'Anzac Day' – 25 April – has generously been ceded by New Zealand to Australia, whose troops landed first. For New Zealanders, the most celebrated day at Gallipoli is 8 August, with the magnificent capture of the height at Chunuk Bair. The most significant day of joint Australian and New Zealand sacrifice is 8 May, not at Anzac but near Cape Helles, at the second battle of Krithia.

What we know as Gallipoli 1915, the Turks think of as the Çanakkale June 1914–January 1916 campaign; but whatever its name, it is

Shrapnel Valley Cemetery contains more identified Australian graves than any other place at Gallipoli.

Map of the Eastern Mediterranean.

as important to them as it is to Australians and New Zealanders. For them, it is about Mustafa Kemal's leadership in fighting off their country's enemies and winning a battle after great sacrifice. Çanakkale has had an increasingly important impact in Turkey, partly in response to our interest, but mostly because it was a significant victory in the making of modern Turkey from the shambles of the Ottoman Empire. Gallipoli – or Çanakkale – however, serves to unite Turkey with its old enemies; in Korea, just 40 years later, Australians, Turks, New Zealanders and British would lie alongside each other in the UN cemetery at Pusan.

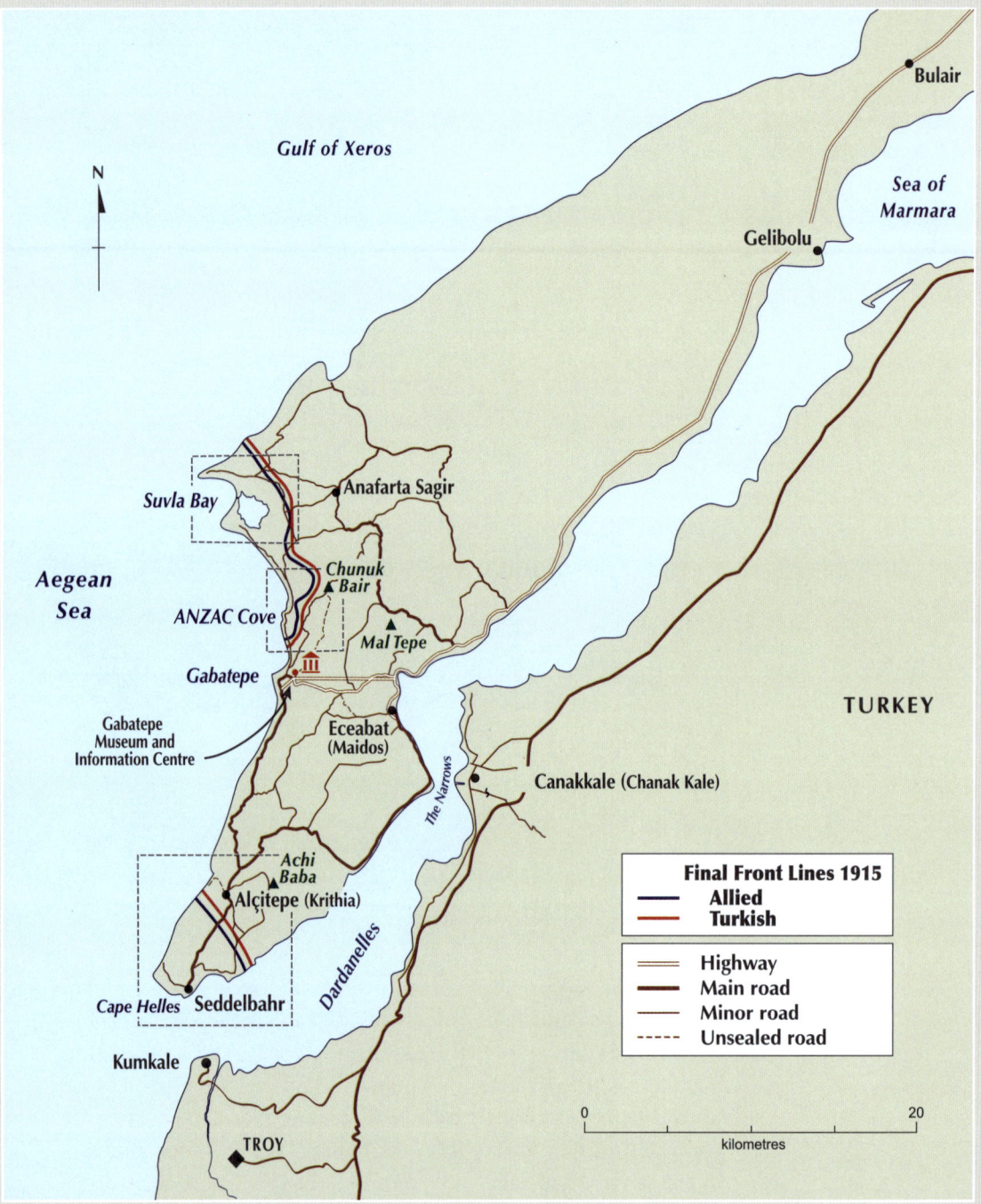

Above: Lieutenant Leslie Morshead (standing right) after Lone Pine, August 1915. As Lieutenant General Morshead, he commanded the Australian garrison at Tobruk in 1941. Private Jim Bryant (standing next to Morshead) later also survived the Thai–Burma Railway. (AWM A02025)
Opposite: Map of the Gallipoli Peninsula region.

The Australians at Gallipoli, 1915

The Landings: Ari Burnu, Anzac Cove and North Beach, 25 April 1915

When the Australians landed, they were a small but crucial distance north of Gabatepe, their intended landing point, and came ashore on a narrow front at Ari Burnu, the point of land at the northern end of Anzac Cove. Gabatepe, though strongly defended, would have provided easier access inland up the gullies between the ridges; instead the Australians had to scale steep cliffs.

The Australians, as Charles Bean wrote, 'had been told to rush across the beach and shelter under a bank such as lines nearly all beaches. They were to drop their packs there, quickly form up, fix

25

bayonets, load their magazines … and then advance.' But they were confronted by a steep hill which rose almost immediately above the water. As the naval commander in charge of the tows put it, 'Explain to the colonel that the damn fools have taken us a mile too far north.'

Initial opposition was from a small number of Turkish riflemen, who nevertheless managed to inflict many casualties from their positions above the confusion at Ari Burnu. By mid-morning, however, the Turkish commander Mustafa Kemal (later to become the first president of Turkey, Kemal Ataturk) had reorganised and reinforced his defenders.

Australian soldiers hauled themselves up with the help of their rifles, clinging to the scrub. Parties of soldiers then plunged down the

The Sphinx, from the landing site on North Beach. On the skyline is Russell's Top and the objectives of the first Anzac Day.

steep sides of gullies, and crawled up steep slopes – some even up the precipitous face they soon named the Sphinx. The fight was carried on in small isolated places. Bean described how, after the first rush, fighting 'became intense again and swayed hour after hour on the second ridge'. During that first morning, with the exception of some thrusting parties, the Australians who landed at Ari Burnu were held up there – and this was about as far as they ever advanced.

Others scrambled up the gravel and mud cliffs next to the Sphinx and gained Russell's Top, clearing it of Turks. These men then advanced northwards along a flat-topped ridge they dubbed Walker's Ridge, where an impassable tangle of small pines flourished, until it

began to narrow at the point known as the Nek. After the senior officers were killed there, others advanced, including Captain Joseph Lalor, grandson of Peter Lalor of the Eureka Stockade, who had come up from Shrapnel Valley. Lalor dug at the stem of the Nek and died there during the day, as the Turks pushed the Australians back from their attempts to take the peak beyond, Baby 700.

By the end of the first day, the position at Anzac was very serious. Although they had a toehold in the area of Lone Pine and 16,000 men had been landed, the Australians had suffered more than 2000 casualties. Bean described the troops 'clinging to a bare foothold on the second ridge little more than 2 mile inland, on a front of a mile ... with only one ridge between them and their landing place'.

Withdrawal was seriously contemplated, but rejected. The overall commander, Sir Ian Hamilton, signalled to the commander of the Anzacs, British General William Birdwood: 'You have got through the difficult business, now you have only to dig, dig, dig, until you are safe.'

Although some small forces were able to climb to their objective, the third ridge, that day, most were stuck on the second ridge along the line from Lone Pine towards the height of Chunuk Bair. This became the Anzacs' home and front line for the duration. The Turkish trenches were just a bomb throw away. Neither side was strong enough to gain any significant ground in the costly fighting over the following eight months.

Left: Looking down from behind the Sphinx to North Beach and Ari Burnu from Russell's Top (2003).
Above: Fisherman's Hut, with Chunuk Bair on the horizon.

The Truce

At the Nek, as at other points on the front line, came a lull in the killing, an armistice, when it was agreed, a few days after the 19 May Turkish attack, that a day's respite was required to bury the dead.

Bean recalled that one Turkish captain said then: 'At this spectacle even the most gentle must feel savage, and the most savage must weep', while another, pointing to the graves, said, 'That's politics,' and, pointing to the dead, 'That's diplomacy.'

At the end of the day an Australian said to a Turk near him, 'Good bye old chap; good luck.' The answer, Bean says, came in Turkish: 'Smiling may you go and smiling come again.' Bean does not say that this Turkish expression, *gule gule*, is always said by the one remaining.

Another Anzac Day: Krithia, 8 May 1915

South of Anzac Cove at Cape Helles, the first British attack on the village of Krithia and the heights behind was mounted on 28 April. This was the first battle of Krithia, and its target was Achi Baba, the ridge that dominates the southern part of the Gallipoli peninsula. Fatigue, however, brought the assault to a halt near Krithia, some kilometres short of the objective. Turkish counter-attacks followed but were repulsed, and for three days, from 6 May, the British and French divisions, reinforced by the Australian 2nd Brigade and the New Zealand Infantry Brigade, carried out a renewed attack on Krithia (2nd Krithia), making some gains but suffering heavy casualties.

So goes a dry official account of operations at Helles after the landing.

Krithia deserves to be remembered as one of the more monstrous days of the First World War, where Australians, New Zealanders, British and French suffered dreadfully from even more than usually inept planning. More than 25 April, 8 May and the battle at Krithia deserves

Before the First World War, today's Turkish village of Alcitepe was known by its Greek name, Krithia. (Gavin Pinar, 2004)

to be remembered as a true 'ANZAC' day, with Australians and New Zealanders fighting and suffering together.

The battle had started on 6 May, but nothing had been gained in two days of slaughter by frontal assault. The Turks were entrenched, and a fifteen-minute artillery barrage on their positions had little effect (after the war, the Turks said they never knew that there had been a barrage). Unbeknown to the attackers and their artillery, the Turks had a line of forward gun pits 200 metres in front of their trenches.

This was a beautiful place – the British official historian described 'cliffs ... carpeted with flowers', 'a smiling valley studded with cypress and patches of young corn', Krithia 'standing amidst clumps of mulberry and oak', and, away to the right, 'the sapphire fields of Troy'. This was the view of the commanders at sea, before General Hunter Weston's mid-morning attack began, preceded by the usual few minutes of artillery to alert the Turks.

The New Zealand Brigade of four battalions, about 2500 men, advanced steadily; as their historian Christopher Pugsley says, this one brigade was asked to succeed where Hunter Weston's 29th Division of some 12,000 had failed on the two previous days.

The New Zealanders, who had been in reserve on those two days, had watched the war in progress on the slope towards Krithia and Achi Baba. They thought it was the sort of scientific war they had trained for – men advancing in line – rather than the desperate improvisation of trench warfare at Anzac, which these men had not yet experienced.

On the night of 7 May, they were ordered forward with a warning that they would continue the advance at 10.30 a.m. the next morning, passing through the British units, but according to Pugsley there is no evidence they received this order.

At 8.55 a.m. on 8 May, written orders were finally received. The attack was to start at 10.30 a.m.: they were to capture Krithia. The battalion commanders had only twenty minutes to get into position and tell the men what they had to do. One apologised to his subordinates: 'The battalion will attack from the frontline trenches at 10.30 a.m. precisely, and I am sorry, gentlemen, that I cannot give you any further information.'

The men did as they were ordered and, twelve paces apart, with heavy packs, marched forward in long lines. They moved past the reserve trenches, under Turkish shot and shell, and were surprised to find them occupied by British troops. Then they advanced further,

Krithia battleground: in 1915 the machine-gun fire was so thick it was like 'walking through a dust storm in Sydney', wrote Charles Bean.

with ever-increasing casualties; the Turkish snipers and machine-guns could now fire from the flanks of the attack.

The New Zealanders rushed 100 metres in some areas, and 300 in another, but had not taken the Turkish trenches. Nor had they seen any Turks. The attackers huddled as best they could in hollows in the ground. By two o'clock they had had enough. Some still ate, even fell asleep in the afternoon sunshine. But Hunter Weston and his intelligent but ineffective superior, General Hamilton, had not finished with the Anzacs. He ordered the New Zealanders to attack again, at 5.30 p.m. Daylight again. Enfilading machine-guns again. New Zealand protests fell on deaf ears. The order was given by Hamilton, who wasn't going to interfere with his junior commander's costly tactics: 'At 4 o'clock I issued orders that the whole line, reinforced by the Australians, should on the stroke of 5.30 fix bayonets and storm Achi Baba.'

The Australian 2nd Brigade had been brought up well behind the reserve line. When the order was issued, they were preparing shelters for the night, and cooking tea. In a repeat of the chaos that morning, Brigadier (later Lieutenant General) James Whiteside McCay, the Australian commander, had half an hour to prepare detailed orders and get to the start line. They were to attack on the right of the New Zealanders for four kilometres under the same Turkish guns, even though the best that had been achieved in the morning was about 300 metres. The 7th Battalion, under Colonel Robert Gartside, had just two minutes to get ready and go, many of them (including Colonel Gartside) to their deaths.

Bean was with them, and watched them advance to the reserve line, which they thought was the front line. But that lay a kilometre or more ahead, across bare, rising country, in clear view of the Turks. Under increasingly heavy fire – Bean likened it to walking through a dust storm in Sydney – the Australians went forward. After an age, they landed in the frontline trenches manned by surprised soldiers from Lancashire (known from there on by the Australians as Tommies Trench) but Brigadier McCay called out 'Onwards Australians!' and forward they went.

From Tommies Trench, Bean watched: 'The fire was terrific ... a twig of olive lying beneath the trees was sent spinning into the air as though the bullets were playing tipcat, and earth from the parapet was constantly showered on to the heads and bodies of the troops in the trench.' Line after line of men scrambled from the trench, clutching rifles and bayonets, forcing themselves forward.

Asked to deliver a message to McCay, Bean followed a telephone line forward into the inferno for about 250 metres and found him behind a little earthwork, 100 metres behind the Australian front line, with the Turkish line perhaps 300 metres ahead of that. McCay's Staff Sergeant Monks had been hit on the way to this spot, his last words: 'I'm hit through the heart.' That night McCay searched for him by lighting matches, but he was never found. (His name is on the Lone Pine memorial.)

The attack simply ran out of men. They dug in where they were that night, at a place that came to be called the Redoubt line.

According to Bean, on 8 May the New Zealand Brigade suffered 771 casualties, including 120 killed and 134 missing believed dead, while the Australian 2nd Brigade suffered 1056 casualties, including 172 killed and 335 missing. The survivors returned to Anzac Cove.

Three weeks later, the British 42nd Division advanced by night and took the Turkish skirmishing positions 250 metres ahead of the Redoubt line, virtually without a shot being fired. This was the final British position at Helles, which then settled into trench warfare until the final evacuation in January 1916.

'Goodbye Cobber': The Charge at the Nek, 7 August 1915

A series of operations was designed in August to take the heights above Anzac Cove, the Sari Bair range. The Anzac front line was situated on one of the ridges running up to the prominent heights, from Lone Pine in the south through Courtney's, Steel's and Quinn's posts to the higher features – Baby 700, and, at the highest point, Chunuk

The Australian Light Horse regiment in the First World War were lightly armed infantry on horseback – 29 officers and 552 men, with 579 horses at full strength, commanded by a Lieutenant Colonel. A Light Horse Brigade comprised three regiments. Three brigades were formed early in the war, and all were in Egypt by early 1915. Sent to Gallipoli without their horses, they suffered terrible casualties, especially the 3rd Brigade at the Nek. After Gallipoli, some went to France, but the majority regained their beloved horses, known as 'Walers', and fought and defeated the Turks in Palestine and Syria in 1918, under the command of Lieutenant General Harry Chauvel. With New Zealand mounted troops and some Indian cavalry, they formed the famous Desert Mounted Corps.

Gallipoli

Opposite: The Light Horse Monument, Albany, Western Australia.

Above: Restored trenches at the Nek, the cemetery lies just beyond.
Right: Trooper Harold Rush lies at nearby Walker's Ridge Cemetery.

Bair, which commanded a panoramic view of the whole battlefield. Capture Chunuk Bair and the whole Turkish position was threatened. This was the Allies' last throw of the dice in the Gallipoli campaign.

At Anzac Cove, the plan was to assault the Turkish positions from two directions – a new attack by the New Zealanders from the north end of Anzac Cove to seize Chunuk Bair, and one from the existing Australian positions on Walker's Ridge at the Nek, and Quinn's Post. Fresh British reinforcements which had landed at Suvla Bay on 6 August were supposed to support this with a quick attack along the ridges from that direction. An attack at Lone Pine was also to be a diversion, dragging Turks away from the main attack.

In a war so wasteful of life, the charge of the Australian Light Horse brigades at the Nek on 7 August 1915 is one of the most futile episodes. Australia would later lose more men a year later in a single day at Fromelles, but the image of the Nek – so beautifully captured in George Lambert's painting *The Charge of the 3rd Light Horse Brigade* – is the image of Australian sacrifice that remains and still hurts. Lambert surveyed this spot with Charles Bean in 1919, when the detritus of the charge was still to be seen, the ground rough and broken up by bombs and digging and battle.

The Turks had themselves charged at the Nek, in April and again on 19 May, when they were scythed down like rows of wheat. Some of their bodies lay unrecovered where they had fallen, and these would provide a skerrick of cover for the Australians in August. (The Turks claim that Mehmet, the Turkish everyman, fought and died here, saying, 'I die happily for my country, and you my comrades will avenge me.' Which, of course, they did.)

Lambert's painting of the 7 August charge shows men – boys – some in shorts and pith helmets, a couple in long trousers and hats, running, falling, bending forward. They carry rifles, bayonets fixed. The Turks rise up in a forward trench, picking off the men without fear of being shot themselves.

Other attacks that day, including one from Quinn's Post, were supposed to support the charge at the Nek, but none distracted the Turks. That murder was called off after one wave of 50 Queenslanders had been cut down by enfilading machine-guns. But at the Nek, there was no one alive who was senior enough to stop the slaughter.

Historian Peter Burness describes how each enemy soldier would have squeezed their trigger as the Australians came into view. Survivors recall the sound of the Turkish storm of fire. Charles Bean, who was nearby, described a 'tremendous fusillade', a 'continuous roaring tempest', and added: 'One could not help an involuntary shiver: God help anyone who was out in that tornado.'

The first line was cut down. Then it was the second line's turn. New Zealand-born Captain George Hore wrote: 'We saw our fate in front of us, but we were pledged to go and ... not a man in the second line stayed in his trench ... We bent low, and ran as hard as we could.' They ran through the smoke and dust kicked up by bullets towards the Turkish trench. Hore recalled: 'I passed our first line, all dead or dying it seemed, and went on a bit further, and flung myself down about 40 yards from the Turkish trenches.' Most of his men had been hit, but Hore had some protection from a small fold in the ground and the body of a Turk 'dead about six weeks!' And then another line of 150 men went. And another.

One of those killed in the second wave was Trooper Harold Rush, of the 10th Light Horse, who is buried nearby on Walker's Ridge. His gravestone reads: 'His Last Words. Goodbye Cobber, God Bless You'.

A descendant of the 'Lonesome Pine', Australian War Memorial.

'The Brigadier came down and congratulated us and said we have added to the reputation and our Glory which will last for ever etc. etc. But you could have my share of all the Glory of the Battle of "Lonesome Pine" (as the Hill is called from the one straggly old pine that once grew on its rugged top but which our Artillery has long since torn to ribbons and splinters) for one of the poor boys who died or was mangled to death there. Goodbye. Pray that war may never come to Australia.'
—Lieutenant Colonel 'Pompey' Elliott – letter to his wife, Kate, 8 August 1915

Four waves of 150 men stood up in the trenches and faced the certainty of being hit and the probability of being killed. To call this anything but a massacre is to demean the bravery of the men who died that day. Their sacrifice achieved nothing, the August offensive was a tragic failure. All that remained was to survive and to wait. Without further massive reinforcement, which in the context of the slaughter in France was never going to happen, Constantinople was a distant dream.

One Long Grave: Lone Pine, 6–10 August 1915

Capturing the hills above Anzac Cove was the essence of a bold plan developed by the commander of the ANZAC forces, General Birdwood, in May. He envisaged a breakout from the north of the ANZAC position, to take the Turks by surprise, although the broken countryside would have made this a tough job, even if executed in strength and with proper reconnaissance and planning.

Instead, when finally carried out under the leadership of commander-in-chief General Hamilton, the August battles were a complex of bravery and sacrifice from the officers and men, and ineptitude and incompetence from their leaders. The German general in overall command of the Turkish defence, Liman von Sanders, replaced one general with Mustafa Kemal, who as a battalion commander had saved the day on 25 April. Kemal's quick and strategic thinking did it again – at Suvla, Chunuk Bair and at Lone Pine, despite the ground gained by the Australians.

There is still confusion about what was the main attack and which were the diversions in the August campaign. Whatever was in the minds of the British generals, the most important strategic aim remained the capture of Chunuk Bair from the north. An elaborate and complex plan was developed, one that depended on separate forces moving with split-second timing over an unmapped twist of ridges. It was undertaken by Australians, New Zealanders, Gurkhas and British on the night of 6 August.

Although many failed to find their starting point, the New Zealanders of the Wellington Battalion did take Chunuk Bair, and held it on the night of 8 August, though they were virtually wiped out doing so, and Mustafa Kemal attacked on 10 August and drove their replacements out. The diversionary attacks by the British at Helles and the Australians had also been costly at Anzac.

The only place where significant Turkish ground was gained was at Lone Pine, at the southern end of the line. Lone Pine had been briefly occupied by the ANZACS on 25 April but had been retaken by the Turks who, on 6 August, occupied the heights looking down the ridge. They had strengthened the Lone Pine end of the plateau with reinforced trenches covered by pine logs and firing points. The position was so strongly defended that the Turks did not imagine anyone would attack from this direction.

But the Australians had prepared by digging tunnels into the narrow no man's land of about 100 metres separating the reinforced Turkish trenches from the Australians' position, 'The Pimple'. After a brief artillery barrage, the Australians moved out of their tunnels at 5.30 p.m. on 6 August after blowing mines in other tunnels to make protective craters. They ran across the gap, suffering surprisingly few casualties, only to discover the covered trenches. Some tried to winkle

Above: William Dunstan (VC) survived the war to become a distinguished newspaper executive with Melbourne's *Herald and Weekly Times*. He was the father of Keith Dunstan, who served in the Second World War and became one of Australia's favourite newspaper columnists, and grandfather of historian David Dunstan. William Dunstan died after going to the Caulfield races in March 1957.
Right: Lone Pine trenches.

out the Turks by poking bayonets between the logs, others by heaving logs up and getting into the weird, musty and dangerous gloom of the maze below. Following troops ran over the frontline trenches to the uncovered reserve system behind.

What followed in the warren of trenches underground was a hellish medieval fight, where Australians and Turks fought with whatever they had – bayonet, bullet, fist, shovel, pickaxe. It was so crowded that to move forward someone had to be killed and walked over. Savage fighting continued into the night, and for five unrelenting days, as the Turks counter-attacked. On 10 August both sides stopped fighting, out of sheer exhaustion.

Private James Croker, of the 11th Battalion, said, 'We was like a mob of ferrets in a rabbit hole ... It was one long grave, only some of us was still alive in it.' Lieutenant Colonel Harold 'Pompey' Elliott, whose 7th Battalion went into the fight on 8 August, said Lone Pine

The Lone Pine battlefield occupied the space of two tennis courts – now the CWGC cemetery and the main Australian Memorial at Gallipoli.

was an 'underground city' except that the entire area would be contained within a couple of tennis courts. His 7th Battalion went into Lone Pine with fourteen officers and 680 soldiers, and lost twelve officers and 342 men.

Lone Pine saw extraordinary bravery, and the awarding of seven Victoria Crosses – four to members of the 7th Battalion – most of them for actions that involved catching and throwing back Turkish bombs or hand grenades; Lance Corporal Leonard Keysor, 1st Battalion, kept returning bombs and grenades for more than two days on

7–8 August, in one of the most spectacular individual feats of the war. Turkish bombs were cast iron jobs, about the size and shape of a cricket ball with an external fuse, and Keysor would judge them, catch them and throw them back, or smother them with a sandbag or his coat. Remarkably he survived Gallipoli, but was wounded re-enacting his feat for a film in 1927. He died in 1951.

Another surviving VC winner was Lieutenant William Symons, 7th Battalion, who was asked to take charge of the defence of a trench by Pompey Elliott, who told him, 'I don't expect to see you again, but we must not lose that post.' Six officers had already been killed or badly wounded there. Symons led the charge to retake the trench, killing two Turks with his revolver. Under fire from three sides and, quite literally, from above, where the woodwork of the trench had been set on fire, he defended the position until the Turks gave up.

VCs were also awarded to Corporal Alex Burton (posthumously), Corporal William Dunstan and Lieutenant Frederick Tubb, of the 7th Battalion, who were in a group of ten men led by Tubb which repelled a sustained Turkish attack on a trench on 9 August.

Tubb was above the parapet, firing his revolver, which encouraged others to get up and do the same. Bean reports him saying, 'Good boy,' and slapping the back of one of his men who had knelt on the parapet and shot a 'sheltering Turk'. That man said later, of Tubb, 'With him up there, you couldn't think of getting your head down.'

When a series of grenades exploded in the trench, killing four men and knocking a fifth down, the wounded Tubb continued to fight, supported by Burton and Dunstan. Then a big explosion knocked down the sandbags in a sap between the Australians and Turks on the other side. The three fought off the Turks twice more, and were rebuilding the sandbags when another explosion killed Burton and temporarily blinded Dunstan.

Corporal Burton from Euroa, who had been wounded on 25 April, is commemorated on the Lone Pine Memorial. Lieutenant Tubb and Corporal Dunstan survived Gallipoli.

The Last Attack: Hill 60, 21–28 August 1915

Hill 60, as described by Charles Bean, was 'little more than a swelling in the plain' about five kilometres north of Anzac Cove, inland from Suvla Bay. Though not very high, it commanded the southern end of the Suvla 'front' and the communications lines back to Anzac.

After the landings at Suvla on 7 August and the heroic failure to retain the height of Chunuk Bair, it was decided that the line between Suvla and Anzac would be better protected by taking Hill 60. It was the last tragic, useless attack of the Gallipoli campaign.

On 21–22 August, the 13th and 14th Battalions of the 4th Brigade, commanded by John Monash, along with the New Zealand Mounted Rifles, the Indian Brigade and three British battalions – no unit now anywhere near full strength – attacked across a dip towards the rise of the 'hill'.

It was like the charge at the Nek all over again. The Australians lost two-thirds of their number in the first two waves. The artillery

Most prominent among the defenders at Hill 60 was Hugo Throssell, who won the VC defending the barricade against the Turkish bombers, refusing to leave his post despite wounds to his shoulder and neck. 'By his personal courage and example he kept up the spirits of his party, and was largely instrumental in saving the situation at a critical period,' said his citation. He later married Katharine Susannah Prichard and, still affected by the war, committed suicide in 1933. 'My old war head is going phut,' he wrote.

barrage alerted the enemy and set the scrub on fire – this 'friendly fire' burned many wounded to death, and set off the grenades and ammunition they carried, killing more.

Reinforcements were required, and on 22 August the Australian 18th Battalion, which had arrived at Gallipoli just three days before, marched in. Its commander, Colonel A E Chapman, was told to charge with bomb and bayonet – but there were no bombs. Chapman complained, but was told to do the best he could. They marched before dawn to the western foot of the hill.

By 4.45 a.m. in nearly full daylight, they stopped behind a hedge. Three hundred metres away was the low summit.

The first the troops knew of their fate was an order to fix bayonets, charge magazines and make two lines – at 5 a.m. they charged towards the summit and reached a newish Turkish trench. That was easy enough, thought the men of the 18th. Some even got out their pipes for a smoko.

But soon the Turks counter-attacked, drenching the trench with

Hill 60 Cemetery stands on the site of the battleground.

machine-gun fire and bombs. Lieutenant Addison, a 28-year-old bank officer from Yass, was observed by Charles Bean 'with dying and wounded all around him' when he 'steadied and waved forward the remnant of his platoon until he himself fell pierced with several bullets'.

At 7 a.m. they were ordered to 'push on to the summit' but there were not enough survivors to achieve this, and by 10 a.m. they had retired to the relative security of trenches held by New Zealanders at the foot of the hill. The 18th had suffered 383 casualties, half of them killed, of the 750 who started.

Hill 60 was still regarded as a threat to communications between Suvla and Anzac. A mixed force of survivors was assembled to renew the battle, but no reconnaissance was undertaken. No one knew just how elaborate or extensive was the trench system constructed by the Turks on Hill 60.

The 9th Light Horse Regiment fought on the night of 27 August, losing their Colonel, Carew Reynell, of the wine-making family from Reynella in South Australia. On the next night it was the turn of the 10th Light Horse – at least, those who had survived the slaughter at the Nek. They were ordered to take 150 yards of Turkish trench near the top of the hill, and did, holding, deepening and barricading it overnight, despite a frenzied Turkish counter-attack using an 'inexhaustible supply of bombs'.

Bomber, sculpted by C. Web Gilbert, was dedicated in Broken Hill in 1925. With the action of Australian fast-bowler Jeff Thomson, *Bomber* recalls the audacity and bravery of Syd Ferrier at Hill 60.

Turkish grenades were on a long fuse and the Australian practice was to catch them like cricket balls and throw them back. This ploy had its dangers, and the Hill 60 champion, Corporal Sutton Henry 'Syd' Ferrier, was said to have returned 500 bombs that night before one blew his arm off at the elbow. Ferrier died on a hospital ship on 9 September.

The captured ground was held until the evacuation in December.

Gallipoli Today

The Anzac Cove area isn't the same as it was in 1915, as any picture from the time will tell you. The shelling, the digging, the construction of Watson's pier, and all the construction involved in supporting a battle between tens of thousands of men for eight months obviously altered the landscape. But nature has been taking it back. Elsewhere on the Gallipoli peninsula, locals have resumed farming.

There are 31 cemeteries at Gallipoli, of which 23 contain Australian burials. Of the more than 22,000 Commonwealth burials, only 9000 have been identified, while 13,000 rest in unidentified graves. In the eight months of this bitterly fought campaign more than 36,000 Commonwealth servicemen died. The more than 14,000 whose remains have never been found are commemorated individually by name on the Helles Memorial (British, Australian and Indian names), the Lone Pine Memorial (Australian and New Zealand names), and the Twelve Tree Copse, Hill 60 and Chunuk Bair Memorials (New Zealand names).

The Imperial (now Commonwealth) War Graves Commission had begun work in France in 1917, and a Graves Registration Unit was at work at Gallipoli soon after the end of the war.

The Australian Historical Mission arrived in February 1919 to report to the Australian government on what was to be done. It was led by Charles Bean, who was accompanied by painter George Lambert.

In the Anzac Cove area, Lieutenant Cyril Hughes of the Australian Engineers, assisted by Sergeant Woolley, had located about 2500 wartime graves by the time Bean arrived. Some lay buried in original cemeteries; the remains of others lay in the scrub, their uniforms still identifiable.

In some cases, especially at Helles, the graves had been disturbed and crosses destroyed, and in others the cemeteries had been 'remade' although not always in the proper positions. But, as Bean commented, 'If men could only be buried where they lay, and their names, so far as known, commemorated there, no one who ever visited Anzac could fail to appreciate their achievements.' He recommended a simple monument at the site of each post where men had fought and died, where the bodies could be gathered, giving 'the name of the post and the names of all men known to have lost their lives before it'.

John McAllister was killed on 20 May 1915, aged 22. He died the same day talks had begun to arrange a truce to bury the dead from the ferocious Turkish attacks which had vainly attempted to drive the invaders back to the beach. The Turks lost some 10,000 dead in the May attacks, Australia lost 160.

He also recommended, as part of the peace terms, that the Imperial Graves Commission be given responsibility for the whole site, that cemeteries and isolated graves be maintained where they were, and that the cemeteries be planted with Australian plants, but without altering the appearance of the battlefield. The final result at Gallipoli was pretty close to what Bean recommended.

After the Treaty of Lausanne was signed in 1923, work was able to proceed, on the land around Anzac and also around Helles, with construction completed by 1926. Except for the New Zealand National Memorial at Chunuk Bair (which was designed by the New Zealand architect S Hurst Seager), all the Commonwealth cemeteries and memorials on the peninsula were designed by the Scottish architect Sir John Burnet, who also designed the war cemeteries in Palestine. These cemeteries are distinguished by the use of stone-faced pedestal grave markers instead of headstones, a walled cross rather than a free-standing Cross of Sacrifice, and the rubble-walled ha-ha to channel flood water away.

The powerful effect that visiting Gallipoli has on Australians today is because the battlefield around Anzac Cove has been mostly left to nature since 1915. It's a small and intimate setting for the big national stories told here. Even a quick visit involves a walk on the beach where the landing took place, and to the cemeteries at both ends of the tiny beach, with their individual sad stories. John Simpson Kirkpatrick is here in the beach cemetery, and many of the men who died in the futile charge at the Nek are at the northern end of Anzac Cove in Ari Burnu Cemetery. Above you can see the impossible tangle of cliffs, and wonder how the landing came to be here.

Above the beach, the road climbs on top of the narrow no man's land between the Turkish and Anzac lines, following the roll-call of names of the positions held – Courtney's and Steel's posts, Quinn's, Walker's Ridge, the Nek, Baby 700 and up to Chunuk Bair, with its great memorial to the New Zealanders and its statue of Mustafa Kemal, the victor surveying the field. You can walk around the staggering list of names on the Australian memorial at Lone Pine, the cemetery occupying the space of two tennis courts covering the infernal maze of trenches where so many died for so little ground gained. Restored trenches across the road from the cemetery, peaceful in the sighing pines, hardly answer the question about what it must have been like here in August 1915, when the hailstorm of bombs was thrown across these tiny plots of land.

Even today the country between the beach at Anzac Cove and the line of frontline posts on the second ridge, from Lone Pine towards Chunuk Bair, is tangled and difficult to walk. There are no tracks up Shrapnel Valley and Monash Gully to the back of Quinn's Post – here the scrub has returned, much as it was before the war.

Nonetheless, natural and human interventions have substantially changed Gallipoli. Bushfires and landslides, especially behind the Australian line along the second ridge and behind Quinn's Post, have changed the landscape considerably. Trenches have filled in naturally, if they were not filled in 1915. There are cemeteries and memorials everywhere, from Helles to Suvla Bay.

The walkers and road builders and those who choose to remember among the vast and growing crowds on Anzac Day might heed the warning found on a gravestone in the Shrapnel Valley cemetery: 'Tread gently on the green grass sod, a mother's love lies here.'

The Gallipoli peninsula was declared a national historical park in 1973, and Anzac Cove was named in 1984, but if there is a management plan for the whole of Gallipoli, no one has put it into practice. The winners of the Gallipoli International Peace Park Project in 1998, a Norwegian architectural firm, recommended that little be changed, but conservation or management work as a result of the competition has not taken place.

In February 2005, excavations in preparation for road widening commenced around Anzac Cove. Apparently this was at the request of the Australian government, concerned about access and convenience, especially on Anzac Day, when thousands of people attend ceremonies at North Beach. Tremendous controversy ensued in Australia about the impact a three-lane road above Anzac Cove would have on the area and the remains still there. The cemeteries and memorials may not have been affected, but the shape of the ground around Anzac Cove has been changed forever.

Further questions were asked after the party that occurred on Anzac Eve in 2005; was success going to spoil Anzac? Is it to become 'Anzacland', a tourist attraction, or a properly conserved and managed battlefield site sacred to the memory of what happened there?

What Gallipoli desperately needs is a park management plan. It would be appropriate if the whole area was placed on the World Heritage List, but this has to be initiated by the Turkish government. It is, after all, their country, and they won. But it would be entirely appropriate for Australia, and other countries, to support a listing, and make a substantial contribution to the conservation of the whole park.

A view of Ari Burnu, with Plugge's Plateau rising behind taken in 2003 from the No. 2 Outpost Cemetery before ill-considered roadworks sliced through the world's best-preserved First World War battlefield.

On Sacred Ground: A walk from Anzac Cove

Charles Bean wrote that when the Australians landed 'they found themselves on the foot of an exceedingly steep, almost precipitous hill 300 feet high which, except for a minor lower knoll around which the boat grounded, rose straight from the bank that bordered the shingle.'

I was privileged to spend a few days in a Commonwealth War Graves Commission gardener's hut in 1996, and did as everyone with the luck to be there does: Bean in hand, I walked as far as I could in the footsteps of the Anzacs, up from the beach to the cemetery at Ari Burnu at the northern end of Anzac Cove, to Plugge's Plateau, and across the wild ravines and the razorback ridge in an attempt to gain the summit at Third Ridge; walking alone, at dawn, during the day, at sunset, and once in the dark of a tremendous thunderstorm. You cannot vicariously experience what the Anzacs did and felt, but you can make a connection with the country and the stories. And the storytellers.

In 2003, Anzac Cove was as it had been, the road winding above Anzac Cove an intrusion on the landscape, but in more or less the same place as a track that had been established in 1915. Any photograph of Anzac Cove at that time will show the tremendous amount of work the Diggers had done in the lee of the hill. While it's difficult to envisage the small town established there, most of the contours of the landscape have remained the same, subject to nature. The soil is a gluggy clay, and there has been much erosion, especially with loss of vegetation during the war, subsequent regrowth and destructive bushfires. But the Sphinx, Plugge's Plateau, the

heights of the ridges at Ari Burnu and Hell Spit are still as they were.

Man-made changes such as the Anzac Commemorative Site, above North Beach, and the controversial roadwork of 2005 mean that the view from the landing beach and the walk up to Plugge's and beyond is no longer possible. The road is a wide scar, the shoulders of the ridges dislocated, and the fill has covered the beach.

The landscape has reverted to normal agricultural use at Helles and Suvla, as it has in France and many other places, but Anzac Cove was unique because it had been left alone – the country was not suitable for anything else. Anzac will still weave its magic on anyone with time to pause for contemplation, but walking the ground near the beach will be a different experience now.

In 1996, the bank at Anzac Cove was shoulder height, when standing on the beach, and gave the impression that it would have afforded some protection from shots fired from higher up. You could see the Sphinx, the prominent formation of the cliffs above, and the impression of ridges beyond the beach – but you could not see much more than the bank, and the steep hill rising above it.

'It was too steep for normal hill climbing – they had to help themselves up by their rifle butts and haul themselves by the stems and roots of the low holly and arbutus scrub that thickly covered the slope. Men could only be seen if they moved. In that respect the Turk had the advantage and a fair number of the climbing men were wounded and left hanging among the scrub,' wrote Bean.

From the top of the bank I saw a ridge above me, perhaps the objective, First Ridge.

High above that a white monument glistened in the weak sunshine. It could be Chunuk Bair, or one of the memorials along the road to it.

Over the bank, across the road, over a drainage ditch and I began to climb the slope in the same way, minus rifle but encumbered with cameras. I struggled up the hill, pulling on branches and finding some of them coming loose – dead from a recent bushfire. Low gorse, and holly, and flowers bent on the cold wind.

After a stiff fifteen-minute climb I reached the top of Plugge's Plateau. It was quiet, with just the wind rushing in my ears. A bird squeaked somewhere near in the bushes. Below at Ari Burnu a bus pulled up, half a dozen people walked to the cemetery.

I walked to the inland end of Plugge's. From there it looked as if this plateau connected directly with the next ridge, where the Sphinx emerges from Walker's Ridge and Russell's Top and the Nek. There seemed to be a way onto the hill known as Baby 700 and one of the ridges down from Chunuk Bair to what is now known as Lone Pine.

But between Plugge's and Russell's Top is a precipitous drop of perhaps 50 metres to a low, narrow spine known to the Diggers as the Razor's Edge. The contorted countryside is folded and twisted like scrunched-up newspaper.

Across from Plugge's on the seaward sides of the ridge line, and along Shrapnel Gully can be seen horizontal bands, like sheep tracks on the side of a hill. These are the remains of 1915 trenches and tracks which had terraced the whole area, providing places sometimes sheltered from snipers, sometimes mined by the Turks, sometimes overrun, sometimes nests for Australian soldiers.

Much has fallen away in landslides and weather. As Peter Stanley has pointed out in his book *Quinn's Post*, the seaward side of the whole position has collapsed.

In 1915 different parties of soldiers plunged down the steep sides of gullies, and crawled up the steep slopes – some even up the precipitous cliff face of the Sphinx. The fight was carried on in small isolated places. Bean found some of their remains on his 1919 expedition lying where they fought and died.

'How in this strange country, amid the sweet smelling thyme on the uplands on that beautiful bright spring day, the fight which after the first rush, had seemed almost over, gradually became intense again and swayed hour after hour on the second ridge until the factor that wins or loses battles – the strain upon nerves – became almost unbearable so that to many brave men the smell of thyme longs afterwards brought a shudder,' he wrote.

During that first morning, some of the Australians, landing to the north of Ari Burnu on North Beach, scrambled up the gravel and mud cliffs next to the protuberance of the Sphinx. One reinforcement said, 'The original men must have been a combination of mule, goat and lion to have succeeded as they did.' This is what I tried to do, scrambling from a pit on the top of Plugge's down the steep sides, aided by the horizontal skeletons of tracks, then up the side of Russell's Top to the Nek and Walker's Ridge. At the top there are many gun pits and trenches, still two or three metres deep. Inside one, the sides washed away by the recent rain, was a length of bone, Turkish or Australian, who could tell. All around are other things exposed by the rain – pieces of pottery, a buttonhole surround, unidentifiable pieces of metal, fragments of bone.

Along Walker's, the small pines flourished in an impassable tangle; you could see over them but could not walk through them. Pictures from the war show this area – most of it was quickly chopped, blasted and destroyed – with no trees. It's hard to imagine charging through this sort of bush.

I walked from the Nek across to Baby 700, and its cemetery of 493 burials, and up the hard road to Chunuk Bair, wind whispering softly, a thrush in the pines.

At the top there is a monument, a tall tapering pylon, next to a double-life-sized bronze of Mustafa Kemal, looking across to the Dardanelles. Around the perimeter are a number of restored Turkish trenches, lined with pine logs. From here you can just see the Straits, far off, and the wisdom of Mustafa

Kemal in knowing that he had to defend this hill no matter what the cost. It still commands everything in the vicinity. Just below the summit of Chunuk Bair is a circle of large monuments, like huge white stone billboards, that tell the story of Mustafa Kemal and his men's deeds in August 1915.

No one else was there on this cold April day. It had taken me perhaps four hours of brisk climbing and walking to make the few kilometres up from the beach to Chunuk Bair.

From here, you can pick the tops of the ridges as they wrinkle down like the fingers in a hand. But from the ground, walking up, there is no such clarity. Even having walked them, it is difficult to convey the impossibility of the terrain. A worse place to stage the first modern amphibious landing and invasion could hardly have been picked.

I began to walk down the hill, along the line of the top of the second ridge, towards Lone Pine. It is steep enough in the beginning so that even on the macadam you have to be careful. I walked down past the roll-call of sacred sites learned each Anzac Day in primary school: Baby 700, Quinn's, Courtney's, Steel's, and that most evocative of all, Lone Pine. The Australian Memorial there has thousands of names of thousands of missing, many of them killed and buried in the captured Turkish trenches beneath your feet. But it's too peaceful, and too beautiful to permit any connection with the savagery that took place in this small spot.

I set out on a course I thought would lead me to somewhere south of Hell Spit and Beach Cemetery. Instead, I plunged across uneven ground and down into a gully – I think it must have been White's Valley – and there was nothing for it but to climb up the other side, and then down again. A steep climb up and along the ridge led me to the intersection of Rest Gully, Monash Valley and Shrapnel Gully. There is a white sand watercourse (dry on this day) at the bottom, with small smooth rocks and dead branches. Some bush-bashing for half an hour through these obstructions, and I emerged at the beautiful Shrapnel Valley Cemetery as the sun dropped over the ridge.

I walked across the modern road to Beach Cemetery and looked north along Anzac Cove and out into the Aegean. The water slapped on the shore, as it always had. I walked back up Anzac Cove, along the sighing sand, onto the road at Ari Burnu where I had started, and down the road to the hut.

Bean, at the end of his mission to Anzac in 1919, quotes from a memorial held in the great museum in Athens to an earlier force that had served in the Dardanelles. This was around 440 BC, when the Athenians battled an insurgency nearby.

Of the soldiers who fought here, the poet wrote:

*These by the Dardanelles laid down
their shining youth
In battle and won fair renown for their
native land,
So that their enemy groaned carrying
war's harvest from the field
But for themselves they founded a
deathless monument of valour.*

Cemeteries, Memorials, Museums: Gallipoli Peninsula

Anzac

The **Anzac Commemorative Site** is located at North Beach where, on the morning of 25 April 1915, troops of the Australian 1st Division came ashore some minutes after the first landings at Ari Burnu and Anzac Cove to the south. North Beach became the site of a major casualty clearing station and resupply area for the Gallipoli campaign, and surviving Anzacs were evacuated from here during December 1915.

The Anzac Commemorative Site, North Beach.

The memorial, which was dedicated on Anzac Day 2000, has a commemorative and educational focus, with panels that tell the story of the Gallipoli campaign. It provides the major venue for the many thousands of Australians and New Zealanders who attend the Dawn Service on Anzac Day, built to take pressure off the small cemeteries at Anzac Cove where the service used to be staged.

Ari Burnu Cemetery lies at the northern end of Anzac Cove, between the beach and the cliff under Plugge's Plateau. Ari Burnu ('Bee Point') was an exposed position subject to shellfire from Turkish positions, useful in 1915 only as a cemetery. The cemetery was made in the first days after the landing nearby. In 1926 and 1927, graves were brought

Ari Burnu Cemetery.

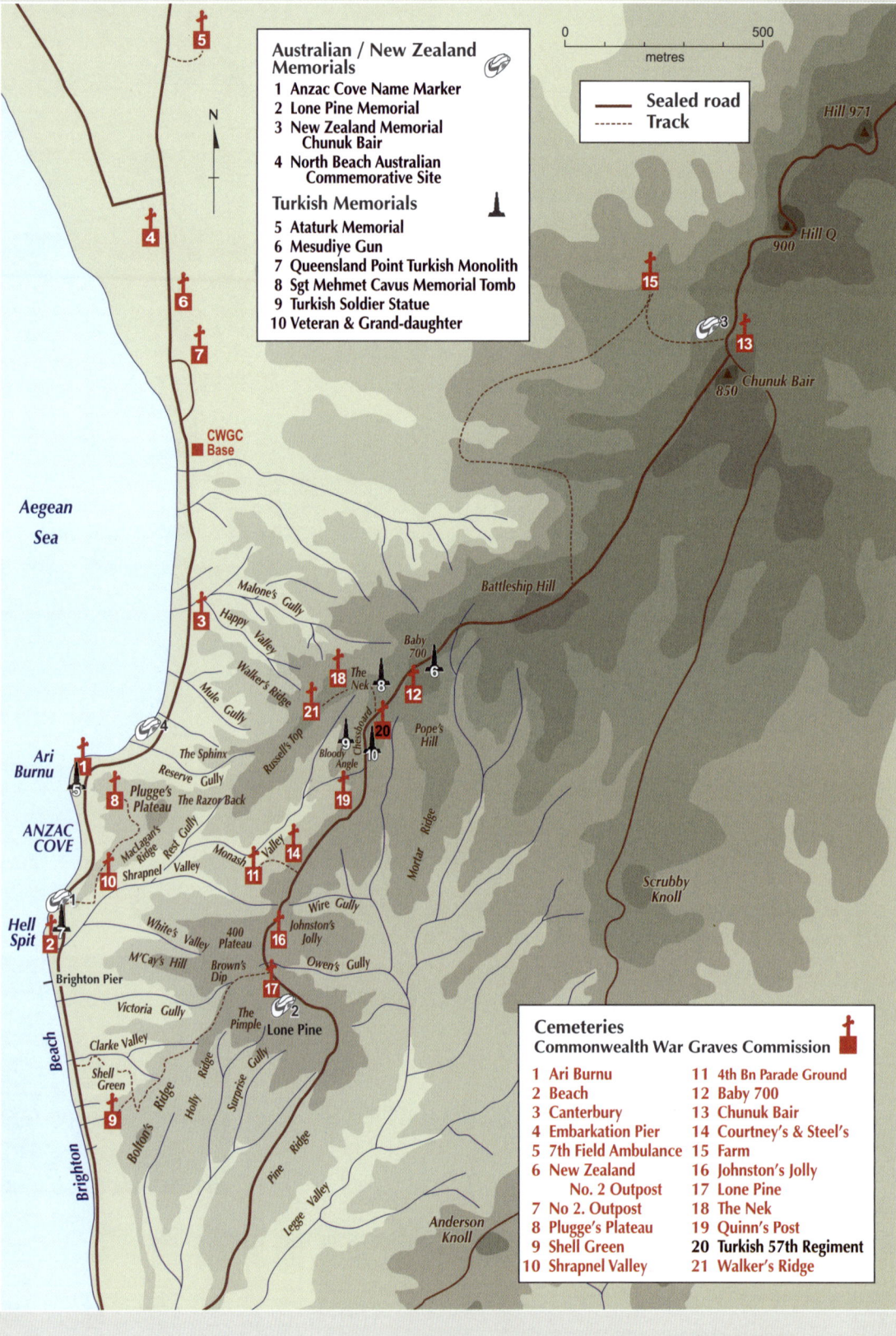

into it from other cemeteries at Kilid Bahr Anglo-French Cemetery and Gallipoli Consular Cemetery.

There are 252 Commonwealth First World War servicemen buried or commemorated here. The 151 Australians include 82 of the Light Horsemen killed at the charge at the Nek on 7 August.

Row A, the first graves above the sea wall, is mostly soldiers of the 8th Light Horse from Western Victoria. The 10th Light Horse, from Western Australia, are in rows E and F, including the grave of Sergeant Duncan Bain, who was on the right of the fourth line and was heard just before the charge 'calling to his men to get ready and that they would be up on Baby 700 for breakfast'. Bain's brother, on the left of the line, did not leave the trench and survived.

Lieutenant Colonel Albert Miell, commander of the 9th Light Horse had returned from Lemnos hospital for the attack at the Nek. He looked over the parapet of an observation post before the charge and was shot through the head. Had he lived, he might have called off the suicidal mess after the first wave had been cut down.

Baby 700 Cemetery was made after the Armistice. There are now 493 Commonwealth servicemen of the First World War buried or commemorated in this cemetery. Special memorials commemorate ten Australian soldiers believed to be among the identified. The 43 identified burials include 32 Australians, one a Light Horseman from the battle at the Nek, ten New Zealanders and one Briton from the Royal Naval Division.

Baby 700 is so called to distinguish it from another hill thought to be about the same height behind, and known as Big 700 or Battleship Hill; in fact, Baby 700 is 590 feet, or 180 metres, high.

The hill was the objective of the Australian 3rd Brigade on 25 April, and was occupied early in the morning by parties of the 11th and 12th battalions. They were joined by part of the Auckland Infantry Battalion later, but in the afternoon they were driven off the hill and it was not taken again.

Bean and the Historical Mission found that the Turks had made a line of burials of 1st, 2nd and 12th battalion men during the 24 May armistice, and nearby were some from the Auckland Battalion, thus finding for certain the men who had fought at this place on Anzac Day.

On the back slope behind Baby 700 is the **Mesudiye Gun**. The gun is from the Turkish cruiser of the same name, sunk on 13 December

Opposite: Map of the Anzac Cove area.

Baby 700 Cemetery.

The Mesudiye Gun.

PILGRIMAGE

Right: Wallace Anderson's small but much-loved 1936 statue of Simpson and his donkey stands outside the Shrine of Remembrance, Melbourne. Eminent historian Ken Inglis remarks that this was the 'first statue anywhere of an individual member of the AIF'.

Below: John Simpson Kirkpatrick's headstone, Beach Cemetery, Anzac.

John Simpson Kirkpatrick, who served as John Simpson but was better known as 'the bloke with the donk', is still where his mates buried him on 19 May 1915 at Beach. An enduring symbol of sacrifice and the Anzac spirit, Simpson was in reality an English merchant sailor, born in 1892. He deserted in Newcastle NSW in 1910, and worked as an itinerant labourer, with distinctly socialist views. He joined up in 1914, looking for a passage back to England, but instead found himself in the Australian Army Medical Corps in 1914, landing at Anzac Cove on 25 April. He soon found work using various donkeys, with names Murphy and Abdul. He was cheerfully brave, or fatalistic, and was killed on 19 May after just three weeks carrying the wounded back down Shrapnel Valley. The 'real' Simpson has been subsumed by the myth. At Gallipoli he was unremarkable for courage and sacrifice, courageous though he undoubtedly was.

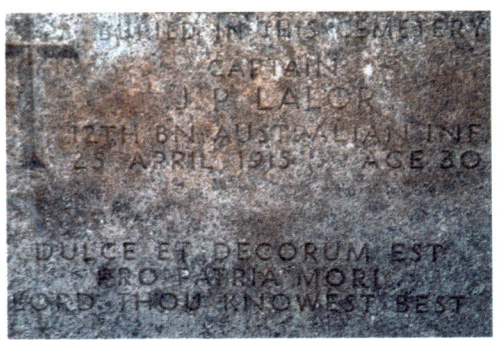

Captain Joseph Peter Lalor had the independence of mind of his grandfather, Peter Lalor of the Eureka Stockade. He is said to have been a wharfie in London, joined and deserted the Royal Navy, served with the French Foreign Legion, fought in a South American revolution before he was 23, when he joined the Australian army, in 1908. He carried a family sword beyond Baby 700 on 25 April – he was killed that day, one of the furthest men out. He is buried at Baby 700.

1914 by the British submarine *B11*. Her guns were salvaged, and this one, which was placed here after the evacuation, was seen by Bean in 1919.

Beach Cemetery is situated on what was known as Hell Spit or Queensland Point, at the southern end of Anzac Cove. It was used from the day of the landing at Anzac almost until the evacuation.

There are 391 Commonwealth First World War servicemen buried or commemorated here, including 295 Australians. The graves are where they were laid in 1915, in a curved cemetery looking out to the Aegean over a retaining wall. South of the cemetery is a concrete Second World War pillbox, falling into the sea.

Buried in Beach Cemetery is Lieutenant Colonel George Braund, a New South Wales MP, vegetarian, theosophist, teetotaller – and a bit deaf – who was killed by friendly fire on 4 May when he failed to acknowledge a challenge by a sentry. Braund was unfairly criticised for his lack of leadership or recklessness in the desperate hours after the landing.

Lieutenant Colonel Lancelot Clarke, commander of the 12th Battalion, was killed on Anzac Day. Clarke, aged 56, was writing a message in his notebook when he was killed, with his batman. Major Sydney Robertson was killed on Baby 700 on 25 April – he reached about as far inland as any Australian on that first day.

Some of the men buried in the Beach Cemetery were killed by shellfire ranging onto the actual beach or pier, such as Commander Edward Cater RN, the 'bloke with the monocle', a beach commander on the original landing day who was killed on the pier in August helping an incoming boat.

The **Turkish Monolith** on the roadside above Beach Cemetery describes the actions of the defenders, the 8th Company of the 27th Infan-

Beach Cemetery.

Second World War pillbox, south of Anzac Cove. (1996)

The Mustafa Kemal Monolith, on which are carved the most moving words about reconciliation after any war, is appropriately located above Ari Burnu. By 1985, when the monolith was unveiled, the Gallipoli victor had become president of modern Turkey, and was known as 'Ataturk', father of the Turks. The monolith bears his words spoken in 1934 to some early pilgrims:

Those heroes that shed their blood and lost their lives
You are now lying in the soil of a friendly country.
Therefore rest in peace.
There is no difference between the Johnnies and the Mehmets to us
Where they lie side by side
Here in this country of ours.
You, the mothers,
Who sent their sons from far-away countries
Wipe away your tears.
Your sons are now lying in our bosom
And are in peace.
After having lost their lives on this land
They have become our sons as well.

Ataturk's words may be read at his memorial in Anzac Parade, Canberra, near the Australian War Memorial. Ataturk is also commemorated in Albany, WA, where the entrance to Princess Royal Harbour was named Ataturk Entrance in 1985.

try Regiment. The **Anzac Cove Marker** nearby was unveiled on 17 April 1985 when this place was renamed Anzak Covu or Anzac Cove. The beach itself had no name or significance before 1915 because it was so small and unimpressive; during the Anzac occupation it became a busy if dangerous small port, with a pier (Watson's Pier), water-making facilities, and primitive warehouses for food and ammunition.

Canterbury Cemetery is a little way inland below Walker's Ridge between Anzac Cove and the No. 2 Outpost cemeteries.

Twenty of the 22 New Zealand graves are from New Zealand's Canterbury Mounted Rifles Brigade, giving the cemetery its name. There are 27 graves in all. The cemetery was made in 1919, and the burials gathered from nearby cemeteries and graves, including deaths recorded from early May until December, just before the evacuation.

Canterbury Cemetery.

Chunuk Bair Cemetery was made after the Armistice on the site where the Turks had buried some of those Commonwealth soldiers who were killed on 6–8 August. There are now 632 Commonwealth servicemen of the First World War buried in this cemetery. Only ten of the burials are identified: eight from New Zealand, one British and one Gurkha.

Chunuk Bair was one of the main objectives in the Battle of Sari Bair, fought 6–10 August 1915. The Wellington Infantry Battalion and some of the Gloucesters and Welsh reached the summit, and were later joined by men of the Auckland Infantry and Mounted Rifles. These troops, after repulsing incessant Turkish attacks, were reinforced by the Otago Battalion and the Wellington Mounted Rifles. The 6th Loyal North Lancashire Regiment relieved them on the evening of 9 August, but the position was taken by a determined and overwhelming counter-attack led by Mustafa Kemal.

The cemetery also contains the **Chunuk Bair (New Zealand) Memorial Wall**. It is one of four memorials erected to commemorate New Zealand soldiers who died on the Gallipoli peninsula and whose graves are not known. This memorial relates to the Battle of Sari Bair and bears 852 names.

Chunuk Bair Cemetery and NZ Memorial.

The **New Zealand National Memorial** was erected on top of Chunuk Bair 'In honour of the soldiers of the New Zealand Expeditionary Force. 8th August 1915. From the uttermost ends of the earth.' It stands at the end of a Turkish trench taken by the Wellingtons on 8 August.

Facing the New Zealand National Memorial is the **Ataturk Statue**, a 10-metre-high bronze of Mustafa Kemal, with four large concrete cannon balls nearby, which mark the spot where he was hit over the heart by a piece of shrapnel, but saved by his pocket watch.

There are also restored trenches at Chunuk Bair.

Above: Ataturk was here: The sign at these restored Turkish trenches at Chunuk Bair indicates where Ataturk gave his famous order.
Below: Courtney's and Steel's Post Cemetery.

The **Turkish Soldiers Memorial** is made up of five stone monoliths between Baby 700 and Chunuk Bair; these give the Turkish story of Gallipoli. Memorial two, second from the left, has the famous order of Mustafa Kemal to his 57th Regiment on 25 April: 'I do not order you to attack. I order you to die. In the time which passes until we die, other troops can take our places and other commanders can master the situation.' Memorial five is about the August battles, which were 'unsuccessful due to the courageous defence operation and the zeal of the heroic Turkish soldier. During the battles which were fought in this sector the Turkish army suffered 9200 casualties and the enemy 12000.'

Courtney's and Steel's Post Cemetery lies west of the road along the former front line on MacLaurin's Ridge, occupying what was Steel's or Steele's Post, the southerly of the two positions. Both places were taken on 25 April, and held against sometimes ferocious attack until

the evacuation in December. It is named for Major T H Steel of the 14th Battalion, about whom little is known. At the time and since, it is often spelled Steele's, but the official spelling is Steel's.

Courtney's Post is named for Lieutenant Colonel R E Courtney, CB, VD, who commanded the 14th Battalion, which arrived here on 27 April 1915. There are 225 Commonwealth servicemen of the First World War buried or commemorated in the cemetery.

Standing in any of the cemeteries along the ridge line it is, as always, difficult to imagine what the scene would have been like in 1915. The eastern wall of the cemetery is about where the Australian frontline trenches were. The road is the narrow no man's land, the Turks throwing bombs and siting machine-guns often in positions behind the Australians; where the cemetery is now was a warren of trenches and tunnels, stretching back for 25 metres where the ridge slopes away steeply. At the back ridge was a shanty town of tunnels, trenches and shelters; much of this part of the ridge has washed away. The positions were held first by men of the 11th Battalion, then on 27 April by the 14th. Lance Corporal (later Captain) Albert Jacka of the 14th won his VC at Courtney's on 19 May.

Many of the men known to be buried in the cemetery are from the bitter fighting of the first two weeks of the campaign. They include sailors turned soldiers from the Royal Naval Division. A survivor, Lance Corporal Walter Parker, won the VC. Parker was a medical orderly who, though badly wounded, showed extraordinary courage in tending the wounded and organising stretcher-bearers under fire. He miraculously survived the war.

Embarkation Pier: Pte John Sutton was, like many Anzacs, English. He was from Darwen, England, his parents lived in Auckland, New Zealand, and he served in the Australian 25th Battalion.

Bill Baker: Brother Bill a'sniping fell, we love him still, we ever will.

Embarkation Pier Cemetery is a little way inland from Embarkation Pier at the north end of North Beach (or Ocean Beach), between the beach and the road from Anzac to Suvla.

Early in August 1915, the Embarkation Pier area was occupied by the headquarters of two divisions, and later by a casualty clearing station. The pier was made to evacuate wounded from the Battle of Sari Bair, but it came under heavy rifle and shell fire and was abandoned after just two days. Apart from five original burials, the cemetery is made up of burials brought in after the Armistice. There are now 944 Commonwealth servicemen buried or commemorated in the cemetery. Special memorials commemorate 262 casualties known or believed to be among the 662 unidentified burials. The identified casualties include seven Australians.

Battalion Chaplain Andrew Gillison from Melbourne is buried here. The morning following the battle for Hill 60, he was conducting a service for the dead when he heard a wounded man calling. With two other soldiers, Gillison rescued the wounded Englishman who was being tormented by ants. But Gillison and one of the soldiers, Corporal Ronald Pittendrigh, were shot by a sniper and died of their wounds. (Pittendrigh, who was buried at sea, is commemorated on the Lone Pine Memorial.)

The **Farm Cemetery** is reached down a steep footpath which runs from the fire-break that starts south of Chunuk Bair Cemetery. It takes about half an hour to walk there and back. It is rarely visited and very peaceful.

The cemetery was made after the Armistice. There are now 652 men buried or commemorated in this cemetery. Special memorials commemorate seven soldiers believed to be buried among them. 645 burials are unidentified. There are just seven identified casualties: six British and one New Zealand.

The Farm was a stone shepherd's hut on the western slopes of Chunuk Bair, known to the Turks as 'Aghyl' (sheepfold), which was passed by the troops who held Chunuk Bair on 6–10 August. On 8 August, it was occupied by the 10th Gurkhas, part of the 9th Royal Warwicks, and the Maoris. Other British units reached it the next day.

The Farm Cemetery.

4th Battalion Parade Ground Cemetery is on the far side of hundreds of metres of Australian trenches – some restored with pine logs, others slowly filling in with needles and Gallipoli soil – across the road from Johnston's Jolly. Bits of barbed wire and rusted tin can still be found here, though decades of scroungers have removed most of the spent bullets and badges. From these trenches, a short walk out to the edge of the 400 Plateau provides a superb view of the heights above Anzac Cove.

The track down to the 4th Battalion Parade Ground Cemetery is found just before reaching the Courtney's and Steel's Post Cemetery. It's a steep and difficult 300-metre descent. The cemetery can also be reached by the more intrepid by walking up Shrapnel Valley and Monash Gully past Shrapnel Valley Cemetery.

The 4th Battalion Parade Ground Cemetery was used from the end of April to the beginning of June 1915. It was enlarged after the Armistice when graves were brought in from the battlefields and from the

4th Battalion Parade Ground Cemetery.

nearby 3rd Battalion Parade Ground and 22nd Battalion Parade Ground cemeteries. The cemetery contains 119 First World War burials, seven of them unidentified. There are 106 Australians, three British who served in Australian units under assumed names, and three members of the Royal Marine Light Infantry, who had been rotated in to defend opposite Johnston's Jolly in early May, replacing the 4th Battalion for a time.

When Charles Bean and the Historical Mission came to Gallipoli in 1919, one of the first things he wanted to do was to locate the single graves of Colonel Henry MacLaurin, commander of the 1st Brigade, and Lieutenant Colonel Astley Onslow Thompson of the 4th Battalion, whom he regarded as 'two of the best leaders we ever had'. Bean knew where the graves were supposed to be, high on the second ridge, and set out to find them; both men are now in the 4th Battalion Parade Ground Cemetery.

Onslow Thompson was killed on 25 April at Johnston's Jolly, which a few of the 4th had taken that day. It was an untenable position, as Onslow Thompson understood. An hour or so after taking the Jolly, according to Bean, 'just as the sun was setting ... Onslow Thompson had tried to walk across the flat surface of the Jolly to the Australian line. Turkish machine-guns opened ... and Onslow Thompson was killed.' During the brief armistice in May, his body was recovered and buried back towards Lone Pine. Later, the Australians digging forward trenches, or saps, from there almost cut through his grave, and erected a plate on the side of the trench to mark the spot.

MacLaurin, 27, was the son of the chancellor of the University of Sydney. The frontline ridge between Johnston's Jolly and Courtney's and Steel's posts was known in 1915 as MacLaurin's Ridge or Hill. This is where Bean conceived the idea of Gallipoli as one big cemetery, and that 'the finest memorial of these men was that they lay where they lay ...' It is Bean's achievement that Onslow Thompson and MacLaurin were brought in from the unstable trench line where they were first laid to rest to the 4th Battalion Parade Ground, so close to where they fell.

Hill 971.

Hill 971, or Kocacimentepe, is the highest point of the Sari Bair range, and there is a Ross Bastiaan plaque and observation platform here, which gives a view back to Chunuk Bair and a sweeping panorama of Suvla. From here you could see everything that the British would have been doing in August 1915.

Gallipoli

Johnston's Jolly Cemetery is just 200 metres from Lone Pine on the road up to Chunuk Bair. It was occupied by elements of the Australian 2nd Brigade on 25 April, and might have been retained if the small numbers had been reinforced. Instead the position was retaken by the Turks and never regained. It gained its odd name from a saying attributed to Colonel (later Brigadier General) George Johnston, who commanded the 2nd Field Artillery Brigade early in the campaign, to the effect that if he had Howitzers rather than field artillery he would have a jolly good time, or would jolly up the Turks at that position. Artillery was always a problem at Gallipoli. There were never enough shells at the right time, and not enough of the right guns; field pieces have a flat trajectory, whereas Howitzer shells, which drop vertically, are much more effective against entrenched opposition.

Johnston's Jolly Cemetery.

The cemetery was made after the Armistice when graves were brought in from the battlefield. For many years the Johnston's name was misspelled at the entrance – this has been corrected. There are now 181 Commonwealth servicemen buried or commemorated here. There are special memorials to 36 Australians believed to be among the 144 unidentified burials, almost all of whom were killed in the capture of Lone Pine in August 1915.

One of the 35 men believed to be buried in or near Johnston's Jolly is Lance Corporal Edwin Hutchinson Taylor, just 23, who was born in India, although his parents Dr Vincent and Maria Jane Taylor lived after the war in Selsey in Sussex, England. Edwin enlisted in Australia in 1914. He was killed with other 4th Battalion comrades in the furnace of Lone Pine between 6 and 9 August. His epitaph is 'How can a man die better than facing fearful odds?'

The single identified grave here is that of Lance Corporal Herbert Norman of the 15th Battalion, who died between 9 and 10 May.

Lone Pine Cemetery began after the battle of Lone Pine with the insuperable problem of disposing of the bodies of the thousands of Australians and Turks; many of them were simply placed in the old Turkish trenches and buried in mass graves at the eastern end of the current cemetery, in front of the cross.

Special memorials commemorate 183 men, 182 of them Australian, who are known to be buried in the area. There are also 46 named graves here, many from graves brought in after the war. The plot at the western end is known as Brown's Dip, from a battlefield cemetery

The Lone Pine.

Above: Lone Pine: An Anzac brave in an Anzac grave.
Below: Lone Pine: The Australian Memorial.

The Nek Cemetery.

brought into Lone Pine in 1919. There are 504 unidentified burials. 1167 men are buried or commemorated in the cemetery.

The cemetery includes the **Lone Pine Memorial**, the Australian memorial to the missing at Gallipoli. It is located where the worst of the fighting took place in August. It names 4223 Australians and 709 New Zealanders who have no known grave. As such it commemorates all the great battles of Gallipoli, as well as commemorating those who died of wounds and were buried at sea.

The most haunting memorial here is the lonesome pine itself. The original tree which gave the place its name was destroyed early in the war, its roots found in a Turkish trench later on. The current tree was propagated in Australia from one found nearby and was planted after the war at the original site.

The memorial includes the names of the two Australian Victoria Cross winners who died or were fatally wounded at Lone Pine, Corporal Alexander Burton and Captain Alfred Shout: 'On the morning of the 9th Aug., 1915, with a very small party, Capt. Shout charged down trenches strongly occupied by the enemy, and personally threw four bombs among them, killing eight and routing the remainder. In the afternoon of the same day, from the position gained in the morning, he captured a further length of trench under similar conditions, and continued personally to bomb the enemy at close range under very heavy fire until he was severely wounded, losing his right hand and left eye.' He died on a hospital ship on 11 August and was buried at sea.

Also in action here were Corporal Fred Wright, 26, of Clifton Hill, Melbourne, and Corporal Harry Webb, an orphan from Essendon, who were with Lieutenant Frederick Tubb's small group that earned three VCs. Asked to stay on the floor of the trench while the rest of the group fired at the Turks from the parapet, Wright and Webb had to throw blankets on Turkish hand grenades or else chuck them back. Unhappily, one blew up in Wright's face, killing him, while Webb's hands were blown off by another. Both men are commemorated on the Lone Pine Memorial.

The **Nek Cemetery** is a short distance up the road from Quinn's Post. The Nek is the track leading along the narrow spur from Russell's Top to Baby 700, and the cemetery stands on what was no man's land.

Sergeant Mehmet's Tomb is the white obelisk in the pine trees first reached on the track to the Nek Cemetery. Mehmet, the Turkish universal soldier, was also a real one: Sergeant Mehmet and his platoon were the last men standing on 25 April as they fought off the Australian attack. The base of this memorial is the only Turkish memorial from 1919 that survived; the obelisk was added later.

The memorial stands at the furthest point reached by the Australians on 25 April – Captain Joseph Lalor started a trench here that day, but was driven off perhaps by Sergeant Mehmet. It also marks the furthest forward any of the Light Horse reached in their futile charge. Behind the cemetery are some deep reconstructed trenches.

The east side of the Nek Cemetery marks the starting point of the Australian attack on 7 August. Imagine a bare field of fire all the way back to the Turkish memorial and the quality of courage it would have taken to run into that hailstorm of machine-gun fire.

There are now 326 Commonwealth servicemen of the First World War buried or commemorated in this cemetery. 316 of the burials are unidentified but there are special memorials to five Australian soldiers known to be buried among them. The ten identified graves are those of four New Zealanders of the Otago Regiment killed in May; Australians Alexander Campbell of the 12th Battalion, killed on 25 April; Private Percy Sherman of the 3rd Battalion, killed on 19 May; and four Light Horsemen killed on 7 August: troopers Ray and Geoff Howell of the 10th; Ern Penny, also of the 10th; and Herb Stanley of the 8th.

Above: The Nek Cemetery.
Below: The Nek: Another hero's part is done, another soul gone west.

No. 2 Outpost Cemetery is a small cemetery a little way inland from the Anzac–Suvla road before Embarkation Pier Cemetery.

No. 1 and 2 outposts were made by Nelson Company of the Canterbury Infantry Battalion on 30 April, for the burial of some of those killed when the 7th and 12th Australian Infantry Battalions landed nearby on 25 April.

No. 2 Outpost was the scene of heavy fighting at the end of May when No. 3 Outpost, higher in the hills above No. 2, was recaptured by the Turks. No. 2 contained the best well in the area, and soldiers used to come from far and wide for the good water. The New Zealand Dental Corps clinic was established nearby, and this was also often visited, though less enthusiastically – hundreds of Australians were evacuated with dental trouble.

No. 2 Outpost Cemetery was made during the occupation and 152 Commonwealth First World War servicemen are buried or commemorated here. Special memorials commemorate 48 casualties known or believed to be among the 66 unidentified burials. It includes seven identified Australians, with special memorials to 29 Australians

No. 2 Outpost: Alfred Baldwin: Just one of the gallant band A.N.Z.A.C.

known to be buried in the area. The headstones nearly all give the date of death as 25 April–2 May, because most of the bodies lay unburied during the week after the landing.

Twenty-eight burials are from the 7th Battalion, killed in the boats or at the landing. One of them is Corporal Arthur Mueller (Joe) Pearce, a champion footballer with Melbourne who played 152 games between 1904 and 1913, mostly at full back. Pearce was killed in the boat taking him and other 7th Battalion men to shore near Fisherman's Hut on North Beach. Joe Pearce was the seventh man to enlist from the Essendon area. Although he was 30, he told his football club, 'I am young, strong, healthy and athletic and I think I ought to go, and if I don't come back, well, it won't much matter.' *The Winner*, a football paper, noted 'a name well known to all footballers and supporters' and described him as 'a fine comrade, a loyal club fellow, and a fair and manly opponent'.

There are also a number of New Zealand Mounted Rifles Brigade casualties buried here – they occupied the outpost from mid-May to August, when they were the starting point for the battle for Chunuk Bair in the hills above.

New Zealand No. 2 Outpost Cemetery was named from the burials carried out by the Nelson Company in one long grave made in September 1915. There are 183 men buried or commemorated in this cemetery. Special memorials commemorate 31 casualties known or believed to be among the 150 unidentified burials. There are special memorials to thirteen New Zealanders and eight Australians known to be buried in the cemetery. Nearly all of them were killed in the battles of August on and around Chunuk Bair.

Buried here is Colonel Neville Manders, the British Chief Medical Officer of the ANZAC Division, who was in charge of getting the wounded off North Beach. He was killed while having breakfast near No. 3 Outpost on 9 August.

Plugge's Plateau. (Gavin Pinar, 2004)

Plugge's Plateau Cemetery (pronounced 'Pluggey's') is on a hill 100 metres above sea level, above the cliff which rises from Ari Burnu. It is unclear what impact the 2005 excavations around Ari Burnu will have on the cliff.

The cemetery is on the north-west corner of the plateau. The smallest cemetery at Gallipoli, it has 21 burials, four of them unidentified, and includes twelve Australians; nine Australians and five New Zealanders who died on the first Anzac Day are buried at Plugge's.

After Plugge's Plateau was captured by the 3rd Australian Infantry Brigade on 25 April it was named for the commander of New Zealand Auckland Battalion, Colonel Arthur Plugge, CMG, who established headquarters there. The plateau, a position on the 'Inner Line' of defences, became a battery position, and housed a reservoir and, on its western slopes, Anzac Headquarters.

Quinn's Post Cemetery was made after the Armistice by the concentration of 225 isolated graves, all unidentified, in the 'little flat as you come out of the sap leading into Bloody Angle', as the historian of the 15th Battalion described it after the war. The post had been established on the afternoon of 25 April by a New Zealand machine-gun crew. In the following months, the post was held by a number of different Australian and New Zealand units and was the subject of incessant attacks and continual hand-to-hand fighting with the Turkish post opposite, who knew it as 'Bomba Sirt' (Bomb Ridge). The post was named from Major Hugh Quinn of the 15th Battalion, Australian Infantry, who was killed there during a fierce attack on 29 May, and is buried in Shrapnel Valley Cemetery.

Quinn's Post Cemetery. (2003)

Peter Stanley in his 2005 history of Quinn's Post concurs that the cemetery site is actually sited at Bloody Angle, 100 metres or more up the road from the major area of Quinn's, on 'the bullet-flecked rise too deadly to be occupied by either side for most of the campaign'. If you are looking for Quinn's Post, walk from the back of the cemetery down the hill.

Stanley writes, 'No one seems to have noticed this before, but it suggests that the bodies in no man's land – now scored by the deep trace of the road – must largely have been recovered and re-buried in a common grave a hundred yards to the north. Some are identified but the bones of Turks, Britons, Australians and New Zealanders must lie together in the great earth platform Greek and Russian labourers built on the ridge 80-odd years ago.' This is Quinn's Post Cemetery.

Quinn's Post: His grave lies southward of the line in Australasian hearts.

There are now 473 Commonwealth servicemen of the First World War buried or commemorated in this cemetery. 105 Australians are known to be buried at Quinn's. There's a special memorial to Lieutenant Francis Leofric Armstrong, a 34-year-old Queenslander of the 15th Battalion who had served in the Boer War and was killed on one of the May raids or attacks from Quinn's up the hill. Successful in capturing a Turkish trench overnight on 9 May, the Australians had to fall back under overwhelming fire. Armstrong helped withdraw his men down three saps cut from the communications trench to the captured trench – 'perhaps the heaviest task ever undertaken by Australian troops', wrote Bean. Armstrong saw the remnants of his men coming back and was 'acutely distressed'. As Bean tells it: '"All my boys are killed or wounded out there," he said, and at once endeavoured to climb out and see if any wounded remained. The men with him tried to pull him down, but he struggled to the parapet and was killed.'

7th Field Ambulance Cemetery.

7th Field Ambulance Cemetery is on low ground, close under the shelter of a hill, about 190 metres east of the Anzac–Suvla road.

The cemetery was named for the Australian 7th Field Ambulance, which landed on Gallipoli in September 1915. There are now 640 men buried or commemorated in this cemetery. Of the 433 graves, 21 are Australian, 20 New Zealand, 130 British and 262 are of unknown nationality. Special memorials record the names of 47 Australians and 160 British known or believed to be among the unknown burials. Many casualties are from Hill 60 in late August, others are from the battle for Chunuk Bair in early August, and from September to the evacuation.

Australians buried here include Private Robert Bethel, aged just eighteen, from Moorina, Tasmania, whose mum wrote 'Though death divides, fond memory clings: 14th Battalion, killed 14 August', and Corporal Frank Hewett, of Carlton, also in the 14th Battalion, who was killed on 10 August and is remembered as 'A good son – he had many friends.'

Shell Green.

Shell Green Cemetery is 300 metres up a track from the coast road that was once called Artillery Road. A sloping cotton field on the seaward side of Bolton's Ridge at the southern end of the Anzac area, Shell Green was captured and passed by the Australian 8th Infantry Battalion on the morning of 25 April, but it remained close to the Turkish line throughout the campaign and was subject to frequent shelling.

The cemetery was used from May to December 1915, largely by the Australian Light Horse and the 9th and 11th Infantry Battalions. Originally two cemeteries a short distance apart, after the Armistice the two were combined and enlarged when graves were brought in from the battlefields and from the cemeteries of Artillery Road, Artillery Road East, Wright's Gully and Eighth Battery.

The cemetery now contains 408 identified Australian burials and eleven unidentified men. Among them is Frank Moorehead, uncle of the great Second World War correspondent and historian Alan Moorehead. Frank, aged 24, was in the 8th Battalion and was killed between the time of the landing and 28 April.

Alex Robertson is buried here. A noted sportsman and brilliant scholar, he played ten games for university in the VFL, graduated from Melbourne University as a Master of Science, and was a finalist in the Rhodes Scholarship. He was working as a geologist in Perth when he joined up.

Shell Green, a field of trampled-down cotton bushes, hosted the only game of cricket Charles Bean observed at Anzac; he noted Major George Macarthur Onslow fielding at cover-point. The cricket match, being played to cover the evacuation, was recorded in a much treasured photograph. The Australian cricket team, under Steve Waugh, posed for a picture in much the same fielding formation in 2001 on their way to England for the Ashes.

Shrapnel Valley Cemetery is in Shrapnel Valley (or Shrapnel Gully), named for the heavy shelling it was given by the Turks on 26 April 1915. Shrapnel Valley was an essential track from the beach up to the Anzac front line at the various posts such as Quinn's Post. Simpson and his donkey Murphy brought wounded down Shrapnel Valley to the more protected area in the lee of the slope above Anzac Cove.

Shrapnel Valley Cemetery. (1996)

The cemetery was made mainly during the occupation, but some isolated graves were brought in from the valley after the Armistice. There are now 683 Commonwealth servicemen buried or commemorated here. Special memorials commemorate 23 casualties known or believed to be among the 85 unidentified burials. With 527 Australians burials identified, this is the largest concentration of Australian graves at Gallipoli. It is perhaps the most beautiful as well, with bright pink Judas trees in flower around Anzac Day.

Major Hugh Quinn of the 15th Battalion, who gave his name to Quinn's Post, is buried here. Quinn arrived at the post on 29 April, and led the desperate fighting and digging there when his unit was in occupation. Quinn, from Queensland, had joined the AIF after volunteering to take part in the expedition to take New Guinea from the Germans at the beginning of the war. Quinn was killed on 29 May, just before he was to lead an attack to retake portions of the warren of trenches and tunnels of the post that had fallen to the Turks the night before. His mother supplied his epitaph: 'Some time, some day I trust to see the dear face I hold in memory.'

Another epitaph, supplied by the wife of Private J E Barclay of the 8th Battalion, killed on 21 June, reads: 'I've no darling now. I'm weeping. Baby and I you left behind.'

Here too is Corporal James Burns, of the 21st Battalion, an ex-student of Scotch College, Melbourne, whose famous patriotic poem 'For England' appeared in the college magazine, *Collegian*, in May 1915:

The bugles of England were blowing o'er the sea,
As they had called a thousand years, calling now to me;
They woke me from dreaming in the dawning of the day,
The bugles of England – and how could I stay?

He was shot in the head on 28 September at Courtney's Post. A comrade wrote that he 'died through being too brave'.

Above: Turkish Soldier, 57th Infantry Regiment Memorial Park.
Below: Walker's Ridge Cemetery.

The **Turkish 57th Infantry Regiment Memorial Park** is between Quinn's and the Nek and includes a number of important Turkish memorials. A large statue of a Turkish soldier – Turk Askerine Saygi Aniti (Respect to the Turkish Soldier) – attacking the invaders from the beach was sculpted by Tankut Oktem and erected in 1992. Over the road is the symbolic cemetery with plaques of the names of the martyrs of the 57th Regiment and where they came from. There were many local men who fought and died here. The statue of the Turkish Veteran and Child is of Huseyein Kacmaz, who died at 108 in 1994, the oldest Turkish veteran, shown with his grand-daughter. The park was opened in 1992.

Walker's Ridge Cemetery is 30 metres down the track from the Nek Cemetery towards the coast. It is named for Brigadier General Walker of the New Zealand Infantry Brigade, who established his command post here on 27 April. It has the finest view at Anzac of North Beach, Ari Burnu and the side of the Sphinx. A Turkish attempt to take the ridge on 30 June was repulsed by the Australian 8th and 9th Light Horse.

The cemetery was made during the occupation and consists of two plots separated by eighteen metres of ground, through which a trench ran. There are now 92 men buried or commemorated in this cemetery. Sixteen of the burials are unidentified and special memorials commemorate 26 soldiers known or believed to be buried in the cemetery, including eighteen Australians. There are 76 identified casualties including twelve Australians, including eight Light Horsemen killed at the Nek in August.

The two plots of the cemetery are in the original form, which was divided by a trench begun on 25 April by the commander of the 2nd Battalion, Colonel George Braund. (Braund was accidentally killed by an Australian sentry on 4 May, and is buried in the Beach Cemetery.) On 27 April Walker's Ridge was taken over by the New Zealanders, and most of their dead are from this time, including eighteen killed in the big Turkish attack of 19 May.

Major Thomas Redford and Quartermaster Sergeant Elias Judell, and Trooper Leo Wyman of the 9th are buried here. Redford was killed in the first wave. 'Our gallant major, whilst lying facing the enemy's trench (10 yards away) in the front of his men received a bullet through his brain as he raised his head slightly to observe. He died with a soft sigh and laid his head gently on his hands as if tired. A braver and honourable man never donned uniform,' wrote Sergeant Judell.

Gabatepe

The **Gabatepe Museum** is a small museum which introduces the Anzac battlefields. There are Turkish memorials and statuary, and interesting relics from the battlefield.

Gabatepe Museum
Address: Kabatepe Eceabat road

Helles

Çanakkale Martyrs Memorial commemorates the 250,000 Turkish casualties – with perhaps 100,000 dead – with a 40-metre high arch. The design won a competition in 1944 and construction commenced in 1954. The memorial opened in 1964.

A verse from 'For Those Fallen at Gallipoli', by Mehmet Akif Ersoy, is engraved on a stone beneath the arch:

Above: Sculpture at Gabatepe Museum.
Below: Material in Gabatepe Museum relating to the three Watt brothers of Gulgong, NSW; Walter and Archie died at Gallipoli, Fred in Flanders.

PILGRIMAGE

Above: Map of Cape Helles and Krithia.
Left: Çanakkale Martyrs Memorial, Helles.

Soldier, you have fallen for this earth
Your fathers may well lean down from heaven to kiss your brow.
Who can dig a grave that will not be too narrow for you?
If I say 'Let us enshrine you in history,'
It will not contain you.

There is a symbolic cemetery with stones for 100 officers and 500 soldiers who died in the Çanakkale campaign and who came from every province of Turkey. There is also a memorial garden and a small museum.

There are many other Turkish memorials, statues and symbolic cemeteries in the Helles area.

Lancashire Landing Cemetery overlooks W Beach, where the 1st Lancashire Fusiliers landed on 25 April. Under tremendous fire they got through the barbed wire entanglements and trenches to the top of the cliff and, with other battalions of the 88th Brigade, made it to the hills above, winning six VCs in the process. W Beach became known as Lancashire Landing.

The greater part of the cemetery was made between the landing in April 1915 and the evacuation of the peninsula in January 1916. Most of the Australians are from the 2nd Brigade's 6th, 7th and 8th battalions, killed in the attack on Krithia or who died later from wounds.

Lieutenant Richard Keiran, aged 26, from Fitzroy in Victoria, was with other officers of the 6th Battalion when he was seen charging out of the trench. He had been rejected as medically unfit when he first tried to join up, but was later accepted as a sergeant, and promoted in the field. Bean described him as a 'born leader of men'.

Major Richard Wells, 37, of the 6th, had made it as far as Lone Pine on 25 April where he formed and held the line. He was mortally wounded in the same action as Keiran.

Corporal Dale Smith, killed in the attack on Krithia.

Pink Farm Cemetery on what is properly Sotiri Farm, took its name from the red soil of the area. The three cemeteries which grew up around the farm were combined after the Armistice on the site of Pink Farm Cemetery No. 3, which was further enlarged when graves were brought in from other small burial grounds in the vicinity. There are now 602 First World War servicemen buried or commemorated in this cemetery. Special memorials commemorate 219 casualties known or believed to be among the 250 unidentified burials.

Pink Farm Cemetery.

Among the 352 identified casualties are two Australians, both from the Australian Field Artillery – Captain Robert Crocker, 27, of Hawthorn, killed on 12 July; and Major John Brier Mills of Claremont, WA, killed on 20 May.

Redoubt Cemetery is on the west side of the road to Krithia, along a track flanked by scented cypress trees. Redoubt was established in May 1915 just behind the rear of two trenches dug by the Australian 2nd Brigade in their attack on 8 May. The spire of the mosque at Krithia can be seen up the gentle slope over which the Australians attacked and returned. The undulations beneath the pine needles in the forest beside the cemetery may well be the old trenches.

Redoubt was greatly increased after the Armistice when the battlefields were cleared and graves were brought in from small cemeteries in the vicinity.

Redoubt Cemetery.

There are now 2027 First World War servicemen buried or commemorated in this cemetery. Special memorials commemorate 349 casualties known or believed to be among the 1393 unidentified burials.

There are sixteen named burials from Australia and one from New Zealand, and four special memorials to Australians, and four also to New Zealanders believed to be buried in the cemetery. At least 200 of the unidentified 1000 'soldiers of the Great War' are Australian, their names recorded on the Helles Memorial. Unidentified New Zealanders from that awful day in May are named on the Twelve Tree Copse New Zealand Memorial.

Among the Australians is Colonel Robert Gartside, a Boer War veteran who would ordinarily have been with the 8th Battalion but was commanding the 7th Battalion at Krithia because Pompey Elliott had been hit in the foot on 25 April. Gartside was 53, from Castlemaine, and became a legend when he led his men from one of the trenches at Redoubt in one of the last rushes on 8 May: 'Come on boys, I know it's deadly, but we must get on ...' The orders to attack had come so Gartside had to lead his troops to show them in which direction to attack. He was killed 400 yards in front of the trench, and was one of the first to be buried here.

Skew Bridge Cemetery was named from a wooden 'skew' bridge carrying the Krithia road across a creek just behind the centre of the line occupied by the Allied forces on 27 April 1915. The cemetery was begun during the fighting of 6–8 May and used throughout the occupation. At the Armistice it contained only 53 graves but was greatly enlarged when further burials were brought in from the battlefields or small burial grounds in the area. There are now 607 First World War servicemen buried or commemorated in this cemetery. 351 of the burials are unidentified but special memorials commemorate a number of casualties known or believed to be buried among them.

There are 256 identified casualties, including five Australians with identified graves and four further Australians known to be buried in the cemetery. They were all killed in the attack on Krithia in May, or with the artillery in June.

Colonel Arnold Quilter, 40, formerly military secretary to the governor-general of Australia, is here; he was killed on 6 May carrying his oversize walking stick while commanding the then Hood Battalion of the Royal Naval Division.

Skew Bridge Cemetery.

Twelve Tree Copse Cemetery is about a kilometre south-west of Krithia. It was made after the Armistice when graves were brought in from isolated sites and small burial grounds on the battlefields of April–August and December 1915. The most significant of these were Geoghan's Bluff Cemetery, Fir Tree Wood Cemetery and Clunes Vennel Cemetery.

There are now 3360 First World War servicemen buried or commemorated in the cemetery. Special memorials commemorate many casualties known or believed to be among the 2226 unidentified burials.

One Australian buried here is Captain Keith Levi of the Australian Army Medical Corps, who graduated from Melbourne University in 1914, joined up in January 1915, landed at Helles on 29 July, was attached to the 2nd Hampshire Regiment, and was killed on 2 August.

Twelve Tree Copse Cemetery.

One of the British heroes commemorated at Twelve Tree Copse is Lieutenant Alfred Smith, of the 1/5th East Lancashire regiment, who was awarded a VC for his selflessness in using his body to cover a grenade he had dropped, in order to protect men in his trench. He had actually cleared out of the trench after he dropped the grenade, but jumped back in when his comrades could not escape.

Twelve Tree Copse (New Zealand) Memorial records the names of the New Zealanders who fell at the second battle of Krithia or in the Helles area and who have no known grave. There are 179 names from the Auckland, Otago, Canterbury and Wellington battalions. Most were killed at the Daisy Patch on 8 May. This is one of four memorials erected to commemorate New Zealand soldiers who fell on the Gallipoli peninsula and whose graves are not known. The other memorials are in the Anzac area at Chunuk Bair, Hill 60 and Lone Pine.

The **French National Cemetery and Memorial** is at Morto Bay and commemorates the more than 10,000 French soldiers who died at Helles. Most remains are in an ossuary, but there are 2235 named graves, on black crosses, *Mort pour La France*. Unlike Commonwealth cemeteries, the French graves are arranged by rank. The French losses were immense; their 27,000 dead was greater than Australia's total casualties.

This cemetery was opened in 1930, drawing from a number of cemeteries and ossuaries on the battlefield.

V Beach Cemetery, Turkish Martyrs Memorial on the horizon.

V Beach Cemetery has no Australians or New Zealanders, but there are now 696 British servicemen buried or commemorated in this cemetery, 216 identified. Of the burials, 480 are unidentified, but special memorials commemorate 196 officers and men, nearly all belonging to the units which landed on 25 April, known or believed to be buried among them.

The landing at V Beach was to be made by boats containing three companies of the 1st Royal Dublin Fusiliers, followed by the collier HMT *River Clyde* which was beached and used as a kind of Trojan horse to bring in more soldiers. For a time it became a killing field. On the morning of 26 April, Lieutenant Colonel Charles Doughty-Wylie and Captain Garth Walford led the survivors on the beach to the capture of the village and the old castle above it. That evening, the main body of the French Corps began to land at V Beach and after the following day, the front line had advanced about three kilometres beyond it.

Doughty-Wylie and Walford were killed during the fight. Both won the Victoria Cross. Captain Walford is buried at V Beach, Colonel Doughty-Wylie is buried in an isolated grave on the spot where he was killed.

Near V Beach is the **Helles Memorial to the Missing**, a 30-metre high obelisk on the tip of the Gallipoli peninsula, which can be seen by ships passing through the Dardanelles. The original inscription reads:

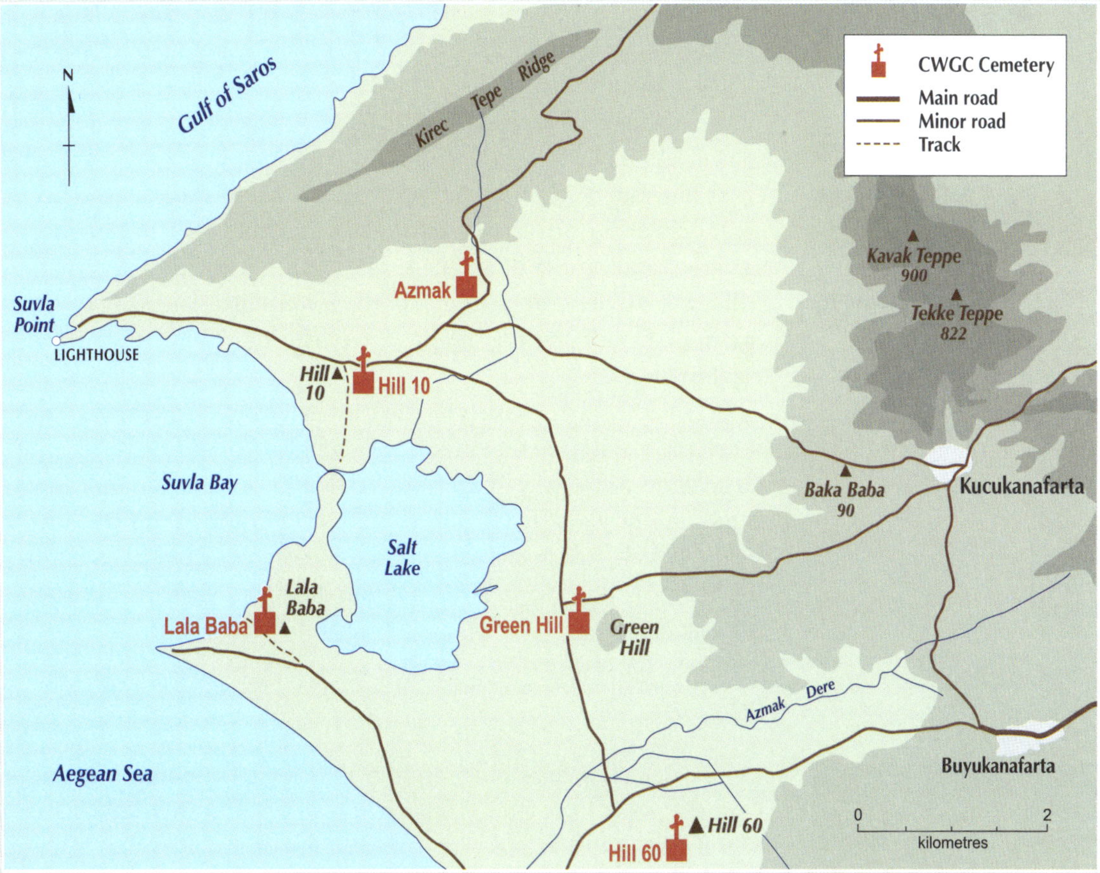

Gallipoli

Above: Map of Suvla.
Left: Poppies, near Azmak Cemetery.

Helles Memorial to the Missing.

In honoured memory of the units and ships which fought on Gallipoli or in the Dardanelles and of these 20,504 British sailors and soldiers and 248 Australian soldiers who fell in this neighbourhood 1914–1916 and have no known graves.

There are now 20,763 names recorded here, including over 1500 from the Indian army. On one side are the names of the ships that fought in the area, and on the other three sides, under the headings Anzac, Helles and Suvla, are the names of the units which fought here. The names of the missing are arranged in panels on the walls surrounding the obelisk.

On weather-worn panels on the west exterior wall, running from panel 201 to 204, are names from the Australian Engineers, the Australian 5th, 6th, 7th and 8th battalions, and Australian Divisional and Brigade Headquarters staff. On panel 332, on the inner southern wall, just inside the entrance, are names from the Australian Army Service Corps, Artillery, and the 21st, 22nd and 23rd battalions at sea.

Suvla

Azmak Cemetery.

Azmak Cemetery was made from a number of smaller cemeteries after the Armistice, and is seldom visited. Barely two kilometres inland from A Beach in Suvla, it marks the furthest point reached by the British. There are no Australian graves among the 1074 First World War servicemen buried or commemorated here. Special memorials commemorate a number of casualties known or believed to be among the 684 unidentified burials here.

Among the unidentified graves are those of 114 officers and men of the 1st/5th Battalion Norfolk Regiment who died on 12 August 1915. They were a 'pals' battalion who enlisted together from the Royal estate at Sandringham. King George V sent the men he knew well a congratulatory telegram before they sailed for Suvla. Landing on 10 August, they were in action on 12 August and suffered catastrophic casualties. A mass grave containing 120 Norfolks was found by the Graves Registration Unit in 1918, and rumours persist that they were massacred by the Turks rather than be dealt with as prisoners of war. A 1999 TV docu-drama, *All the King's Men*, had them marching off into the mist.

Green Hill Cemetery is on a hill a kilometre inland from the salt lake, which was taken on the 7 August. No further advances were made, and the cemetery is at the mid-point of the final British line. The cemetery was made after the Armistice when isolated graves were brought in from the battlefields of August 1915 especially from the attack on Scimitar Hill, where there were 5300 casualties from 14,300 men who attacked with no ground gained.

There are now 2971 men buried or commemorated in this cemetery. Special memorials commemorate a number of casualties known or believed to be among the 2472 unidentified burials. There are no Australians among the identified casualties.

Hill 10 Cemetery is on a ten-metre bump at the north end of Suvla Bay. The cemetery was made after the Armistice by the concentration of graves from isolated sites and cemeteries. There are now 699 servicemen buried or commemorated in this cemetery. There are two Australians among the 549 identified casualties: Chief Petty Officer Edward Perkins, 21, of Essendon, from the Royal Australian Naval Bridging Train, who was killed on 6 September; and Lance Corporal Herbert Peters, 39, of Glenorchy, Victoria, from the 8th Light Horse, who was killed on 30 August, probably at Hill 60.

The view from Hill 10 Cemetery.

Also buried here is Corporal Hubert Esme Govett of the British 67th Field Company, who was born in Geelong in 1890 and educated at Melbourne Grammar, then studied engineering in London and joined the Royal Engineers. On 18 December he was standing by his gun, ready to blow it up as the evacuation from Suvla proceeded, when he was killed by a Turkish artillery shell.

Hill 60 Cemetery is on the 60-metre-high mound at the southern end of the final front line, in Turkish territory also known as Kaiajik Aghyl, or Sheepfold of the Little Rock.

The cemetery was created among the trenches of the Hill 60 actions after those engagements, and was enlarged after the Armistice. There are now 788 men buried or commemorated in this cemetery, including 25 identified as Australians. Special memorials commemorate 34 casualties known or believed to be among the 712 unidentified burials.

Private Thomas Durack of the 18th Battalion lies in Hill 60 cemetery.

Hill 60 (New Zealand) Memorial within the cemetery is one of four memorials erected to commemorate New Zealand soldiers who died on the Gallipoli peninsula and whose graves are not known. This memorial relates to the actions at Hill 60. It bears more than 180 names.

Lala Baba Cemetery.

Lala Baba Cemetery is on a 146-metre hill on the southern side of Suvla Bay which commands the bay. The hill had been raided and shelled several times before the landing there, including one commando raid by 50 intrepid Kiwis from the Canterbury Battalion, on 2 May.

The cemetery was formed after the Armistice from nine small cemeteries and a few isolated graves in the surrounding area. There are now 216 First World War servicemen buried or commemorated in this cemetery. Special memorials commemorate sixteen casualties known or believed to be among the 53 unidentified burials. There are no Australians among the identified casualties.

Cemeteries, Memorials, Museums: Turkey

Çanakkale

The **Cemenlik/*Nusret* Museum** is 400 metres from the ferry wharf in Çanakkale (past the clocktower) and houses a replica of the small minelayer the *Nusret*, the little ship that turned the war.

The Turks had lined the Dardanelles with artillery batteries, from the old fortresses at Kum Kale at Seddulbahr at the entrance to the Dardanelles, to Kilitbahir and Chemenlik and Hamidieh at the Narrows between present-day Çanakkale and Eceabat. They had set lines of mines across the Dardanelles, but also parallel to the Asian shore fifteen kilometres to the east of Çanakkale, at the widest part of the

The Australian submarine *AE2* was in action on 25 April 1915, torpedoing a Turkish cruiser in the Dardanelles. After expending all its torpedoes, it was scuttled in the Sea of Marmara. A part-replica was constructed and is on view in the West Australian Maritime Museum, Fremantle.

channel, where Allied ships had been observed turning. There were no secrets about this battle between ship and shore artillery – each side knew where the other's weapons were – except this single line of mines, which was laid by the *Nusret*.

The real *Nusret* was laid down in 1910 in Germany, and entered the Ottoman Navy in 1913. She survived the war, and worked as a minesweeper and later as dive support ship until decommissioned in 1955, and laid up at Golcuk. In 1962 she was sold to a private shipping company and used as a cargo ship until she sank in Mersin harbour in 1990. Refloated, she is still there, now owned by the nearby city of Tarsus, and there are plans for restoration and display in a museum.

Some historians believe the Turks were so low on ammunition that another determined attempt to burst through the minefields would have succeeded.

Nusret Turkish minelayer.

The **Dardanelles inscriptions** are visible to anyone travelling on the ferry from Çanakkale across the Dardanelles to Eceabat; you will see a soldier, a flame, a memorial with the words etched in the hills above:

Dur yolcu
Bilmeden gelip bastýöýn,
Bu toprak, bir devrin battýöý yerdir.

These are the first few lines of a poem by Necmettin Halil Onan called 'To a Traveller'.

To a traveller.

It is a reminder of what the battle the Turks know as Çanakkale means to them. Gallipoli has been appropriated by Australians, in need of a violent and heroic episode as part of our national story, but it is also a significant moment in the Turkish national story.

Translated by S Tanvir Wasti, the whole poem reads:

Stop wayfarer! Unbeknownst to you this ground
You come and tread on, is where an epoch lies;
Bend down and lend your ear, for this silent mound
Is the place where the heart of a nation sighs.

To the left of this deserted shadeless lane
The Anatolian slope now observes you well;
For liberty and honour, it is, in pain,
Where wounded Mehmet laid down his life and fell.

18 Mart 1915.

Above: Ataturk, in the Istanbul Military Museum.
Below: The Janissary Band performs most afternoons in the courtyard of the Istanbul Military Museum.

This very mound, when violently shook the land,
When the last bit of earth passed from hand to hand,
And when Mehmet drowned the enemy in flood,
Is the spot where he added his own pure blood.

Think, the consecrated blood and flesh and bone
That make up this mound, is where a whole nation,
After a harsh and pitiless war, alone
Tasted the joy of freedom with elation.

Further down the Dardanelles is another memorial – with the words '18 Mart 1915' enclosed by garlands of victory.

Istanbul

The **Istanbul Military Museum** is the equivalent of the Australian War Memorial, with a very interesting display of Turkey's long military history. The Çanakkale (Gallipoli) campaign forms a small, and slightly disappointing, part of the whole.

The museum had its origins in the weaponry owned by Sultan Ahmed III and kept in the former Aya Irini church behind the great Hagia Sophia church in 1726. It became a formal museum in 1826. In 1955, the museum was transferred to its current location. It was renovated in 1959, again in 1986, and 1993.

The collection includes military uniforms of different periods of the Ottoman army, weaponry ranging from bow and arrow to flintlocks, seals, armour, tents of the Sultans, and the chain used by the Byzantines to close the Golden Horn. On the upper floor objects from the First World War, the Battle of Çanakkale/Gallipoli, and the War of Independence, and uniforms from more recent times are displayed. There is also an Ataturk room. The Janissary Band gives concerts in the afternoons.

Istanbul Military Museum
Address: Vali Konagi Caddesi, Harbiye

Travel Tool Kit

Independent travel in Turkey, especially for Australians and New Zealanders, is about the safest and most fun you can have anywhere. Turkey's history stretches back about as far as Egypt's, and Istanbul, one of the world's most extraordinary cities, is 2000 years old. The Greek and Roman ruins around the Mediterranean coast, at Miletus, Priene, Ephesus and Pergamum, are better than you will find in Greece or Rome. The bus network is safe and cheap, the food fantastic and accommodation easy to find. Compared to Europe, all of this is inexpensive. And when the locals discover that you are an English speaker from the Southern Hemisphere, doors and conversations tend to open up.

Everyone should go to Gallipoli if they are able, but not just to Anzac Cove and not just on Anzac Day. The more time you can spend at Gallipoli the better, but even a single afternoon at Anzac can be a profound experience. (That's what happened to me, and this book is the result.)

Tens of thousands of Australians and New Zealanders now come to Turkey to be at Gallipoli on Anzac Day, which could be an entirely appropriate way of commemorating 25 April and all that it has come to represent, but has become a version of the Big Day Out, with rock music, drinking and overcrowding, and restrictions on where you can go and for how long.

Anzac Day is not the best time to discover what Gallipoli is all about. This is better done alone or in a small group, giving you a chance to stand silently on the beach at Anzac Cove or survey the tiny and terrible killing grounds at the Nek or Lone Pine. There are plenty of dates to commemorate besides 25 April. Summer is hot, it has snowed in winter, spring and autumn. I have a few favourite places

Take the *feribot* across the Dardanelles.

Shrapnel Valley Spring. (2003)

and people. The recommendations below are for places where I have stayed, and services I have used and trust.

Tours and Guides

There are plenty of tour operators who do a one-day tour of the main sites at Anzac. I took one to see what it was like, and it was pretty good because I had the good fortune to have Captain Ali as a guide. He is ex-Turkish Navy, his grandfather was killed at Lone Pine, and he spent his childhood at Gallipoli. Captain Ali had a group of fifteen enthralled with his even-handed explanation of events. An excellent guide makes all the difference to a short visit.

It is possible to 'do' Gallipoli in one long day from Istanbul if that is all the time you have. The recommended hotels will be happy to put you in touch with an Anzac tour operator or tell you how to catch a bus to Çanakkale. You'll be picked up by minibus from your hotel at around 6 a.m., taken on a five-hour drive with an assortment of Australians and New Zealanders, meet with a local guide in Çanakkale, and will visit Gabatepe Museum, Lone Pine, Johnston's Jolly, the Nek, Chunuk Bair, Anzac Commemorative Site, Ari Burnu and Beach cemeteries before catching a bus back to Istanbul about 6 p.m.

You can also join a one-day tour but stay the night at a hotel or hostel in Çanakkale. You can contact Anzac House in Çanakkale for details of tours operated by Hassle Free Tours. Despite the daggy name, their service is efficient, reliable and friendly. See: **www.anzachouse.com** or contact **hasslefree@anzachouse.com**

But with brief tours you don't see all of Gallipoli. They necessarily focus on the areas around Anzac Cove and on the ridge from Lone

Pine to Chunuk Bair. That's not the half of it; it leaves out Cape Helles, the area around Krithia and Suvla, for example. You won't get to these places with a standard tour, especially one oriented around Anzac Day.

The best way to see these places is to arrange a 'private' tour with an experienced guide in a car. Two full days on your own tour is adequate, but three or four would be more relaxed. Some places require a bit of walking.

Several years ago I had the privilege of staying for a number of nights and dawns at Anzac, and walked and climbed the Anzac area; more recently I spent a few days with the excellent guide Guven (Gavin to Australians) Pinar, driving to places I had not been. This is the best way to 'do' Gallipoli. Contact Gavin at **gavin@downundergallipoli.com**

Longer tours can also be booked from Australia through your travel agent. I can recommend Tempo Holidays tours, which start in Istanbul; they offer a 17-day tour of Turkey, including the Anzac Day Dawn Service (about $2500 in 2005, twin share); a 4-day tour of Anzac (from around $600 in 2005 in hostel accommodation); and a 7-day Anzac and Ephesus tour, including a flight from Istanbul to the airport at Izmir, near Ephesus (from $1700). See **www.tempoholidays.com**

The Australian War Memorial runs comprehensive and fully guided tours of Gallipoli and the Western Front that include the Anzac Day Dawn Service. This is the most comprehensive and authoritative guided tour from Australia, with seven days at Gallipoli. See **www.awm.gov.au**

Further Information

C E W Bean (ed. Kevin Fewster), *Frontline Gallipoli*, Allen & Unwin, Sydney, 1983.

C E W Bean, *Official History of Australia in the War of 1914–1918*, Volumes I & II, 'The Story of Anzac', Angus and Robertson, Sydney, 1924. (The full text and maps of the Official History are available on-line at the Australian War Memorial site **www.awm.gov.au**)

C E W Bean, *Gallipoli Mission*, ABC Books, Sydney (1948), 1990.

Peter Burness, *The Nek*, Kangaroo Press, Kenthurst, 1996.

Les Carlyon, *Gallipoli*, Pan Macmillan, Sydney, 2001.

Peter Cochrane, *Simpson and the Donkey*, Melbourne University Press, Melbourne, 1992.

Hasan Basri Danisman (trans.), *Lone Pine (Bloody Ridge): Diary of Lieutenant Mehmed Fasih*, Denizler Kitabevi, Istanbul, 1997.

Ronald East (ed.), *The Gallipoli Diary of Sergeant Lawrence*, Melbourne University Press, Melbourne, 1981.

Kevin Fewster, *Vecihi Hatice, Hurmuz Basarm: Gallipoli, The Turkish Story*, Allen & Unwin, Sydney, 2003.

John Hamilton, *Goodbye Cobber, God Bless You*, Pan Macmillan, Sydney, 2004.

Tonie and Valmai Holt, *Major & Mrs Holt's Battlefield Guide: Gallipoli*, Leo Cooper, Barnsley, South Yorkshire, 2000.

Robert Rhodes James, *Gallipoli*, Angus & Robertson, Sydney, 1965.

Ross McMullin, *Pompey Elliott*, Scribe, Melbourne, 2002.

Alan Moorehead, *Gallipoli*, London, 1956.

John North, *Gallipoli: The Fading Vision*, Hamish Hamilton, London, 1936.

Christopher Pugsley, *Gallipoli: The New Zealand Story*, Hodder & Stoughton, Auckland, 1984.

Peter Stanley, *Quinn's Post, Anzac, Gallipoli*, Allen & Unwin, Sydney, 2005.

Nigel Steel, *Gallipoli*, Leo Cooper, Barnsley, South Yorkshire, 1999.

Phil Taylor and Pam Cupper, *Gallipoli: A Battlefield Guide*, Kangaroo Press, Kenthurst, 2nd ed., 1997.

Turkish General Staff Directorate of Military History, *A Brief History of the Çanakkale Campaign*, Turkish General Staff Printing House, Ankara, 2004.

2.

PALESTINE

In the First World War, present-day Israel, Jordan and Syria were part of the Ottoman Empire, and at the outbreak of war Turkish forces – with help from their German allies – were engaged in attempts to seize the British-controlled Suez Canal in Egypt, Britain's vital supply to the East. The biblical land of Israel was known, at the time, as Palestine.

After their return from Gallipoli the Australian Light Horse regiments regained their beloved horses and became part of General Harry Chauvel's Australia and New Zealand Mounted Division in Palestine. With other British and Indian units of the Egyptian Expeditionary Force, they defeated a Turkish attack near the Suez Canal at Romani in August 1916, and advanced into the Sinai, beginning the campaign to push the Turks back.

p.83: Gum trees in an abandoned village outside Beersheva.
Opposite: Map of First World War Palestine and Beersheva.

By early 1917, however, the campaign against the Turkish and German forces, which were holding the whole of the Middle East – from Suez through Palestine and Syria to what is now the Turkish border – was stalled. Gaza, the key to the coastal route, had been bombarded by French warships in April 1915, and at the end of March 1917, it was attacked and surrounded by the Egyptian Expeditionary Force in the First Battle of Gaza, but the attack was broken off when Turkish reinforcements appeared. The Second Battle of Gaza, 17–19 April, left the Turks in possession.

In June, Lieutenant General Edmund 'Bull' Allenby, the replacement for General Sir Archibald Murray as commander of the Egyptian Expeditionary Force, was given much-needed reinforcements, and reorganised and re-energised the forces. Australia's General Sir Harry Chauvel was given command of the Desert Mounted Corps of three divisions composed of all the mounted troops – Australian, New Zealand, British and Indian – and including both horses and camels. The Arab Army, an irregular army under the guidance of Englishman T E Lawrence, or 'Lawrence of Arabia', based in the desert of the Hejaz, in Arabia, was harassing the Turks, while Allenby's conventional troops fought along the coast, and up the valley of the Jordan River towards Damascus and Aleppo.

Australians, particularly the Light Horse regiments, were prominent in the successful battles fought in this very successful campaign, after Allenby took over. The capture of Beersheba on 31 October 1917 was the first of these successes, followed by the raids around Jordan at Es Salt, the Light Horse's most costly engagement, and on Amman in April 1918.

The decisive battle was fought and won at Megiddo (site of the biblical Armageddon) on 19 September, all of which culminated in the taking of Damascus on 1 October 1918. Australians, not the forces of

The official historian of the Palestine campaign H S (Harry) Gullett, a former journalist on the *Sydney Morning Herald*, was plain-writing but evocative. He was certainly the best writer who also became a cabinet minister; he was Minister for External Affairs in the first Menzies government in 1939. He was killed in an air crash on 13 August 1940 near Canberra.

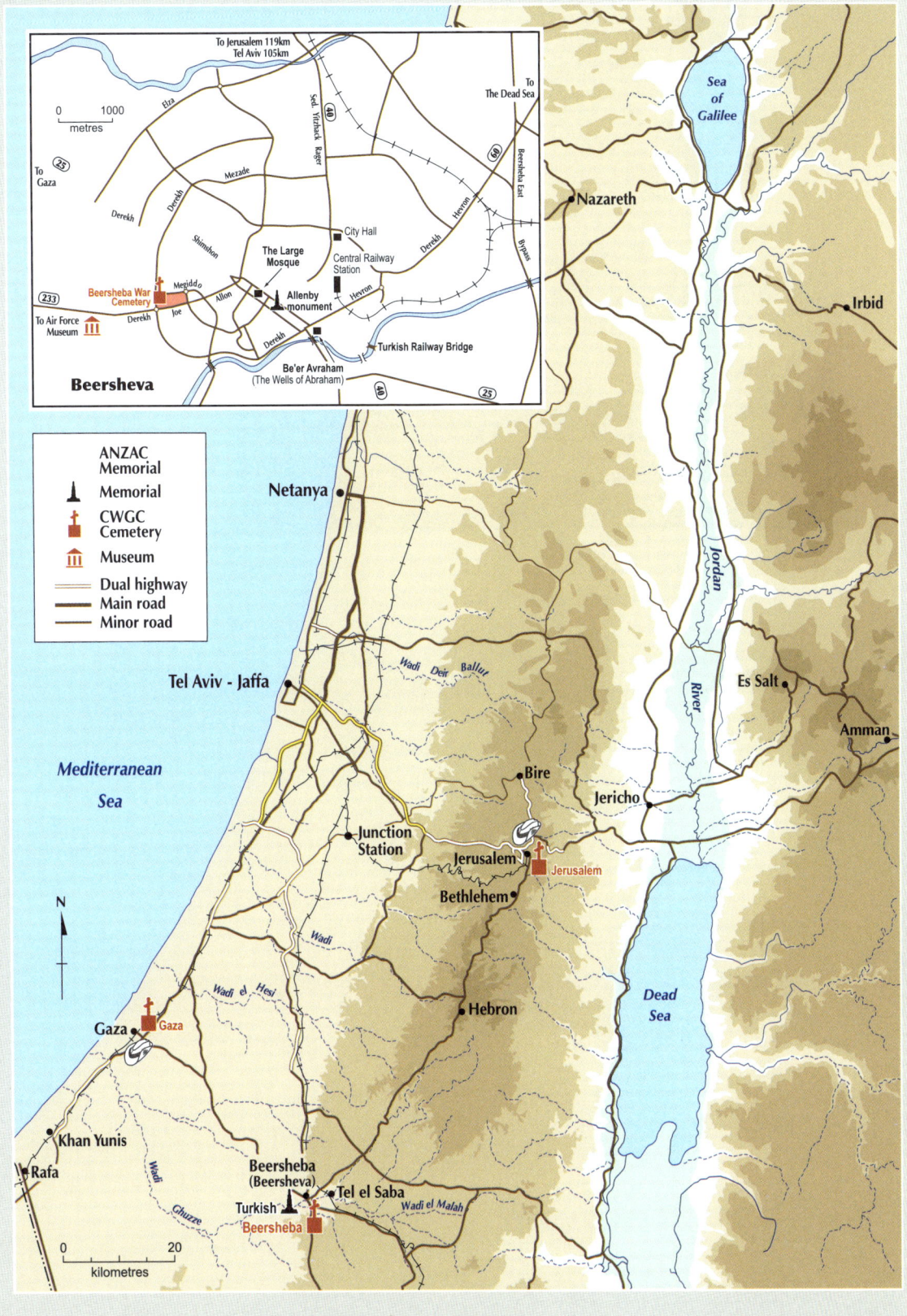

Beersheva, seen from Tel Sheva. Formerly named Tel el Saba, this strategic height was captured by New Zealanders as a necessary prelude to the capture of the town on 31 October. The site was first occupied 3000 years ago.

Lawrence of Arabia, accepted the surrender of Damascus, but quickly headed north to Aleppo, where Mustafa Kemal, by then in command of the remaining Turkish forces, thought he had better leave. By war's end, the Ottoman Empire had collapsed. A few years later, in 1923, Mustafa Kemal was to become the first president of modern Turkey, and took the name Kemal 'Ataturk', or 'Father of the Turks'.

Harry Gullett, the official war historian, captured the essence of the men of the 2nd Light Horse Brigade when he described them at Jerusalem: 'Careless of what awaited them east of the Jordan, they explored the cities with the zest of pilgrims ... The curiosity of the men was boundless; and their diligent reading of the Old and New Testaments, combined with a true reverence, strangely broken by skeptical challenges and even lapses into daring, good-humoured blasphemy, imposed a heavy strain on the physical endurance, the biblical knowledge of the regimental padres ... Full of significant suggestion was this spectacle of young Australian Light Horsemen, led by churchmen in military dress and emu feathers, heavy boots, and clinking spurs, proceeding along the Via Dolorosa or gathered round the traditional Stations of the Cross.' One of these padres, the Rev Maitland Woods, once shrewdly if romantically said in a Thanksgiving service after victory, 'I would describe the Light Horseman as a man who, while denying he is a Christian, practises all the Christian virtues.'

Turkish forces in retreat on the Jericho to Jerusalem road.

The Australians in Palestine, 1916–1918

'Put Grant straight at it': Beersheba, 31 October 1917

The last cavalry charge in history was staged not by cavalry but by the mounted infantrymen of the Australian Light Horse regiments. That charge, at Beersheba, marked the beginning of the end of the war for the Turks and Germans in Palestine.

The Australians' task on 31 October was to turn the flank of the Turkish line that extended from Gaza on the coast to the fortified town of Beersheba, with its vital wells. Numerous ruses had been used in the weeks beforehand to convince the Turks that the attack was to be on Gaza, not on Beersheba. However the Turks were well dug-in at Beersheba, and held up the initial attack by British forces

Above: The old railway bridge was one of the objectives of the Light Horse in 1917.
Right: Debris, probably from the 1973 Arab–Israeli War.

on 31 October in the south-west of the town. Later that day New Zealanders with some Australians captured the fortified Turkish position on Tel el Saba, the hill that dominated the town. Genesis gives Tel el Saba as the southern boundary of the land of Israel and recent archeological excavation reveals occupation going back nearly 3000 years. In a successful ruse, the horsemen had galloped up the hill and dismounted, sending their horses back down. The Turks thought this was a retreat, and fired in the direction of the horses – by which time their attackers were upon them.

But by late in the day, more had to be done if the objective was to be achieved. Frank Dalby Davison, in *The Wells of Beersheba*, has Chauvel thinking, at 4.30 p.m.: 'Water was 30 miles behind him – or three miles in front. To retire on the wells from which his horses had last drunk would be to leave victory in the hands of the enemy …' Chauvel clearly had a galloping attack in mind; the question was, who should mount it? Both Brigadier P D Fitzgerald, commander of the British 7th Yeomanry Brigade and Brigadier William Grant, commander of the 4th Light Horse pleaded for the honour.

As Harry Gullett tells it: 'Fitzgerald's yeomanry had their swords and were close behind Chauvel's headquarters; Grant's Australians had only their rifles and bayonets, but they were nearer Beersheba. After a moment's thought, Chauvel gave the lead to the Light Horsemen. "Put Grant straight at it," was his terse command … '

The men of the 4th and 12th regiments mounted. They began at a trot, then cantered, and as the Turkish fire increased, gave the horses their heads and at full gallop crashed into the Turkish trenches.

An observer, watching them race forward as darkness descended, through deafening noise and clouds of reddish dust, noted: 'They seemed to move silently, like some splendid, swift machine. Over the Turks they went, leaping the two lines of deep trenches, and, dismounting on the farther side, slung themselves into the trenches with the bayonet.' Something of the rush and vigour of the charge can be seen in George Lambert's painting at the Australian War Memorial: the power of the horses leaping over the stunned and dying Turks, the dust, the confusion, the closeness of stinking battle, man to man, horse to man. By 5 p.m. the Light Horse had taken 1000 prisoners, at the price of 31 killed and 32 wounded.

T E Lawrence, fighting with the Arab irregulars further east, noted in *Seven Pillars of Wisdom* that the Light Horse regarded war as a kind of 'point to point race'. Chauvel and his men would have taken that as a compliment.

Tibby Cotter's Last Bowl

Among the Australians killed at Beersheba, one worth special notice is Albert 'Tibby' Cotter, the fastest bowler in world cricket in the early years of the 20th century. Young, fast and erratic, he was a bit of a larrikin and had been popular with the denizens of the Hill at the Sydney Cricket Ground. He smashed a lot of stumps, and the great Victor Trumper, who played with him for Australia once, carried his broken stump from the ground in a club game as a trophy.

He had made his debut for NSW in 1902, and was selected for the fourth Test against England at the SCG in February 1904, when he had just turned nineteen. He took three wickets in the English second innings, and made a defiant 34 at number eleven as Australia went down by 157 runs, losing the Ashes.

Cotter's greatest claim to fame was bowling a beamer at the ancient W G Grace during the 1905 tour of England. He was so fast that the English complained about him. He played three Tests in unfavourable conditions, and took a Herculean 7/148 from 40 overs in the fifth Test, his best Test return. In all, he played 21 Tests and took 89 wickets at 28.64.

By the time the 1914–15 season came around, the First World War had broken out, and Cotter had decided to join up. Despite being a city boy, he joined the glamorous Light Horse, which had suffered traumatic casualties fighting at Gallipoli, and served in the 12th Light Horse as a stretcher-bearer.

Cotter first came to notice at the Second Battle of Gaza in April

Tibby Cotter was a fast and furious bowler, the Brett Lee of his day – and the only Australian Test cricketer to lose his life in the First World War.

1917 where Gullett noted that he was 'prominent all day among the stretcher-bearers' under heavy fire. Gullett later described how the mounted stretcher-bearers at Beersheba 'rode forward, as they always did, with the advanced Light Horse lines, and worked coolly in the midst of the dismounted fight around the earthworks', and recorded that, 'while so engaged Private A Cotter, the famous Sydney fast bowler, was shot dead by a Turk at close range ... He behaved in action as a man without fear.'

Cotter's bravery and spirit endeared him to his comrades in the Light Horse. Although it is alleged by some that he stupidly stuck his head out of a trench and was shot, this is unlikely given the situation at Beersheba: Australians weren't in trenches – the Turks were.

A better story is the one told by his mate Bluey: 'I was Tibby Cotter's cobber in the 12th Light Horse, and on the night of October 30, 1917, we were at Khallassa in Southern Palestine, the most remote portion of the southern position. We watered our horses there, and prepared to move off in the attack on Beersheba.

'Tibby was one of the best foragers in the AIF. He'd come to light with a bottle of champagne in the middle of the desert, and the lads in the section all looked to him to turn up with something unusual.

'About 1.30 on the morning of the attack, Tibby, who'd received instructions to report to Echelon on a guard, turned up at the unit. He said to me, "Bluey, I've skittled a Turk in one hit, and what do you think he had on him? A yard of ling."

'He wasn't going to Echelon, he insisted, but said he would treat the boys to a Stammell fish supper in Beersheba, and be damned to the consequences.

'We moved off at 4.30 a.m. from Khallassa and attacked Beersheba that afternoon. Tibby was next to me on one side in the charge, and Trooper Jack Beazley on the other. Rex Coley was there also. The other three were skittled by a machine-gun.

'And after we'd cleared the Turks out, the troops went back half an hour later to bury the dead. Tibby was still alive when I got to him, and he recognised me. "Blue," he said, "you can have the fish supper on your own."

'He died shortly afterwards. He should never have been in the charge. Had he obeyed orders, he would probably have been alive today.

'Just before we left Khallassa, Tibby – who in a bowling competition at Tel-el-Fara bowled over 18 single stumps at full pace out of 24

Tibby Cotter was one of the 171 Australians killed in the Palestine campaign, and buried in the Beersheba War Cemetery.

Palestine

Amman, today capital city of Jordan, was captured by the Australians in September 1918, after earlier costly attempts.

– took up a ball of mud and, throwing it into the air, said, "That's my last bowl, Blue, something is going to happen."'

Trooper 924, A Cotter, 33, is buried in the Beersheba War Cemetery with Jack Beazley and Rex Coley, along with another 171 Australians killed in the Palestine campaign.

The Raids on Amman: 1918

At the end of March 1918, the Australian Light Horse, the Camel Corps and the British 60th Division forded the flooded Jordan River to raid the Hejaz railway at Amman. This bloody episode was the most costly of all the actions in which the Light Horse participated.

The Hejaz Railway, from Damascus north to Constantinople and south to Medina in Arabia, was the main communication and supply route for the Turkish forces in the Great War. Destroying it or cutting access to it was a way of shortening the war in the area, and of keeping the Turks occupied. Lawrence and the Arab Legion destroyed sections of the line but the Turks always repaired them. However, if the railway tunnels and viaducts through the hills around Amman could be destroyed, they would not be so easily repaired.

The March attack was focused on the main hill in the city, Hill 3039, or Jebel Amman, where embassies are now concentrated. It guarded the Hejaz railway tunnels and viaducts to the east, which still exist, although the railway is now only used for freight. Conditions at Hill 3039 were muddy, and the attack was undermanned and over-ambitious. There was little or no artillery to help clear the Turkish machine-gun defences.

There were the usual heroics, but adverse weather conditions and the opposition encountered prevented the objects of the raid being completely obtained. Gullett wrote that 'damage was trifling and of very little embarrassment to the enemy. The failure was expensive.' The Anzac Mounted Division lost 118 officers and men killed, 551 wounded and 55 missing. It was the blackest day of the Light Horse campaign in Palestine.

In Gullett's words: 'Troops feel some failures more sharply than others ... the Australians and New Zealanders felt their reverse on the bleak tableland more deeply than any other reverse in the long war, with the single exception of Gallipoli ... every Australian and New Zealander who fought at Amman prayed for the day he would fight there again ...' Amman would not be taken for another six months.

On 25 and 26 September 1918, the Australians and New Zealanders, showing great dash and courage, on their horses and with the bayonet, finally captured Amman. The old Roman citadel was taken by elements of the 5th Light Horse and New Zealand's gallant Canterbury's. Turkish resistance all over Palestine was already wavering, and collapsed on the appearance of the Queenslanders of the 7th Light Horse. Other Australians captured the Amman railway station and cut off the Turkish forces to the south, which were concentrated near

No. 1 Squadron Australian Flying Corps played a prominent role in reconnaissance and bombing enemy positions during the Palestine campaign, against generally superior German aircraft. There were many casualties including Lieutenant N L Steele of Kew, killed on 20 April 1917; Lieutenant J S Brasell of Melbourne, on 25 June 1917; and A H Searle on 13 July 1917. With five airmen from the Royal Flying Corps, they are commemorated in a curious memorial in Tel Aviv. It notes that it was generously erected by one of their enemies, and restored by friends in 1918.

the railhead at Maan, near Al Jiza, where Amman's Queen Alia Airport is situated.

These Turks were threatened by 10,000 men of the Arab Army, but would not surrender to them. One of those wonderfully improbable moments in the Australians' war followed. An advance guard of Light Horse galloped to the Turkish position and decided to 'join forces' with the Turks for the night of 28 September, taking two sheikhs from the Arab Army with them for protection. The Light Horse detachment entered the Turkish camp, told the Turks to keep their weapons and maintain their positions, and indicated to the sheikhs that if the Turks were attacked by the Arabs, the first people shot would be the sheikhs.

Gullett: 'The sheikhs sent out messengers to inform their followers of this threat, and the Turks and the Australians proceeded, after years of bitter fighting, to bivouac together. They gathered about the same fires, exchanging their food, making chapattis together, and by many signs expressing reciprocal respect and admiration. The Australians, although outnumbered eight to one, had no concern for their safety, and the confidence with which they moved about the armed lines was a tribute to the honour of the Turks. Perhaps in all their campaigning, the Light Horsemen were never so richly entertained.' Next day everyone marched back to Amman, in Allied hands. This time the campaign casualties in capturing Amman were light: 27 killed, 105 wounded, seven missing.

The Australians Ride First into Damascus: 30 September 1918

On the night of 30 September 1918, the rule of the Ottoman Turks had virtually ceased in Damascus. All night the streets and bazaars were in a tumult as the Arab people thronged the streets, carrying the Hejaz flag of independence, and firing rifles in the air, exulting in a new-found nationalism, and threatening the fearful but expectant Christians of the city. Allenby's capture of Jerusalem in December 1917 had seemed to the Christians the answer of Providence to their centuries of prayer; the news of Chauvel and the Australians' rushing approach to Damascus was a miracle of Divine dispensation.

Damascus then, as described by Gullett, was 'the home of a rich and numerous people ... [a] great city set in a beautiful forest of orchards and plantations, brilliant with the vivid flowers of sub-tropical climes'. None of this exists now, except the city: the Barada River is a drain, the orchards are built over by modern Damascus.

Above left: Turkish soldiers left behind in the village of Rayak, now in Lebanon near the Syrian border.
Above: Captured German trucks on the road to Damascus, 1918.

The Australians were coming from nearby Dumar at the eastern end of the Barada Gorge, where the enemy had been caught and killed by the Australians when they refused to surrender on the day before. The Australians, according to Brigadier Wilson of the 3rd Light Horse, were 'restricted to a walk by the terrible effects of the previous evening's slaughter: The roadway was heaped up with over 370 dead and wounded Turks and Germans, vehicles and killed and maimed teams of cattle and horses ... [But] the Western Australians, long seasoned alike to the horrors and risks of war, rode with light hearts through the early morning shadows of the winding pass. The train at Dumar (taken with 480 prisoners) had contained besides great wealth in gold and silver coin, a store of German cigars; and as the troopers passed out of the gorge, and the sun-touched minarets of the city rose above the beautiful tangle of green gardens splashed with ripening fruit and gay with flowers, they blew forth clouds of smoke, and seemed to have no thought beyond their keen relish of the moment.'

The approaching Australians bowled along beside the Barada into the city, not knowing what might be waiting. This is the moment caught in H Septimus Powers' painting *Into Damascus*, in the Australian War Memorial, swords at the ready, hats firm on head, solid in the saddle, emu feathers fluttering, the blue Barada a creek beside them, the walls of the wadi rising behind, a blue sky. Two hundred Australians about to invade the most ancient city.

The Light Horse rode past the Orient and Victoria Hotel, and the Palace Hotel, now Al Quaitby Street where the National Museum is, swinging around towards the railway station to what was then the Town Hall, and along the northern wall of the Old City, past the tomb of Saladin himself.

At the Town Hall, Lieutenant Colonel Olden of the 10th Light Horse told the Emir Said, who seemed to be in charge, that he was surrounded by thousands of Chauvel's troops and that resistance was impossible. He demanded the Australian troops not be molested. The Emir agreed, and said, 'In the name of the civil population of Damascus, I welcome the British army.' Olden was too polite to point out that this was the bloody Australian Light Horse. The Emir formally wrote out these assurances, and Olden left on the Homs road, chasing more Turks.

'The Australians on this wonderful morning were the only calm purposeful men in this clamorous city,' wrote Harry Gullett: 'They rode with drawn swords, dusty and unshaven, their big hats battered and drooping, through the excited people of that ancient city, with the same easy casual bearing, and the same quiet self confidence, which marked their bearing on the country tracks at home ... And their lean long-tailed horses ... found nothing in the shouting mob or banging rifles of the Arabs, or in the narrow ways and vivid hues of the bazaars, to cause them once to shy or even cock an ear.'

Wilson rode off chasing the Turks with 'every man in his brigade' and cleared the streets. T E Lawrence then rode into the town with a few Arab horsemen, on the heels of the advance guard of the Indian 14th Cavalry Brigade. The Arabs believed that they and the Indians shared the honour of first entry into Damascus, and made a melodramatic demonstration which contrasted with the casual bearing of the Australians. 'The Turkish tragedy was culminating in Damascus,' wrote Lawrence. Twelve thousand Turks surrendered that day, sick with typhus and other diseases.

Allenby's army poured into the city. Harry Chauvel wrote home from Jemal Pasha's house in Damascus: 'We have had a great and glorious time, and the Chief [Allenby] ... has just told me that our performance is the greatest cavalry feat the world has ever known ... '

Gullett wrote that, '[T]he wide vineyards were laden with grapes of rare quality, and the city stalls glowed with pomegranates and other luscious fruits. After their long summer ride over the bare plains, the men delighted in the widespread plantations, and rested and slept within sight and sound of cold clear running water.'

That clear running water harboured diseases – malarial mosquitoes, cholera and typhoid. In the next month, a number of the Australians, including some who had fought through the war from Gallipoli onwards, died of illness.

Israel, Syria and Jordan Today

After the First World War, with the collapse of the Ottoman Empire, the lands where the Palestine campaign was fought eventually became the modern states of Israel, Syria, Lebanon and Jordan. The area has continued to be torn by war and civil strife, including during the Second World War. There is plenty of evidence of present-day conflict, in all four countries.

Beersheba is now called Beersheva, and is a thriving Israeli city, the gateway to the Negev Desert. The population has more than doubled to nearly 200,000 since the 1990s. It's a go-ahead sort of place with thousands of students, high tech industries and archeological sites. Tel Sheva, formerly Tel el Saba, is very ancient and quite interesting, in a dusty-dig sort of way. Many of the places mentioned in accounts of the charge of the 4th Light Horse – including wells, the railway station and railway bridge – can still be seen.

Syria, which was under French control following the First World War, has recently begun to open up to Western travellers. Syria, and especially Damascus, are surprisingly friendly and welcoming, with an extraordinary heritage from biblical and pre-Christian days. However, except for the cemeteries in Damascus and Aleppo, there isn't much evidence of Australia, or even of either world war. There is, on the other hand, mighty evidence of more ancient wars – at the crusader castle at Krac des Chevaliers for example.

Right: The old Beersheba railway station, site of a future First World War museum.
Above: The nearby Turkish Memorial. The inscription says: 'This monument is dedicated to 298 honourable Turkish Army soldiers fallen at the Beersheva front for the sake of their country.'

Palestine

Jordan has two of the wonders of the ancient world within reach of the capital Amman – the extraordinary Petra, and the equally interesting Jerash. Both tourists and terrorism have increased in recent years. Australian sites are nonexistent, though readers of Lawrence of Arabia's *Seven Pillars of Wisdom* will recognise the wadis beyond Petra.

Cemeteries, Memorials, Museums: Israel

Beersheba (now Beersheva)

Beersheba War Cemetery was built immediately on the fall of the town, remaining in use until July 1918, by which time 139 burials had been made. It was greatly increased after the Armistice when burials were brought in from a number of scattered sites and small burial grounds. The cemetery now contains 1241 Commonwealth burials of the First World War, 67 of them unidentified. There are 174 Australians buried here, including Tibby Cotter and his mates Jack Beazley and Rex Coley, and Lieutenant Colonel Harry Maygar VC, commander of the 8th Light Horse.

Maygar was on his grey horse before the Beersheba battle when his unit was bombed by a German aircraft. He was wounded and his horse bolted. Troopers dashed off in pursuit and found the horse but not Maygar, who was picked up during the night by some other troops, but died the following day. Lamented by all, Maygar had won his VC in the Boer War with the 5th Victorian Mounted Rifles, and had done fine work at Gallipoli. Gullett described him as 'a true fighting commander'. Troopers of the 8th Light Horse shot down one of the German aircraft on 1 November.

Left: Lieutenant Colonel Harry Maygar won the VC in the Boer War.
Far left: Corporal Bill Hutchinson of Essendon, 3rd Light Horse Machine-gun Section, killed in the charge.

Above: Abraham's Well.
Below: The Allenby Monument, without the statue of the great general.

A First World War Museum commemorating the charge at Beersheba and Australia's role is being established in the old railway station in Beersheba. There is a **Turkish Memorial** close by.

Abraham's Well is one of the hundreds of wells in Beersheba that the Light Horse wanted to capture in 1917. Abraham's Well was mentioned in Genesis, and perhaps this is it: 'And Isaac digged again the wells of water, which they had digged in the days of Abraham his father; for the Philistines had stopped them after the death of Abraham: and he called their names after the names by which his father had called them.'

The original form of a historic well has been preserved, and you might find a bit of preaching going on here, as I did.

The **Allenby Monument** in Beersheba, an extraordinary monument, was erected in the 1920s next to the ancient mosque. It was in the form of a double life-size bust, atop a column many metres tall. Sometime in the 1930s, the column and bust were destroyed. All that remains today is the plinth.

The **Anzac Memorial** was built by the Keren Kayemeth Leisrael (JNF) with the help of Jewish communities in Australia and New Zealand and dedicated in April 1967. The memorial is in memory of the Australia and New Zealand Army Corps who fought in Israel during the First World War.

Jerusalem

Jerusalem War Cemetery and within it, the Jerusalem Memorial, is located on the Mount of Olives, north of the old city. It was begun after the Turkish defeat in December 1917. Fifty-nine Australians of the First World War (and eleven of the Second World War) are buried here, among 2514 Commonwealth burials. The Jerusalem Memorial commemorates by name 3300 Commonwealth servicemen who died in Palestine and who have no known grave.

Jerusalem War Cemetery.

Cemeteries, Memorials, Museums: The Palestinian Territories

Gaza

Gaza War Cemetery is 1.5 kilometres north-east of Gaza City, some 45 kilometres from Beersheva in the Palestinian Territories and 65 kilometres south-east of Tel Aviv, and is difficult to visit. Some of the earliest burials here were made by the troops that captured the city. About two-thirds of the First World War burials were brought into the cemetery from battlefields after the Armistice, and the remainder were made by medical units during the occupation.

The cemetery contains 3217 Commonwealth burials of the First World War, 781 of them unidentified, as well as 210 Second World War burials, 30 postwar burials and 234 war graves of other nationalities.

The Anzac Memorial is near the border crossing from Israel into Gaza. (Kelvin Crombie)

Cemeteries, Memorials, Museums: Syria

Aleppo

Aleppo War Cemetery, 1.5 kilometres north of the city, was created in 1941 and now contains 114 Commonwealth burials of the Second World War, eight of them unidentified. There is also a memorial to 127 Indian soldiers who died during the First World War. The cemetery also contains one Czech and twelve Greek war graves.

The **Cavalry Memorial** is fifteen kilometres from the city centre, on the road to Bab Salami, and marks the site of one of the last actions of the First World War. Covered on my visit in election posters, and threatened with demolition because of the widening of a road, it records the names of a number of members of the Imperial Cavalry Division who died here on 26 October 1918.

Aleppo War Cemetery.

The **Baron Hotel** is a small, famous and slightly down-at-heel hotel, which hosted some notable figures during the First World War. On the wall in the sitting room is T E Lawrence's unpaid bill from 8 June 1914, for £76.20. He must have eaten well back in those days.

Lawrence's and the Australians' principal opponent, Turkish commander Mustafa Kemal, stayed here in October 1918 while in charge of the retreating but still fighting Turkish armies. Ill with a kidney complaint, he was in bed at the Baron one afternoon when a commotion outside caused to him get up. Aleppo was under attack, and a crowd of locals was storming the hotel, in anticipation, it seemed, of the arrival of the Australian and British forces and the Arab irregulars. Kemal drove the rioters out with his riding crop and surveyed the situation from the balcony of the Baron. 'Certain inhabitants of Aleppo, whom I wish to defend, are throwing grenades at me from the roof,' he told another officer, and ordered a machine-gun attack on the rioters. Soon afterwards the Turkish army withdrew from Aleppo, fighting a number of stiff rearguard actions.

Damascus

Damascus Commonwealth War Cemetery.

Damascus War Cemetery is approximately five kilometres south-west of the city centre in an area known as Sabara (Arabic for prickly pear). The cemetery dates from the First World War when Damascus was entered by Commonwealth forces. The first medical unit, arriving the next day, found the Turkish hospitals crowded with sick and wounded, and a few days later an epidemic of influenza and cholera broke out. The First World War burials in this cemetery were mostly from these hospitals.

One of the Australians buried here was Trooper James Smyth, a jockey of Hamilton in Victoria, who, during the ride into Damascus with his mate Norm Halliday, surprised a party of three Germans and 85 Turks setting up a machine-gun. Smyth charged in under fire, grabbed the officer in charge, disarmed him of his revolver and turned it on the rest, who, surprised and browbeaten by the audacity of the stunt, abjectly surrendered. Smyth and Halliday were awarded the DCM for their feat. Smyth died of illness on 25 October.

The cemetery contains 661 Commonwealth burials and commemorations of the First World War, including 74 unidentified burials, and 504 Second World War burials, of which fourteen are unidentified. A special tablet in the new part of the cemetery commemorates six men of the Indian army who were buried in Damascus Indian War Cemetery but whose graves are now lost.

Travel Tool Kit

Independent travel is certainly possible everywhere in the Middle East. Risks are involved, and careful thought should be given to where and when you go. The situation can change quickly. Thought also has to be given to the structure of an itinerary that includes Israel and Syria.

Aside from the normal personal security caveats about travel to Israel, it is an easy country to travel in, although expensive by comparison with elsewhere in the Middle East. Accommodation of all kinds is readily available, there are gum trees everywhere, and you might think you are in outback Australia.

Visitors will, of course, have to observe the protocols – make sure you get your Israeli visa stamped on a separate piece of paper if you want to visit other countries in the region; you will not be admitted to Syria, for example, with an Israeli stamp in your passport or exit/entry stamps that suggest you have visited Israel. Check with the Embassy of Israel for the latest information on visas and security. See **www.canberra.mfa.gov.il** or contact **info@canberra.mfa.gov.il**

Tourists should not have any trouble crossing the Allenby Bridge from near Amman over the Jordan River to near Jerusalem. Make sure you have valid re-entry visas if you need to cross back – they are not available at the border. The crossing is sometimes closed at short notice at times of heightened tension in Israel or Jordan. Check with the Embassy of the Hashemite Kingdom of Jordan for the latest on visas and travel arrangements.

Syria is more open to visitors now than at any time for 50 years, despite war in neighbouring Iraq, and rumbling trouble with Lebanon and Israel. Accommodation ranges from the spectacular to the historic, the food is splendid, and I was very comfortable wandering

Tracks in the desert hills of the Sinai near present-day Beersheva. Wars have been fought here for thousands of years.

around Damascus by myself. For visa forms and other information go to the Embassy of Syrian Arab Republic.

Tours and Guides

I hired a car and driver to get to Beersheva from Tel Aviv, as it is easily reached as a long day trip. In Syria, I travelled around by bus, and hired car and driver, and visited the Commonwealth War Graves cemeteries in Damascus and Aleppo, as well as other sights.

For those who want an individual or group itinerary, my recommended travel agent is Tempo Holidays, formerly Ya'alla Tours, who have been of great service to me over ten years in the region. See **www.tempoholidays.com** or contact **info@tempoholidays.com**

Further Information

Lindsay Baly, *Horseman, Pass By*, Kangaroo Press, East Roseville, 2003.

Kelvin Crombie, *Anzacs, Empires & Israel's Restoration*, Vocational Education & Training Publications, Osborne Park, 1998.

Frank Dalby Davison, *The Wells of Beersheba*, Angus & Robertson, Sydney, 1933.

H S Gullett and Chas Barrett (eds.), *Australia in Palestine*, Angus & Robertson, Sydney, 1919.

H S Gullett, *Official History of Australia in the War of 1914–1918*, Volume VII, 'The Australian Imperial Force in Sinai and Palestine, 1914–1918', Angus & Robertson, Sydney, 1923.

Rex Hall, *The Desert Hath Pearls*, Hawthorn Press, Melbourne, 1975.

Ion L Idriess, *The Desert Column*, Angus & Robertson, Sydney, 1932.

Jill, Duchess of Hamilton, *First into Damascus*, Kangaroo Press, East Roseville, 2002.

Elyne Mitchell, *Light Horse*, Macmillan, Melbourne, 1978.

3.

THE WESTERN FRONT

THE WESTERN FRONT WAS AN INDESCRIBABLE QUAGMIRE of shell-raked trenches that ran for about 750 kilometres from Nieuport on the Belgian coast, past Ypres, Vimy, Albert, Reims, Verdun and Nancy to Belfort on the Swiss border. It stabilised in October 1914 after the initial German attacks failed to take Paris, and barely moved until the decisive battles of August 1918, in which the Australian Corps commanded by General Sir John Monash played such a decisive part. The Western Front was the name accepted by both sides, even though it was originally the German description, as the Germans had also attacked Russia to their east; they were fighting on the Eastern Front until it collapsed following the 1917 Russian Revolution.

The Australians, who had regrouped and been reinforced in Egypt after the evacuation of p.103: Villers Bretonneux Cemetery from the tower of the Australian National Memorial.

Gallipoli in December 1915, were a well-trained and experienced force, eagerly awaited on the Western Front. The Australian 1st and 2nd divisions arrived in Marseilles in March 1916, and were soon in the action. The 4th and 5th divisions arrived in June, and the 3rd Division, after completing training in England, followed in early 1917. By May 1918 all five divisions were fighting as the Australian Corps, commanded for the first time by an Australian, General Sir John Monash.

Much of the significant Australian action on the Western Front took place in three areas: around Fromelles, in northern France; on the battlefields of the Somme, between Amiens and Péronne including the village of Villers Bretonneux; and in the fields of Flanders in Belgium around Ypres (now Ieper).

The battles of the Somme in July 1916 were among the most wasteful of lives of any in the First World War. The grand plan involved coordinated attacks by more than three-quarters of a million men,

The peaceful view towards Villers Bretonneux from the top of the Australian National Memorial. The Australians attacked from this direction in April 1918.

aimed at a significant breakthrough. A German attack involved the French forces south of the Somme, but the British attacks north went ahead anyway, at a ghastly cost incurring 60,000 casualties on 1 July. The Australians were first involved in a feint (which the Germans knew was not a serious attack) further to the north at Fromelles. This was the first major action by Australians on the Western Front, by the 5th Division on 19 July 1916. An ill-planned daylight charge saw 5533 casualties in 24 hours. It was the Nek or Krithia on an even

Map of the Western Front, 1916.

bloodier scale. The Germans consolidated their strong defensive positions even further with more cement, tunnels and machine-guns, and the frontline at Fromelles barely moved for two years after the battle.

The other Australian divisions were sent into the line 75 kilometres further south, near the town of Albert and a small village on the higher ground, named Pozières. Between 23 July and 27 July, the 1st Division also suffered catastrophically – 5285 casualties, or about a third of its strength. The 2nd Division took over, and by 4 August, it had suffered even more – 6848 casualties – in taking Pozières, gaining a section of the ridge that runs up to Thiepval, just a few kilometres to the north-west. It was then the 4th Division's turn, on this ridge that Charles Bean said 'was more densely sown with Australian sacrifice than any other place on earth'. In four days, 7000 men were killed or wounded. Overall, Pozières cost around 23,000 casualties.

That winter of 1916–1917 saw the Australians fighting in the freezing mud of trenches not far from Pozières, which ended in a German withdrawal and the Allied offensive of April 1917. The Australian commitment to this large offensive was around Bullecourt, where two battles were fought in April and May by the four Australian divisions for a small gain in ground, at the cost of nearly 6000 casualties.

Later in 1917, all five AIF divisions were involved in the series of battles east of Ypres at Messines, Polygon Wood, Menin Road and Broodseinde. Some 38,000 Australians were killed or wounded in those two months.

Restored trench at Australian Corps Memorial, Hamel, the village church visible across the 1918 battlefield.

The Eastern Front collapsed after the 1917 Russian Revolution, enabling the Germans to swing tens of thousands of soldiers to the west, and launch what turned out to be their final offensive in March 1918. The Australian 3rd and 4th divisions arrived in the Somme on 23 March 1918 to stiffen the retreating British forces.

One of the Germans' major aims in those last offensives was to capture Amiens and the Channel ports and the vast British and French forces north of the Somme. They powered through Armentières and were at the gates of Ypres, to the north, by April, but were checked 30 kilometres from Amiens when the Australians held the line at the Somme River. On 4 April the Australians helped defend Villers Bretonneux, an important town on a ridge overlooking Amiens, just sixteen kilometres away. Villers Bretonneux was taken on 18 April by the Germans from the British, who had replaced the Australians. But on 24–25 April, the Australians recaptured the town in fierce fighting, halting the German advance towards Amiens for the last time.

General Sir John Monash took command of the Australian Corps of all five divisions on 30 May, after which it participated in a series of offensive actions which for the first time successfully co-ordinated all arms of modern warfare – tanks, aircraft, artillery and infantry. The battle at Hamel, east of Villers Bretonneux, on 4 July was a small-scale pilot for what was to come. The battle of Amiens commenced on 8 August. It was also the famous 'black day' of the German army. All five Australian divisions were involved together for the first time. Significant actions were the capture of Péronne and Mont St Quentin on 2 September. The final Australian action in this tremendous advance was the capture of Montbrehain on 5 October 1918. The Armistice was declared at 11 a.m. on 11 November 1918.

The Diggers' spirit is everywhere, still, in northern France and Belgium, reinvoked whenever you say 'g'day' to someone at a cemetery – there always seems to be another Australian there, if you wait awhile. Or when you introduce yourself to a puzzled local in atrocious French as someone who is lost and looking for an Australian place – half the time, she will get in the car and guide you there. Australian-related places are everywhere, and the deeds of the Diggers are remembered in the roll-call of battle honours: Fromelles, Pozières, Mouquet Farm, Menin Road, Hill 60, Polygon Wood, Passchendaele, Amiens, Villers Bretonneux, Hamel, Mont St Quentin.

The strong affinity between this part of France and Australia was created especially in the grim days at the Somme in March and April 1918, and that area today has a close connection with Australia – the Australian memorial is located at Villers Bretonneux, the Unknown Soldier came from the nearby Adelaide Cemetery to be reinterred at the Australian War Memorial in Canberra and, most movingly perhaps, the school at Villers Bretonneux was rebuilt with the pennies of Victorian schoolchildren.

This bond was inspired by the incorrigibly civilian Australian soldiers. Some French refugees, seeing the Australians heading into the line, took their bags from the wagons, and put them on the ground. Asked why, one replied '*Pas necessaire maintenant. Vous les tiendrez!*' It's not necessary now. You'll hold them! A Digger stopped for a smoke on his way to the front was heard to say to Madame, '*Fini retreat, beaucoup Australiens ici!*' Don't bother retreating, the Aussies are here! That's the laconic, confident, practical Digger we love. Speak French? Of course! Take any nonsense from anyone? Of course not! Win the war? No worries!

Never Forget Australia: The sign on the shelter shed at the Villers Bretonneux school.

Looking at a map, it's easy to trace the Australian battlefields along the Western Front. They stretch along about 250 kilometres, revealing a line fought over at the cost of some 180,000 casualties, including 53,000 dead, from the 313,814 soldiers who sailed to war from Australia.

The dead are to be found in some 500 cemeteries in France and Belgium. Many of these cemeteries have only one Australian burial, some have over 1000. Many others who fought on the Western Front died of wounds or illness and are buried in Britain. Eighteen thousand of those who died on the Western Front have no known grave. They are named on memorials at Menin Gate in Ypres, at Tyne Cot and Passchendaele in Belgium, at VC Corner at Fromelles, at the Arras Memorial and at the Australian National Memorial at Villers Bretonneux.

The thanks of the French and the Belgians are recorded too, in the place names and memorial plaques, in the cathedral at Amiens, and on the shelter shed at Villers Bretonneux which says Never Forget Australia. And they do not.

Cross of Sacrifice,
VC Corner, Fromelles.

Medical orderlies, 45th Battalion, on the Somme battlefield, near Dernancourt, September 1917.

The Australians on the Western Front 1916–1918

'The stock of a thousand butcher-shops'; Fromelles, 19 July 1916

What happened to the Australians at Fromelles in July 1916 was all the more tragic for having such a predictable result. A bad half-idea led to sloppy staff work and criminally inept planning at the higher levels of British command, especially by Lieutenant General 'Butcher' Haking. Thousands of Australian casualties were the direct result of his decision to order an attack across flat sodden ground against entrenched German positions on slightly higher ground, with concrete pillboxes and machine-guns commanding the open killing field.

McCay, the Australian commander of the inexperienced 5th Division, which had been in France just a month, was an unlikeable martinet who had only recently been appointed to the job. According to Pompey Elliott, commander of the 5th Division's 15th Brigade, McCay wanted to lead the first Australians to have a big fight in France, 'and to get a big splash'. Elliott said he would have protested about having to attack such a position, but he never blamed McCay for what happened at Fromelles, as the move was ordered from above. Elliott noted, however, that 'McCay was terribly anxious that it shouldn't be stopped and made no mention of the difficulties facing us …'

The idea, such as it was, was for the Australians and the British 61st Division to take a kilometre of German trenches across a stretch of no man's land between 100 and 500 metres wide, and guarded by a cement bunker complex of machine-guns known as the Sugarloaf. There was no cover, and the Germans, the experienced 6th Bavarian Reserve Division, were well dug in and supported by effective artillery and observation from the Aubers ridge behind their lines. The Germans inhabited strong, deep positions with tunnels and concrete bunkers, and had settled in to a kind of permanent defence. The attackers' trenches were temporary and swampy; the ground between the two positions, boggy.

There were supposedly three lines of German trenches, and the assault's objective was to dig in at the third line. The Australians were on the left, the British on the right, with the Sugarloaf close to the boundary between the British troops and the Australian 15th Brigade, at no man's land's widest point. If the British failed to take the German defences in the trenches to the right of the Sugarloaf or failed to do their bit in attacking that position, there would be a wholesale slaughter of any attackers who did make it to the German lines.

Opposite: Map of Fromelles area.

Below left: German concrete pillboxes at Fromelles photographed by Charles Bean in 1918.
Below: One of the same pillboxes in 2004.

The Western Front

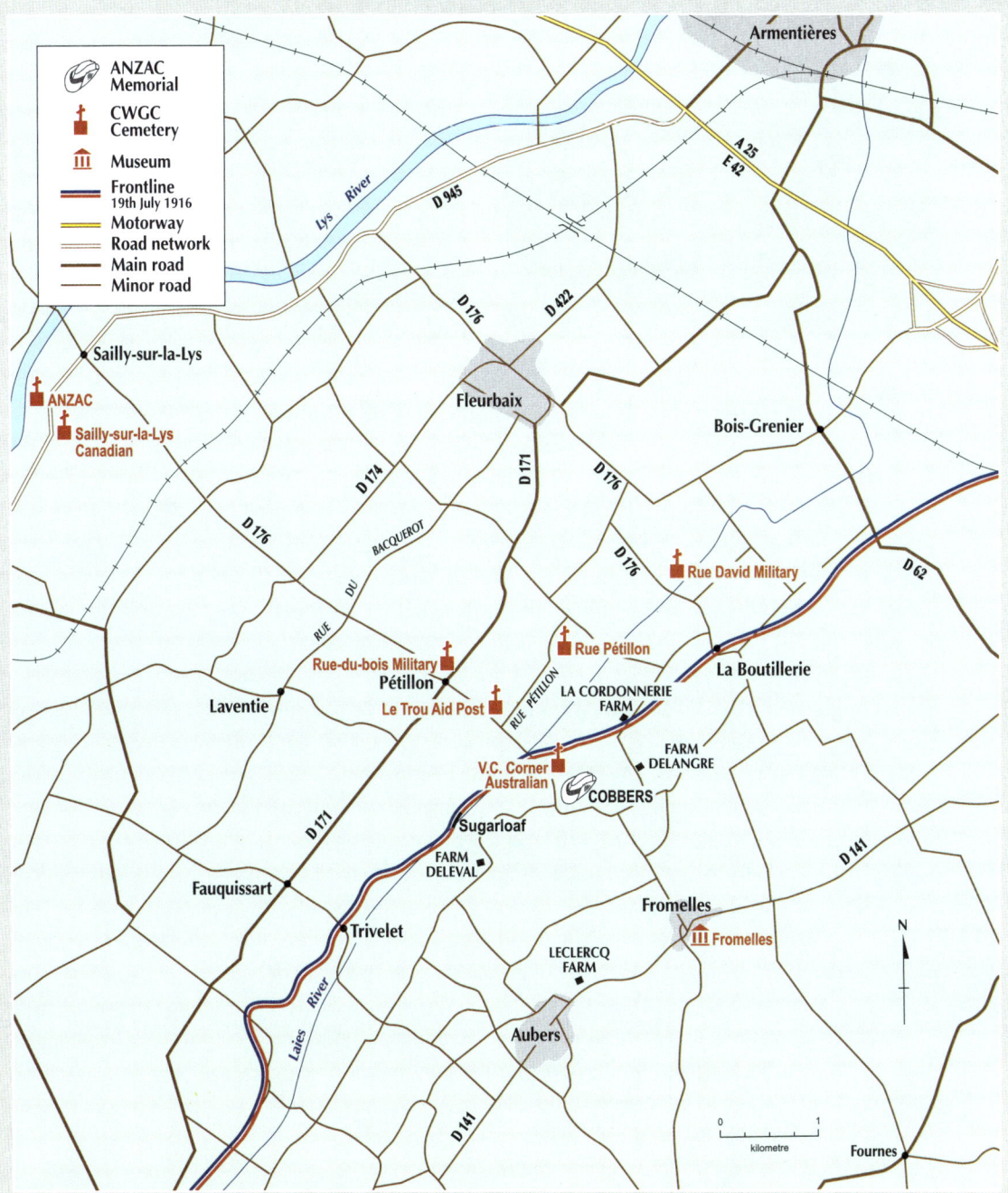

Fromelles, 19 July 1916: The Australians attacked across this ditch in their first action on the Western Front, and suffered terrible casualties.

The plan to keep German reinforcements away from the battle further south on the Somme was ill thought out; from their observation post, the Germans could see that preparations were being made for a small attack on a narrow front, and the artillery bombardment that began on 16 July served to warn the Germans of the attack.

The Australians had been force-marched to the start-line for the attack, planned for 17 July, but it was foggy and the attack was postponed. Two days later, the opportunity to cancel or further postpone the attack having been missed, the attack was ordered to commence on the afternoon of 19 July.

Although the 15th Brigade, under Pompey Elliott, had the toughest task, the narrower crossing of the Australian 14th and 8th brigades to their left was still deadly. The Germans began shelling the communications trenches where the Australians formed up, and the 8th Brigade suffered hundreds of casualties as they waited to advance, receiving fire, too, from the German lines further north, who had returned to the trenches when the British artillery had finished. But like the 14th Brigade in the centre of the Australian attack, these men 'only' needed to cross 150 to 250 yards of no man's land before they reached the German frontline trenches.

Amid the confusion and casualties, the Australians started the advance at six o'clock. A few hours of daylight remained. Suffering heavy casualties as they advanced, they cleared the German front trench and advanced to where the third line of trenches was supposed to be. But there were no trenches, just some watery ditches.

After the surviving men of the 8th and 14th gained their objective, they momentarily 'strolled on through the grass, like sportsmen after quail, occasionally shooting at Germans who had settled in shell holes and who now started to run farther'.

At the other end of the attack, the British 61st Division had one brigade (182nd) which took the front trenches, one which barely moved off the start-line, and one (184th), which was to take the all-important Sugarloaf, that did not move at all. The German machine-gunners in the Sugarloaf blocked their exit points with dead, and unlike the Australians, the British were not willing to go over the top.

Two battalions of Pompey Elliott's 15th Brigade (the 59th and 60th) were to attack the Sugarloaf across 500 metres of machine-gun-ripped mud crossed diagonally by a water-filled ditch called the Laies River, a death ditch that soon filled with Australians, as wave after wave fell. Just fifteen minutes after the attack by the 15th began, German firing stopped. Elliott thought for a moment that they had succeeded – but the firing had stopped because nearly all his men were dead or wounded. The two assault battalions of the 15th Brigade suffered terribly – the 60th Battalion suffered 757 casualties from 900 who started out, the 59th Battalion, 695 casualties.

Because the Germans still held the Sugarloaf, the right-hand section of the 14th Brigade was exposed. Here one of the heroes of Fromelles, Captain Charles Arblaster of the 53rd, aged just twenty, stationed himself to face the inevitable German counter-attack. It came at about nine o'clock that night, when the Germans counter-attacked down the trenches from the Sugarloaf towards their old front trenches, which had been emptied by the Australians. Arblaster organised a famous defence, but through the night was outflanked by the Germans: 'Where the youngster held out, the din of bombing ... became continuous, and white flares, blurred by dust and smoke, constantly curved through the air ... Captain Murray, farther along the front, would nod to one of his officers after another to move off with their men into the inferno. Of every ten men who went barely one came back.' In the end, Arblaster had to fight back through the old German trenches re-taken by their original occupants. He was killed as he led the charge.

Lieutenant Colonel, later Brigadier General, Harold 'Pompey' Elliott was one of the first AIF's most caring and popular commanders. It has been speculated that he was nicknamed Pompey after the famous footballer, Fred 'Pompey' Elliott – Carlton's 1908 premiership captain.

Meanwhile the British 61st Division was planning another attack on the Sugarloaf, and Pompey Elliott's 15th was asked to help. All he had left were two companies – half of the 58th Battalion – under the command of 21-year-old Major Arthur Hutchinson, a Tasmanian Duntroon graduate and 'a boy of the finest type this country produces' according to Charles Bean. They attacked as requested, but the 61st failed to move. No one told Elliott or Hutchinson that the 61st had decided not to attack. Elliott has been criticised for not checking the order, but his actions in the heat (and fog) of battle are understandable. Hutchinson made it to the German wire before being riddled with bullets. By the end of the battle, these two companies had suffered 248 casualties.

Finally, the order to withdraw back to the Australian lines was given at 8 o'clock in the morning. Many could not get back, fighting until after 9 o'clock. Many episodes of heroism as well as much confusion ensued, as small groups had to decide when and how to gain their own lines. A number were killed or captured in the attempt.

Elliott wrote later that the 'whole operation was so incredibly blundered from beginning to end that it is almost incomprehensible how the British staff, who were responsible for it, could have consisted of trained professional soldiers ... and why, in view of the outcome of this extraordinary adventure, any of them were retained in active command'.

Trenches Fromelles: 'If you had gathered the stock of a thousand butcher-shops, cut it into small pieces and strewn it about it would give you a faint conception of the shambles those trenches were.
'There was another heart-rending spectacle for anyone looking out towards no man's land, where Australians could be seen everywhere raising their limbs in pain or turning hopelessly, hour after hour, from one side to the other.'
—Corporal Hugh Knyvett, 59th Battalion

Bean noted that the attack at Fromelles had the opposite effect to that intended, being revealed as 'a mere feint', and this would quiet any German doubts about '"milking" that front for reserves for the Somme'. Bean concluded that 'the impression already created in the AIF that the new British armies lacked something in fighting capacity, was noticeably strengthened by this episode.'

By noon on the 20th, the guns had ceased, 'the artillerymen both sides being worn out'. The survivors were back where they started, but in front of them were the forward saps dug into no man's land and the ditch of the Laies, filled with the dead and the dying.

Corporal Hugh Knyvett (59th) likened it to 'the stock of a thousand butcher-shops, cut into small pieces and strewn about'. Elliott, alone among the commanders, visited the trenches crowded with dead and dying. Afterwards, recalled Lieutenant Neil Freeman (58th), 'I will always have before my eyes the picture of Pompey, the morning after Fromelles, tears streaming down his face, shaking hands with the pitiful remnants of his brigade.'

Charles Bean returned to Fromelles with a photographer on the day the war ended, 11 November 1918, and took pictures of the German blockhouses. He 'found the old No Man's Land simply full of our dead. In the narrow sector west of the Laies River and east of the Sugar-loaf salient, the skulls and bones and torn uniforms were lying about everywhere. I found a bit of Australian kit lying 50 yards from the corner of the salient, and the bones of an Australian officer and several men within 100 yards of it ...'

The village hardly had one brick on top of another; the battlefield was a swamp punctuated by smashed cement.

The Truce that Never Was

After the guns had stopped, according to Charles Bean, 'there was a stillness never again experienced by the 5th Division in the front trenches. The sight of the wounded lying tortured and helpless in no man's land, within a stone's throw of safety but apparently without hope of it, made so strong an appeal that more than one Australian, taking his life into his hands, went out to tend them.' What followed, the truce that never happened, is an extraordinary story, best told in the words of Sergeant William 'Billy' Miles of the 8th Brigade (29th Battalion) in a letter to Bean. (Bean had mentioned the wrong Miles in his account of the truce in the Official History, and Miles, who had subsequently suffered shell shock, wanted to protect his pension entitlements so his son, officially named 'Aussie', was looked after.) On the afternoon of 20 July, Billy had volunteered to go out into no man's land to tend to the wounded and look for Captain Ken Mortimer:

'I offered and was given a red cross badge for my arm and over I went landing in a shell hole and ricking my knee. I asked two or three wounded if they had seen Capt. Mortimer but could not find him.' After tending to some wounded men, dodging from shell hole to shell hole, Billy heard a voice.

'I jumped as well as I could into another shell hole, which, however, was not deep enough to hide in, and heard someone call out from the German lines; looking over I saw a man beckoning to me. I got up and walked slowly towards him, stopping once to pick up a pair of field glasses. I stopped at the edge of the wire.' The following conversation took place with the officer Billy named Fritz:

Sergeant Billy Miles, 29th Battalion.

> Fritz: What are you supposed to be doing?
> Billy: Tending wounded men, giving them a drink, and cutting their equipment off so they will lie more comfortable till we can get them in.
> Fritz: You may be laying wires, this is not the usages of war.
> Billy: Oh yes it is, the Red Cross is always allowed to work unmolested.
> Fritz: What did you pick up just now?
> Billy: A pair of field glasses.
> Fritz: It might have been a bomb.
> Billy: I'll show you.
> Fritz: Don't put your hands in your pocket, put your hands above your head.

Billy waited by the German wire as 'Fritz' spoke on the telephone to his superiors; after a devastating battle which had caused 8000 casualties, the dead and dying just a few paces away, an Australian private was having a matter-of-fact conversation with a German officer while others were taking photographs of him. The German officer put down the telephone and Billy promptly asked whether he could lower his hands.

Fritz answered, 'I forgot, your arms must be aching.' And then added, 'I want you to go back to your lines and ask an officer to come over here and we will have a "parliamentaire" and see if we can arrange about collecting the wounded. Will you come back and let me know what they say?'

Billy promised and returned with Major Alex Murdoch, distributing water bottles as they walked across. 'Fritz' explained, according to Billy, that if an Australian officer would allow himself to be blindfolded and held as a hostage in the German trench, each side could collect the wounded in the half of no man's land nearest them. (Bean, in the official version, has this as a suggestion from Murdoch.) Murdoch and Miles returned to the Australian lines, and asked General McCay for permission for this informal truce, while Australian stretcher-bearers were busy bringing in as many wounded men as they could, and the Germans were repairing their parapet and looking after their own wounded.

McCay refused Murdoch's request for the truce, claiming that instructions from higher headquarters were explicit and unambiguous. It is a decision which has remained controversial ever since. It is clear that truces were permitted under military law, however much British commanders wanted to argue the contrary. But, in practice, once asked, McCay had to obey the spirit of his instructions; if the request for permission had not happened, local conditions might have applied and many lives been saved.

'The horror of knowing that a mate – his living body the prey of flies and ants – is slowly being done to death within two minutes of the succour to which, without military disadvantage, he could be brought, is less present to distant staffs than to officers and men in the line, and was estimated (though doubtless only after severe internal conflict) as a trifle when balanced against the mighty issues at stake ...

'A great part of both the nation and the army would probably have favoured a policy more rigidly consistent with the principles of chivalry and humanity, for which the Allies genuinely stood, but a divisional general can hardly be blamed for rigid adherence to the orders of the commander-in-chief.'

In these tortuous sentences Bean, who was at Fromelles on the afternoon of the 20th, put the best face on McCay's attitude, but also conveyed his – and our – view that it would have been better if the men had been saved.

There was no truce, but for the next three days and nights Australians went out into no man's land under enemy fire to bring in the wounded.

Hitler at Fromelles

Not among the estimated 1500 German casualties at Fromelles on 19–20 July 1916 was one Adolf Hitler. He had joined the 16th Bavarian Reserve Infantry Regiment in 1914 and survived the first battle of Ypres in October 1914 when the regiment had over 3000 casualties. He was a despatch rider – a messenger – a role not much less dangerous than serving on the front line. He received the Iron Cross in December 1914. In the 1920s he described it as the 'most memorable time of my life'. The regiment was at Fromelles from 8 July to 25 September, holding the Sugarloaf, and here Hitler failed to fulfil one of his fantasies and die in battle, though he was wounded on the Somme when the regiment faced the 5th Division again on 7 October 1916.

A couple of his regimental comrades were remembered when Hitler took up his political career – Friedrich Wiedemann, a lieutenant in the war and Hitler's immediate superior became Hitler's personal assistant and later consul-general in San Francisco and China. Tried at Nuremberg, he served a couple of years and died in his bed in 1970, aged 79. Rudolf Hess was another member of the regiment, as was Sergeant Major Max Amann, a particular friend of Hitler's. Amann later became the biggest media baron in Nazi Germany and was responsible for the royalties on *Mein Kampf* that made Hitler extremely rich. Amann received ten years at Nuremberg and died poor, but in his bed, in 1957, aged 66.

Fromelles was extremely important to Hitler; he stayed here during the Second World War when the Armistice with France came into effect at 1.35 a.m. on 25 June 1940. The French had been made to sign the surrender on 21 June, in the same train in which Germany had signed her surrender in 1918. This was perhaps the peak of Hitler's career – he'd finally won the First World War; he toured Paris, he toured the Somme and then he went back to Fromelles with a couple of mates from the war – Amann and his old sergeant, Ernst Schmidt. He looked for bits of cement that marked the battlefield and, according to some sources, found them – perhaps they were the old blockhouse that today provides the basis for the Australian memorial.

On 20 April 1942 a plaque was placed on the building in nearby Fournes-en-Weppes where Hitler had been billeted. It is now in the museum in Fromelles.

If an Australian bullet or shell had found its mark in 1916, history would have taken a different course.

Fromelles Museum: The plaque from the village of Fournes, near Fromelles, where Adolf Hitler had billeted in 1916. It was erected on 20 April 1942 on the occasion of Hitler's visit to his old battlefield.

The Western Front

Above: The Pozières battlefield near the Windmill position in the winter of 1916. Charles Bean said it was a formless, featureless landscape 'as in the world's dawn'.
Above right: The remains of the Windmill today.

'Densely sown with sacrifice': Pozières, July–August 1916

The British attack on the Somme was a costly failure in most parts of its 32-kilometre front east of Albert. Of the 140,000 men involved, 60,000 were casualties by the end of the first day, 1 July. The Australian 1st Division became involved at the strategically important village of Pozières on 23 July. Three previous British attacks to take the ruins had failed, but the Australians achieved the objective in two days, suffering 5285 dead and wounded.

The next objective for the Australians was the high ground between Pozières and Mouquet Farm near Thiepval. Nine attacks were launched by the 1st, 2nd and 4th divisions between 28 July and 3 September for a gain of 1500 metres and the loss of 16,847 men. In total, nearly 23,000 casualties were incurred in barely six weeks, easily the greatest loss suffered by Australia anywhere in such a short time.

Australia's Greatest Frontline Soldier

On 7 August 1916, not far from the German position known as the Windmill, about 500 metres north-east of Pozières, Albert Jacka, who had won Australia's first VC at Gallipoli, performed 'the most dramatic and effective act of individual audacity in the history of the AIF', according to Charles Bean. Bean thought this 'stunt' should have earned him another VC – instead Jacka was awarded a Military Cross.

The Germans on this day overran a part of the Australian line including Jacka's portion. Jacka, having just returned to his dug-out from a personal survey of the front, was surprised to see Germans in the entrance. A grenade was lobbed in, killing two of Jacka's mates,

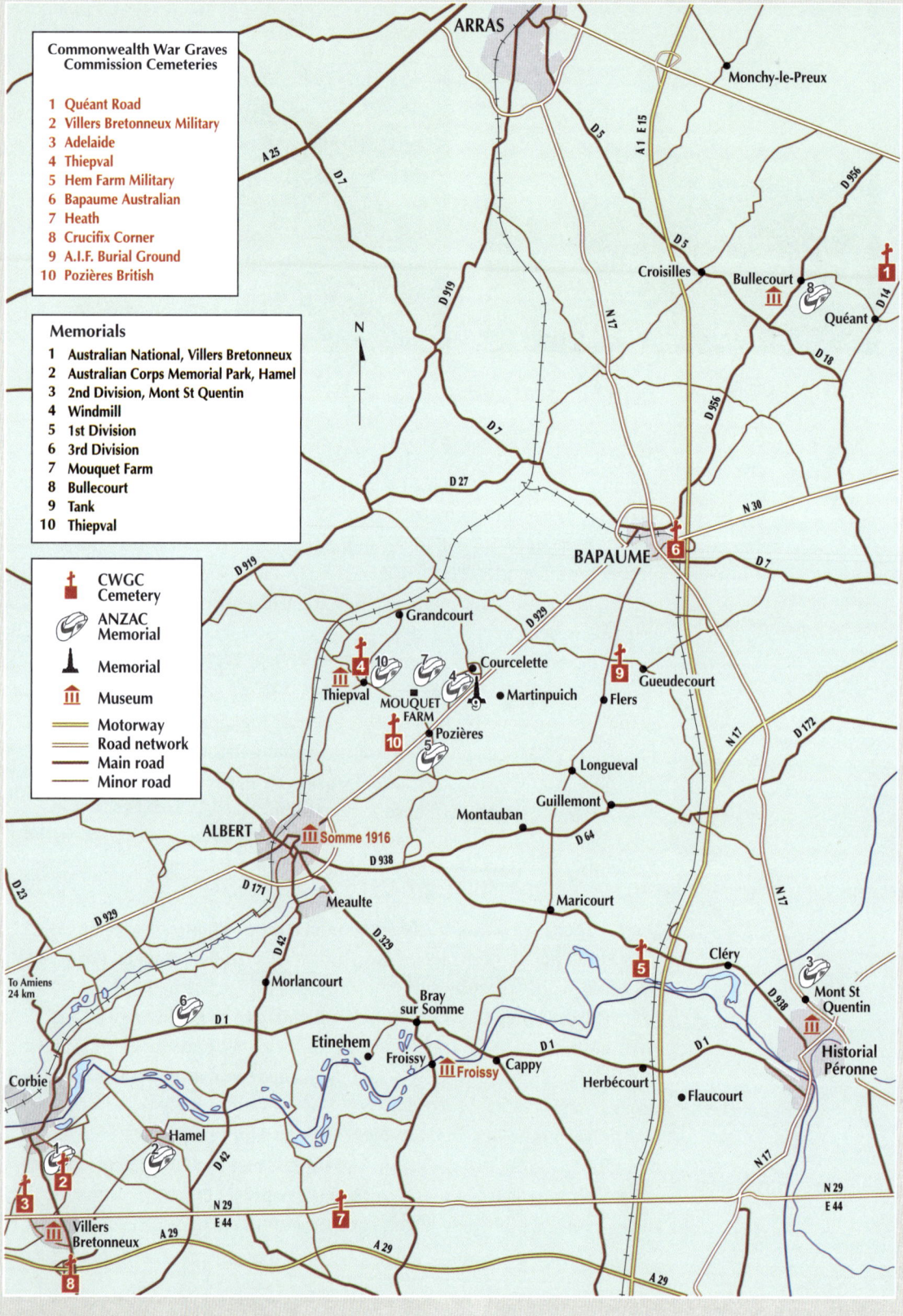

The Western Front

Opposite: Map of Villers Bretonneux and the Australian area of operation 1917–1918.

whereupon he charged out up the steps and found the enemy in possession of the trenches.

Australians were being rounded up and taken prisoner. Jacka with a couple of others promptly charged the Germans, and in a furious han-to-hand fight, he was wounded three times. His actions inspired the Australian prisoners to join in, and the situation was saved. Instead many Germans were made prisoner, and the line was retaken.

Captain Jacka was an inspiring leader, and the guiding light of the 14th Battalion – which became known as Jacka's Mob. He was badly gassed in 1918, and after recovery he was demobbed in 1920 when he finally returned to Melbourne. His business was lost in the Depression, but he was elected Mayor of St Kilda in 1930. He died on 17 January 1932, Australia's greatest frontline soldier.

The Pozières VCs

Private John Leak of the 9th Battalion won a VC for his conspicuous bravery in capturing a German trench on 23 July down in the hellholes of Pozières.

On the same day Lieutenant Arthur Blackburn of the 10th Battalion won his VC for leading his men to capture over 300 metres of trench in the face of fierce opposition, and holding it. Blackburn was one of the most remarkable soldiers of two wars – he had landed at Gallipoli and was one of the few who penetrated to the Third Ridge. Invalided home after his exploit at Pozières he joined the CMF and was appointed to command the 2/3rd Machine-gun Battalion in the Second World War. He fought in Syria in 1941, and was one of the 7th Division who landed in Java in 1942. He commanded a rag-tag crew known as Blackforce but without support had to surrender in February. He was a POW for the duration, in Japan, Korea and China. He survived captivity as well. A lawyer, he was appointed to the Conciliation and Arbitration Commission 1947–1955, and died at the age of 68, in 1960.

Two other VCs were awarded at Pozières, posthumous awards to Private Thomas Cooke, 8th Battalion; and Sergeant Claud Castleton, 5th Machine-gun Company, on 28 July.

Cooke was awarded his VC 'for most conspicuous bravery. After a Lewis gun had been disabled, he was ordered to take his gun and gun-team to a dangerous part of the line. Here he did fine work, but came under very heavy fire, with the result that finally he was the only man left. He still stuck to his post, and continued to fire his gun. When assistance was sent he was found dead beside his gun. He set a splendid example of determination and devotion to duty.' He is commemorated on the Australian National Memorial at Villers Bretonneux.

Castleton's citation notes, 'For most conspicuous bravery. During an attack on the enemy's trenches the infantry was temporarily driven back by the intense machine-gun fire opened by the enemy. Many wounded were left in "No Man's Land" lying in shell holes. Sergeant Castleton went out twice in face of this intense fire and each time brought in a wounded man on his back. He went out a third time and was bringing in another wounded man when he was himself hit in the back and killed instantly. He set a splendid example of courage and self-sacrifice.'

Castleton is one of 690 Australians buried in the Pozières British Cemetery, Ovillers-La-Boisselle, which is within the walls of the Pozières Memorial on the D929 south of Pozières.

'Come on boys, don't turn me down': Bullecourt, April–May 1917

Bullecourt was the site of two costly battles for the Australians, the first beginning in the bitterly cold dawn of 11 April 1917, when, after a night lying in the snow, the Australians were ordered to attack the main German defensive position, the Hindenburg Line. They were supposed to be backed up by British tanks and artillery, but neither of these eventuated, and when the Australians advanced, they were cut off by German artillery and machine-guns. After ten hours, a withdrawal was ordered, and the surviving Australians had to fight their way back to their original positions. The 4th Brigade suffered 2339 casualties from 3000 men sent into battle; the 12th Brigade, 950 from 2000. The battle was later used by the British staff as a model of failed planning.

Albert Jacka added a bar to his MC at Bullecourt. In a night reconnaissance before the battle he brought in a German patrol who had seen him lay the start-line for the attack, and achieved this without his pistol, which had failed. Jacka's actions saved the Australians from discovery and bombardment.

The second battle at Bullecourt, from 3 to 17 May, was somewhat better planned. The 2nd Division was to take the German positions

The Bullecourt Digger by Peter Corlett was unveiled in 1993.

in the village of Bullecourt, and they succeeded, using 96 Vickers machine-guns instead of the unreliable tanks, but even with better planning, the attack cost the four Australian divisions another 10,000 casualties.

Corporal George 'Snowy' Howell of the 1st Battalion won a VC for his actions at Bullecourt on 6 May, when he single-handedly repelled a German attack which threatened to outflank his unit, and, although wounded, inspired a counter-attack.

In the closing stages of the battle of Bullecourt, Lieutenant Rupert Moon of the 58th Battalion also won a VC. On 12 May, the 58th were sent to clear three German positions – a large dug-out, a cement machine-gun post, and another trench. After a horrendous night of bombardment from the Germans, Moon's platoon set off for the machine-gun emplacement, and Moon suffered his first wound. They took this position after Moon rallied his men, saying, 'Come on, boys, don't turn me down.'

By the time the position was secure, Moon had been wounded four times in the four stages of the advance – in the face, the shoulder, the foot and leg, and, finally, with a mutilating wound to the jaw. His leadership and courage had been decisive. After the war Moon was a successful businessman in Geelong, Victoria, and died in 1986, aged 94 as the most senior VC winner.

'You can't do it – you'll all be killed': Villers Bretonneux, 1918

Villers Bretonneux is on a slight rise just twenty kilometres from Amiens, now the transport hub for today's department of the Somme. The Australian defence helped beat the German advance back from Villers Bretonneux on 4–5 April 1918, but the Germans, desperate for a breakthrough, attacked again on 17 April using mustard gas, causing more than 1000 Australian casualties. On 24 April they attacked yet again, using tanks in the dawn mist, and succeeded in pushing an inexperienced British division out of the town. This was a tremendous blow; if the German offensive succeeded in reaching the Channel, the war might well be lost. Villers Bretonneux had to be retaken, and quickly.

That night, Pompey Elliott's 15th Brigade was to attack from the north while Brigadier (later Major General) Charles Rosenthal's 13th Brigade, including the 51st Battalion, attacked from the south, with orders to take Monument Wood, south-west of the town, 'and nothing is to stop you getting there'. As the 51st set off just after 10 p.m., however, flares lit the area and they came under deadly fire from German machine-guns on their left.

When Sergeant Charlie Stokes of the 51st asked Lieutenant Clifford Sadlier what they should do, Sadlier explained, 'Carry out the order – go straight to our objective,' to which Stokes responded, 'You can't do it, you'll all be killed.'

Sadlier's answer was to attack the machine-guns first. He found the nearest German machine-gun position, directed his own Lewis gun to cover him and, with Stokes, charged the gun. In Charles Bean's words his 'extraordinarily bold' move surprised the Germans and 'before they recovered from their surprise, the Western Australians were in among the trees, firing wildly in the dark, advancing through

the fringe of the wood, firing and being fired at around bushes and trees, stumbling on unsuspected posts.' Of the leaders of this reckless foray, Sadlier was wounded twice but Stokes carried on with a few others, silencing all the German guns.

Pompey Elliott's 15th Brigade, meanwhile, swept up the slope where the Australian Memorial now stands, heading around the back of the town towards Monument Wood, and the 13th fought in from the south; by dawn on Anzac Day 1918, Villers Bretonneux had been retaken. The German attack was petering out, apparently, but the men of the 3rd and 4th divisions didn't know that, and beat back determined German attacks using gas and tanks.

Both Sadlier and Stokes were recommended for the Victoria Cross; Sadlier received it, and Stokes was awarded the Distinguished Conduct Medal. (Although Sadlier was living in WA and returned there after the war, he was born in Camberwell and went to my school, University High School, where I first heard his story, because the

Above left: A postcard showing the Villers Bretonneux school in ruins in 1918.
Above: The school today, rebuilt with the help of pennies raised by Victorian schoolchildren in the 1920s.

school's 'houses' were named for students killed in the First World War.)

Three other VCs were won around Villers Bretonneux: by Corporal Walter Brown of the 20th Battalion, on 6 July; Lieutenant Albert Borell of the 26th Battalion, on 17–18 July; and Lieutenant Alfred Gaby of the 28th Battalion, posthumously, for conspicuous bravery on 8 August.

8 August 1918 was the beginning of the August offensive where the whole Australian Corps of five divisions led by Sir John Monash broke the German line in the area east of Villers Bretonneux, centred on the old Roman road. The Australians were supported by British on their left, and Canadians on the right. Using tanks and aeroplanes, this meticulously planned attack was executed with great skill and was described by the German commander Ludendorff as *der Schwarze Tag*, the 'blackest day' of the war. For the Germans, it was the beginning of the end. While it wasn't the all-Australian effort that won the war, it was a great victory nevertheless, and could not have occurred without Monash's leadership and Australian skill and determination.

Monash summed it up in his postwar book *The Australian Victories in France in 1918:* 'The tactical value of the victory was immense, and has never yet been fully appreciated by the public of the Empire ... but no better testimony is needed than that of Ludendorff himself, who calls it Germany's "black day", after which he himself gave up all hope of German victory. Ludendorff in his memoirs, republished in the *Times* of 22 August 1919, writes: "August 8th was the black day of the German Army in the history of the war. This was the worst experience I had to go through."'

Who Shot Down the Red Baron?

Baron Manfred von Richthofen, the 'Red Baron', was a German fighter ace credited with shooting down 80 aircraft. His Fokker triplane was painted bright red; his squadron was known as 'the Circus' because all the aircraft were brightly coloured. Their base was at Cappy, about nineteen kilometres east of Villers Bretonneux. On 21 April 1918, just before the battle at Villers Bretonneux, the Circus was engaged in a dogfight with British aircraft, including that of Captain Roy Brown, a Canadian wrongly credited with shooting down the Red Baron.

PILGRIMAGE

'The Australian Corps also captured 173 guns capable of being hauled away, not counting those which had been blown to pieces. These captures included two "railway" guns, one of 9-inch and the other of 11.2-inch bore. The latter was an imposing affair. The gun itself rested on two great bogie carriages, each on eight axles; it was provided with a whole train of railway trucks, some fitted to carry its giant ammunition, others as workshops, and others as living quarters for the gun detachment. The outfit was completed by a locomotive to haul the gun forward to its daily task of shelling Amiens, and hauling it back to its garage when its ugly work was done.'
Sir John Monash – 8 August 1918

Top: The 'abandoned Bertha' at Chuignes, 1918.
Top right: *General Sir John Monash*, the sculpture by Leslie Bowles, in the Kings Domain, Melbourne, was unveiled in 1950.
Above: The 28-centimetre railway gun souvenired by the Australians after the 8 August offensive, now at the Australian War Memorial.

Monash's order of the day
Corps Headquarters, 7 August 1918.
To: The Soldiers of the Australian Army Corps.

For the first time in the history of this Corps, all five Australian divisions will to-morrow engage in the largest and most important battle operation ever undertaken by the Corps.

   I entertain no sort of doubt that every Australian soldier will worthily rise to so great an occasion, and that every man, imbued with the spirit of victory, will, in spite of every difficulty that may confront him, be animated by no other resolve than grim determination to see through to a clean finish, whatever his task may be.

   The work to be done to-morrow will perhaps make heavy demands upon the endurance and staying powers of many of you but I am confident that, in spite of excitement, fatigue, and physical strain, every man will carry on to the utmost of his powers until his goal is won for the sake of Australia, the Empire and our cause.

   I earnestly wish every soldier of the Corps the best of good fortune, and a glorious and decisive victory, the story of which will re-echo throughout the world, and will live for ever in the history of our home land.

   JOHN MONASH, Lieut.-General. Cmdg. Australian Corps.

Above: Baron Manfred von Richthofen who was shot down on 21 April 1918.
Right: Richthofen was initially buried at Bertangles on 22 April 1918, but was later reinterred in Germany.

Robert Buie believed he was the man who shot down the Red Baron. He died on Anzac Day, 1964.

But it was a single shot from the ground that killed Richthofen, fired by one of the Australian machine-gunners based at Vaux. It seems that either Sergeant Cedric Popkin of the 24th Machine-gun Company, or Private Robert Buie of the 53rd Battery fired the shot that killed the Red Baron, who came down two kilometres north on the road from Corbie.

Bean and others give the benefit of the doubt to Popkin, but it seems that contemporaries, including a number of generals, thought it was Buie. Long after the war, Buie said that a month after the shooting down a 'dispatch came from General Rawlinson to the 53rd Battery and to me, giving me credit for shooting down the German ace.' Buie said, 'I have the proof in my possession.' Other generals followed in person, including General Birdwood, who told Buie, 'Keep on bringing them down.' Bob Buie died on Anzac Day 1964, still not credited with one of the most famous feats of the war.

As for Richthofen, he was buried with full military honours by the Australians at Bertangles. Richthofen has been disinterred and reburied several times since, and is currently in Schweidnitz in Germany.

Robinvale – Vale Robin

Second Lieutenant George Robin Cuttle was an Australian serving as an observer with the Royal Air Force when in 1918 his aircraft was shot down, crashing ten kilometres from Villers Bretonneux near the village of Caix. Cuttle was just 22, a big man, over two metres tall, and possibly for that reason he was rejected by the AIF when he volunteered in 1914. Determined to serve, Robin went to England and joined the artillery. He won the Military Cross in 1916 at Butte de Warlencourt on the Somme for 'great courage and determination in endeavouring to relieve a wounded observation officer under intense fire ... and was on duty continuously for some 20 hours.'

Too big to be a pilot, in late 1917 he joined the 49th Squadron of the RAF as an observer. He was on a reconnaissance flight with Canadian Lieutenant George Leckie when he was killed. His body was never recovered, but his mother Margaret Cuttle went to France in 1923 to search for the site of the crash, and found it. Cuttle and Leckie are commemorated on the Arras Flying Services Memorial, among nearly 1000 men of the Royal Flying Corps and Royal Air Force, which came into being on 1 April 1918.

Robin Cuttle was from Ultima, near Swan Hill in Victoria, and had been managing a property for his father in an area known as the Cliffs, on a bend of the Murray. In 1924, after the railway was built, the area was being sold off and needed a name. The story is told that Robin's mother had sewn a sign for display at the station. It said 'Robinvale' – vale, farewell, Robin – as a tribute to her son. The old Cuttle homestead is still named Robinswood.

Robinvale became the twin town (*jumelage*) of Villers Bretonneux, on 5 May 1984. A plaque on Robinvale's Villers Bretonneux Walk commemorates the *jumelage*. In Villers Bretonneux, you'll find a celebration of Robinvale in the town hall.

The Bell: After signalling the start and finish to the school day at Victoria College, Villers Bretonneux, for almost 60 years, the bell was presented to the people of Robinvale at the twinning ceremony in Villers Bretonneux on 5 May 1984.

The Western Front Today

In many places around the world where I've been looking for evidence of Australian involvement, the search has been frustrating and disappointing. Whatever the rights or wrongs of Australian participation, I wanted to find some evidence that we were there, and we are remembered. Most of the time a cemetery marks the place, a memorial the lonely location of one of our stories. Sometimes there's nothing, Australia's role overwhelmed by the greater numbers of our allies or enemies. But it's not like that in northern France. Here, despite being in a numerical minority, Australia is not forgotten.

We are remembered not only in the memorials at Villers Bretonneux, Hamel, Pozières, Fromelles, Polygon Wood and Bullecourt but in the work of the local people you meet when you call in at the museum at Fromelles and talk to Martial Delebarre, whose family has lived there for generations, and is literally digging up Australian stories.

Or having a cup of tea with Jean Letaille at Bullecourt – the museum is attached to his house, around the corner from the bronzed slouch hat at the church.

Or finding the streets named Rue Victoria and Rue de Melbourne in Villers Bretonneux, and the plaque thanking Australia in Amiens Cathedral.

Without over-exaggerating the Australian achievement in saving the Channel ports in April, it included great victories, achieved at awful cost, and established an Australian relationship with Villers Bretonneux that has been maintained ever since. Villers Bretonneux remains Australia's home in France. As neat as a new pin today, it is impossible to summon up the images of 1918, yet here in the square, next to the Town Hall is a tall granite plinth with a statue of a mourning woman, a little flower garden, and the words *A nos morts* (To our dead) *1914–1918*, and in front of that, a small remembrance plaque, *Souvenir aux Australiens* – to those who died in the liberation of Villers Bretonneux. And beside this is yet another plaque, bearing the names of the French soldiers and citizens of Villers Bretonneux who died in the First World War, and in the Second World War – soldiers, civilians, resistance, and fourteen citizens of Villers Bretonneux deported to Nazi labour camps – and also those who died in Indochina, and Algeria: The history of France in the 20th century in one small village.

The Australian plaque in the Amiens Cathedral. 'To the Glory of God and to the memory of the soldiers of the Australian Imperial Force who valiantly participated in the victorious defence of Amiens from March to August 1918 and gave their lives for the cause of justice, liberty and humanity. This tablet is consecrated by the government of the Commonwealth of Australia.'

N'oublions jamais l'Australie – **Never forget Australia**

Beaucourt en Santerre is a tiny village just a few kilometres from Villers Bretonneux. I was staying there, at the bed and breakfast owned by Jean-Marc and Colette Roisin, and using it as a base for exploring some of the Australian places nearby.

Jean-Marc was sitting at the kitchen table trying to communicate in broken English – in response to my fractured French – the impact of the First World War on this part of France, and on Australia. We had maps and books and postcards – the images were language enough.

Jean-Marc is a great collector, and brought out a book of before and after postcards of Villers Bretonneux and the other villages of the area, including his own.

There was life before the war – the station, the school, the town hall, Jean-Marc's great-grandmother outside the boulangerie – these were peaceful, ordinary streets with people dressed up for the photographer.

Then there was the wartime series. Scenes of utter destruction. The station in ruins, the town hall collapsed, the church tower a broken ruin, M. Outrequin's house a shell. Village after village within reach of the guns along the front line was destroyed, not from the air but by artillery shelling.

I showed pictures in books – of Sir John Monash, of the 15th Brigade's great leader, 'Pompey' Elliott, of the 13th Brigade's Bill Glasgow. There was one of VC winner Donovan Joynt, and the place where he won it, just up the road at Chuignes. We found Chuignes on the map, and looked for the woods near the Roman Road where Donovan Joynt had performed his great deed winning the VC in August 1918.

Jean-Marc pulled some postcards from his book and gave them to me.

The Western Front

the Roman Road, now more prosaically the N29.

Then he flipped over something truly wonderful, a postcard dated 22 July 1938 of the Australian Memorial at Villers Bretonneux the day of the *Inauguration du Monument Australien*.

We tried to translate the faded and hard-to-decipher handwriting. Here was someone in 1919, on the railway station card, writing to a dear brother and sister. Great to receive your card. Something about a work and pension and father's heart and always … Alive! That was it.

And here was Jacques, in 1938, just a year before another war, on the back of the Memorial card writing quickly to catch the post on that day; he's OK, and sends good kisses for you all, presumably his parents, not far away in Gournay en Bray.

Villers Bretonneux was not unique in its destruction, but was unique in its attachment to Australia.

One pictured the big railway gun that had pounded Amiens – La Bertha – abandoned by the Germans at Chuignes. Little Bertha! I told Jean-Marc that a smaller version of the 185-ton, 72-foot-long barrel had somehow been transported back to Australia, eventually being displayed in the Australian War Memorial, where it made a lasting impression on me. Other cards. Villers Bretonneux, the chateau before the war; the ruins of the railway station, photographed in 1918. There was the marker stone from Villers Bretonneux showing the furthest advance of the Germans in 1918, a helmet with gas mask, water bottle and grenade and the victor's laurel carved on top. *Ici fut repousse l'envahisseur 1918*. Here the invader was brought to a standstill. By the Australians. The stone is still there on

A Nos Morts. Souvenir aux Australiens. Mort pour le liberation de Villers Bretonneux.

Opposite: Map of Flanders Fields: the battlefields around Ypres.

Cemeteries, Memorials, Museums: Belgium

Ieper (Ypres)

In Flanders Fields is a superb museum, located upstairs in the 13th century Cloth Hall, which was shelled flat by the Germans but sublimely reconstituted – now you wouldn't know that two world wars had blown through at all. The museum tries hard, often successfully, to evoke a museum experience of war. There are touch-screen computers, smoke-filled rooms, environmental films, eye witness accounts, memorabilia, and spoken words.

Cemeteries and memorials are quite properly places for reflection and mourning, but the museum can use sound and image to provoke a response, as hearing 'In Flanders Fields', a poem written by the Canadian medical officer John McCrae, did for me:

Soldiers, In Flanders Fields museum, Ieper, Belgium.

> *In Flanders Fields the poppies blow*
> *Between the crosses, row on row,*
> *That mark our place, and in the sky*
> *The larks, still bravely singing, fly*
> *Scarce heard amid the guns below.*
> *We are the Dead. Short days ago*
> *We lived, felt dawn, saw sunset glow,*
> *Loved and were loved, and now we lie*
> *In Flanders Fields.*

McCrae wrote that in 1915, near Ypres, and it had an immediate impact when published that year. He died in France in 1918, and the poem inspired the wearing of the red poppy in remembrance.

In Flanders Fields
Address: Lakenhallen – Grote Markt 34
B 8900 Ieper Belgie
Website: www.inflandersfields.be

The **Menin Gate Memorial**, not far from the Cloth Hall, has the names of 6176 Australians who died in Flanders fields inscribed on it. There are 54,896 names in total on the memorial which was opened in 1927. A Ross Bastiaan plaque stands outside.

The Last Post has been played nightly at the Menin Gate Memorial

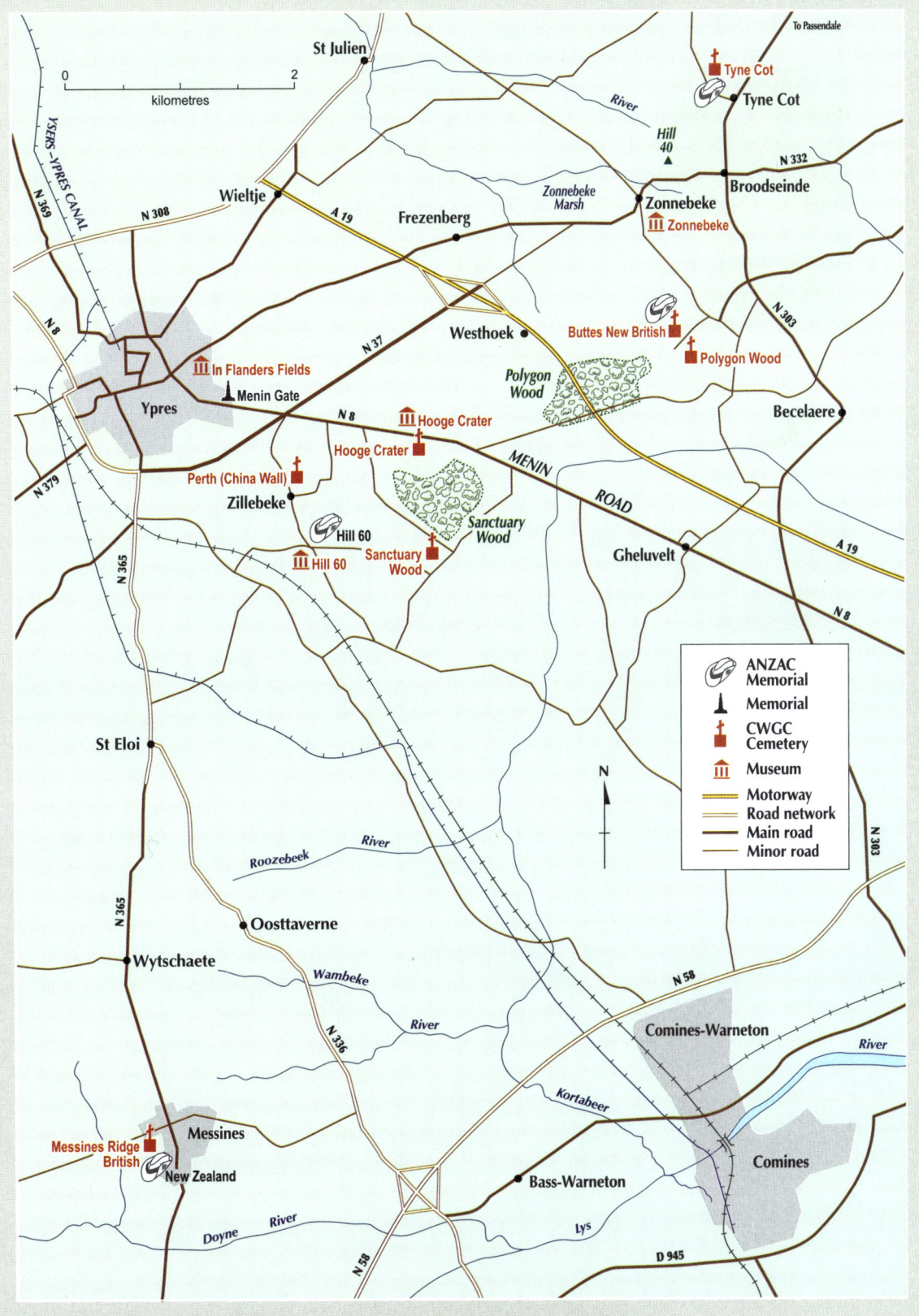

PILGRIMAGE

Above: The Menin Gate.
Below: Ross Bastiaan bronze plaque outside the Menin Gate, Ypres.

since 1929, just two years after the memorial opened. This has continued ever since, except during the Second World War. At eight o'clock precisely, the traffic is stopped, and three buglers play that saddest of all tunes.

That devotion to the remembrance of a war long ago is notable enough, but even more remarkable is that there is generally an audience of several hundred people – including locals, tourists and busloads of children from Britain.

Passchendaele (Passendale)

Tyne Cot Cemetery is located nine kilometres north-east of Ieper. 'Tyne Cot', or 'Tyne Cottage', was the name given by the Northumberland Fusiliers to a barn which stood near the level crossing on the Passchendaele–Broodseinde road. The barn, which had become the centre of five or six German blockhouses, or pillboxes, was captured by the Australian 2nd Division on 4 October 1917 in the advance on Passchendaele. One of these pillboxes was unusually large and was used as an advanced dressing station after its capture. From 6 October to the end of March 1918, 343 graves were made on two sides of it by the 50th (Northumbrian) and 33rd divisions, and by two Canadian units. The cemetery was in German hands again from 13 April to 28 September, when it was finally recaptured, with Passchendaele, by the Belgian Army.

Tyne Cot Cemetery was greatly enlarged after the Armistice when remains were brought in from the battlefields of Passchendaele and Langemarck, and from a few small burial grounds. Designed by Sir Herbert Baker, it now has the most burials of all Commonwealth war cemeteries. At the suggestion of King George V, who visited the cemetery in 1922, the Cross of Sacrifice was placed on the original large pillbox captured by the Australians. A plaque and a small part of the original blockhouse can be viewed through an opening in the base. There are three other pillboxes in the cemetery.

There are now 11,953 Commonwealth servicemen of the First World War buried or commemorated in Tyne Cot Cemetery, which includes 1368 Australian graves. There are two Australian VCs in Tyne Cot, Captain Clarence Jeffries, 34th Battalion, and Sergeant Lewis McGee of the 40th Battalion. Captain Jeffries, from NSW, won his posthumous VC at Passchendaele on 12 October 1917 when his company was held up by enemy machine-gun fire: 'Organising a party, he rushed one emplacement, capturing four machine-guns and 35 prisoners ... Later, he again organised a successful attack on a machine-gun emplacement, capturing two machine-guns and 30 more prisoners. This gallant officer was killed during the attack, but ... his example had a most inspiring influence.'

On the same day, Sergeant McGee also died winning a VC. His citation describes how, single-handed, he 'rushed the post armed only with a revolver. He shot some of the crew and captured the rest, and thus enabled the advance to proceed. He re-organised the remnants of his platoon and ... his coolness and bravery were conspicuous and contributed largely to the success of the Company's operations.'

The **Tyne Cot Memorial** forms the north-eastern boundary of Tyne Cot Cemetery and commemorates nearly 35,000 servicemen from the United Kingdom and New Zealand who died in the Ypres Salient after 16 August 1917 and whose graves are not known.

Zillebeke

Hill 60 Memorial commemorates the Australian 1st Tunnelling Company, which took over the tunnels and mines in the Zillebeke area east of Ypres. A tremendous amount of tunnelling went on under what used to be Hill 60, in preparation for a big explosion under the Germans on 16 December 1916. The tunnels saw explosions, counter explosions and ferocious fighting by both sides to protect the positions. It was a nightmarish place.

Hooge Crater Museum is located in a renovated chapel on the Menin Road four kilometres from Ieper at Hooge. It was opened in 1994 and has a collection of First World War uniforms, displays and artefacts. There is a café.

Above: Hill 60: German pillbox.
Below: The Australian tunneller's memorial in front of the preserved battleground.

Museum Hooge Crater
Address: Meenseweg 467, B-8902 Zillebeke-Ieper

Perth (China Wall) Cemetery contains 2763 burials including 134 Australians, among them Second Lieutenant Frederick Birks, who won a VC at Polygon Wood. No one knows why this cemetery was called Perth, but China Wall is from a nearby breastwork (a mound or 'trench' made above the ground) known as the Great Wall of China.

Sanctuary Wood Cemetery contains 88 Australian burials, most killed at Polygon Wood in 1917.

Zonnebeke

The **Memorial Museum Passchendaele 1917** was opened in Zonnebeke Chateau on 25 April 2004. It was formerly called the Streekmuseum and is located in the centre of the village in the chateau of Zonnebeke.

> **Memorial Museum Passchendaele 1917**
> Address: Ieperstraat 5, 8980 Zonnebeke, Belgium
> Email: info@passchendaele.be
> Website: www.zonnebeke.be, www.passchendaele.be

Polygon Wood is a large wood 1.6 kilometres south of the village of Zonnebeke which was completely devastated in the First World War. The wood was cleared by Commonwealth troops at the end of October 1914, given up on 3 May 1915, taken again at the end of September 1917 by Australian troops, evacuated in the Battles of the Lys, and finally retaken by the 9th (Scottish) Division on 28 September 1918.

Buttes New British Cemetery at Polygon Wood was taken by the Australian 5th Division on 26–28 September 1917. The **5th Division Memorial** stands on top of the former butt of the rifle range. A **New Zealand Memorial** is at the other end of the cemetery.

Above: Buttes New British Cemetery at Polygon Wood.
Below: The Australian 5th Division Memorial.

The memorials are reached down a shaded path from the road, elevated above the headstones, and provide one of the most contemplative places on the Western Front. This burial ground was made after the Armistice when a large number of graves (almost all of 1917, but in a few instances of 1914, 1916 and 1918) were brought in from the battlefields of Zonnebeke. There are now 2103 Commonwealth servicemen of the First World War buried or commemorated in this cemetery.

Buttes New British Cemetery (New Zealand) Memorial, which stands in Buttes New British Cemetery, commemorates 378 officers and men of the New Zealand Division who died in the Polygon Wood sector between September 1917 and May 1918, and who have no known grave. The majority died in the trenches, or in working and carrying, and the conditions in the Salient during the winter of 1917–18 must explain the comparatively large number of names on this memorial, which deals with only one set attack on a German position. This is one of seven memorials in France and Belgium to those New Zealand soldiers who died on the Western Front and whose graves are not known. The memorials are all in cemeteries chosen as appropriate to the fighting in which the men died.

Polygon Wood Cemetery is across the road from Buttes cemetery. It is an irregular frontline cemetery made between August 1917 and April 1918, and used again in September 1918. The cemetery contains 103 Commonwealth burials of the First World War; 60 of those buried here served with the New Zealand forces. There is also one German grave within the cemetery.

Polygon Wood Cemetery, in a field of Brussels sprouts.

Cemeteries, Memorials, Museums: France

Albert

The **Somme 1916 Museum** is in the original crypt of the rebuilt basilica of Albert's church. In the niches, scenes from trench life are displayed with original uniforms and equipment.

The basilica had a golden statue of the Virgin Mary which was hit by German shelling in 1915, and leaned precariously and horizontally over the road. Legend had it that when she finally fell, the war would end. She remained leaning until the Germans took Albert in March 1918 and the town was shelled by the British. The Virgin fell on 16 April, but the war, unhappily, continued until November. The **crypt** was used as an air raid shelter in the Second World War.

The Virgin Mary hanging from the Albert basilica in early 1918.

> **The Somme 1916 Museum**
> Address: Rue Anicet Godin 80300 Albert
> Email: musee@somme-1916.org
> Website: www.somme-1916.org

Bapaume

Bapaume Australian Cemetery has 74 burials, most of them from the first battle of Bullecourt, who died of wounds at the 3rd Australian Casualty Clearing Station established in Bapaume in March 1917. Twenty-five Germans as well as twelve British are also buried here.

Above: Inside the museum at Bullecourt.
Below: The Slouch Hat Memorial sits on the wall outside the Bullecourt church. The museum is just across the street.

Bellenglise

The **4th Division Memorial** is an obelisk standing on the Hindenburg Line north of St Quentin, marking the easternmost point reached by the Australians in 1918.

Bullecourt

Bullecourt Museum is in the tiny village, which had 396 inhabitants in 1914, and after rebuilding would not have many more today. It is run by a great friend of Australia, Jean Letaille. This terrific small museum of the Bullecourt battles is in a barn and outbuilding at his house at No. 1 rue d'Arras. Most probably you will be given a guided tour, and a cup of tea.

A **walking tour of the battlefield** is detailed in a pamphlet you can pick up at the museum. This eight-kilometre, two-hour signposted walk includes the Australian memorials and battle sites, which are not far away.

The **Slouch Hat Memorial** in the Town Hall Square, to the right of the church, is actually a bronzed First World War felt hat given by the Australian War Memorial and erected by Souvenir Français in 1981. It sits on a brick plinth near a track from a tank, with marble inscriptions to the Australian 1st, 2nd, 4th and 5th divisions, and the 58th (London), 62nd (West Riding) and British 7th divisions, all of whom fought near Bullecourt.

It is dedicated 'In memory of the Australian and British soldiers who fell in this area – April–May 1917, Lest We Forget.' In English and French – *passant souviens toi*.

The **Australian National Memorial** is in the rue des Australiens on the road to Riencourt, and features Peter Corlett's larrikin bronze *Digger*, which was dedicated in 1993. It is 'Sacred to the memory of the 10,000 members of the Australian Imperial Force who were killed or wounded in the two battles of Bullecourt, April–May 1917, and to the Australian dead and their comrades-in-arms who lie here forever in the soil of France. "Lest we Forget."'

Buissy

Queant Road Cemetery, in Buissy, near Bullecourt, was made by the 2nd and 57th Casualty Clearing Stations in October and November 1918. It then consisted of 71 graves (now Plot I, Rows A and B) but was greatly enlarged after the Armistice when graves were brought in from the battlefields of 1917–1918 between Arras and Bapaume, and from certain smaller burial grounds in the area. There are now 2377 Commonwealth servicemen of the First World War buried or commemorated in this cemetery. It includes the graves of two significant Australians who died around Bullecourt.

Sergeant John White was listed as missing during the second battle of Bullecourt and remained so until December 1994 when his remains were unearthed with his wallet, a letter and identity discs. He was given a military funeral, attended by his daughter Myrtle, who was ten months old when her father went to war. She and the late historian John Laffin wrote his epitaph: 'The deep peace of the quiet earth, so far from the land that gave you birth.'

Also here is Captain Percy Cherry VC MC, who was killed at Lagnicourt on 27 March 1917 when his company was required to storm a village. His citation explains: 'After all the officers of his company had become casualties he carried on with care and determination in the face of fierce opposition, and cleared the village of the enemy. He sent frequent reports of progress made, and when held up for some time by an enemy strong point, he organised machine-gun and bomb parties and captured the position. His leadership, coolness and bravery set a wonderful example to his men ... Wounded about 6.30 a.m., he refused to leave his post, and there remained, encouraging all to hold out at all costs, until, about 4.30 p.m. this very gallant officer was killed by an enemy shell.'

Flers

The **AIF Burial Ground, Grass Lane** is the only cemetery bearing the name AIF and was begun by Australians in November 1916. It was greatly expanded after the end of the war, and now contains 402 Australians among 3450 burials.

Froissy

The **Museum of Military and Industrial Railways** in Froissy, ten kilometres from Albert, displays many of the vehicles used to transport supplies during the battles of the Somme, including a narrow gauge railway, 'Le P'tit Train de la Haute-Somme', running on the line used during the war.

Fromelles

Fromelles Museum is a superb private museum organised by the Association Souvenir de la Bataille de Fromelles (ASBF). It is currently located in the attic of the Mairie (Town Hall), and has a staggering array of material on display, some of it recovered from the battlefields around Fromelles. Because of the Australian action in July 1916, there is a great emphasis on the AIF. The museum is open on specified weekends throughout the year, but members of ASBF will open it up by prior arrangement. A small fee is charged, and groups can be accommodated. Not to be missed if you visit the area.

Above: The Fromelles Museum.
Below: Martial Delebarre in the tunnel he discovered at La Cordonnerie farm.

Martial Delebarre is the prime mover of the ASBF, and works as supervisor for the Commonwealth War Graves Commission, caring for the graves of the thousands who died around Fromelles. His family has lived for generations in Fromelles; the family house was destroyed in the war, and Martial attended school at the Mairie. Martial is a great friend of Australia, and has an intimate knowledge of the Fromelles battle and battlefield. He was awarded the Order of Australia Medal (OAM) in 2005.

As everywhere on the Western Front, literally tons of material is turned up every year, but Martial has also undertaken archaeological excavations with the ASBF, which has uncovered a fantastic tunnel system dug after the battle, at La Cordonnerie.

Fromelles Museum
Website: www.asbf14-18.org

The **Australian Memorial** is two kilometres north of Fromelles. Here the Australian and French flags fly proudly over muddy fields, and nearby buildings still bear the names they had in 1916: la Cordonnerie, le Trou, la Boutillerie. But Rue Delvas is now the D175, and has

The Western Front

Peter Corlett's *Cobbers*, the Australian Memorial at Fromelles.

Cobbers was unveiled on 5 July 1998. It shows Sergeant Fraser carrying a wounded mate who still holds his slouch hat. The sergeant looks as if he has much work left to do in this solitary place. The sculpture is mounted on some old German blockhouses, built after the battle, which are on the site of the 1916 German trenches.

a bit of traffic, but this is not on the main Western Front tourist route, and is not visited as often as it should be.

Cobbers, a sculpture by Peter Corlett, is the focus of the **Australian Memorial Park.** The most moving Australian memorial in France, it was inspired by the deeds and face of Sergeant Simon Fraser (57th Battalion), from Byaduk in Western Victoria, who was mentioned in despatches for his heroism at Fromelles. Fraser, who was commissioned 2nd Lieutenant in April 1917, was killed in action at Bullecourt with the 58th Battalion on 12 May 1917 and his body never found; his name is recorded at the Australian Memorial at Villers Bretonneux.

In one of his letters, Fraser described his work bringing in the wounded: 'I must say Fritz treated us very fairly, though a few were shot at the work. Some of those wounded were as game as lions and got rather roughly handled; but haste was more necessary than gentle handling ... splendid specimen of humanity trying to wriggle into a trench with a big wound in his thigh. He was about 14 stone weight, and I could not lift him on my back; but I managed to get him into an old trench, and told him to lie quiet while I got a stretcher. Then another about 30 yards out sang out "Don't forget me, cobber." I went in and got four volunteers with stretchers, and we got both men in safely ...'

VC Corner Australian Cemetery, 200 metres up the road from the Australian Memorial, is the only all-Australian cemetery on the

VC Corner Cemetery.

Western Front. It was established between the Australian and German lines after the war, just where the 15th Brigade attacked and died. 'One foggy morning in particular, I remember, we could hear someone over towards the German entanglements calling for a stretcher-bearer; it was an appeal no man could stand against, so some of us rushed out and had a hunt. We found a fine haul of wounded and brought them in; but it was not where I heard this fellow calling, so I had another shot for it, and came across.' From the few steps up to the cemetery, you can look across the road towards the farm and trees in the distance. The Sugarloaf was a little to the right of those trees.

The **Great Cross** within the cemetery stands in front of a screening stone wall which records the names of 1299 Australian soldiers who fell out there in those fields. Many of them are still there – their bodies have never been recovered. The 410 Australian bodies found after the war are buried in four plots between the front of the cemetery and the screen wall. Unique among Australian cemeteries, there are no headstones here.

The **Laies** is barely a creek, let alone a river and runs diagonally across the D175 just to the north of VC Corner. Starting at the intersection of the Laies and the road, a walk 500 metres south-east along the ditch will bring you to about the spot where the **Sugarloaf** was.

This is the distance the Australians had to cover. Although the Sugarloaf has long been demolished and ploughed under, it's not difficult to understand the horrific death rate as the Australians charged across those 500 metres of shell-churned bog, swept by machine-guns from this elevated bunker.

Rue-du-Bois Military Cemetery.

Rue-du-Bois Military Cemetery is on the D171, turning right 1.2 kilometres north-east of VC Corner on the D175. Of 832 burials, 242 are Australian, including Major Geoffrey McCrae, CO of the 60th Battalion.

Other cemeteries with Fromelles burials are Anzac Cemetery on the D945 (begun as an advanced dressing station in 1917), and Sailly-sur-la-Lys. One hundred and eleven Australians are buried here, many from Fromelles and 31 Battalion. Another nineteen Australians are in the Sailly-sur-la-Lys Canadian Cemetery across the road.

Rue David Cemetery at Fleurbaix includes 353 Australians, 256 of them unnamed, from Fromelles. Billy Ellsdale, the first Aboriginal soldier killed in France, on 7 July 1916, is buried here.

Le Trou Aid Post Cemetery is on Rue Petillon, the first cemetery on the left after taking a right turn 500 metres north of VC Corner. Le Trou, where Pompey Elliott had his battle headquarters, was an aid post where wounded soldiers were treated in 1916; a cemetery had been established here as early as 1914. Of the 351 graves here, 56 are Australian and only four are identified.

Above: Le Trou Aid Post Cemetery.
Below: Rue Petillon Cemetery.

Rue Petillon Cemetery is a kilometre from the Le Trou Aid Post Cemetery, on Rue Petillon. It has 1507 burials, of which 291 are Australian. Only 22 of them are unidentified. Most of them are from Fromelles, including George Challis, a sergeant in the 58th Battalion, who played Australian Rules football for Carlton in its 1915 premiership.

Hamel

The **Australian Corps Memorial Park** in Hamel is an important recent Australian memorial, a few kilometres east of Villers Bretonneux. The park was dedicated in 1998, and is on the site of the objective captured by the Australians on 4 July 1918.

The battle of Hamel is where all the planning and tactical genius of Sir John Monash, by then the first ever commander of an Australian Corps, comprising all five divisions, came to fruition, using tanks and aircraft for both offensive and resupply purposes. It was a great triumph. The battle was all over in 93 minutes, although victory came at a cost of 1400 Australian casualties.

The casualties included the remarkable Private Harry Dalziel of the 15th Battalion, who won the VC by single-handedly capturing a machine-gun and its crew, and then, after his trigger finger was shot off and he was ordered back to an aid post, continuing in the fight by carrying ammunition back to his comrades until severely wounded in the head.

Dalziel survived the war, and surgery. He worked on the railways and as a miner, before becoming a successful songwriter. One of his songs was titled 'You Never Know What You Can Do Til You Try.' He returned to Hamel in 1956, but was unable to recognise the spot

Hamel, Australian Corps Memorial Park.

where he won the VC: 'The whole place was covered with greenery – wheat, poppies – all kinds of agriculture. It just didn't seem to be the same place.' He died in 1965, aged 72.

There are some preserved German trenches at the Australian memorial, and a short walking track.

Harbonnières

Heath Cemetery is located along the arrow-straight old Roman road, now the N29, about ten kilometres east of Villers Bretonneux at Harbonnières. It was made after the war, and contains 985 Australians and nearly 900 other Commonwealth servicemen. The Australians come from all round the 1918 battlefields, but most particularly from Villers Bretonneux.

Lieutenant Alfred Gaby who won a posthumous VC at Villers Bretonneux on 8 August 1918 is buried here, as is Private Robert Beatham who won his 'east of Amiens' on 9 August.

Mont St Quentin

Replica of the lost 2nd Division memorial at Mont St Quentin in the Villers Bretonneux Museum.

The **2nd Division Memorial**, the figure of a Digger, at ease, surveying the battlefield at Mont St Quentin, was erected in 1971, replacing Web Gilbert's powerful statue of a belligerent Digger bayonetting a German eagle, which was destroyed in 1940 (a small replica of it can be seen in the **Villers Bretonneux Museum**). Mont St Quentin, a small village on a hill near Péronne, was the site of one of the Australians' finest hours in World War One, when three VCs were won on 1 September 1918 in taking the village.

Hem Farm Military Cemetery was begun by British troops in January 1917, and used until the following March, and again in September 1918. There are now nearly 600 First World War casualties commemorated in this site.

Among 138 Australians buried at Hem Farm Military Cemetery is Private Robert Mactier, 23rd Battalion, who initiated an action, during the attack on Mont St Quentin, which he had no hope of surviving. He exemplified the bravery and sacrifice of the Australians in capturing this important area.

His citation explains: 'It was necessary to clear up several enemy strong points close to our line ... Pte. Mactier single-handed, and in daylight, thereupon jumped out of the trench, rushed past the block, closed with and killed the machine-gun garrison of eight men with his revolver and bombs, and threw the enemy machine-gun over the parapet. Then, rushing forward about 20 yards, he jumped into another strong point held by a garrison of six men who immediately surrendered. Continuing to the next block through the trench, he disposed of an enemy machine-gun which had been enfilading our flank advancing troops, and was then killed by another machine-gun at close range ...'

Pozières
....

The **Windmill, 2nd Division Memorial** is a few kilometres north-east of Pozières on the D929, in the direction of Bapaume. A few remains of a windmill remain on a small grassy hillock. An inscription on a stone bench at the end of a flagstoned walk explains their significance: 'The ruins of Pozières windmill which lies here was the centre of the struggles for this part of the Somme battlefield in July and August 1916. It was captured on 4 August by Australian troops, who fell more thickly on this ridge than any other.'

The Australian troops were from the 27th and 28th battalions led by Captain Maitland Foss. There had been a windmill here since 1610,

Far left: Windmill Australian Memorial, near Pozières.
Left: The Tank Memorial, near Pozières.

but it became a German blockhouse – which was also destroyed. The view of the flat fields beyond, like all of the Somme battlefields, makes what happened here impossible to imagine.

The **Tank Corps Memorial** is across the road from the windmill. It is in the form of an obelisk with, at each corner, a small model of a British war-time tank, and is enclosed by a fence made from **6-pound gun barrels** and driving chains.

The **1st Division Memorial** at Pozières was erected on the site of a German trench on the forward side of the Pozières ridge, which the 1st Division attacked on 23 July 1916. The obelisk is easily visible from the road that leads past Mouquet Farm to Thiepval Memorial, visible on the horizon.

Across the road from the 1st Division Memorial in Pozières is the German post **Gibraltar,** known to the Germans as a *panzersturm* (armour post). A lookout tower has been constructed here on the site of a three-metre-high German blockhouse, of which little remains. There is an orientation table and information panels at the top of the lookout.

Above: 1st Division Memorial, Pozières.
Below: Mouquet Farm Memorial.

Mouquet Farm, nearby, was bitterly fought over between July and September 1916 by Australian forces, including the 16th Battalion in their first full-scale action on the Western Front.

The 16th relieved the 15th Battalion on 9 August, and over the next four days attacked and held a trench line under intense bombardment from the Germans higher up the ridge. Irish-born Private Martin O'Meara of the 16th Battalion, who had come to Australia as a young man, won a VC here for actions over all four days. His citation explained: 'During four days of very heavy fighting he repeatedly went out and brought in wounded officers and men from no man's land under intense artillery and machine-gun fire. He also volunteered and carried up ammunition and bombs through a heavy barrage to a portion of the trenches which was being heavily shelled at the time.' His health was never good after the war, and he spent the years until his death in 1935 in a military hospital in Perth.

Nothing remains of Mouquet Farm today, though there is some cement on the ridge beyond the present-day farm. The **Mouquet Farm Memorial**, a battle exploit plaque by the side of the road, explains the Australian role in the battle.

Péronne

Historial de la Grande Guerre in Péronne is unlike many war museums, which are often overburdened with battlefield souvenirs. The Historial (so named to evoke history and understanding, rather than

The Western Front

simply 'remembrance'), opened in 1992, is in a new building inside the grounds of Péronne's medieval chateau. Both the town and the chateau were liberated by Australians on 1 August 1918.

The Historial shows an evocative selection of materials about civilian and military life during the First World War. The showcases on the wall contain civilian objects, in three tiers, for Germany, France and Britain; the centre of each of the five exhibition halls is devoted to military objects, uniforms (including Australian), weapons and objects of daily life. There are also many individual video screens with a rotating set of films, including film of the funeral the Australians gave 'Red Baron' Richthofen. The effect of the museum is informative and contemplative.

Above left: Entrance to the Historial in Péronne.
Above: Display of uniforms in the Historial.

Historial de la Grande Guerre
Website: www.historial.org

Thiepval

The **British Memorial to the Missing** is a towering memorial, designed by Sir Edwin Lutyens, that honours 72,087 British soldiers with no known grave, including many of the 58,000 lost on the first day of the battle of the Somme in September 1916.

Thiepval Visitor Centre, which opened in 2004, is discreetly hidden out of sight near the Memorial to the Missing, and adds a welcome perspective to the memorial's bare listing of names. Display panels put the war and the Battle of the Somme into context, and the 'Missing of the Somme' panel displays photographs of 600 of them. Further information on many can be found on the *Missing of the Somme* database at

Thiepval Memorial to the Missing.

the centre. A brochure marking an informative walking tour is available from the shop – this is perhaps the best place for Commonwealth-related maps, books and information.

Villers Bretonneux

Musée Franco-Australien is situated in a school rebuilt with the help of donations by Victorian primary school children in the 1920s. There are two plaques which read – one in French, one in English: 'This building is the gift of the school children of Victoria Australia to the school children of Villers Bretonneux, as a proof of the love and goodwill toward France. Twelve hundred Australian soldiers, the fathers and brothers of these children, gave their lives in the heroic recapture of this town on 24th April 1918 and are buried near this spot. May the memory of great sacrifices in a common cause keep France and Australia together forever in bonds of friendship and mutual esteem.'

Above: The plaque thanking the children of Victoria.
Below: Inside the museum.

Upstairs, in a spacious room, the museum is a quiet but bright place devoted to telling the story of the Australians in France, and Villers Bretonneux, through objects including a piece of Little Bertha, photographs, documents, flags, uniforms and testimony.

An evocative collection of well laid-out Australian memorabilia – letters, personal photographs, battlefield souvenirs – tells the story of the battle that recaptured Villers Bretonneux, and there's a diorama of the battlefield, such as you find at the Australian War Memorial.

Musée Franco-Australien
Address: 9 rue Victoria, 80800 Villers Bretonneux
Email: museeaustralien@aol.com

The **Australian National Memorial** is located here because, as the president of France put it at the opening of the memorial, in 1938, 'There is no spot on the tortured soil of France which is more associated with Australian history and the triumph of Australian soldiers, than Villers Bretonneux'; here (with some British help) the Australians fought and won two important battles, recapturing the town, and saving Amiens.

A few minutes' drive from the town, the memorial is a 30-metre tower in front of a three-sided court on which are inscribed the names

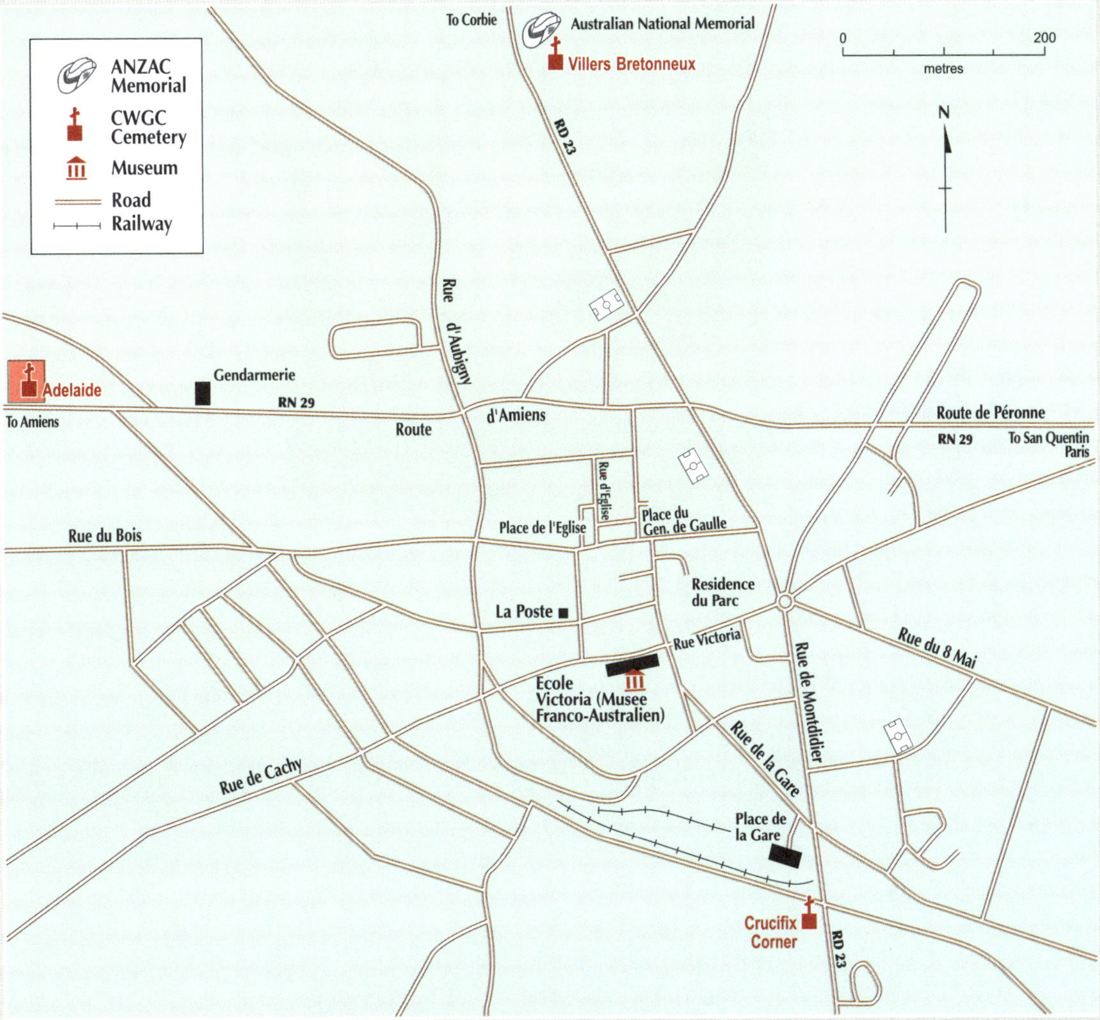

The Western Front

Above: Street map of Villers Bretonneux. The Unknown Soldier's original grave was in the Adelaide cemetery.
Left: The Australian National Memorial is just outside the town.

The Australian National Memorial, Villers Bretonneux.

of 10,982 Australians who died in France and have no known grave. Walking up the hill from the road, the tower is slowly revealed, flanked by the Australian and French flags, as you walk slowly through the cemetery. It is a majestic piece of theatre.

Controversy, apathy and the Depression meant the memorial was the last one of the national memorials to be completed. It is situated near Hill 104, which was taken by the wild men of Pompey Elliott's 15th Brigade very early on Anzac Day 1918 when they charged straight up the hill, bayonets fixed, at the enemy lines. Among the leaders of the assault was the remarkable Colonel Norman Marshall of the 60th Battalion, who won a DSO and two bars (that is, the DSO three times), at Polygon Wood, then at Villers Bretonneux, and later at Péronne.

Inside the memorial are the marvellous words written by Don Watson for Paul Keating at the 1993 re-interment in Canberra of the Unknown Australian Soldier, who was previously buried at the Adelaide Cemetery, on the other side of Villers Bretonneux: 'Out of the war came a lesson which transcended the horror and tragedy and the inexcusable folly ... It was a lesson about ordinary people ... the soldiers and sailors and nurses – those who taught us to endure hardship, show courage, to be bold as well as resilient, to believe in ourselves, to stick together ... That is surely at the heart of the Anzac story, the Australian legend which emerged from the war. It is a legend not of sweeping military victories so much as triumphs against the odds, of courage and ingenuity in adversity. It is a legend of free and independent spirits whose discipline derived less from military formalities and customs than from the bonds of mateship and the demands of necessity.'

The memorial was damaged during the Second World War – you can still see the pockmarks made by German artillery – and when a Melbourne *Herald* correspondent inspected it in December 1944, he found it to be 'one of the saddest sights in France. It looked forlorn and neglected and many displaced granite blocks lay among the uncut grass. At least five 88 mm shells hit the main walls. Each caused damage over an area 6 ft in diameter. The main tower ... is badly chipped ... stone Australian flags on the corners of the two wings are bullet pocked.'

The mayor of Villers Bretonneux, who had kept the Australian flag hidden in the town hall, hung out under a banner when the town was liberated: 'Welcome to the Australians'. He was disappointed to learn that there were none coming.

It is a very evocative place, with its directions and mileages to battlefields and to faraway Australian cities, and the peaceful view of orderly fertile fields and the spires of Villers Bretonneux and Corbie and Hamel in the distance.

The **Villers Bretonneux Military Cemetery** is on the slope you walk up on your way to the Australian National Memorial. It was made after the Armistice when graves were brought in from other burial grounds in the area and from the battlefields. Plots I to XX were completed by 1920 and contain mostly Australian graves, almost all from the period March to August 1918. Plots IIIA, VIA, XIIIA and XVIA, and rows in other plots lettered AA, were completed by 1925, and contain a much larger proportion of unidentified graves brought from a wider area. Later still, 444 graves were brought in from Dury Hospital Military Cemetery.

There are now 2141 Commonwealth servicemen of the First World War buried or commemorated in this cemetery. The cemetery also contains the graves of two New Zealand airmen of the Second World War.

Adelaide Cemetery was begun early in June 1918 and used by the Australian 2nd and 3rd divisions. It continued in use until the Allies began their advance in mid-August, by which time it contained 90 graves (the greater part of the present Plot I, Rows A to E).

After the Armistice, a large number of graves were brought into the

'Not dead, but a soldier of the immortal 60,000'
Second Lieutenant E S Davidson, Australian Engineers, killed in action 4 July 1918, Villers Bretonneux Cemetery.

The Unknown Australian Soldier lay here for 75 years. His remains were exhumed and reinterred in the Tomb of the Unknown Soldier, Australian War Memorial in 1993.

cemetery from small graveyards and isolated positions to the north, west and south of Villers Bretonneux. Without exception, these were men who died between March and September 1918; Plot III was filled almost entirely with Australians. There are now 955 Commonwealth servicemen of the First World War buried or commemorated in this cemetery, including 519 Australians. The cemetery was designed by Sir Edwin Lutyens. On 2 November 1993, following a request by the government of Australia, an unknown Australian soldier killed in the First World War was exhumed from Plot III, Row M, Grave 13, and is now buried in the Australian War Memorial in Canberra.

Crucifix Corner Cemetery is just south of Villers Bretonneux on the D23, and marks an important Australian place – this is where much of the fighting to recapture Villers Bretonneux on Anzac Day 1918 took place. There are 60 burials from the battle of Hamel among the 236 Australians buried here. There are 660 Commonwealth burials in all, and 141 French and two Russians.

Vimy

The Canadian National Memorial, Vimy.

The **Canadian National Vimy Memorial** commemorates the 66,655 Canadians who died in the First World War. Vimy Ridge – taken by the four Canadian divisions on 9–12 April 1917, at a cost of 10,162 casualties, making it the Canadian Gallipoli – dominates this area of the northern Somme. Carved on the walls of this, the most striking of all the Western Front memorials, are the names of 11,285 Canadians who have no known grave. The monument is set in 100 hectares of parkland, and includes restored trenches and a very good museum interpretive centre.

Travel Tool Kit

To see all the Australian-related sites on the Western Front would take months. But even a couple of days around Fromelles in northern France, or the battlefields in the Somme 'triangle' of Amiens–Péronne–Pozières that includes Villers Bretonneux and Bullecourt, or around Ypres in Belgium will be as inspiring as any Australian place on earth.

On the road to Villers Bretonneux.

The independent traveller is very well cared for in the Somme, with the materials and maps supplied by the Somme Tourist Authority (Comité du Tourisme de la Somme), and by the Office of Australian War Graves. There are plenty of tours to be found for those who don't care to drive from Ypres, Albert, Péronne and Amiens. Some are outlined here. But your first port of call in organising a trip should be the Comité du Tourisme de la Somme website at **www.somme-battlefields.com**. From there you can order all the relevant brochures. Contact **accueil@somme-tourisme.com**

If you are already in the area, the museums at Péronne, Villers Bretonneux and Ypres have the brochures as well including *The Australians in the Somme Tour Guide 18 Sites of Memory*.

The most helpful publications available in Australia are *Australian World War 1 Battlefield Tour – Villers Bretonneux to Hamel*, with maps and an explanatory CD, and *A Guide to Australian Memorials on the Western Front*, as well as the booklet of Michelin maps overprinted with the hundreds of cemeteries.

The Australian guides can be purchased at the Australian War Memorial in Canberra or from their online shop or at the Shrine of Remembrance in Melbourne, or ordered from the Office of Australian War Graves, PO Box 21 Woden ACT 2606, email **wargraves@dva.gov.au**

The Somme Tourist Board also publishes the useful booklet *Le Circuit du Souvenir – The Circuit of Remembrance* – a 60-kilometre driving tour of Somme battlefields (self-guided, or in a guided group arranged through the Historial) which runs from Péronne to Albert via Rancourt, Longueval, Pozières, Thiepval and Beaumont-Hamel. A brochure and map can be downloaded at **www.somme-battlefields.com/en/index.aspx**. A red poppy symbol in the pavement marks the sites on the tour. Nearby, also indicated on the tour map, are Le Hamel and Villers Bretonneux, essential sites for Australians.

Tours and Guides

The Western Front is a highly organised and competitive tourist operation in France and Belgium, and in Britain; wherever you go, you are likely to come across minibuses of battlefield tourists or large coaches of school students. Tours operating on the Somme and Ypres battlefields are naturally oriented around the needs of British visitors. You will also almost always find (this happens all over the world) a couple of Aussie individuals contemplating one of our special places.

From Amiens, the Taxi Groupement Amiénois has five different taxi itineraries that take you to the main sites of the battles of the Somme, each taking a maximum of seven people. Contact Taxis Groupement Amiénois at 2, passage Alphonse Fiquet, Amiens.

For those with limited time, and who happen to be in Ypres or Albert, Salient Tours offer a three-hour minibus overview of the battlefields. They operate from Easter to November; pay on the day, booking not necessary. They leave from outside Albert railway station for the Somme twice a day (not Mondays). They also leave from Ypres. See **www.salienttours.com** or contact **info@salienttours.com**

Other guides can be contacted through the Historial at Péronne, Péronne Tourist Office, The Somme 1916 Museum in Albert, The Albert Tourist Office, or the Amiens Tourist Office.

Somme Normandy Tours offer a personalised half-day or day-long tour. See **www.somme-normandy-tours.com** or contact **colingillard@infonie.fr**

Australian-related tours are offered, and can be booked from Australia through French Travel Connection. See **www.frenchtravel.com.au/contact**

There are many escorted tours from Australia to the Western Front, often in combination with an Anzac Day tour to Gallipoli. The Australian War Memorial tour is the best of these. See **www.awm.gov.au**

These are organised through Boronia Travel, whose experience would be of benefit to anyone organising their own individual or group travel to the Western Front from Australia. Email John Waller at Boronia Travel Centre at **john@boroniatravel.com.au**

However, Anzac Day is definitely not the only time to be on the Western Front – any time of year except the depths of winter and August is fine. Driving yourself with a patient navigator is easily the best way to see the battlefields at your own pace.

The extraordinary Michelin website (**www.viamichelin.com**) allows you to plot and print out routes between any two places in Europe, and is essential to navigation planning before you leave Australia.

The Michelin map booklet overprinted with the Commonwealth War Graves Commission Cemeteries is also essential – order it from the Department of Veterans' Affairs. See **www.dva.gov.au/commem/oawg/publication.htm** for details.

The relevant larger scale 1:25000 (1 centimetre = 250 metres) maps from the Institut Geographique National are also necessary for field by field navigation. Buy them on the spot or from their equally remarkable website **www.ign.fr** where you can buy 1:25000 aerial photographs of anywhere in France.

It is possible to do a quick tour of the Western Front, though part of the experience is to leave time for walking, not just ticking off cemeteries and memorials visited. Accommodation can be found in small hotels and *gites* (B&Bs) everywhere – although not right in Fromelles.

Further Information

Serge Barcellini et al., *Première Guerre Mondiale des Flandres à l'Alsace*, Editions Casterman, Tournai, Belgium, 1996.

C E W Bean, *Letters from France*, Cassell, London and Melbourne, 1917.

C E W Bean, *Official History of Australia in the War of 1914–1918*, Volumes III–VI, 'The AIF In France'. The Official History (with maps) is available at the Australian War Memorial website, **www.awm.gov.au**

Nigel Cave, *Polygon Wood*, Leo Cooper, Barnsley, South Yorkshire, 1999.

Peter Cochrane, *The Western Front*, ABC Books, Sydney, 2001.

Robin S Corfield, *Don't Forget Me Cobber: The Battle of Fromelles*, Corfield and Company, Rosanna, 2000.

W H Downing, *To the Last Ridge*, Duffy & Snellgrove, Sydney, (1920) 1998.

Tonie & Valmai Holt, *Major & Mrs Holt's Battlefield Guide to the Somme*, Leo Cooper, Barnsley, South Yorkshire, 2000.

Tonie & Valmai Holt, *Major & Mrs Holt's Battlefield Guide to the Ypres Salient*, Leo Cooper, Barnsley, South Yorkshire, 1997.

Graham Keech, *Pozières*, Leo Cooper, Barnsley, South Yorkshire, 1998.

John Laffin, *Guide to Australian Battlefields of the Western Front*, Kangaroo Press, East Roseville, rev. ed., 1999.

John Laffin, *The Battle of Hamel*, Kangaroo Press, East Roseville, 1999.

Ross McMullin, *Pompey Elliott*, Scribe, Melbourne, 2002.

Peter Oldham, *Messines Ridge*, Leo Cooper, Barnsley, South Yorkshire, 1998.

Peter Pederson, *Hamel*, Leo Cooper, Barnsley, South Yorkshire, 2003.

Peter Pederson, *Fromelles*, Leo Cooper, Barnsley, South Yorkshire, 2004.

Edgar John Rule, *Jacka's Mob*, Military Melbourne, (1920) 1999.

Geoffrey Serle, *John Monash*, Melbourne University Press, Melbourne, 1982.

Lionel Wigmore, *They Dared Mightily*, Australian War Memorial, Canberra, 1962.

4.

NORTH AFRICA & THE MEDITERRANEAN

German forces invaded Poland on 1 September 1939. A British ultimatum demanding their withdrawal expired at 8 p.m. Australian Eastern Standard Time on 3 September, when British prime minister Neville Chamberlain announced that Britain was at war with Germany. Shortly afterwards a naval signal was received in Canberra, with the order 'Commence hostilities at once against Germany.' At 9.15 p.m. Australian prime minister Robert Menzies made a radio broadcast to inform Australia that it was therefore at war.

The Australian army at that moment was 82,800 strong, but 80,000 were part-time militia

PILGRIMAGE

p.157: The old Turkish fort, Ras el Medauur, Tobruk.

– citizen soldiers. On 15 September, Menzies announced that the 6th Division would be formed in Australia for service overseas (there had been five First World War divisions). Lieutenant General Sir Thomas Blamey was appointed to command the new force, soon to be named the 2nd Australian Imperial Force (2nd AIF). By the end of 1939, three more divisions were formed – the 7th, 8th and 9th. Conscription for military service in Australia – defined to include New Guinea – was introduced for 21-year-olds at the outbreak of war in October 1939, when militia numbers had to be replenished because of the numbers volunteering for overseas service.

The first battalion of the 6th Division to set sail was the 2/16th (the Second World War AIF battalions being given the prefix '2' to distinguish them from First World War units). In early 1940, I Australian Corps, comprising the 6th and 7th divisions, had been formed in the Middle East, and the 9th was in training in England. The situation in the Middle East changed fundamentally in June 1940 when Mussolini's fascist Italy entered the war on the side of Hitler's Nazi Germany. France had fallen, the Battle of Britain was taking place in the skies over London. Italy invaded Egypt in December, but was driven back towards Bardia in Libya by the British. The 6th Division, commanded by General Iven Mackay, was called into the offensive.

The first AIF action of the Second World War was the capture of Bardia, a Libyan town situated on a headland above a harbour on 3

Bardia in Libya was captured by the 6th Division on 3 January 1941.

January 1941. For some days, according to war correspondent Alan Moorehead, Rome radio had been broadcasting that 'Australian barbarians' had been turned loose by the British in the desert.

The attack, by the 16th and 17th brigades of the 6th Division, began at dawn, and by nightfall on 4 January, the Italians – all 38,000 of them – had surrendered, with copious amounts of war material and foods that many Australians had never seen before, including wheels of cheese, cans of tomato paste, and coffee-making equipment. Moorehead wrote that the deed was done while singing 'The Wizard of Oz', but lovely as that would be, it seems that the song was actually 'South of the Border'.

Moorehead described the Australians, 'cigarettes in the corner of their mouths and steel helmets down over their lined eyes', and noted how 'These men from the dockside of Sydney and the sheep stations of the Riverina presented such a picture of downright toughness with their gaunt dirty faces, huge boots, revolvers stuffed in their pockets gripping their rifles with huge shapeless hands, shouting and grinning – always grinning – that the mere sight of them must have disheartened the enemy troops.'

The Australians were on their way to the crucial Italian-held port of Tobruk, which was captured by the Australian 6th Division's 19th Brigade (with the British 7th Armoured Brigade) on 21–22 January 1941. Soon the Italians were rolled up – from the Egyptian border all the way to Benghazi and beyond.

The Germans invaded mainland Greece on 6 April, after the Greeks had successfully resisted an attempted invasion by the Italians. The Germans had overwhelming superiority, on land and in the air, and began operations even before the complete Allied force had arrived. Only the New Zealand Division and part of the Australian 6th Division were in place on the day of the invasion, without adequate armour or air cover. The defence of Greece was a token effort, more political than strategic, and described by the British official history as 'from start to finish a withdrawal'. By Anzac Day 1941, the withdrawal began from Athens and the Peloponnese. Forty-eight thousand of the 62,000 troops sent to Greece were evacuated in the next week, including many but not all Australians. The Greek fiasco cost 814 Australians killed or wounded, and over 2000 made prisoners of war.

The bulk of the 6th Division was evacuated to assist in the defence of Crete, which was an even greater tragedy than the defence of mainland Greece. The defending 'Creforce' comprised 6500 Australians,

The Greek National Monument, Heraklion, Crete.

The airfield at Malame, Crete, seen from the German cemetery on Hill 107. German paratroops landed here on 20 May 1941.

7750 New Zealanders, 15,000 British (a high proportion of whom were not trained soldiers, but base-camp support troops) and around 10,000 Greek soldiers, with little training. With virtually no air cover and little artillery, Creforce was charged with what Churchill called the 'stubborn defence' of Crete. General Bernard Freyberg VC, the great Kiwi hero of the First World War, had command, and allocated his forces to defend the three airfields on Crete, with most of the Australians sent to Retimo (modern Rethymno, or Rhetimno) in the centre of the island.

When German paratroopers and glider-borne troops invaded Crete on 20 May 1941, their objective was to capture the island's airfields, facilitating quick reinforcement by transport aircraft. These initial landings resulted in heavy German casualties; the German paratroopers suffered so severely they were never again used as an airborne assault force. Initially Malame airfield was only partly captured, while at Retimo and Heraklion (now Iraklio) the Germans were contained. Over the next two days of fierce fighting the battle hung in the balance, but after German reinforcements arrived at Malame, the Allies were forced to withdraw to a line near Canea (now Hania or Chania), while the Australians at Retimo were cut off.

On 27 May 1941, the British high command in Egypt ordered the evacuation of Crete. At Retimo, where the Australians had contained the Germans, they received orders to evacuate too late, and with no escape route available, were forced to surrender. Of the Commonwealth force of around 33,000, about half were evacuated.

A report to the Australian government in late 1941 estimated that there were between 4000 and 5500 Allied soldiers still at large in Greece, approximately 500 of them in Crete, while another 1400 were calculated to have escaped from captivity or been evacuated to Egypt. There are dozens of amazing stories involving service with Greek and Yugoslav partisans, long-distance treks through Greece, journeys by boat through the Greek islands, single-handed feats of navigation across the Mediterranean to North Africa and, for some, eventual return to Egypt and Palestine. The help given to the escapers by the Greek people – who risked their lives to provide food, clothing and shelter – was vital. Twenty-five thousand Greeks were shot by the occupying forces.

The Nazis saw Crete and mainland Greece as simply another country to plunder for their war effort, and they diverted Greek industrial and agricultural production to this end. As a result, it is estimated that in four years of occupation over 450,000 Greeks died from malnutrition. Around 25,000 were executed for guerrilla activities or during reprisals for partisan activities. Of Greece's pre-war 80,000 Jews, only 10,000 survived the war. Crete was badly damaged, and its population suffered greatly. The Cretan guerrillas harassed the enemy throughout the four years of the occupation until Crete was liberated on 28 May 1945.

For Australians, the relationship with modern Turkey forged at Gallipoli has overwhelmed many other important relationships, where sacrifice and service were equally present. In Greece, and especially in Crete, there is evidence of an equally strong relationship with Australia as there is in Turkey or France. The memories of the defeat in 1941 are fresher, as is the ultimate victory in 1945. In Greece, after all, Australia, Britain and New Zealand fought as Allies with the Greek forces, regular and irregular, and a tremendous amount of suffering was endured by the civilian population, some of it directly attributable to the help these people gave to our soldiers.

Of the 6203 Australians taken prisoner by the Germans and Italians in the Second World War, 83 per cent fell into enemy hands in Greece and Crete, and nearly 40 per cent of the 17,125 Australians in Greece at the beginning of the campaign were killed, wounded or made POW by its end. The Australian losses in Greece and Crete were virtually all from the 6th Division AIF.

Meanwhile, Syria, which included the territory of Lebanon, had been under French control since France was given a mandate by the League of Nations in 1920. Following the German occupation of France in 1940, the collaborationist government established at Vichy under Marshal Petain maintained control over many French

Syria: the unchanging landscape.

possessions around the world, Syria among them. The policy of the British, who had a similar mandate over Palestine (as Australia did over New Guinea), was that it would not permit Syria or Lebanon to be used as a base for hostile operations against neighbouring countries or to be occupied by a hostile power.

This set-up was disturbed by a coup in Baghdad by Rashid Ali early in April 1941 that not only threatened oil supplies but which, had it been enthusiastically supported by Germany, might well have seen a major geopolitical back door opened up. The coup failed and British control in Iraq was restored, but the German threat to Syria, via the Vichy French, was still thought to be real.

There was no hard intelligence that the Germans intended to attack Syria – in fact, they had been trying to avoid giving the British an excuse to invade, as Hitler's focus was now on the invasion of Russia, which began in June 1941. Nonetheless, the British wanted to secure Syria before the Germans recovered from their victory in Crete. In May, General Wavell, commander-in-chief in the Middle East, was ordered to put together, as best he could, a force to capture Syria and Lebanon. The main elements were the Australian 7th Division, commanded by Major General Lavarack, which would see its first action of the war, 5 Indian Brigade and the Free French Division. The whole force was commanded by British General Henry Maitland Wilson, who kept himself at the King David Hotel in Jerusalem.

The attack began from Palestine, in a memory of the First World War, on 8 June, but progress was slow. General Lavarack, in the field, was given operational command on 18 June, and things began to

General Leslie Morshead, by Ivor Hele, Australian War Memorial.

happen. On 21 June, Indian troops captured Damascus and on 11 July the 7th Division was eight kilometres from Beirut, after hard fighting at Damour. Next day the Vichy French, military honour satisfied and defeat in sight, sought an armistice.

When the Australian 6th Division had left Tobruk for Greece in March 1941, they had been relieved by the 9th Division. As this changeover was taking place, the heavily armoured German Afrika Corps arrived in North Africa, under their aggressive commander General Erwin Rommel, and immediately went on the offensive, bypassing Tobruk in a push to the Egyptian border where they paused, en route to the Suez Canal.

Tobruk was a serious problem for the Germans, as it meant that supplies had to be trucked overland for hundreds of miles rather than shipped via the port. If the Allies lost control of Tobruk, Egypt and the Suez Canal would be threatened. The Allies had to hold Tobruk for as long as possible.

Between April and November 1941, the Afrika Corps laid siege to the city, and tried repeatedly, without success, to capture it. An attempt at Easter to breach the defences was repulsed by superior Australian tactics, and while the attack in May at Hill 209 was more successful, it managed only a small dent, or salient, in the Australian line. This place, called Ras el Medauur, was the site of a stone fort built by the Turks 100 years earlier on Roman foundations, and was used by the Italians as the centrepiece of their defence of Tobruk.

The aggressive defenders of Tobruk were Australians of the 9th Division with British artillery support, commanded by 'Ming the Merciless', General Leslie Morshead, and supplied with great courage and determination by the Australian and British navies. When Lord Haw Haw, the Nazi broadcaster, disparagingly referred to the defenders of Tobruk as 'rats', they took up the epithet as a badge of honour.

In December 1941, with most of the Australian forces having been relieved, the siege of Tobruk was finally lifted, and the remaining Australian 2/13th fought its way out during Operation Crusader. Tobruk was the Germans' first defeat on land during the Second World War. It was a ray of light in an otherwise unrelieved year of gloom in which the Allies had suffered defeat from Europe to the Pacific.

The legend of Tobruk has since joined Gallipoli and Kokoda as a defining crucible of the Anzac. A thousand Australians lie buried in Libya. Tobruk's two cemeteries commemorate 962 men; the others lie in Benghazi and Tripoli. They are not alone. Although Australia,

being the aggressive spearhead of Tobruk's defence, suffered a proportionately higher casualty rate than the sixteen other Allied countries and territories, the total number of dead in Tobruk is 6128.

Tobruk was besieged by the Germans again in June 1942, and lost by the British and South African defenders. Some 35,000 were taken prisoner.

By June 1942, the Germans had reached El Alamein, the last natural defensive line before Alexandria and the Suez Canal. With the wasteland of the Qattara Depression to the south and the Mediterranean to the north, the defenders could not be outflanked. Rommel paused at the end of his long supply route, confident of taking the last 100 kilometres. The Australian 9th Division, fresh from Syria and Lebanon, was given the task of first holding the line in the offensive Australian manner at the northern end in June and July, and then taking the weight and the casualties in the conclusive October attack, the battle of El Alamein. The work of the 9th Division, by absorbing all that the Germans could throw against them, opened the door for the British forces under Montgomery in the south, and was critical in winning the battle of El Alamein. Success was slow, but Rommel's forces suffered massive casualties, and eventually had to withdraw, all the way beyond Libya, to Tunisia.

The Australians did not participate in the final pursuit and defeat of the Afrika Corps following the victory at El Alamein in November. Tobruk was retaken for the last time on 13 November, Tripoli on 23 January 1943, and the final surrender took place on 13 May 1943 in Tunis.

Above left: White Mountains, Crete. Thousands of Allied soldiers walked through here to Sfakia on the south coast, hoping to be evacuated.
Above right: The El Alamein battlefield today.

Members of the 2/13th Battalion at El Alamein. The writer Geoffrey Fearnside is seated on the left.

The Australians in North Africa and the Mediterranean

'There will be no Dunkirk here': Tobruk, January–October 1941

Twenty-six years after Australian soldiers first landed in the Eastern Mediterranean, at Gallipoli, some of the same blokes were back in the same pond, backs to the sea, defending what was to become another iconic place – Tobruk.

These Diggers, the worthy sons and younger brothers of the original Anzacs, brought additional fear, fame and friendship around the Middle East, and not just to the enemy – again. The larrikin band of brothers had the great good fortune to be commanded by one of our under-sung commanders, General Leslie Morshead – Ming the Merciless.

Tobruk, like Bardia, was protected in the Italian style. The fortress was made for defence, with a 48-kilometre string of Italian-made concrete emplacements and strong points, protected by barbed-wire fences and anti-tank ditches, that ended about ten kilometres east and west of Tobruk harbour, with the small town of Tobruk at its centre. While Bardia was being invested, Australian forces headed up the road to Tobruk, and laid siege on 9 January 1941, taking the city almost two weeks later.

Morshead said, 'There will be no Dunkirk here. If we should have to get out, we'll fight our way out. There is to be no surrender and no retreat.' Between April and October, when the last Australians left, they never surrendered, and they never retreated. They defeated Rommel twice, the first time the Nazi war machine had suffered any setback in the war. This was due in equal part to the brilliant tactical leadership of Morshead, his manipulation of the British artillery, and the toughness and tenacity of the Australians.

The Allied defenders at Tobruk were the 20th, 24th and 26th brigades of the 9th Division, and the 18th Brigade of the 7th, plus four regiments of British artillery. The strength of the garrison lay in its fire-power, supplemented by captured Italian weapons, and the extensive use of minefields, which offset to some extent the weakness in infantry.

Morshead's idea was to defend in depth – if necessary, to allow German tanks to penetrate past the outer ring of defences, the 'red line', but then to try and cut them off. Later, when the siege had settled in, he also had a policy of defending aggressively by taking the fight to the Germans beyond the red line, patrolling in the dark, snatching prisoners and making life extremely uncomfortable for them.

The Germans made their first major attack on Tobruk on the night of 13–14 April 1941. Rommel personally directed this attack, but found to his very great surprise that even when the Panzers had breached the ditch to the west of the road, they were unable to exploit and widen the gap. As the tanks came through a second time, they were allowed to travel across what is today a bare rubbish-strewn desert field. A few hundred metres in, they were crunched by artillery, and the soldiers supporting the tanks were mown down by the Australians. In the dark there was savage hand-to-hand fighting, reminiscent of ancient Rome.

Opposite: Map of Tobruk and North Africa.

One of the Italian-built defensive positions used by the Australians, on the Red Line at Tobruk.

The German blitzkrieg tactic of forcing a passage through the defences with tanks and allowing their infantry to walk through the gap had been turned into a trap by Morshead's strategy.

The Germans had some limited success at Ras el Medauur (Hill 209) in May, but it was achieved at great cost to them in men and armoured vehicles. The Salient, as this area was soon known, was held by the Germans throughout the rest of the siege, despite frequent and costly attacks by the Australians. But Morshead's policy of aggressive patrolling kept the Germans off balance – besieging the besiegers.

War correspondent Chester Wilmot described life with the Rats of Tobruk at the Salient, where 'from dark until midnight you could safely move around the Salient posts, but about twelve o'clock the fun started'. With no chance of digging communication trenches back to HQ through the Libyan rock, he concluded that it was safer to be in the frontline posts than on the plain behind them. 'You had to keep the upper hand by giving the Germans more than burst for burst. Some nights these private machine-gun battles developed into willing combats with fire from mortars and artillery added. During the night you took your turn in the listening post a couple of hundred yards out in no man's land – lying in an 18-inch trench; straining your eyes and ears; slowly growing numb with cold. Then came the stand-to, and you waited for dawn with its uneasy quiet.'

An Afrika Corps diarist, Lieutenant Schorn, noted, 'Our opponents are Australians – not trained attacking troops but men with nerve and toughness, tireless, taking punishment with obstinacy, wonderful in defence,' adding, 'Ah well, the Greeks also spent ten years before Troy.'

By July, with casualties mounting, the Australian government had decided that the Australian forces should be relieved. By October, all had been taken back to Egypt by sea, except the 2/13th Battalion, which saw out the siege after its ship was forced back to Alexandria. The British attack to relieve Tobruk began on 18 November, and at some cost forced Rommel to withdraw from 10 December. The siege had lasted for 242 days.

Australian casualties in Tobruk were over 3000, with 941 taken prisoner; the RAN destroyer *Waterhen* and the sloop *Parramatta* were sunk in supplying the defenders.

Above left: The anti-tank ditch near where Jack Edmondson won the VC.
Above: The position today.
Left: Some of the Rats of Tobruk at the Salient.

Australia's first Second World War VC

Jack Edmondson's platoon commander in the 2/17th was Lieutenant Austin Mackell. At Post 33, on the night of Easter Sunday 13 April 1941, near El Adem crossroads, he saw that the Germans had got over the anti-tank ditch and brought up light artillery and machine-guns. This was Rommel's first attempt to take Tobruk. If the Germans stayed there, the whole position would be threatened; Mackell had to get them out.

He told war correspondent Chester Wilmot: 'About a quarter to twelve we set out, Corporal Jack Edmondson, five men and myself – with fixed bayonets and two grenades each. The Germans were dug in about 100 yards to the east of our post, but we headed northwards away from it, and swung around in a three-quarter circle to take them in the flank.

'As we left our post there was spasmodic fire. They saw us running and seemed to turn all their guns on us. We didn't waste any time. After a 200-yard sprint we went to ground for breath; got up again, running till we were about 50 yards from them. Then we went to ground for another breather, and as we lay there pulled the pins out of our grenades. Apparently the Germans had been able to see us all the way, and they kept up their fire. But it had been reduced a lot because the men we'd left behind had been firing to cover us. They did a grand job, they drew much of the enemy fire upon themselves.'

Mackell had arranged that as his group rose for the final charge they would start shouting, and the men covering them would stop firing and begin shouting too. 'The plan worked. We charged and yelled, but for a moment or two the Germans turned everything onto us. It's amazing we weren't all hit. As we ran, we threw our grenades and

'Henceforth for me a crown of righteousness': Jack Edmondson VC is buried in the Tobruk War Cemetery.

'In the dead flat desert the machine-gunners and snipers on both sides could see every move. And so for thirteen hours of daylight both sides lay quiet and fought vermin and boredom. In most parts you couldn't even stand up, for the unyielding Libyan rock made the digging of deep trenches impossible ... You might stretch your legs going back to Company HQ after dark to guide the ration party forward. That was exercise but it was no pleasure stroll, for you never knew when the Hun would forget the rules and start sweeping the desert with machine-guns.'
—Chester Wilmot, 1941

The desert beyond the perimeter, near the Salient, Tobruk.

when they burst the German fire stopped.' Jack Edmondson had been hit in the neck and also seriously wounded in the stomach by machine-gun fire, but ran on with his comrades.

As the Australians reached the Germans, the enemy dropped their guns and fled: 'In their panic, some actually ran slap into the barbed wire behind them, and another party that was coming through the gap turned and fled. We went for them with the bayonet. In spite of his wounds, Edmondson was magnificent. As the Germans scattered he chased them and killed at least two. By this time I was in difficulties wrestling with one German on the ground [Mackell's bayonet had broken in the German, and he'd been grabbed by the legs] while another was coming straight for me with a pistol. I called out – "Jack" – and from about fifteen yards away Edmondson ran to help me and bayoneted both Germans. He then went on and bayoneted at least one more.'

Not surprisingly the Germans fled, leaving behind twelve dead. Mackell reported, 'We've been into 'em, and they're running like —— .' Official reports don't say what they were running like. Edmondson had fought till he could not stand, and died next day. His was the first Australian VC of the war.

'Bogin Hopit': Crete, April–May 1941

The main task of the Australians in Crete was to defend the airstrip at Retimo. German paratroops landed almost on top of the Australians dug in on the hills above the strip on 20 May, the day they launched their invasion of Crete. However, in a series of small actions the Germans were forced off the hills and into the nearby villages of Stavramenos and Perivolia. The Germans held out for a time in an olive oil

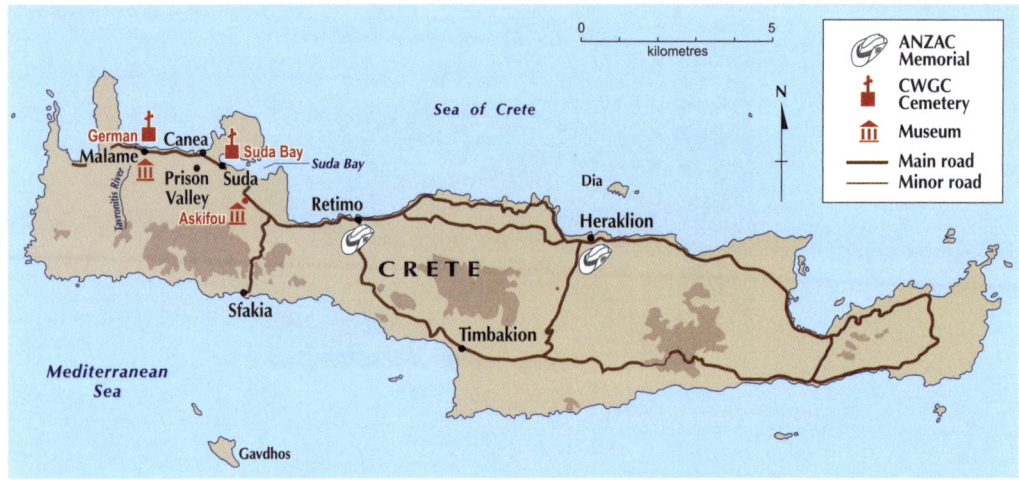

Map of Crete.

factory at Stavramenos, but were finally forced out on 26 May, however they were not dislodged from Perivolia, despite valiant efforts by Australians of the 2/11th Battalion. In one action, eight men of the 2/11th were killed trying to get their Bren gun into position to cover an advance on the village.

The savage small-scale battle in the area's villages, olive groves and vineyards saw some 400 Germans and 100 Australians killed – but the position held.

The Kiwis, meanwhile, inflicted enormous casualties on the German paratroopers and gliders who landed at Malame airfield on 20 May, overlooked by Hill 107 (where the German cemetery is now located), and for a couple of days it looked as if the success of the German invasion was in the balance, before the New Zealanders withdrew, having lost half their number.

Communications were difficult for both sides. The German commander, back in Athens, had to send an officer to Malame to find out what was going on; he found that the Malame airfield was now open for transport aircraft to bring German reinforcements, which they did.

None of the defenders were in touch with one another. Colonel Campbell at Retimo never received a message that, with the loss of the Malame airfield to the Germans and the reinforcement that could now land there, the main Allied force around Canea was withdrawing to the south coast to Sfakia.

One message which failed to reach Campbell, who had no code books, was in a distinctly Australian lingo: 'Waratahs Bulli Puckapu-

North Africa & The Mediterranean

Stavramenos, Crete: Scene of savage small battles in May 1941.

nyals St Kilda Gropers Albany Bogin Hopit ... Australians fight your way south.'

Various sharp actions were fought as the Germans pushed out from Malame, and the Allies withdrew towards the south coast. At one of these actions, on 27 May, at a rural lane known as 42nd Street and flanked by olive trees, a force of Australians from 2/7th Battalion and New Zealanders from the 28th Maori Battalion charged the Germans, killing nearly 300 of them, for the loss of four Australians.

The thirteen-day battle for Crete was lost. Campbell surrendered on 29 May.

Gunner Jager's War

The Allied retreat across the mountains to Sfakia was memorably fictionalised by Evelyn Waugh in the middle book of the *Sword of Honour* trilogy, but this hardly captures the black tragedy it was for many Australians, such as Charles Jager of the 2/2nd Field Regiment.

The regiment was without its 25-pounders, spiked and left behind in mainland Greece a few weeks before. They had not fired many shots. Although the regiment had rifles, they had not been called in to help the Kiwis at Malame airstrip, a few kilometres away. They had been shuffled around Crete for three weeks, in Jager's words, as the 'pawns of a military mind that moves us constantly over a map of Crete by means of pins; pins which can neither sweat nor curse him'. They ended up in an olive grove of a village, a few kilometres from Canea, the main town of western Crete.

On 28 May, after orders had been received to abandon Crete, Jager and his mates set out to walk the 50 miles to Sfakia on the south coast, where they had been told the navy would ferry them to Alexandria.

Some 15,000 odds and sods were marching south. Jager remembers many of them as being British noncombatant units, who carried banjos and threw away their water bottles, or officers who had their servants carry suitcases on the trek.

On the second night, hungry and thirsty, Jager and a mate came upon the deserted village of Askifou in a high valley, about halfway to Sfakia. They found no people, nor water in the wells, but a barrel of

wine, a scrawny chicken, and a twist of onions. The aroma of cooking food attracted a party of Maori soldiers, fresh from the loss of the airfield at Malame. Gunner Jager drank too much and slept too soundly – and didn't notice one of the Kiwis pinching the boots he was using as a pillow. He had to walk the rest of the way in bare feet.

Left: The valley of Askifou, crossed by Charles Jager and mates as they headed down the Imbros Gorge, above, on the way to Sfakia.

At Sfakia Jager was captured, a bit ashamed and determined to get out, to become one of the *escapades*, of whom it was said every village had two or three. Forced to march back to Canea, Jager and a mate took the opportunity to escape from camp. They were found by children, and with a few other escapers were led to a village where the mayor, Yorgo Dimitrakis, hid them. When things became too hot, Dimitrakis asked his daughter Evangelia to lead them to a safer place. The next day, 106 males from the village were forced to dig their own graves. The youngest was thirteen, the oldest 93. Dimitrakis was among them. The women had to fill in the graves. Jager had survived, but as he has written: 'I was alive but better men, perhaps, than me, had died.'

After surviving for some time on the charity of other villagers, Jager was captured for the second time. Once again he was lucky not to be shot as a spy. He managed another escape, and was smuggled to Agios Nikolaos on mainland Greece, where his plan was to walk to Palestine via Turkey and Syria to rejoin the unit. That's a very long walk.

As it happened, while being sheltered by the family of another brave Greek, Dimitri Livanos, mayor of Agios Nikolaos, Jager bumped into a bloke from Brisbane who knew of a plan to pinch a boat and sail it to Egypt. Which they did, on 9 October 1941. Their boat ran out of fuel and food, but luckily had a cargo of figs, which the *escapades* survived on. The boat was bombed twice, by the British and the Germans, but nine days later landed at Mersa Matruh in Egypt.

There are many extraordinary stories of escape from Crete, but few have the ending that Jager's story has. After the escape, Livanos was badly beaten and jailed and his sixteen-year-old daughter shot, but they did not give up the *escapades*, who before they left had signed a testimonial letter. Fifty years later, the granddaughter of Mayor Livanos was living in Australia and found Jager through that letter.

'A close run thing': Syria, June–July 1941

The Australian 7th Division, commanded by Major General Lavarack, saw its first action of the war in the campaign to capture Syria and Lebanon.

Gavin Long, the Official Historian, described how 'Geography imposed on the commander of an army invading Syria from Palestine three possible lines of advance – (i) through a defile between sea and mountains, (ii) along a winding mountain road, or (iii) over an area of broad desert highways.'

The British plan depended on the Vichy French cooperating by only lightly defending their territory. The French had different ideas. Some 35,000 regular troops, including 8000 Frenchmen with artillery and some 90 medium tanks, fought the three-week campaign in defensible country with professionalism and a disinclination to obey Free French imprecations.

Phase one of the British plan was for a brigade of Australians (21 Brigade) to attack along the coastal route towards Beirut, a single road over steep spurs and narrow valleys, where they could be easily blocked or delayed. A second brigade (25 Brigade) was to attack along the valley of the Litani River towards Merdjayoun, a route guarded by a formidable mountain barrier. The Indians and Free French were to take Damascus through the desert, where the Vichy French were well prepared.

Opposite: Map of Syria and Lebanon.

The attack commenced on the night of 7 June 1941. Until 13 June, each of the attacking forces made ground, though the coastal route was tough fighting, especially crossing the Litani River. By 13 June the ancient town of Sidon had been taken by the Australian 21st Brigade, and Merdjayoun taken and lost, and the Free French and Indians were on the way to Damascus.

The next week or so was different. The Vichy French counter-attacked the Indians and Free French and recaptured Merdjayoun from the Australian 25th Brigade when a small force was left to defend the position while the bulk was sent to reinforce the coastal advance. Major General Lavarack responded quickly, reinforced the position and prevented any attack by the enemy to the south. General Wavell, commander-in-chief in the Middle East, sent additional British forces to recapture positions on the Damascus route.

On 18 June Lavarack was, at last, put in command of all forces in Syria and ordered to make Beirut the primary objective while exploiting any other success when he could. The 7th Division under Major General Allan would go to the coast, and the other forces under British Major General Everts would head for Damascus, which, if taken, would help unhinge Beirut.

Damascus fell on 21 June. Merdjayoun was recaptured by Australians on 24 June. A British force from Iraq was headed for Palmyra, north-east of Damascus. The defenders were being ground down from many directions.

The Australian 21st Brigade was advancing beyond Sidon on the Damour River, about 50 kilometres south of Beirut. It attacked Damour on the night of 5 July. The plan was to attack the strong

Australian Bren carriers parade after the fall of Beirut, 9 July 1941.

Australians make their way through rough country of the Anti-Lebanon mountains, near Damour.

defences from the front and turn them with an attack from the eastern, or inland, side. When the defences cracked, the 17th Brigade was to pass through and head for Beirut. A French Colonel commented, 'Until I saw your [Australian] infantry crossing the Damour River and fighting in the mountains, I believed the Foreign Legion were the toughest troops in the world.'

By 9 July, after hard fighting – a 'slogging match in which infantry supported chiefly by 25-pounder field guns again and again attacked well-trained regular forces supported by tanks, artillery and mortars', according to the Official History – the Vichy defences were so widely stretched that their commander, General Dentz, with military honour satisfied, asked for an armistice, which was signed on 13 July at Acre.

General John Coates: 'Syria had been close run, and success had come about more by good luck and hard fighting than by special prescience in the British high command ...'

Allied victory in Syria was hard won. Australia had about 1600 killed and wounded from 18,000 troops; Free French 1100 from 5000, British and Indian 1200. Nevertheless, it was a victory in a year where there was little to celebrate.

Cutler VC

On 7 July 1941, four French Legionnaires carried a stretcher bearing a badly wounded Lieutenant Roden Cutler of the 2/5th Field Regiment down the main coast road between Sidon and Beirut, towards the village of Yerate, accompanied by the medical officer Captain Adrian Robinson and Sergeant Jack Johnson. French shelling was still going on in the distance.

This journey to safety and survival was the final act in an extraordinary sequence of courageous acts between 19 June and 6 July

1941, two weeks of heroism that resulted in Cutler being awarded the Victoria Cross.

Lieutenant Roden Cutler had the dangerous job of 'spotting' or registering the range for his regiment's 25-pounder guns; he was often kilometres forward of the guns. Communication was by telephone – radios wouldn't work in the fragmented country of Lebanon – and miles of heavy telegraph wire had to be carted forward. This was often cut by enemy gunfire, and Cutler and comrades would have to try and repair it out in the open.

Cutler cleared a number of these machine-gun positions himself, through sheer force of surprise at his audacity, and with the help of a revolver. On one occasion he turned back two Vichy tanks with well-directed solo fire at their tracks, after which he got the wounded out. Cutler found himself cut off when sent into Merdjayoun to register the only road out of the town, did the job, hid out overnight, and made his way back through enemy lines to his unit. The successful recapture of Merdjayoun on 24 June was due in good part to Cutler's actions.

On 5 July, Cutler was sent as forward observer for the 2/16th Battalion, but in the confusion of bombardment found himself part of the

French Legionnaires carry the badly wounded Lieutenant Roden Cutler to Sidon. Cutler was governor of NSW from 1966–1981.

attack across the Damour River. He was instrumental in clearing a number of machine-gun nests and taking some not unwilling prisoners, one of whom was wounded. Cutler gave his water bottle to him.

With more machine-guns causing problems, Cutler set off to try and find the telephone line to call in some help from the artillery, when he was severely wounded in the leg. Cutler, wearing shorts, could see how bad the wound was. He applied a tourniquet himself, then lay there for 26 hours, now without water. He was rescued after this long period of agony by his comrades, with the help of disarmed Legionnaires, who knew of him, and knew where he might be found. There is a photograph of these Legionnaires, escorted by Cutler's mates, carrying him back down the road to Sidon where his leg had to be amputated.

'Homeric fighting': El Alamein, July–November, 1942

In early 1942, having withdrawn from Tobruk to western Libya, Rommel's resupplied Afrika Corps with substantial Italian forces resumed the offensive. They finally captured Tobruk on 20 June, and Rommel then advanced quickly to a railway halt at El Alamein, 120 kilometres west of Alexandria, where the British established a defensive line between the sea and the impassable Qattara Depression. Rommel attacked on 1 July, but could not break through.

The Australian 9th Division, just back from Syria, became part of the British Eighth Army, and was in action at Ruweisat Ridge near El Alamein on 7 July. This was the first of a series of actions in July which eventually exhausted both sides.

On 22 July, at Ruin Ridge, near the Tel el Eisa railway halt a few kilometres west of El Alamein, Stan Gurney won the first of three El Alamein VCs from the 2/48th Battalion when his D company suffered heavy casualties from machine-gun fire during a daylight attack on a strong German position. Most of the officers were killed or wounded, which left the success of that day's attack in the hands of the ordinary soldiers.

A hundred metres from the enemy machine-guns, Private Gurney understood what had to be done and unhesitatingly did it. He charged the nearest machine-gun nest, threw a grenade and used the bayonet on the remaining Germans. He eliminated a second post, and after being knocked over by a grenade was last seen vigorously using his bayonet in a third, where he was killed. As the attack was not sup-

Opposite: Map of El Alamein.

North Africa & The Mediterranean

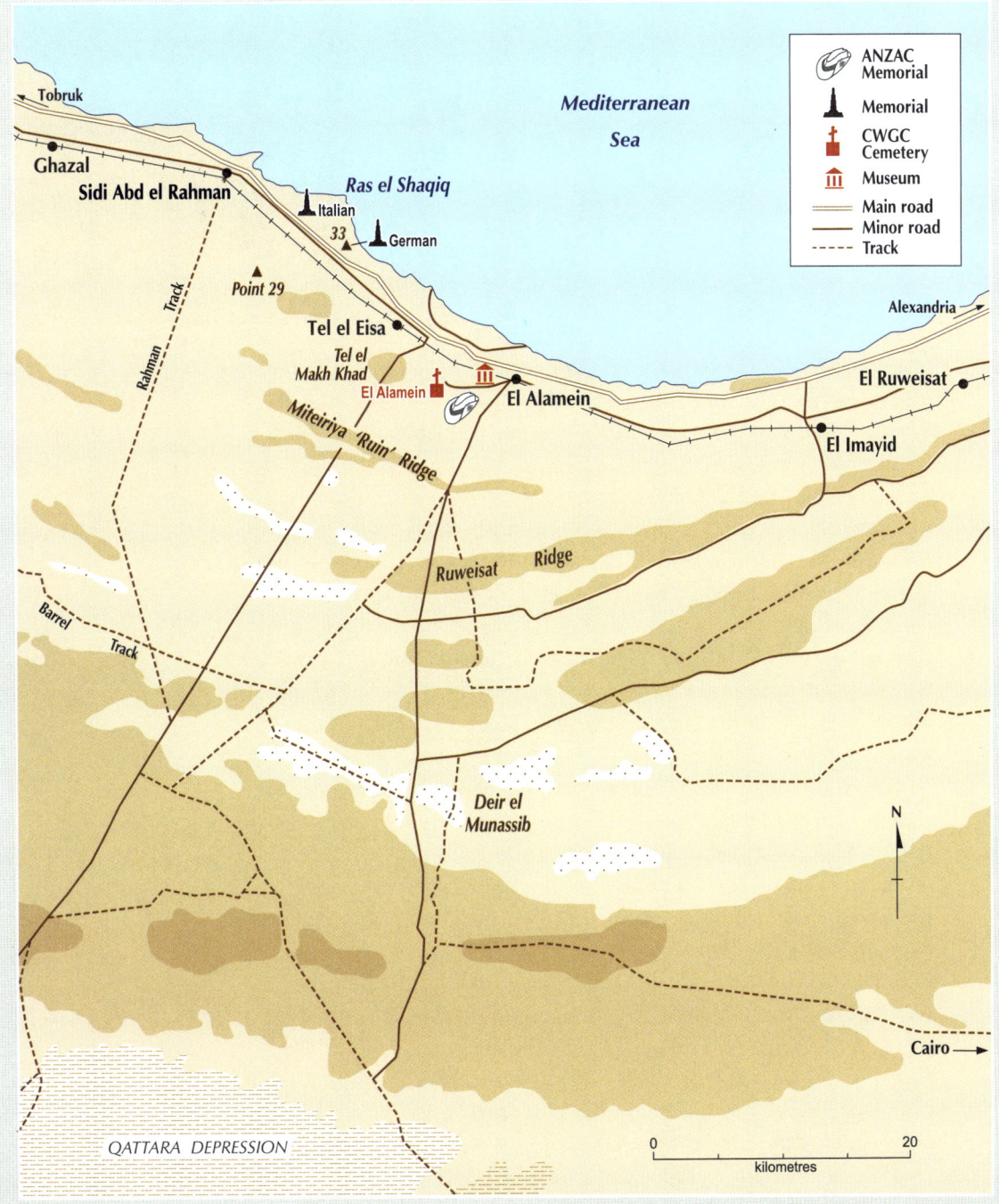

Left: The 1942 El Alamein railway station today.
Above: Weapons pit near the El Alamein Military Museum.

ported by tanks, the survivors were condemned to lie low in the sun all day, before those that could withdrew under cover of darkness. They had killed 60 Germans, and had themselves suffered 49 killed, three missing and 63 wounded.

On 13 August 1942, General Bernard Montgomery was appointed to command the Eighth Army, and immediately improved morale in his forces. His plan was to build up overwhelming force, and use the Corps under his command (which included the 9th Division) near the coast to occupy the Germans while the British armour punched through on the inland side. The battle commenced on 26 October with a massive artillery barrage, and after much heavy fighting Rommel ordered a withdrawal on 4 November. This was the beginning of his end in North Africa.

G H Fearnside of the 2/13th described how 'at 2140 [on 26 October] the guns began their barrage, hundreds upon hundreds of tongues of flame licking ceaselessly at the darkness of the night. Then the sound of the guns came as a drum-beat to the troops waiting forward of them on the start lines. The percussion of them came swimming forward, like the shock waves of sound they were. The ground vibrated, like the skin of a kettledrum and the flames went licking up and down the ridges and the air was filled with the sound of the high, whispering, urgent rushing of tens of thousands of shells passing overhead. And then the sound of the shells exploding merged with the endless clamour of the guns and went on and on in a nether world of half light of fog and dust and cordite fumes.'

The Australians attacked at 2200, including Sergeant Bill Kibby of the 2/48th, who began a series of actions of personal bravery and leadership that resulted in his winning the 2/48th Battalion's second VC at El Alamein. He took command when his platoon commander was killed, and decisively attacked a German post with a tommy-gun. He's supposed to have said 'Follow me' to his men, but no one heard him in the noise of battle, so he did the job by himself.

Action commenced again on 25 and 26 October, and the 2/48th attacked a position on a sand hill, otherwise known as Miteiriya or Ruin Ridge, called Trig 29. Private Percy Gratwick could see that something needed to be done about the German fire from the heights of the ridge. Corporal Frank Dillon recalled that 'Suddenly, without saying a word, Percy took out a grenade, climbed to his feet and galloped forward, holding his rifle in his left hand. It was so crazy and so quick that the Jerries didn't realise what was happening. Percy gave them the grenade, dropped onto one knee, got out another one, and let fly with that.' Gratwick had no more grenades and charged more Germans using automatic weapons with his bayonet. He was killed dealing with the last enemy, the third 2/48th VC.

A few days later, attacking further west beyond Tel el Eisa railway station, where his first VC exploit had occurred, Bill Kibby was killed. His comrade, Private Tom Martin said later that his section had been driven to ground scarcely twenty yards in front of a Spandau machine-gun which was ripping them to pieces. 'We seemed to be in a serious position, but Kibby saved the bunch of us. We saw him run forward with a grenade in his hand and throw it. Then he disappeared, but after that grenade exploded there wasn't any more firing from that quarter.'

After this action, the 2/48th were down to fewer than 50 men. The company commander, Captain Peter Roberts, was among the dead. In his pocket was found a recommendation for Kibby to receive the 'highest possible decoration' for his actions during the previous week.

Gurney, Gratwick and Kibby are all buried in the El Alamein War Cemetery.

El Alamein was the most costly action in the two years Australians fought in the Mediterranean theatres. From July to November 1941, 1177 Australian were killed, 193 were missing, and 3629 wounded: 5794 casualties in all, from a force of 15,000. Making up only 10 per cent of Montgomery's Eighth Army, Australia suffered 20 per cent of its casualties.

'I am quite certain that this breakout was only made possible by the Homeric fighting over your divisional sector,' said Lieutenant General Oliver Leese, who commanded the men of the Australian 9th Division who had borne the full weight of the Germans.

Kenneth Slessor and 'Beach Burial'

Kenneth Slessor was Australia's official war correspondent, and while perhaps technically and temperamentally unsuited to the censorship and hard news of war, he provided in his diaries, despatches and poems some of the best writing about Australians at war.

Slessor saw some of the fighting in July, when Rommel was stopped, or ran out of petrol, at El Alamein, but he was in hospital when the October battle commenced. Afterwards, on 15–17 November, he drove up and down the 200 miles of the 'road to ruin' west from El Alamein, and surveyed the detritus of the retreating enemy – 'a corridor of dusty death, lined with ruin, leading to ruin'. He describes the desert campaign, fought in the absence of a civilian population, as a 'battle in a vacuum, a campaign of mechanised destruction, full of the fury and humiliation of machines'.

Kenneth Slessor.

On 9 December Slessor wrote 'Honouring the Fallen', a story about Australian war graves at El Alamein: 'Here at this little speck on the map, between the huddle of stone huts which is El Alamein railway station and the lonely coast road which they helped to guard so stoutly, they are burying Australia's dead ... Day after day the living battalions of the AIF have gathered their dead comrades from the battlefield and brought them here to simple burial and makeshift memorials ... There have been services of all kinds. Some have been attended by whole battalions, listening stiff-faced and silently to the age-old words of burial, now loud, now faint, in the wind from the sea which flutters the white surplices of the chaplains. Others have had an audience of only two or three, clustered with a padre round a solitary grave. Australians mixing cement for headstones close by, and men from other units, down tools for a moment and stand to attention, joining in the familiar hymns with hushed voices. Then the Last Post, with its utter finality and long echoes over the sandhills, a brief inarticulate pause, and work starts again on the headstones and cement.'

Slessor came out of retirement as a poet to write two poems during the Second World War. 'Beach Burial', written after El Alamein, is the result of Slessor's observation and meditation on the universality of death. It revives some of the themes in his most famous poem, 'Five Bells', an elegy for a mate who drowned in Sydney Harbour and the inability of poetry to bring him back.

In 'Beach Burial' the dead are sailors of all nationalities washed ashore on the brilliant beaches in front of the cemetery at El Alamein, buried in the sand hills under improvised crosses. They came to represent everyone.

Beach Burial

Softly and humbly to the Gulf of Arabs
The convoys of dead sailors come;
At night they sway and wander in the waters far under,
But morning rolls them in the foam.
Between the sob and clubbing of the gunfire
Someone, it seems, has time for this,
To pluck them from the shallows and bury them in burrows
And tread the sand upon their nakedness;

And each cross, the driven stake of tidewood,
Bears the last signature of men,
Written with such perplexity, with such bewildered piety,
The words choke as they begin –
'Unknown seaman' – the ghostly pencil
Wavers and fades, the purple drips,
The breath of the wet season has washed their inscriptions
As blue as drowned men's lips,
Dead seamen, gone in search of the same landfall,
Whether as enemies they fought,
Or fought with us, or neither; the sand joins them together,
Enlisted on the other front.

El Alamein

North Africa and the Mediterranean Today

Egypt

Egypt's struggle for independence goes back 2500 years, to when the country was run by the Persians. Since then, Egypt has been liberated and occupied by the Greek (or Macedonian) Alexander the Great; the Umayyad Arabs from Damascus; Saladin and the Ayyubid; Mamelukes; Napoleon; the Albanian Mohammed Ali and the Ottoman Turks; and then by the British, who left the Ali dynasty on the throne but effectively took over running the country and the vital Suez Canal.

In 1919, there was serious agitation for independence in Egypt which the Light Horse participated in putting down, something many older Egyptians still remember. During the Second World War, a number of Egyptians looked forward to a German victory as they thought this would lead to Egyptian independence. Fortunately for Egypt, Nazi intentions were not put to the test. With the riots of 26 January 1952, or 'Black Saturday', many foreign-owned businesses in Cairo and elsewhere were burned down, and six months later, on 26 July, a coup of army officers led by Colonel Gamal Nasser ousted Farouk, the descendant of Mohammed Ali. Nasser nationalised the Suez Canal in 1956, staring down the British and the French.

The complex relationship between Egypt and Israel (itself only gaining independence from the British in 1948) has seen shooting wars in 1967 – the Six Day War, which saw the loss of the Sinai and the closure of the Suez Canal for eight years – and in 1973, which eventually resulted in the Camp David peace accord in 1979, follow-

By the side of the road from Alexandria to El Alamein, an Italian memorial. It was bad luck, not a lack of courage that lost them the war in Egypt.

ing which Israel withdrew from the Sinai in exchange for Egypt's recognition of Israel's right to exist. This compromise, by Egypt's second president, Anwar Sadat, resulted in his assassination in 1981.

Sadat was succeeded by Hosni Mubarak, who was re-elected in a limited form of democracy in 2005. Mubarak has survived assassination attempts and the rise of Islamist fundamentalism by a fairly brutal suppression of fundamentalist groups. There have been periodic outbreaks of violence including massacres of tourists in the 1990s and other disturbances (including the hijacking of an aircraft on which I was a passenger). Tourism has survived these events. Egypt has too much to offer for people to stay away – about 5000 years of battles, occupations and liberations. El Alamein and the Second World War are a tiny aspect of this extraordinary heritage, but highly significant for Australians and the Commonwealth.

Cemeteries, Memorials, Museums: Egypt

Alexandria

The **Alexandria (Chatby) Military Cemetery** is on the eastern side of Alexandria. It was used in the First World War. There are 1259 First World War burials and 503 from the Second World War.

The **Alexandria (Hadra) War Memorial Cemetery** is in the main Alexandria cemetery complex and has 1700 burials from the First World War, including 23 Australians, and 1305 from the Second World War.

Cairo

Cairo War Memorial Cemetery, with 2057 First World War and 340 Second World War burials (including twenty Australians), and **Cairo New British Protestant Cemetery**, with eleven First World War and fifteen Second World War burials, adjoin each other inside the massive Old Cairo cemetery complex. The cemeteries are surrounded by a high wall, and are located near the Maronite section of the cemetery.

One of the 158 Hutchinsons who died in 1918. Private C Hutchinson, 20, of 115 Brixton Rd, Kennington, and the London Regiment is buried in the Cairo War Memorial Cemetery.

El Alamein

The **El Alamein War Cemetery** entrance is down a path from the road. There are 7367 burials in the cemetery, of which 821 are unidentified

El Alamein War Cemetery, the old 9th Division Memorial in the background.

by name. The names of a further 603 men whose remains were cremated are commemorated on the **Cremation Memorial** within the cemetery. There are 1188 Australians buried here.

You will pass the **Australian 9th Division Memorial** and the **South African Memorial** and enter the cemetery via a cloister opened by Montgomery in 1951. The memorial cloister, some 80 metres long, is entered through three arches leading from the forecourt, and at each side there are steps leading to the flat roof of the memorial, from which there is a view of the cemetery, the surrounding desert and, to the north beyond the road, the sea.

Above the arched entrance to the cloister the dedicatory inscription reads: 'Within this cloister are inscribed the names of the soldiers and airmen of the British Commonwealth and Empire who died fighting on land or in the air where two continents meet and to whom the fortune of war denied a known and honoured grave. With their fellows who rest in this cemetery, with their comrades in arms of the Royal Navy and with the seamen of the Merchant Navy they preserved for the west the link with the east and turned the tide of the war.'

The **El Alamein Memorial** bears the names of 11,874 Commonwealth soldiers and airmen who have no known grave. The 8687 missing soldiers died in the campaigns in the Western Desert (8392), Iraq (184),

Syria and Lebanon (116) and Persia (33). The 3187 missing airmen died not only in these four campaigns but also in the operations in Greece, Ethiopia, Eritrea, Madagascar, and the French, British and Italian Somalilands.

Australian VC winners Kibby, Gratwick and Gurney were among those whose comrades had scoured the ridges and sand dunes around Ruin Ridge and the other fateful places; they now are 'at rest' with all the other Australians who have been brought 'home' to El Alamein.

Kenneth Slessor finished his piece about the El Alamein cemetery with this: 'Today all is quiet at El Alamein. The vital coast road to Alexandria ... is now as peaceful as a country lane. The war has gone west with the 8th Army. Towards noon as the sun grows warmer, birds come singing to the purple desert gorse which fringes the cemetery, and butterflies blow across the sand. The war has gone far away but, it seems, Australia is closer now, to these men who had died for Australia, than it has ever been.

'The guns have stopped, the air is quiet, and peace has come also to the fresh graves on the farther side of the cemetery where they had buried Hans W Reidel of the Afrika Corps and Ermino Cyrillo Feronza of the Italian Army.'

So it is still, at El Alamein.

Sergeant William Kibby VC, El Alamein War Cemetery.

The **Australian 9th Division Memorial** stands outside the El Alamein War Cemetery. The four sides of the plinth feature four symbolic reminders: on one, the words 'We will remember them', on another, the Australian Coat of Arms, then the Rising Sun badge above the words 'The Australian Memorial to honour the participation of the Ninth Australian Division and its supporting arms and services in the battles of the El Alamein campaign, July–November 1942' and finally the 9th Division patches T (Tobruk) and the platypus above a boomerang.

The memorial was badly damaged by high desert winds in 2005, and in October 2005 it was announced that the memorial would be demolished and replaced with the same badges and inscriptions. Work was to be completed in 2006.

The 9th Division Memorial surveys the El Alamein battlefield.

The **El Alamein German Memorial** is on the seaward side of the main road 110 kilometres from Alexandria, not far from the El Alamein War Cemetery. It was built after, and along the same lines as, the German memorial at Tobruk, using equipment from there and a reddish

Afrika Corps plaque in the German Memorial, El Alamein.

sandstone quarried in Mersa Matruh. It is an octagonal shape, with a tower at each corner, 42 metres in circumference and twelve metres high. In the central courtyard is an obelisk. Seven niches on each wall correspond to the seven tombs underneath, each with 600 dead buried there – a total of 4300. Each niche has six tablets inscribed with the names of the dead.

Dedicated on 28 October 1959, it is an austere, solemn and defensive sort of place, but impressive and strong.

There is a text dedicated to the soldiers of unknown nationality buried there, which a sign inside indicates 'can be interpreted as the message of the whole memorial':

Here rest 31 soldiers of unknown nationality.
Here death took all: Name, age, nation,
Took every earthly measure, made it anomalous.
Only one thing remained as a clear tone in the dark legend
Of this unbridled war in the world without God:
Where you stood here in combat – Foe, friend or brother,
Sons of Germany, Italy, England. Chivalrous was your
Manner, human here the law. God alone knows you all. He
Knows your names, he fits them into his strict, true order.
In His hands He holds the plea of the living and dead,
The plea for peace.

El Alamein Italian Military Shrine.

El Alamein Italian Military Shrine is at the 120-kilometre mark from Alexandria at Trig 33, on the site of the cemetery established by the British after the war for German and Italian dead. There is a white octagonal tower commemorating the dead. The shrine contains 4634 war dead; there are 2447 known and 2187 unknown soldiers buried or commemorated here.

There is a mosque and cemetery on the left of the entrance, and various divisional and other memorials in the courtyard leading to the shrine. There are four 47 mm guns from the turrets of tanks of the XI brigade at the entrance.

'To 4800 Italian soldiers, sailors and airmen. The desert and sea did not give back 38,000 who are missing.'

Inside the memorial it is bright and clean, somehow stylish with white marble, and the names inscribed in niches reach to the high ceiling. Outside at the back is a fine view of the Mediterranean.

Nearby on the highway is one of the more evocative memorials, in

Italian, marking the furthest point east they reached. It says '*Manco la Fortuna, Non Il Valore – 1.7.1942, Alessandria*'. Literally, 'Lacking fortune, not valour', but perhaps 'Bad luck not lack of courage cost us the war' might have been the thought.

The **El Alamein Military Museum** has a terrific collection of vehicles and guns outside, with uniforms and displays inside a modern building opened on the 50th anniversary of the battle, 21 October 1992. Outside is a restored bunker supposedly used by Montgomery during the battle. Australia and the 9th Division are not especially remembered here.

Above: The El Alamein Military Museum.
Below: The war cemetery at Sollum.

Sollum

Halfaya Sollum War Cemetery is on the main coast road that runs from Egypt's border with Libya to Alexandria. The cemetery is about twelve kilometres down an escarpment at Halfaya Pass, where there was heavy fighting in 1941 and 1942. Graves were brought in from Bardia, Sidi Barrani and other places after the war. There are 1823 identified casualties, 238 unidentified, including 169 Australians.

Greece

In the wake of the German withdrawal in 1944, civil war broke out in Greece, between the communist Democratic Army of Greece and various monarchist and right-wing forces, supported by Britain and America. The monarchists won in 1949, a pyrrhic victory that saw millions of Greeks leave for a better future in Australia and elsewhere. Periods of social democratic government, punctuated by the right-wing Colonels Coup in 1967–1974, have seen Greece slowly emerge as a modern, stable if still passionate country. The costly but successful 2004 Athens Olympic Games, the admission of Cyprus to the EU despite its continuing division, and a growing rapprochement with Turkey are all good news. Greece's history has gifted Australia a special relationship, especially in Crete.

After the war it was decided to bring the bodies of all British and Dominion servicemen killed in 1941 from smaller burial grounds all over Greece and Crete into either the Phaleron War Cemetery in Athens or the Suda Bay War Cemetery on Crete. On the Greek mainland, British units were assisted in this task by the Australian 21st and 22nd Graves Registration Units. The Australians themselves undertook the work on Crete.

Crete today is one of Europe's favourite holiday destinations – aeroplanes arrive at the airport in Heraklion in an endless stream, to be met by convoys of buses which take tourists to the resorts which litter (literally) the north coast of Crete.

Some of the places of interest to Australians and New Zealanders, such as Rethymno, have been affected by development – the airstrip defended at such great cost has been swallowed up in a somewhat tawdry beach development.

The old Venetian part of Canea around the harbour, well known to Second World War *escapades*, is stunning, and being truthful has some of the worst food found in the best locations anywhere in the world. Sfakia, now Chora Sfakion, is probably not much bigger than it

was during the war, though it does have much better food. The drive across the plain of Askifou under the White Mountain and along the rim of the Imbros Gorge is alone worth a trip to Crete.

Above left: The Askifou plain.
Above: Canea Harbour.

Today, in spring, the Askifou plain is covered in fields of yellow daisies and olives, and rings with the musical bells of goats. And signs leading to Askifou village, and the George Hatzidakis War Museum. Here the unwary traveller can fall victim to the hospitality of George Hatzidakis, who, like all Cretans, is a great friend of Australia. George has a splendid collection of wartime relics from all participants: bits of aircraft and weapons, Marsden matting, a Cretan partisan coat. He doesn't speak much English, but has slips of paper with the appropriate pieces of information on them – including the fact that he was wounded as a small boy, and that it is time to toast the bravery of Australians and Cretans 60 years before. The ouzo is not the most potent I have ever tried, but warming and smooth, and, on reflection, pretty silly.

I left Askifou with my boots, but perhaps a bit too relaxed for the spectacular drive to Sfakia on the narrow road of switchback turns and blind corners and buses coming the other way that skirts the rim of Imbros Gorge. Sfakia, which took Gunner Jager more than a day of hard walking in bare feet to reach, now takes an hour of careful driving. In 1942 it was a place of mayhem and tragedy, as thousands of soldiers were left behind to surrender; today, it is a picture-perfect village.

The war is long gone, but it is still alive in the people of Crete, especially for Australians and New Zealanders. When you get away from the tourist areas, and drive into the mountains and sit in a taverna somewhere, it might feel a bit threatening. But strike up a conversation, let it be known that you are from down under, and most likely you will have a new set of best friends, even if their English is a bit rusty, not to mention a whole lot of new relatives in Melbourne.

Cemeteries, Memorials, Museums: Athens

Athens

Phaleron War Cemetery is on the coast south-east of Athens, more easily accessible from the airport and the city after roadworks for the 2004 Athens Olympics were completed.

The site was a burial ground for Commonwealth casualties of the Greek Civil War of 1944–1945. It was decided by military authorities, in conjunction with the Greek government and the Army Graves Service, that it would be the most suitable site for a Second World War cemetery for the whole of mainland Greece. Australian and British war graves units worked together to bring in graves of the 1941 campaign from the battlefields, temporary military cemeteries and civil cemeteries.

There are now 2028 Commonwealth servicemen of the Second World War buried or commemorated in this cemetery.

Among the Australians buried here is Colonel W E Kay, who was mortally wounded on 24 April 1942 during the evacuation of Allied forces from Greece. The large yacht *Hellas* had taken on board nearly 1000 passengers, including civilians and sick and wounded from the 2/5th Australian General Hospital. She was hit by two German bombs,

Phaleron War Cemetery.

the gangway destroyed, and many of the passengers were trapped in burning cabins. Colonel Kay was among the estimated 500 to 742 death toll. A doctor from Waverley NSW, Colonel Kay had commanded the 2nd Field Ambulance in 1917–1918.

Among the 694 New Zealanders buried at Phaleron or commemorated on the Athens Memorial within the cemetery is George Cook, a member of the 1932 Olympic rowing team, who was killed on Crete in 1941.

The cemetery is dominated by the large stone panels of the **Athens Memorial**, which commemorate nearly 3000 members of the land forces of the Commonwealth who lost their lives during the campaigns in Greece and Crete in 1941 and 1944–1945, in the Dodecanese Islands in 1943–1945 and in Yugoslavia in 1943–1945, and who have no known grave.

Those whose bodies were never recovered, or who were unidentifiable at burial, are commemorated on the **Athens Memorial to the Missing** at Phaleron. There are 331 Australian names on this memorial representing 56 per cent of the Australian dead of the Greek campaign.

The following words, attributed to the ancient Greek poet Simonedes, are inscribed in English above the north entrance to the memorial and in Ancient Greek above the south entrance: 'We, who to clothe Hellas in freedom fought, lie here at rest in praise that fadeth not.'

Cemeteries, Memorials, Museums: Crete

Askifou

George Hatzidakis War Museum houses a fine collection of relics. Follow the plentiful signs from the road from Canea to Sfakia, and call out loudly. The museum is before you get to the village.

Heraklion

The **Monument of National Resistance**, in the heart of Heraklion on Dimokratias Street, is the Greek national war memorial. The heroes' names are being carved in stone, scenes from the battle of Crete shown in plaques around the memorial. One of Ross Bastiaan's bronze plaques, unveiled in 1992, is situated nearby and tells the Australian story.

George Hatzidakis War Museum.

Malame

The **German Military Cemetery** is on Hill 107, which overlooks the airfield at Malame. There are 4465 burials here, two names inscribed on each tablet, set in a field of sea marigolds. It is a very open and beautiful cemetery, unlike the inward-looking German fortress memorials in Egypt and Libya. The cemetery was opened in 1974.

The **airfield at Malame** is still visible from Hill 107 above, where the German cemetery is located. It can still be looked at, but visitors are not welcome. It seems to have become some kind of tatty aircraft museum, with old American jet fighters such as an F104 visible through the locked gates.

German Cemetery, Malame.

Preveli

Preveli Memorial was unveiled on 24 May 1985 by the Australian Ambassador to Greece. It recognises the debt owed to the local people by the escapers in the Preveli area of southern Crete. On the memorial are these words:

'This tablet commemorates the deep gratitude of British, New Zealand and Australian servicemen befriended by the monks of Preveli Monastery and Cretans from surrounding villages, who, at great personal risk, helped them to escape by British submarines, HMS *Thresher* and *Torbay*, in July and August 1941.'

Rethymno

The **Hellenic–Australian Memorial Park**, dedicated on 19 May 2001, is located at the corner of Igoumenou Gavrill Avenue and 44th Syndagmatos Street. It has been designed to symbolically represent the Greek people fighting side by side with Australians during the battle for Crete in 1941. The two flanking pillars, clad in a rough-surfaced local limestone, represent Greek soldiers and civilians, while the Australian forces are portrayed by the central pillar clad in a polished black granite from South Australia. All three pillars are equal in size.

The **Stavromenos Memorial** was erected in 1975 by the local community at Stavromenos, near Rethymno, to commemorate where Australian and local Greek forces held back the German paratroopers in May 1941. A plaque on the memorial records, with attendant colour

Above: Greek Australian memorial, Preveli. (John Rerakis)
Below: The Hellenic–Australian Memorial, Rethymno.

The Australian Hellenic Memorial, in Anzac Parade, in front of the Australian War Memorial, takes the shape of an amphitheatre in which a Doric column symbolises the birth of civilisation. The column is embossed with the cross of the Greek Orthodox Church. It represents a hero's grave and it contrasts with the harshness of the bomb-damaged steel fragment representing the destructive forces of war. The memorial stands on a mosaic pavement incorporating a graphic interpretation of the Greek mainland and outlying islands. The memorial was dedicated 21 May 1988.

patches, every major Australian unit that fought the Germans in the Retimo area, including at Stavromenos and Perivolia. In 1977, the Australian government presented the Stavromenos memorial with two anti-aircraft Bofors guns, the type used by Australian anti-aircraft gunners in action against the Luftwaffe in May 1941. The guns were brought from Australia by the flagship of the RAN – HMAS *Melbourne* – while on a visit to Suda Bay.

Suda Bay

Suda Bay War Cemetery.

Suda Bay War Cemetery is at the north-western corner of Suda Bay, five kilometres east of Canea and three kilometres north of the main east–west highway on the northern coast of Crete. The cemetery is in an olive grove and is well sign-posted from the main road.

The site was chosen after the war, and graves were moved there by Australian 21st and 22nd War Graves Units from the four burial grounds that had been established by the German occupying forces at Canea, Heraklion, Retimo and Galata, and from isolated sites and civilian cemeteries.

There are now 1502 Commonwealth servicemen of the Second World War buried or commemorated in the cemetery.

There are also nine non-Commonwealth burials and 37 non-war graves. They include three Germans – two civilians and Corporal Alfred Hamann; Hamann died in May 1941, but was buried at Suda Bay rather than the German cemetery at Malame due to a mistake in identification.

Lebanon

Lebanon has a complex and ancient history – travellers will find evidence of the Phoenicians who had a thriving trade in glass and other goods around the Mediterranean from 2500 BC from cities like Byblos (Gebal), Saida (Sidon) and Berytus (Beirut). All the great conquerors, from Rameses II and Alexander the Great passed down the coast on the way to battle and left their names at Nahr al Kalb (Dog River). St Paul, born in Tarsus in southern Turkey, also passed through on his way to Damascus.

Lebanon became a Christian country, part of the Byzantine Empire, in the 5th century. The Lebanese Christians are Maronites, who joined with the invading Crusader armies against the Arab Muslim rulers, who arrived in the 7th century, in the new millennium. The great general Saladin (Salah ad-Din) took Jerusalem in 1187, and the Crusaders were finally beaten at Tripoli, in northern Lebanon, in 1289.

Lebanon was part of the ramshackle but mostly tolerant Ottoman Empire for the next 500 years, although open warfare occasionally broke out between Maronite Christians, local Druze, Sunni Ottoman Muslims and southern Shiite Muslims. Modern sectarian divisions have their origins in these divisions.

Modern Lebanon began with French intervention on the Christian side in 1860 in a conflict with the Druze. The Ottomans agreed to set up a separate province in Lebanon, under a Maronite governor, guaranteed by European powers. Lebanon prospered, and after the First World War and the defeat of the Ottoman Empire, France was awarded

The extraordinary Crusader castle, Krac des Chevaliers, flourished as a defensive position east of Homs in Syria from 1099 until surrendered to the Mameluke Sultan Baibars on 7 April 1271.

a League of Nations mandate and attempted to create a new nation-state in the area from the mountains to the coast. A constitution with power-sharing between the various religious groups was drawn up, which formed the basis of the independent Lebanon declared after the Second World War in 1946.

Israel's independence in 1948 resulted in a flood of Palestinian refugees into Lebanon, and the next half-century of tension, invasion and civil war, as Lebanon was involved in the Middle Eastern maelstrom of ethnic, religious and political differences. The civil war between right-wing Phalange Christians, Palestinian and other Muslims began in 1975 and continued for seventeen years. It resulted in Syrian intervention, Israeli invasion, more massacres, the division and destruction of much of Beirut, kidnappings and the creation of powerful groups such as Hezbollah.

Peace has broken out gradually since 1992. Beirut has been rebuilt, Israel withdrew from southern Lebanon in 2000, and following the assassination of prime minister Rafiq Hariri in 2005, Syria has withdrawn its more obvious forces and the former terrorist organisation Hezbollah has become a political party representing the Palestinians in Lebanon (even if it is not viewed that way by everyone outside the country).

Tensions remain. There are hundreds of thousands of Palestinians in Lebanon unable to return to their former homeland. But given the condition of other Middle Eastern countries, and despite setbacks, Lebanon is on the way to a stable future. Visitors will find 5000 years of history on view.

Cemeteries, Memorials, Museums: Lebanon

Beirut

Beirut War Cemetery. (CWGC)

Beirut War Cemetery is in two sections. One section, originally known as Beirut British War Cemetery, was begun in October 1918 and was later enlarged when graves were brought in from other burial grounds in the area. The older part of the adjoining section, originally known as Beirut (Saida Road) Indian and Egyptian Cemetery, contains three memorials to soldiers of the Indian Army and the Egyptian Labour Corps who died during the First World War. This section was later extended for Second World War burials, and the two sections combined under the name of Beirut War Cemetery.

Commonwealth burials and commemorations at Beirut War Cemetery now total 628 for the First World War and 531 for the Second World War. There are 24 Australians from the First World War and 243 from the Second World War here.

Nahr al Kalb (Dog River)

The **Inscriptions at Dog River** are about twenty kilometres north of Beirut, on the conqueror's coastal road from Europe and the Near East, or vice versa. Alexander the Great crossed the present-day river at Nahr al Kalb heading south, as had the armies of the Egyptian pharaoh Rameses II, also the Great, 1000 years before him. Other leaders, from Nebuchadnezzar in the 6th century BC to the Roman emperor Caracalla and Napoleon III, have had inscriptions carved here. The tradition continued in the 19th and 20th centuries, with inscriptions caused to be carved by a variety of commanders of greater or lesser quality. The last inscription made in the 20th century was by Hezbollah in 2000.

Nahr al Kalb. The freeway has replaced the 1941 Australian-built railway bridge; Jesus surveys the inscriptions from across the river.

The Romans knew the river as the Lycus, but Nahr al Kalb came to be called Dog River after a legendary statue of a wolf said to have stood guard at the entrance to the river. It was supposed to have included a cleverly designed mouth vent so when the wind blew in the right direction, it howled. Australians building the Second World War bridge are supposed to have found a statue of a wolf, which later vanished.

There is a very large highway crossing the river, and a few hundred yards upstream the 'modern' bridge constructed in the 1930s, and beyond that, the 'Arab' bridge built in the 14th century.

There are seventeen ancient inscriptions here, all easily accessible beside the road and on a track above, on the south bank of the river, except Nebuchadnezzar's, which is hard to find on the north bank.

There are two Australian-related inscriptions. In the cliff above the Napoleon III tablet from 1860–1861 is one celebrating the capture of Damascus in 1918: 'The Desert Mounted Corps composed of British, Australian, New Zealand and Indian cavalry. With a French regiment of Spahis and Chasseurs d'Afrique and the Arab forces of King Hussein captured Damascus Homs and Aleppo October 1918'.

The 1930 inscription which General Chauvel demanded replace one that failed to mention the Australians.

This records, of course, the epic of the Australian Light Horse, and the legend of Lawrence of Arabia. The inscription was controversial, only being put in place in 1930 after General Harry Chauvel,

The 1941 inscription made on the order of General Blamey.

Australian commander of the Desert Mounted Corps, intervened to have the original replaced – it had referred to the 'British' Desert Mounted Corps.

A few metres down the road from the Arab bridge is one from 1941 commemorating the liberation of Lebanon and Syria from the Vichy French.

Kenneth Slessor and General Blamey

Kenneth Slessor visited Dog River in November 1941. In a despatch dated Cairo 31 January he outlined the story of the inscriptions and stated that the Australian sculptor/soldier Lyndon Dadswell was to carve a new inscription 'with the approval and personal interest of General Blamey'. (Dadswell, as Slessor pointed out, was wounded at Damascus, and was responsible for the interior panels at Melbourne's Shrine of Remembrance.)

Slessor was there again on 18 May 1942, when he photographed the finished inscription and had a look at the great Australian engineering work in the Middle East, the Haifa–Beirut–Tripoli Railway. South Africans worked on the section from Haifa to near Beirut, completed in December 1941, and the Australians began constructing the northern section to Tripoli in early 1942, covering miles in a year, six months ahead of schedule. At Dog River, a 270-foot bridge was constructed across the river. The link was finished on 20 December 1942 – allowing, theoretically at least, travel from London to Cairo by train.

There was no love lost between Slessor and Blamey – for a variety of reasons. Blamey, who some thought was more concerned with his own comforts than those of his men, apparently believed Slessor was one of those responsible for spreading rumours about allegedly dubious activities in the Middle East; Slessor, for his part, plainly thought Blamey was about to have his name carved alongside Nebuchadnezzar's, which got up his nose.

Blamey may have been hubristic but, contrary to popular belief, he did not have his name carved in the inscription. The inscription reads: 'June–July 1941 The first Australian Corps captured Damour while British, Indian and Free French troops captured Damascus, bringing freedom to Syria and the Lebanon.' Hardly exceptional, and in fact a well-deserved tribute to a short but hard campaign that cost more than 300 Australian lives. They deserve remembrance at Dog River – as Slessor fervently agreed.

The poem 'Inscription for Dog River' (with 'Beach Burial' one of only two Slessor wrote after retiring in 1939 with 'Five Bells') leads us down the garden path by saying that 'our general' has his name inscribed next to a Persian king. However, it remains one of the finest memorials of the ordinary soldier ever written.

An Inscription for Dog River
Our general was the greatest and bravest of generals.
For his deeds, look around you on this coast –
Here is his name cut next to Ashur-Bani-Pal's,
Nebuchadnezzar's and the Roman host;
And we, though our identities have been lost,
Lacking the validity of stone or metal,
We, too, are part of his memorial,
Having been put in for the cost,
Having bestowed on him all we had to give
In battles few can recollect,
Our strength, obedience and endurance,
Even our descendant's right to live –
Having given him everything, in fact,
Except respect.

Field Marshal Sir Thomas Blamey, King's Domain, Melbourne. Sculpture by Raymond Ewers, 1960.

Sidon

Sidon War Cemetery is about a kilometre inland from Sidon harbour in Barghout Street in the suburb of Durukman, and is about 60 kilometres south of Beirut. The entrance to the cemetery is in a small road called Sahl al Sabbagh, leading right off the Rue Iskandarani. When looking for the cemetery ask your driver to ask the locals where the British cemetery is. They have forgotten Australians, it seems.

The cemetery is officially open Monday to Friday between 7.30 and 14.30; outside these hours there is a convenient hole in the fence in the road to the left of the entrance.

The cemetery was opened in 1943 by British occupation forces and originally used for the burial of men who died while serving with them. Later, the graves of a number of the casualties of the 1941 campaign, such as the La France brothers, were moved into the cemetery from other places in Lebanon. There are now nearly 200 Second World War casualties commemorated in this site, 185 of them identified.

Sidon War Cemetery.

Their duty nobly done: Ray La France.

Duty well done for the country he loved: Merv La France, Sidon War Cemetery.

Pour La France

Among the graves brought in to this cemetery are two that had caught the eye of Ken Slessor. He had 'stopped at a smashed police post not far from the Litani River [just north of Tyre] and stood for a few moments at a little cluster of Australian graves ... huddled together, as if taking cover on a slope of a hill. Behind them a ripple of young maize came to life in the wind, still defiant of the shells which had ploughed it.'

He described the crosses made from the sides of packing cases nailed together and the inscriptions in indelible pencil, and noted that 'two comrades lay side by side facing the white beach and the blue sea ...

'It was not their relationship nor the fact that both had been killed on the same day that held me there so much as the tragic irony of their names. That was four months ago. Last week, revisiting the battlefields of the Lebanon, I came to a little cemetery in lonely Bergouliye, just south of the Litani. It was a neatly kept square in the middle of an empty plain, fenced with barbed wire, with paths of white pebbles in the rich soil and a gate painted battleship-grey.

'Here the bodies of those British soldiers who died in the surrounding territory have been removed by the War Graves Commission ... There was a red poppy on each of the 70 graves, for it had been Remembrance Day a few days earlier. English, Scots and 33 Australians lie in precise ranks, and the crosses are now of smooth white wood with painted inscriptions ... I found the two comrades here still side by side as they fought against Vichy France. Inscriptions on their crosses are lettered neatly in black – "SX 4756 Private M La France 12/6/41" and "SX 3104 Private R La France 12/6/41".'

Slessor, writing in fastidious haste in Cairo, didn't know whether Merv and Ray were brothers, and noted in his diary that after a night's pondering he had opted for safety by naming them 'comrades'.

But they *were* brothers, sons of Pierre and Florence La France of Port Augusta West, South Australia. Merv was 27 and Ray 22 when they were killed. Their deaths might have been recognised on 12 June, but they had been killed on the two nights prior, as their unit, the 2/27th Battalion, fought up the coast from Tyre to Sidon.

By the afternoon of 10 June the battalion was in a creek bed three kilometres south of Adloun, some eighteen kilometres from Sidon. Vichy defences at Adloun were on a set of north–south ridges above the main road, with a cliff above a couple of hundred metres of flat terrain on the sea side. The battalion was tired, hungry and thirsty after three days of hard fighting and no sleep, as they waited for the French to attack.

Ray La France was in Captain D R McPhee's B Company, which attacked a position above Adloun just after midnight, early on 12 June, and reached the top before 2 a.m. He was killed with four others in the same company in that hour and a half.

Merv was in D Company, and was killed later that same day in the fighting along the river bed and the ridges above. One cannot imagine what was in his mind, knowing his younger brother had been killed.

Slessor returned that way on 17 May 1942, and noted in his journal that he photographed their graves at Bergoulive cemetery 'astonishing how quickly the earth covers the scars of a campaign – not even craters or bomb-holes now visible on the fields over the Litani ...'

Now the brothers are buried, but not side by side, in the meticulously cared-for cemetery in Sidon.

Libya

Following World War Two and the defeat of colonial power Italy, Libya, comprising the two ancient provinces of Cyrenaica in the east, and Tripolitania in the west, became independent. The UN approved the creation of the new state in 1949, and it was declared the United Kingdom of Libya under King Idris on 24 December 1951. Elections and various forms of government were tried in the 1950s, as Libya signed treaties in exchange for aid with Britain and the United States, and good relations established with other European countries. Oil was discovered in 1959.

A hitherto unknown group, the Revolutionary Command Council led by Colonel Muammar Gaddafi staged a coup while King Idris was in Turkey, on 1 September 1969. Since then Gaddafi has led Libya on a strange secular socialist journey, through an involvement in some of the more disgusting terrorist plots such as the Lockerbie bombing to a reopening of Libya to investment and tourism in 2005. Gaddafi came in person to Benghazi to set me and my companions free after being hijacked in Egypt in 1996, so I have a bit of a soft spot for him.

But Libya has, rightly or wrongly, been regarded as a pariah state, and only the most determined travellers have visited in the past ten or fifteen years. The visitors' books at Tobruk show just four Australian names among a hundred English – the McKay family from WA came

Colonel Gaddafi on display in Tripoli, Libya.

Graffiti at Cyrene, Libya. (2003)

to visit their father and grandfather, who died here in August 1941, aged just 22.

Like the Middle East in general, Tobruk gives the impression of not having been reconstructed to a great extent since the war – buildings look like they are being renovated or demolished, at the same time. But progress has come to Tobruk. In 1941 it was a handful of streets and a port; now it has a population of about 140,000, with developments and housing going up inside the blue line.

Time and progress are the enemies of battlefield discovery, but less so in the desert than in the jungle or city. From this point of view there is a lot still to be discovered in Tobruk, although finding Tobruk is more difficult than finding Gallipoli or even the Kokoda Track.

Finding a meaning among the headstones and loss of life is perhaps easier for the Second World War than for the First. If it wasn't a good war, even a just war, it was close enough. Regime change in Nazi Germany was vital, the dictator in question was the definition of evil. But even if the war in North Africa was more honourably fought than most, between armies in the sand sea, not involving civilians, it had its horrors. The human results are here for us to mourn.

On Anzac Day, 2003, there were no other Australians at the major cemetery in Tobruk, the Tobruk War Cemetery. I organised a wreath made of gum leaves and wild flowers, jumped the fence and laid it on the Australian memorial. I stood for a minute's silence with my guide, Abdul, and driver Idris. Libyans understand our desire to make a pilgrimage. They have their own memorials of their own struggles, and their own pilgrimages.

Anzac Day, 2003.

As a sign of the changing times, an Anzac Day ceremony was held at Tobruk in 2005, with the Australian minister for defence present.

Salaam Alikoum: Peace Be With You.

Looking for the place where Corporal John Edmondson won the first Victoria Cross at Tobruk, we drove along the Adem road towards where the red line, and the two-metre-high Italian-made anti-tank ditch still exist. This place is just a decrepit field beside the road now, a few buildings going up or coming down, a paddock, the anti-tank ditch. It evokes nothing.

Hoping for more, we drove west down the Derna road towards Benghazi looking for the site of Rommel's attack on the night of 30 April. Turning south off the road into the stony desert, our four-wheel-driver, Abdul Jawad, looked for and found what they call the Roman road – which is really the Italian road circumscribing the red line.

There is plenty of evidence that soldiers have been here – the desert winds bring the dust and blow it away from the straight stone-lined tracks made by Australians between the piles of stones they used as shelters. There are rusty cans, broken glass and other detritus from the armies which had passed this way.

Rommel was called the Desert Fox, and there was a real one looking at us curiously from his fox hole as we rumbled by. The desert here is neither trackless nor unpopulated. Herders tend their fat sheep and goats. Cameleers look after the dark brown ships of the desert. They live in shacks, and are perennial optimists who have ploughed fields where they will plant wheat after it rains. Everyone invites us around for a meal – offering to kill a sheep or two. Hospitality is the rule out here.

Eventually we find what we are looking for, the point the Germans attacked that cold April night. It is marked by a stone fort; it's only 60 or 70 metres above the coastal plain, but from here, dust allowing, you can see everything that moves down there, and everything that is coming from the south-west. In that direction, 50 metres from the fort, is an elaborate system of trenches and tunnels, one of the strong points, Post S. It has collapsed in places from shelling or bombing, and some of the bunkers are full of sand and rubble. This and the hill above were what the Germans managed to capture by early May after stout defence by the Australians against heavy tanks and overwhelming numbers and a fierce sandstorm.

On the clear, cool April day of my visit, the peace and silence here were overwhelming. Imagination is just not good enough to bring back the terror of night fighting down that dark tunnel, where one Rat said that he just charged on, bayonet in the lead, stabbing anything and anyone, friend or foe.

Abdul made a little fire, we drank tea, and were at peace.

Cemeteries, Memorials, Museums: Libya

Bardia

The Bardia mural by John Brill.

The **Bardia murals** are found in a flat-roofed Italian building on the headland overlooking the harbour. Some rooms are in ruins but one, locked and barred on my visit in 2003, contains some surprising murals, the best of them painted by a British soldier, Private John Brill, in April 1942. Brill's black and white mural is full of symbols – a boxer, coins turning into skulls, pleading women, coffins, six novels of Dickens, musical instruments. Private Brill was in the 5th Battalion, East Yorkshire Regiment, and probably left Bardia in June as Rommel besieged Tobruk. Brill was killed on 1 July, and is buried in the El Alamein War Cemetery.

Benghazi

Benghazi War Cemetery.

Benghazi War Cemetery is about seven kilometres south-east of Benghazi in the Fuihat area, about 300 metres from the children's hospital on the opposite side of the road. From the city centre, take the road following the coast past the sports stadium. Approximately two kilometres beyond the stadium is a large roundabout with a flyover on to the Tripoli road. Turn left at this roundabout, and the war cemetery is found three kilometres along this road on the left-hand side. There are now 1214 Commonwealth servicemen of the Second World War buried or commemorated in Benghazi War Cemetery. 163 of the burials are unidentified. There are 1075 identified casualties. Many of the Australians in Benghazi are RAAF, or soldiers who fell in early 1941 in the fight against the Italians.

Derna

There is a dearth of museums to the Second World War in Libya, but there is one in a backstreet in Derna, which your compulsory Libyan guide will be able to find. It has a small collection of relics, which is worth a look if you are in town and like the detritus of the desert, rusting helmets of different armies, shell casings, fragments of Libyan history. The proprietor is very enthusiastic about any foreign visitor.

Tobruk

Tobruk War Cemetery is about seven kilometres inland on the main road from the port of Tobruk to Alexandria, set back about 100 metres along an access track branching from the left side of the main road. It is generally open in the mornings, but the stone wall is easy to climb over at other times.

Tobruk War Cemetery incorporates the burial ground used during the siege; the memorial erected there at the time by the Australians has been replaced by a permanent memorial of similar design. Many battlefield graves in the desert have been brought into the cemetery. There are now 2282 Commonwealth servicemen of the Second World War buried or commemorated in Tobruk War Cemetery. 171 of the burials are unidentified but special memorials commemorate a number of casualties known or believed to be buried among them. The cemetery also contains 171 war graves of other nationalities, most of them Polish. The Poles fought in Tobruk after the Australians had been withdrawn. There are 559 identified Australians at Tobruk. The **bell from HMS** *Liverpool*, sunk in Tobruk harbour, is fixed to the cemetery entrance wall, and a **memorial to the Black Watch** stands by the track on the way to the entrance.

Tobruk War Cemetery entrance, with Ross Bastiaan bronze plaque.

The Australians built a memorial obelisk during the war, which was destroyed. The **Australian Memorial** was rebuilt in 1948. Below the word 'Australia' and a map of the country surrounded by a laurel wreath are the words: 'This is hallowed ground for here lie those who died for their country.' (The original dedication, carved on a stone step from the Tobruk Post Office, is now at the Rats of Tobruk memorial in Canberra.)

Australian Memorial, Tobruk War Cemetery.

Chester Wilmot, in a description of the ceremony at the dedication of the memorial, wrote, 'Their real monument is their name and their most honoured resting place is in the grateful hearts of their fellow men.'

Knightsbridge War Cemetery (Acroma) is located about 25 kilometres west of Tobruk, 750 metres south of the main road from Benghazi to Tobruk, and is easily visible from what the locals call the Roman road, which is roughly paved with stones. This was one of the tracks around the Knightsbridge defensive 'box', one of the defensive strong points, linked by deep minefields, which were supposed to hold up Rommel in 1942. The graves of many of those who gave their lives

Knightsbridge War Cemetery (Acroma).

during the campaign in Libya were later gathered into Knightsbridge War Cemetery from the battlefield burial grounds and from scattered desert sites.

There are now 3651 Commonwealth servicemen of the Second World War buried or commemorated in Knightsbridge War Cemetery. 993 of the burials are unidentified and special memorials commemorate a number of casualties known or believed to be buried among them. There are 2677 identified casualties, including 240 Australians. Another 63 Australians are unidentified.

The simple ochre-coloured **French Cemetery** is on the El Adem road, where the dead from the epic battle of Bir Hakim are buried. This stark place is well cared for, but you get the feeling it is not often visited.

German Memorial, Tobruk.

The **German Memorial and Cemetery** in Tobruk was built on land on a dominating ridge south of the harbour, given by the then Libyan government in 1953. In 1951 the Volksbund, the private organisation founded in 1919 which is the German equivalent of the Commonwealth War Graves Commission, had begun the recovery of German dead in Libya. Within two years it had recovered 5350 remains, 98 per cent of the total. These men were laid in individual stone coffins in a church in Tobruk.

The German cemetery opened on 20 November 1955. It is a forbidding square castle-like structure, fourteen metres high, with 40-metre-long walls with round towers at the corners. The tomb, with 6026 dead in individual stone coffins, is below the central courtyard; in the middle is a fire bowl supported by four large angels; in arcades around the courtyard, the names of the dead are inscribed in mosaics. There is no mention of religion, or politics (or Nazis).

The monument is overwhelming, closed off from the outside, unlike the design of 'our' cemeteries such as the Tobruk War Cemetery, where you can jump the fence. The Germans are in their stone coffins beneath your feet, in a desiccated Valhalla. I felt uncomfortable, and not just because it was the enemy's memorial; it was almost as if in some grail quest in the future they might all rise up.

Al Watany Museum, Tobruk.

The official **Al Watany Museum** is housed in the former Church of St Anthony in Tobruk's main square. This church was badly damaged during the siege, but was one of the few buildings that remained more or less intact. Inside are well-kept displays of artefacts and photographs. Australians will be heartened by the appearance of Chester

North Africa & The Mediterranean

Wilmot's poster of the *Siege of Tobruk* with the map by James Emery, published by Gordon and Gotch in the 1940s. There are pictures of Rommel, bits of bombs and radios – a random assortment, but tidily presented.

In a square nearby is what is said to be a **bunker used by Rommel** in his relatively short time in Tobruk. This seven-room complex has the distinction of having also been used by Montgomery. When it was found, it still contained the sand table used to make sand maps.

On my visit, Mansour el Shuieb, the friendly and very helpful tourism chief in Tobruk, showed me around the empty rooms and talked of a better International Military Museum to tell the wartime story of Tobruk, very soon. In the square above are some large artefacts – the mount of a big Italian coastal gun, a 25-pounder.

There is also the **wreckage of the *Lady Be Good***, an American B24, brought in from the desert in 1994. The aircraft crashed in April 1943 after running out of fuel 600 kilometres south of Benghazi in the Great Sand Sea, having missed a radio beacon and become disoriented after a raid on Naples. Eight of the crew survived a parachute jump but died trying to walk out of the desert. The aircraft was located in 1958, and the remains of seven of the eight crew in 1969. The bodies were repatriated to the United States.

Stump of an Italian gun at the proposed International Military Museum, Tobruk.

Above left: The fig tree, 2003.
Above: The fig tree, 1941.

The **Fig Tree** growing on the lip of an escarpment a kilometre below Ras el Medauur was a famous landmark at Tobruk, and still is. There was a regimental aid post in a cave beneath it, now filled with sand, and a battalion headquarters 100 yards to the south had been made by the Italians. Before the end of the siege in 1941 the tree's canopy had been shredded by shrapnel – it is back better than ever now.

Tripoli

Tripoli War Cemetery and **Tripoli Military Cemetery** are co-located in the Mansura district of Tripoli, 2.5 kilometres west of the city centre. They are located off the western end of Sharia Jamahuriya, close to the major roundabout at Bab Gargaresh. Access to the war and military cemeteries is via the now disused Italian Municipal Christian Cemetery.

The burials in the war cemetery were almost entirely from the hospitals, which included, from March 1943, Nos. 2, 48 and 133 General Hospitals and from April 1944, No. 89 General Hospital.

Tripoli War Cemetery contains 1369 Commonwealth burials of the Second World War, 133 of them unidentified. The number of identified casualties is 1262.

Among the fourteen Australians at Tripoli are six RAAF casualties from 1943.

For Syria, see Chapter 2, 'Palestine'

RAAF officers were fighting until the end of the campaign in North Africa. Flying Officer A E H Tonkin was killed on 14 January 1943; he is buried in the Tripoli War Cemetery.

The Salient was the only section of the Tobruk defensive perimeter captured by the Germans while the Australians were in occupation.

Left: 9th Division patches on the division's memorial at El Alamein.

The Rats of Tobruk memorial (left) on Anzac Parade in Canberra is based on the 1941 memorial in the Tobruk War Cemetery, built by Australian soldiers during the siege, which was destroyed. The inscription stone, the only surviving relic of the 1941 memorial, and at one time a front step of the Tobruk Post Office, is incorporated into it.

The inscription reads:

THIS IS HALLOWED GROUND FOR HERE LIE
THOSE WHO DIED FOR THEIR COUNTRY
'AT THE GOING DOWN OF THE SUN,
AND IN THE MORNING
WE WILL REMEMBER THEM'

The memorial takes the form of an obelisk. Surrounding walls portray the perimeter defences and the design recalls the area in which the siege took place. The coastline and harbour are to the front and the defence positions flank the rear of the memorial.

Travel Tool Kits

Egypt

Egypt has been a travel destination since the world's first travel writer and historian, Herodotus, visited the pyramids when they were already 2000 years old. There are 5000 years of sites to see.

Alexandria is Egypt's traditional summer resort, favoured since the days of Cleopatra, and a place that still lives with its cosmopolitan past. Lawrence Durrell's wartime *Alexandria Quartet* hints at what the mood was like when the city was under threat of German invasion. Aside from its own unique attractions, Alexandria is the best base for a visit to the Egyptian battlefields; El Alamein is 106 kilometres to the west.

Coming from Alexandria, El Alamein town, cemetery and museum are in a smaller road off to the left on the main highway that goes to Mersa Matruh and on to Libya. The old railway line is south of the road, beyond the El Alamein War Cemetery. The German and Italian memorials are on the right off the main highway, nine kilometres further west – you can't miss them.

Any time is a good time to visit, though Alexandria is crammed with holidaying Cairenes in the very hot summer. There is no accommodation to speak of at El Alamein, but a great range of it in Alexandria.

Around El Alamein, the cemetery, the Australian 9th Division Memorial, the military museum and the Italian and German memorials are best visited by car in a longish day, which would also allow access to less-visited places such as the old El Alamein station and Tel el Eisa railway halt, and the rebuilt mosque at Sidi Abd el Rahman, significant sites for Australian visitors. It is very difficult to see anything by using public buses.

It is helpful to know what you want to see, as most driver/guides will only know the El Alamein War Cemetery, the 'British' cemetery and the museum. My own recommendation is to contact Emeco Travel, either in Cairo or Alexandria. They have a lot of experience with Australian travellers, and I found them completely reliable.

Greece

Phaleron War Cemetery is a few kilometres to the south-east of Athens, on the coast road from Athens to Vouliaghmen. A new road was completed in 2004 for the Olympic Games – I visited before it was completed and it took a Bangkok-style two hours in a taxi from the airport. Now there is a new tram that also goes past the cemetery, and this is much easier than driving. Take a tram towards Glyfada from Syntagma Square and after half an hour you will see the cemetery to your left. Get off at the stop immediately after the cemetery.

By contrast, getting around the Australian war sites in Crete is easy, especially if you like driving. A splendid highway runs east–west across Crete, with significant places like Rethymno, Stavromenos, Canea, Galatas and Malame easily accessible. Suda Bay War Cemetery is on the northern side of the bay, but well signposted from the highway. It's a beautiful place, as they all are, nestled in an olive grove, with a view across the water to Suda. Greek naval vessels are often berthed there, giving the view an added poignancy. Any time is a good time to visit Crete, even in the winter. Accommodation is plentiful, and best away from the ugly resorts of the north coast.

Lebanon

Lebanon's later wars have given the country a reputation as a dangerous place to visit. It's no more problematic than anywhere else in the world, though the increase in the number of bombings after the Syrian withdrawal in 2005 have made the situation more fragile. While scarred buildings can still be found along the Green Line in Beirut, the downtown area has been rebuilt, and the place once again thrives on its passion for beach, food and business.

Australians are made welcome. While the experience is not quite the same as in Athens where every second taxi driver has a cousin in Melbourne, you will be sure to meet plenty of Lebanese people with Australian connections. The main difficulty is explaining to them the difficulties of migration. Lebanon, even for the Lebanese, has a very temporary feeling. A lot of people still want out. Anyone who can afford it has their children educated outside the country, in hope that they might be successful somewhere safer.

Beirut has once again become the place where, as everyone will tell you, it's possible to swim in the morning and ski in the afternoon.

Eating at any of the beachside restaurants and cafés is good fun. Beaches are mostly privately owned, but cafés are plentiful.

Libya

Things are changing for the better, in regard to travel to Libya. A Libyan Embassy was been established in Canberra in 2003, and there will be an Australian equivalent in Tripoli in the near future.

But organising a visa is not a straightforward process. Visas are generally not available to individuals at all. You have to be part of a group, and be guided on your trip. Getting a visa from Egypt is not possible, even as a group. You should arrange a visa with a travel agent from Australia well in advance of intended departure. Contact the Libyan People's Bureau in Canberra for the latest updates.

Things are changing quickly, but when I travelled to Libya in 2003 there was no reliable method of arranging a visa and the tour in Australia. I contacted a company in Libya, who proved utterly reliable, despite communications difficulties. In my case I did travel by myself, and turned up at the airport in Tripoli with a visa, trusting my email correspondent, Mr Hussein Founi. It was *inshallah* all the way. After a great deal of agitation, running around and time in regard to stamps and permissions and other matters, I was granted permission to enter. I would not recommend this to anyone else but I would recommend that a group arrange with Mr Founi's travel company, Robban Tourism Services. The visa process can take a considerable amount of time, generally requiring your passport being translated into Arabic, and a good deal of to-ing and fro-ing. See ginfo@robban-tourism.com

Travel in Libya would not normally simply involve visiting wartime sites at Tobruk, but also the best preserved Greek and Roman sites anywhere in the world, and the most Saharan of all deserts. Leptis Magna and Sabratha near Tripoli are simply spectacular, Cyrene, Apollonia and Qasr Libya near Benghazi equally so. The scenery is awesome.

The food is a wonderful mix of cuisine between Morocco and Egypt, with touches of Italy and while you cannot drink alcohol, the coffee and tea are excellent. And it means that the driving is that much safer. Best of all, save for a few busloads of French and Italians, I met no other tourists at all.

Libya has no ATMs and you can't use credit cards. The nearest are in Tunis and Alexandria. You will need to take cash, most usefully US dollars or Euros to pay for everything.

There are more or less direct flights to Tripoli from Australia on Emirates via Dubai and Valetta in Malta. While the land border between Egypt and Libya is generally open, and it is possible to drive from Tobruk via the Umm Sa'ad crossing to Sollum, El Alamein and Alexandria (as I did), going in the other direction is impossible. Be aware that the crossing can take anything up to eight hours, as squads of customs, security and immigration officials from both countries inspect you and your goods, and take lunch or tea. You can exchange any excess Libyan dinars for Egyptian currency at one of the many unofficial dealers on the Libyan side of the border. Accommodation ranges from the super luxury of new hotels in Tripoli, to clean and friendly in smaller places in Tobruk.

Syria

For Syria, see Chapter 2.

Further Information

John Burns MM, *The Brown and Blue Diamond at War*, 2/27 Bn Ex-Servicemen Association, Adelaide, 1960.
Peter Cochrane, *Tobruk 1941*, ABC Books, Sydney, 2005.
J S Cumpston, *The Rats Remain: The Siege of Tobruk 1941*, Melbourne, 1966.
G H Fearnside, *Sojourn in Tobruk*, Ure Smith, Sydney, 1944.
G H Fearnside, *Half to Remember*, Haldane Publishing, Sydney, 1975.
Charles Jager, *Escape from Crete*, Floradale Books, Melbourne, 2004.
Mark Johnston & Peter Stanley, *Alamein: The Australian Story*, Oxford University Press, South Melbourne, 2002.
Eric Lambert, *The Twenty Thousand Thieves*, Newmont, Brunswick, 1991.
Lew Lind, *Flowers of Rethymnon*, Kangaroo Press, Kenshurst, 1991.
Gavin Long, *Official History of Australians in the War of 1939–1945*, Volume II, 'Greece, Crete and Syria', Canberra, 1953.
Colleen McCullough, *Roden Cutler VC*, Random House, Sydney, 1998.
Barton Maughan, *Tobruk and El Alamein*, Australian War Memorial, Canberra, 1966.

Alan Moorehead, *African Trilogy*, London 1944, Text Publishing, Melbourne, 1997.

Richard Reid, *A Great Risk in a Good Cause*, Department of Veterans' Affairs, Canberra, 2001.

Clement Semmler (ed.), *The War Dispatches of Kenneth Slessor*, UQP, St Lucia, 1987.

I McDougall Stewart, *The Struggle for Crete*, London, 1966.

Lionel Wigmore & Bruce Harding, *They Dared Mightily*, Australian War Memorial, Canberra, 1963.

Chester Wilmot, *Tobruk 1941*, Angus & Robertson, Sydney, 1944.

5.

SOUTH-EAST ASIA

THE WAR IN SOUTH-EAST ASIA AND THE PACIFIC began at Kota Bharu, Malaya, at 12.30 a.m. Malayan time on 8 December 1941, 75 minutes before the Japanese attack on the American naval base at Pearl Harbor, Hawaii.

Most of the Australian 8th Division, commanded by Major General H Gordon Bennett, was already stationed in Malaya, and Australian battalions were in place on the islands beyond Singapore, at Rabaul, Ambon and Timor (the western half of which was part of the Dutch East Indies).

The Indian troops at Kota Bharu and in northern Malaya were without effective air cover, as all the airfields in northern Malaya were lost within 48 hours. They were rapidly pushed

Westforce (27th Brigade plus three Indian brigades) was stationed across the main road and along the Muar River. Crucially, few troops were on the beach road, and the Japanese were able to get behind the defenders. An effective ambush was staged on the main road at the Gemenceh River near Gemas on 14 January, though it only temporarily delayed the Japanese. Over the next week Australians fought well, especially at Bakri where Lieutenant Colonel Charles Anderson won a VC commanding the 2/19th. But all this was in vain, because General Bennett's plan called for no withdrawals but without prepared positions or sufficient supplies. As Australians were to discover later in 1942, on the Kokoda Track, the Japanese operated on thin supply lines, and if you could delay them and outlast them, you might win.

p.217: The view across the River Kwae from where the Chungkai POW camp stood, Kanchanaburi, Thailand.

back by the well-trained and agile Japanese, who used everything from bicycles to motor transport to drive down the Malayan Peninsula. The Japanese commander General Yamashita famously said that Malaya would be conquered by cheap Japanese bicycles using expensive British roads.

The British battleships *Repulse* and *Prince of Wales* were sunk by Japanese aircraft off the coast of Malaya on 10 December, with a huge loss of life, and the Japanese had taken Kuala Lumpur by early January 1942. The battle for Malaya was over.

Australian forces were divided into two – Westforce to deal with the main Japanese thrust from Kuala Lumpur and Malacca towards Singapore; and Eastforce, from Kuantan down the coast road.

By 31 January 1942, all 130,000 Australian, British and Indian troops were concentrated in Singapore. Singapore was supposedly impregnable because it was defended by big artillery batteries guarding the eastern approaches to the Johore Strait. Unfortunately for the pre-war planners, the Japanese arrived by road from the north, and prepared to cross the Singapore Strait where the Australians, who had fought their way to Singapore from Malaya, were thinly spread on the north-west side of the island.

The attack came, primarily in the Australian sector, on 8 February, when fourteen Japanese battalions overwhelmed the thinly spread Australians. Brave small defensive actions were not sufficient to overcome strategic ineptitude by General Percival, overall

Map of South-East Asia.

commander, and mistakes by General Bennett. With the loss of the reservoirs, Percival surrendered on 15 February. Bennett, controversially, escaped, leaving the 8th Division to suffer as prisoners of war.

Australian casualties – killed, wounded, missing and prisoners of war – were 18,490. British casualties were 38,496, Indian 67,340, local volunteers 14,382. Of the total 138,708, more than 130,000 were made prisoner.

After the surrender of Singapore there was a widespread belief that invasion of Australia was imminent. Most women and children had been evacuated from Darwin after the Japanese entered the war, leaving about 3000 people in the city. The Australian mainland came under direct attack for the first time on 19 February 1942, when the Japanese launched two air raids on Darwin. Some 250 people were killed, civilians and military, and 400 injured. The raids were organised and led by Admiral Chuichi Yagumo, who had also commanded the Japanese forces in the attack on Pearl Harbor two months before, and some of the aircraft flew from carriers that had been at Pearl Harbor. There were also 54 heavy bombers from Japanese bases in the Celebes, in what was the Dutch East Indies. Air raids on Darwin continued until 12 November 1943. By this time the Japanese had bombed Darwin 64 times and other northern Australian towns, including Broome, Wyndham and Townsville, 34 times, in support of Japanese activities in Java and Timor.

The Japanese may not have intended to literally invade Australia, but their relentless advance through the islands in the north certainly made Australians at the time think it was a possibility. Tarakan in Borneo was taken on 12 January, Rabaul fell on 23 January, and Ambon was captured on 3 February. No respecters of any country's neutrality, the Japanese wanted Timor's airfields and invaded on 19–20 February 1942, and Timor surrendered on 23 February. (Australian commandos and the Timorese fought on for another year, the Australians waging an effective guerrilla war.) Lae and Salamaua on the north coast of New Guinea were taken on 8 March, and the Kokoda

Diorama of the Japanese invasion of Singapore, Singapore History Museum.

Above: A wartime Japanese bicycle, Kota Bharu War Museum.
Above right: The Johore Strait 1942, looking towards the Sultan of Johore's palace from the Australian position.

Track campaign began on 21 July. General MacArthur had left the Philippines on 11 March, vowing to return, and the Americans surrendered on 3 April.

More than 22,000 Australians were prisoners of the Japanese by early April 1942 – mostly the 17,000 men of the 8th Division in Singapore, but also 3000 7th Division men who had been sent to Java on the way back from the Middle East. Others were soldiers who had been captured or surrendered in Ambon and Timor, or nurses whose ship had been sunk while trying to escape from Singapore and survived the Japanese massacre, or sailors such as Ray Parkin, who was on HMAS *Perth* sunk on 1 March in the Battle of the Sunda Strait.

In Singapore, the Australians (and British) were concentrated at the POW camp at Changi, where they had to organise themselves and provide working parties for the Japanese around Singapore. Compared to what was to come later in Burma and Thailand, Changi at this time was a relatively benign experience.

Aside from invading South-East Asia, the Philippines and New Guinea, the Japanese had designs on India. A plan was formulated to invade India in the dry season of 1943–1944, via Burma. The problem for Japan was supplying the vast force which would be required. Supply by sea was subject to attack by submarines and aircraft, so it was decided to build a 415-kilometre train track from Thailand to Burma across country that had previously been thought impossible. It was to be built in fourteen months, starting in June 1942 simultaneously from existing track at Thanbyuzayat in Burma and Ban Pong in Thailand, joining near the border at Konkoita, near Three Pagodas Pass.

More than 60,000 POWs were transported to the railway project during 1942 and 1943. The conditions for everyone working on the railway – Australian, British, Dutch, *romusha* (Burmese conscripts) or starving Malay 'volunteers' – were appalling. Disease, starvation

PILGRIMAGE

A life for every sleeper: The Thai–Burma Railway today.

rations, overwork, poor or no accommodation or sanitation, and the individual brutality of Japanese and Korean engineers and guards took their inevitable toll. Some 2646 Australians died of disease, starvation, or were killed by the Japanese and Korean guards.

Thousands of other Australian and British prisoners were sent to Borneo to build an airfield at Sandakan, and there suffered even more than those on the railway.

The Thai and Burmese sections of line were joined near Konkoita in October 1943, after just sixteen months – a remarkable engineering feat – and POWs were transferred from remote jungle camps to base camps and hospitals. Some, after recovery, formed new work parties destined for Japan, others returned to Singapore. The majority of the Asian labourers remained in the jungle camps to operate the railway and undertake maintenance work. Over 13,000 POWs taken by the Japanese perished between late 1942 and late 1945. The numbers of Asian labourers who died is harder to calculate; around 100,000 is a likely figure.

In 1943, the area for Australian service by militia units was named the South-West Pacific Zone – which included New Guinea, southern Borneo, eastern Java and Timor. The larger South-West Pacific Area, which included all of Borneo and the Philippines, but not peninsular Malaya or Thailand, was the overall area of operations of General Douglas MacArthur's Allied command. The AIF divisions were composed of volunteers from the militia, and new recruits. Though there was conflict between the AIF volunteers and the so-called 'chockos', ('chocolate soldiers' who melt in the sun) or 'koalas' (not to be exported or shot) of the militia, some 200,000 of them volunteered for the AIF, and militia battalions, such as the 39th, were the equal of the AIF on the Kokoda Track.

Australian forces were occupied through 1943 and 1944 in grinding the Japanese in New Guinea, while the Americans 'island hopped' their way to the Philippines. Supreme commander in the South-West Pacific, General MacArthur, had fulfilled his promise to return to the

Mt Kinabalu towers over Ranau, final destination of those on the Sandakan death marches.

Philippines, landing at Luzon in January and Mindanao [in] 1944. Australian forces were not wanted or required for t[he opera]tions in the Philippines, but there was a need for an Austr[alian role,] both military and political – elsewhere in the region, in or[der to defeat] Japan, and Australia wanted a place at the postwar settlement in the Malay and Dutch East Indies.

MacArthur began planning operations in Borneo in 1944, and these commenced in 1945. The idea was to take the oil-rich island of Tarakan in the Dutch north-west of Borneo, Labuan and Brunei in the north-east, and oil town Balikpapan in the south-west, which would provide bases for an invasion of Java and the restoration of Dutch control, while depriving the Japanese of oil. In addition, it was hoped that the POWs held in atrocious conditions at Sandakan in British North Borneo (now Sabah) might be liberated.

Tragically, this never happened. Instead, beginning in January 1945, the 2434 surviving POWs at Sandakan, almost three-quarters of them Australians, were force-marched 360 kilometres to Ranau. Except for six Australians, all died on the track, or were executed by the Japanese – the last after the Japanese had surrendered.

Japan had wanted to transform the countries of South-East Asia into the self-serving Greater East Asian Co-Prosperity Sphere by military means – direct conquest in Indonesia, Burma, Malaya and Singapore, or military pressure in Thailand and Vietnam. False promises of independence were given until Emperor Hirohito said in his surrender speech that the military situation was not necessarily to the Japanese advantage. It is a cliché to note that the Japanese economic aims have been achieved by other means – postwar independence and the rise of the Asian 'tiger' economies have seen to that.

Australia's role, paid in blood in Borneo, was supposedly to have a seat at the table in the postwar carve-up. This did not occur, except in Papua and New Guinea. Britain more or less willingly gave up everywhere east of Suez. The Dutch, unwillingly, had to be ejected from Indonesia, while Australia cheered from the sidelines. Other wars were fought in the 1960s in Malaysia and Indonesia involving Australia forces, and of course in Timor in 1999. But Thailand, Borneo, Singapore, Indonesia and soon Timor-Leste became part of Australia's travel consciousness – we land at the airport at Changi for some shopping, perhaps visit the Bridge over the River 'Kwai', and maybe travel to Sandakan to visit the orangutans, with barely a memory of what happened at these places 60 years ago.

Somewhere in Malaya: Australians push through the jungle in early 1942.

The Australians in South-East Asia

Syonon Tu: Malaya and Singapore, December 1941 – February 1942

By 10 January 1942, the Australian 8th Division had been split – 22 Brigade becoming part of Eastforce under the command of III Indian Corps, and 27 Brigade part of Westforce under the Australian General Gordon Bennett – with Westforce defending the main road from Kuala Lumpur to Singapore, where the Japanese were expected to attack. Westforce was made up of 2/15th Field Regiment with 25-pounder guns, 2/26th, 2/29th, 2/30th battalions, and some anti-tank gunners. In addition there was the 45 Indian Division defending the coast road at Muar. Lieutenant General Arthur Percival, the Allied

The Changi Chapel in 1999 before it was reconstructed at the new Changi Museum.

theatre commander, told Bennett that if his position was lost, Singapore was lost.

On 13 January, the Australians of the 2/30th with gunners of the 2/15th Field Regiment and the anti-tank gunners set up the first of the engagements with the Japanese that would hold up their advance on Singapore. At the Gemenceh River, ten kilometres west of Gemas on the main road to Malacca, was an ideal spot to ambush the overconfident enemy. The plan was for the Indians to disengage and quickly pass through the Australians, who were waiting at the river and a few hundred metres back at a roadblock in a four-metre-high road cutting. The Japanese would ride through on their bikes, after which the bridge was to be blown up leaving them trapped in a killing zone between the river and the roadblock in the cutting. Any enemy on the other side of the river would be attacked by artillery fire after the bridge was blown.

The ambush worked well. On the afternoon of 14 January, the Japanese rode arm-in-arm unconcernedly across the bridge, helmets and guns strapped to their bikes, into the trap. About seven or eight hundred Japanese were allowed through before the bridge was blown up, and they were then attacked with everything the Australians had before withdrawing to the roadblock. But only six hours later the bridge had been repaired by the Japanese, and on 15 February they attacked the roadblock with tanks. These were destroyed or disabled in a terrific fight, with the artillery firing over open sights. The Australians withdrew that night to the main battalion position at Gemas. The 2/30th lost seventeen killed and 55 wounded, and nine missing. The 25-pounders had one killed and one wounded, and lost three of their guns.

Meanwhile the Japanese were advancing down the coast, forcing the Indians back from Muar on the road to Bakri. Here the 2/29th Bat-

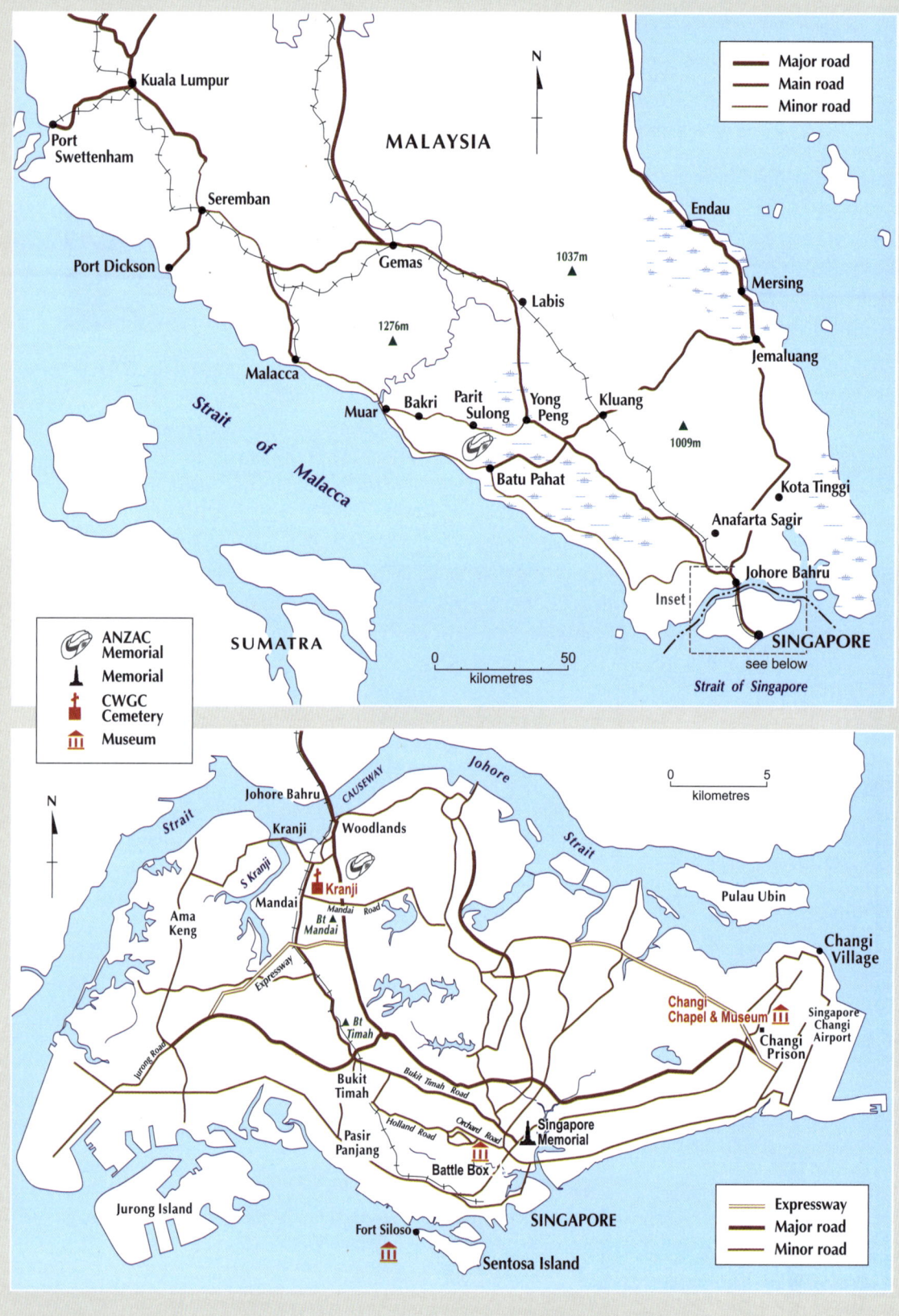

Opposite: Map of Malaysia and Singapore.

Right: The Gemenceh River, scene of the successful ambush on 14 January 1942.

talion fought off the Japanese, and Lieutenant Colonel Charles Anderson, commanding the 2/19th Battalion which had been sent to help out from Eastforce, won a VC for outstanding brave work over four days, 18–22 January. Anderson and his small force destroyed ten tanks, fought their way out of several encirclements and ambushes, and personally attacked the Japanese holding a bridge, destroying several guns. Eventually caught in an indefensible position between the approaching Imperial Guards Division commanded by General Nishimura and another unit holding the bridge at Parit Sulong, Anderson and his men were ordered to evacuate and find their way back as best they could.

Withdrawing through a swamp, only 500 Australians and 400 Indians from the 4000 originally in the force made it back to Singapore. They were forced to leave about 150 badly wounded comrades behind – all but two of whom were massacred at Parit Sulong, in one of the most odious acts of the Japanese in Malaya and Singapore.

Two Australians escaped the massacre. One of them was Lieutenant Ben Hackney. Hackney's evidence, buried in a shell case at Changi, eventually hanged Nishimura on 11 June 1951. The War Crimes Tribunal held after the war sentenced Nishimura to life imprisonment for the *Sook Ching* massacres of the Chinese in Singapore, but ultimately he was hanged for what he ordered at Parit Sulong.

After the Gemenceh River ambush, and the battles at Muar and Bakri, the Australians fought back to Singapore, and were stationed thinly on the north-east of the island, facing the Japanese across the narrow Strait of Singapore. With no air cover, inept leadership, and difficulty getting the heavy artillery at Changi and Fort Siloso on Sentosa Island to fire in the direction of the invasion, they and the other

100,000 defenders had no hope, especially after losing control of water and fuel supplies.

Rather than use a fresh British division, Percival had placed the battered and barely half-strength Australian 8th Division in the north-west of Singapore island, the most likely place for an invasion. Both Australian brigades were forward, spread over a wide front. After a heavy bombardment, the Japanese sent thirteen battalions over the narrow strait, beginning at 10.30 p.m. on 8 February 1942, against the Australian 22nd Brigade of three battalions. The Australians inflicted many casualties, but were forced back. Another Japanese division came across the Causeway and attacked the 27th Brigade in the Kranji area. The next night, Percival failed to commit reserves where they were needed, and the Australian General Bennett made a number of tactical blunders. With water and all but one airfield in Japanese hands, the last defending aircraft were evacuated on 11 February, and Percival surrendered Singapore on 15 February.

Australians comprised just 14 per cent of the ground forces defending Singapore, but were 73 per cent of those killed in action. Some 18,500 Australians were killed, wounded or among the 130,000 made POWs. For those survivors, the worst was yet to come. One-third were to die.

Above left: An artillery piece at Fort Siloso on Sentosa: in 1942 the guns were pointing the wrong way.
Above: Kranji War Cemetery, Singapore.

Changi

In 1941 Changi was a pretty little village on the Singapore coast, and gave its name to the area around it. Australians had camped in the area in the months before the Japanese invasion of Malaya.

There was a large garrison complex nearby, Selarang Barracks, an airy three-storey-high verandah-enclosed compound with a large parade ground, which had been occupied during the 1930s by British units such as Gordon Highlanders. The Royal Artillery were lodged in nearby Roberts Barracks, and the Royal Engineers in Kitchener Barracks.

The Changi area had been established as a military base by the British in the 1920s as part of the Singapore defences. The huge 16-inch guns from the old British battleship *Queen Elizabeth* were part of these coastal defences. In 1941 these guns were pointing west, out to sea, and guarded the battleships the *Prince of Wales* and the *Repulse* in the weeks before they sailed to their tragic rendezvous with the Japanese airforce off Kuantan, on the east coast of Malaya, in December 1941. Unfortunately, as Stan Arneil noted in *One Man's War*, the magnificent weapons couldn't be turned when it counted to face the enemy coming from the north-east.

On the fall of Singapore, over 100,000 British, Indian, Dutch and (European) Singapore civilians were made prisoner – many of them kept in separate sections of the Changi area. The Australians were under the command of their own officers, responsible for their own discipline and food. The early months, when the 'Changi University' (a system of lectures and classes given by academically trained POWs) flourished, were somewhat better than later times, when malnutrition set in.

The portrayal of the 'dreaded Changi' camp brings a smile to the faces of many former POWs, who longed for Changi as almost a heaven on earth compared to some of the dreadful places to which they were taken. It was possible to remain at Changi and rarely see a guard; 'the camp was administered by Brigadier "Black Jack" Galleghan almost as it would have been at any Australian army camp' wrote Arneil. The captured war correspondent Russell Braddon, after his experiences in Kuala Lumpur and on the Thai–Burma Railway, wrote that Changi was 'phoney captivity'. But as Dr Roy Mills, a survivor of F Force on the railway wrote, 'The description of Changi as HOME or being like HEAVEN must be seen in context. The survivors of F Force had been through HELL.'

Operation Jaywick

Z Special Unit commandos sailed the ex-Japanese fishing tender *Krait* from Exmouth, WA, to near occupied Singapore and on 26 September 1943 they paddled canoes into the harbour at Singapore and used

The *Krait* is now berthed at the Australian National Maritime Museum in Sydney.

limpet mines to sink or damage 40,000 tons of enemy shipping. This was Operation Jaywick.

The *Krait* was originally a Japanese 24-metre teak-plank copper-sheathed fishing boat named *Kofuku Maru*, working from Singapore. She was seized and interned. Bill Reynolds sailed her to Ceylon and on to Bombay, where she was renamed the *Krait*, after the deadly snake. Her next voyage was to Fremantle, where she was fitted for her secret mission. After the Singapore raid, the *Krait* was sent to Darwin to join the Lugger Maintenance Patrol of the famous Z Special Unit. At the end of the Second World War she was taken over by the occupation authorities at Labuan Island off British North Borneo and sold to a local trading company which for the next twenty years used her to haul timber down the jungle rivers of Borneo.

Acquired from postwar owners in Borneo in the 1960s, the *Krait* was operated by the Royal Volunteer Coastal Patrol for many years. The vessel is now on loan from the Australian War Memorial and is berthed at the Australian National Maritime Museum in Darling Harbour, Sydney. A memorial plaque was placed by the Australian *Krait* Committee at the World Trade Centre Singapore on 28 September 2003.

Sparrow Force: Timor, December 1941–December 1942

When the Japanese invaded northern Malaya in an assault hours before the attack on Pearl Harbor, and the Second World War broke

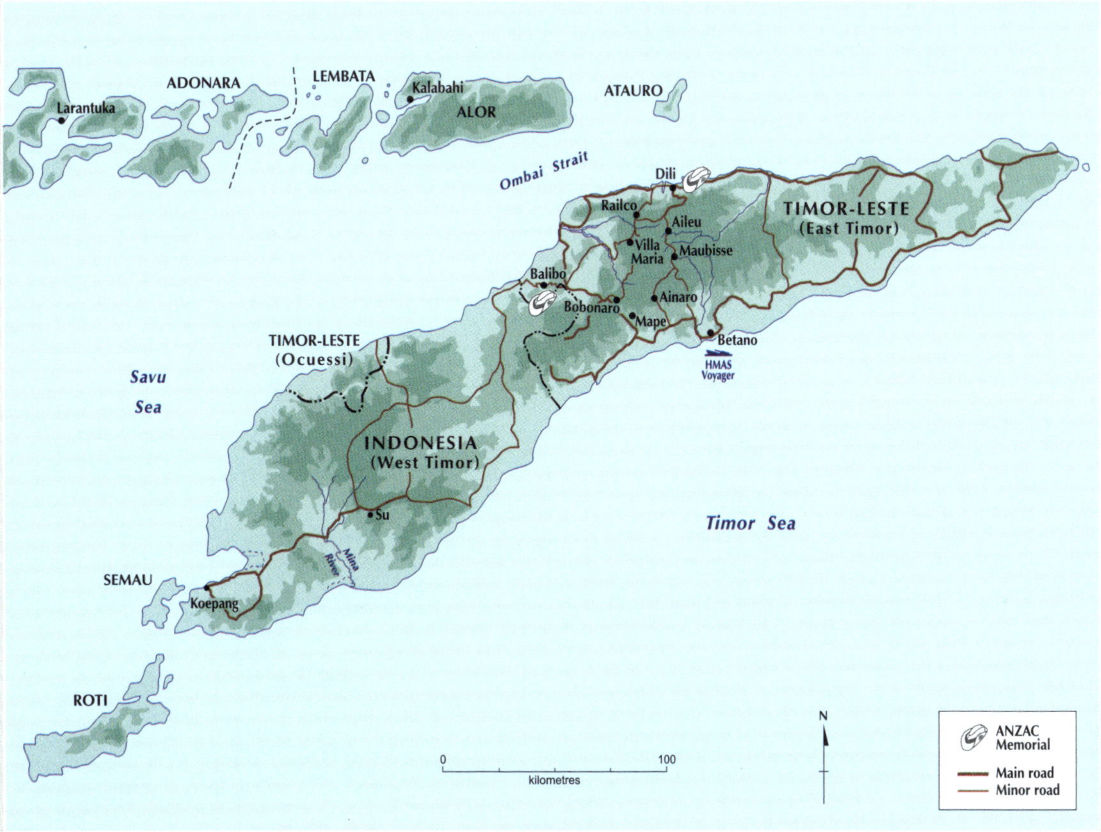

South-East Asia

Above: Map of East Timor.

'My *creado* Patricio was very slim and fairly tall for a Timorese. He would have been about nineteen years of age. I went to Mass in Ainaro for Easter Sunday, 1942. The beautiful Gregorian chant of the natives' singing was wonderful and when I came down from the church, Patricio and a mate were there and they said in Tetun that they wanted to join the Australians. I had no money at all. All I could do was give him a feed when we got down to where our mates were, but he stayed with me.'
John 'Paddy' Kenneally, 2/2nd Independent Company

'Each of us had his *creado*. They carried our packs so we were free with our guns, and without them we just couldn't have fought like we did.'
Lance Bomford, 2/40th Battalion

From Michele Turner, *Telling East Timor: Personal Testimonies 1942–1992* out in South-East Asia, Timor was one of the thousands of islands sheltering behind Fortress Singapore, but to Australians, if they thought of it at all, Timor was an airfield on the way to Europe, with a Qantas office and an Australian consul.

In 1941, before the outbreak of war with Japan, plans had been made for an Australian military presence in Dutch (West) Timor; Portuguese (East) Timor was officially neutral territory. Australians were also dispatched to Ambon, a strategic airfield on an island to the north of Timor in the Halamaheras, and to Rabaul, on New Britain, an administrative centre of New Guinea. The small forces were named after small birds: Sparrow Force (2/40th Battalion and 2/2nd Independent Company, a specially trained commando force) went to Timor, on 12 December 1941; Gull Force (2/21st Battalion) to Ambon on 17 December; and Lark Force (2/22nd Battalion) to Rabaul, in April 1941.

The Japanese wanted neutral Timor's airfields. They invaded in overwhelming force on the night of 19–20 February 1942, near Kupang in the west, and near Dili in the east. The 2/40th at Kupang surrendered after a brave three-day fight; the 2/2nd at Dili withdrew into the interior after inflicting significant damage on the enemy.

Although Portuguese authorities had protested at the arrival of Australian and Dutch forces in East Timor before the Japanese came, the protests were made redundant by the invasion. (Some claim there would not have been an invasion if the Australians had not been there – the 2004 *Lonely Planet* guide to East Timor says the Australian presence 'inevitably drew the region into the conflict' – but the Japanese always wanted the airfield and port at Dili, and the Australian defenders cannot be blamed for the subsequent brutal Japanese behaviour towards the Timorese people.)

Far left: Australians in 1999 patrolling the same places as their grandfathers did in 1942.
Left: Surveying the countryside near Maubisse.

Above: Near Ainaro today.
Above right: Australians re-enact radio contact with Australia for Damien Parer. (AWM 13764)

Sparrow Force, initially commanded by Lieutenant Colonel William Leggatt, was sent to provide a token defence of Timor in what was then thought of as the unlikely event of Japanese invasion. The small force arrived at Kupang in Dutch (West) Timor on 12 December 1941, five days after the Japanese invasion of Malaya. The total of 70 officers and 1330 men of the 2/40th Battalion and the Australian 2/2nd Independent Company had little artillery or air support. However spirited their efforts, there was not much hope of them defending a large island against serious invasion.

The Dutch had an even smaller number of defenders – 500 – in Kupang. The neutral Portuguese, for their part, had 150 troops in their part of Timor and an intact administration. If East Timor were invaded, the Portuguese expected they would ask for Australian and Dutch assistance.

After the Japanese capture of Ambon on 3 February 1942, Timor was next on the list – the airfields were useful staging posts between Singapore, which had surrendered on 15 February, and Darwin, which would be first bombed on 19 February.

It was clear that Sparrow Force should be expanded, and Brigadier W C D Veale was sent to take overall command of the force. Unfortunately, most reinforcements were prevented from arriving by the Japanese invasion, on 20 February.

Two companies of the Australian 2/40th Battalion were used to defend Kupang in the west, with the Dutch. Two companies were to be used as a mobile reserve. The 2/2nd, about 250 officers and men, had been 'pre-deployed' to defend Dili airport, to the official annoyance of the Portuguese.

Kupang was defended by the 2/40th, which exacted a heavy toll on the Japanese, in particular Japanese paratroops at the airport. But the small and divided force could not withstand the superior numbers and firepower of the invaders – which included not only aircraft but also tanks. Communications between Veale and Leggatt, who was with the 2/40th, were difficult. Leggatt's Australians were eventually driven back from Kupang, and cut off from food and ammunition supplies, and he had to surrender on 23 February. Some 250 of the force's headquarters troops then moved with Veale into East Timor, hoping to make contact with the 2/2nd.

The Japanese attack on the airfield at Dili began on the night of 19 February 1942. They faced a tiny force of the Australian 2/2nd Independent Company, which inflicted significant casualties on the Japanese marching from their unopposed landing in Dili harbour towards the airport, some kilometres outside Dili. Communications between

The Australian 2/2ndCommando Squadron Memorial (originally the 2/2nd Independent Company) is located in King's Park, Perth WA, in Forrest Drive. A rough-cut granite memorial cairn incorporates a memorial bronze plaque with the names of the 52 members of the 2/2nd who lost their lives in Timor, New Britain and New Guinea during the Second World War. Individual plaques line the roadway, each with its own tree. The memorial was erected in 1973.

the section holding the airport and Captain (later Major) Bernard Callinan in Dili and with Veale in Kupang were very difficult.

Lance Corporal Cyril Doyle famously rode a bike from the airport to Dili through the Japanese lines to let Callinan know the state of play. The Official History quotes Corporal S A Robinson explaining how 'the sight of a dashing Australian riding a push bicycle hell for leather through their lines must have amazed the Japanese to such an extent that they did not open up.' Doyle told Callinan that the Bren gun had been knocked out, and the airfield was being held by just a section of soldiers. He then volunteered to go back with a return message, but this time he wasn't so lucky. The Japanese knocked out the bike from under him, forcing him 'to leave his vehicle at top speed, to land on his feet, and crouching low disappear along the side of the

2/2nd Independent Company Honour Roll, King's Park, Perth.

road'. (Doyle was killed in action with the 2/2nd in New Guinea on 29 September 1943, and is buried at the Lae War Cemetery.)

Communication between the scattered groups of the 2/2nd was sparse on the day following the Japanese landing. Some groups had seen or heard the action at the airport, or the shelling of Dili, and had been in action. Others were unaware that anything was going on at all, and left their positions for Dili for a look around or to pick up supplies.

Lieutenant Archie Campbell, with some of 7 Section, was patrolling at Tibar, a few kilometres to the west of Dili, and spotted the Japanese warship shelling the town and the enemy in the village. He sent word to the rest of his comrades at their base in the hills at Three Spurs advising of the situation, but the messenger arrived after sixteen men left on a truck to get rations from Dili. Most of them were from Campbell's section. They were captured by the Japanese outside Tibar; and all but one had their hands tied behind their backs before being shot. All appeared, mercifully, to have died quickly, except for Keith Hayes, who had a bullet in the neck. Hayes revived and moved, prompting the Japanese to bayonet the men again.

But Hayes did not die. The Japanese had looted the bodies, and had needed to free Hayes' hands to get at his watch. Later, he was able to crawl out of the ditch; under the care of the Timorese, he survived, and after evacuation from Timor he went on to fight again in New Guinea. 'The boys on the ration truck' were apparently incinerated – they are commemorated at the Northern Territory Memorial. The remaining soldier, Private Peter Alexander, was taken away for interrogation, which he survived as he did the Thai–Burma Railway.

Small parties of the 2/2nd staged a sabotaging, fighting, ambushing withdrawal into the interior. By 7 March, all surviving members of the 2/2nd had gathered inland from Dili at a place called Hatu Lia. As a formed unit, in high spirits with relatively few casualties, they spurned a Japanese call to surrender. The Japanese had not yet ventured in strength into the rugged and twisted Timor interior, but this was just what the 2/2nd had trained for, and they would fight on.

The commandos' headquarters was near Mape, about 50 kilometres as the crow flies south-west of Dili, protected by the crumpled terrain and the Timorese people. Platoons patrolled vigorously from the villages on the same line 50 kilometres from Dili – Ainaro, Same, Bobonaro, Maliana – relying on their *creados*, or Timorese mates, and the small sturdy Timorese ponies.

On 20 April a radio – called Winnie the War Winner – had been improvised and contact made with Darwin, which the Australians were relieved to hear had not been invaded, despite being bombed. This 'masterpiece of improvisation' was built in a kero tin, with stolen batteries, on a picturesque mountain ridge (it can now be seen at the Australian War Memorial).

In July, the Japanese began sending stronger forces to the interior to try and track the Australians, threatening the Timorese into betraying their positions. The 2/2nd was reinforced by the 2/4th Independent Company, which arrived on 23 September at Betano on the south coast of Timor aboard HMAS *Voyager*. Betano is an exposed anchorage with reefs and strong currents, but with deep water close to the shore. Unfortunately, *Voyager* swung on her anchor, and could not use her engines to move, as this would have endangered the troops disembarking in barges. Just 23 minutes after anchoring, *Voyager*'s stern touched ground, and at noon on the next day the ship was abandoned. The officers and crew were successfully returned to Darwin on the corvettes *Warrnambool* and *Kalgoorlie*, sent from Darwin. *Voyager* was demolished – aided by Japanese air raids.

The Australian commandos formed lasting friendships with many *creados*. They helped with transport on the Timorese ponies, information and food, and many paid a penalty at the hands of the occupiers.

The 2/2nd was evacuated from Timor on 10–16 December 1942, by which time the Japanese pressure on the local population meant less information was being provided and less useful work was being done. The last Australian commandos were evacuated in January 1943. The war then passed Timor by until the final Japanese surrender. On Timor, the Japanese commander surrendered his 3235 men at a ceremony aboard HMAS *Moresby* on 11 September at Kupang. This surrender included a small number of Japanese in Portuguese Timor. Here, at least, pre-war colonial authority was retired smoothly.

Damien Parer and Winnie the War Winner

Damien Parer, the great photographer and Academy Award-winning filmmaker, was sent by the Department of Information to Timor to film the Australian resistance in November 1942. There hadn't been much good news for the Australian public that year – the successful guerrilla war in Timor was being kept secret while the commandos were still in operation – but now the story of Australian activities in Timor could be told.

Parer left on HMAS *Castlemaine* on 5 November 1942 with journalists Dixon Brown, a colossal Brit; and Bill Marian, from the ABC. They were supposed to land at Betano, but were dragged by the strong currents 50 miles to the west and had to steam back in the morning – in full view of everyone. Parer was excited by the Timorese countryside and started filming straight away, as they journeyed to the commando headquarters at Bobonaro in the mountains south-west of Dili.

Major Bernard Callinan was annoyed about his former St Kevin's schoolmate turning up – not happy that their operation was 'being turned into a fun place for journalists'. But Parer, fresh from his work with 2/5th Independent Company at Wau, soon won their trust. 'I'm just trying to get the truth ... you help me get it ...' Parer told them.

Parer had the perennial problem of obtaining film of events that had already taken place, and had to restage them. He filmed a recreation of the broadcast of the first message to Darwin over Winnie the War Winner, which had been made on 20 April 1942 by Signaller Joe Loveless. Loveless by this time had been repatriated to Australia, and Parer filmed Corporal John Sergeant, Lance Corporal John Donovan and Signaller K Richards.

Parer also filmed a re-enactment of an ambush of invisible Japanese in a Timorese village. Parer saw 'a patrol getting into position and then their speedy getaway. With this tactic they had the Jap so bamboozled that for every one man of ours killed in action, we bumped off 90 Japs.' They built and burnt a village especially for the camera.

Men of Timor was edited on Parer's return in December 1942 and shown in cinemas in January 1943. The images Parer made, of the wild and bearded Australian commandos attacking the Japanese, gave Australians a much-needed propaganda boost after the dark days of 1942 when almost nothing went right.

Parer, like other independent-minded journalists, eventually fell out with the restrictions of working for Australian organisations, and joined the American film company Paramount. He joined the American reconquest of the Philippines, and was killed filming the landing at Peleliu on 20 September 1944, aged just 32. He is buried at Ambon War Cemetery.

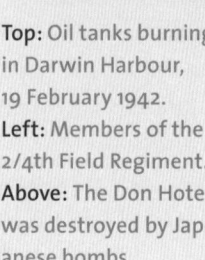

Top: Oil tanks burning in Darwin Harbour, 19 February 1942.
Left: Members of the 2/4th Field Regiment.
Above: The Don Hotel was destroyed by Japanese bombs.

'Australia's Pearl Harbor': Darwin 1942

Supposedly impregnable Singapore had just surrendered; 16,000 Australians were now POWs, many of them destined for the hell of the Thai–Burma railway; Java and Timor were about to fall. There was widespread pessimism about Australia's prospects in the war. Many believed that we were next on the list.

In 1942, Father John McGrath, mission priest on Bathurst Island north of Darwin, made two great contributions to the life of Australia, one tragically ignored, and one spectacularly successful. The success was the introduction of Australian Rules football to the Tiwi people; the tragedy was that his radioed warning of large numbers of suspicious aircraft coming from the north-west was lost, ignored or not taken seriously. The warning wouldn't have changed the course of the Japanese attack, but it might have prepared the people of Darwin for attack.

In Darwin there was a widespread belief that invasion was imminent, but there was little or no preparedness for what was about to happen, except for the coast-watchers. There was no air patrolling. Radar was not yet installed. Most women and children had been evacuated from Darwin after Pearl Harbor, but some were not evacuated far enough away. About 3000 people were left in the city.

There were 45 ships in the harbour at Darwin, including the American destroyers USS *Peary* and *William B Preston*. These ships, with the cruiser USS *Houston*, had turned back from reinforcing the Australian forces on Timor after coming under heavy attack. The convoy returned on 18 February. The *Houston* refuelled and departed Darwin that night, bound for the Java Sea and its terrible fate with HMAS *Perth*. The *Peary* had also departed but, after it spent the night chasing a Japanese submarine, returned for fuel early on 19 February.

The first Japanese attack began at about 10 o'clock that morning, when high altitude heavy bombers pattern-bombed the town and harbour for about 40 minutes. This had a devastating impact – killing many civilians and destroying the post office and telegraph station. Low-level Mitsubishi Zero fighters also bombed and strafed ships in the harbour, and the civilian and military aerodromes. An hour later the RAAF base was also bombed from high altitude for about 25 minutes. In all, twenty military aircraft were destroyed, eight ships at anchor in the harbour were sunk, and most civil and military facilities in Darwin were destroyed.

Among the soldiers who hadn't made it to Timor was 'Snow' Dicker with the 2/4th Field Regiment. He saw what happened in the harbour: 'The USS *Peary*, being a warship, was the main target, and although they had all available guns firing, they suffered a number of direct hits by the dive bombers and did not stand much of a chance against such odds, as the first bomb immobilised them. They suffered 92 casualties as a bomb went down one of their funnels and blew the ship to pieces. She still had guns firing as she went below the surface. There was plenty of heroism throughout that one-sided battle.'

Herb Kriloff was on the bridge of the *William B Preston*, a Catalina (flying boat) tender and a 'floating gas tank': 'It was a calm, windless, hot day full of sunshine. About 10 a.m. our general alarm sounded,

Anti-aircraft gun at East Cape Military Museum.

calling all hands to battle stations. Looking up, the sky was black with enemy aircraft ... Within five minutes, many ships were under attack. *Peary* detonated in an immense ball of flame which rose hundreds of feet in all directions. At this moment bombs struck the afterdeck of *Preston*. We lost steering control and one of our two propellers. We were on fire astern, concerned that we were about to make *Peary* appear as a minor blast ... Fifteen men had been killed, many more badly wounded. Bombs had broken the main deck of the ship aft, so that the ship was now in two pieces – with one piece about two metres above the other, moving up and down. Would it snap off? On the deck aft where the bombs hit, lay several men in pieces. The deck was covered in blood and human parts.'

The *Preston* made it out of the harbour, under duress, and made an epic voyage almost circumnavigating Australia from Darwin to Sydney, where she was eventually repaired.

Dudley Vose, in command of the 14th Anti-Aircraft Battery, remembered the bravery of the men rescuing their comrades from the inferno of the harbour, in which oil quickly spread because of the big tides and caught fire. There were 33 awards for bravery on that day, including the award of two Military Medals, one to John Waldie, whose civilian job had been servicing flying boats, Darwin being the main Australian landfall for services from Europe. When the *Neptuna* exploded, Waldie commandeered the tender *Halcyon*, and went into the burning harbour five times, saving over 200 lives.

'Snow' Dicker, not yet eighteen years old, had come ashore on the evening of 18 February but had returned in the morning to get his equipment. After witnessing the devastating results of the first raid on the harbour, he was back at his campsite beyond the end of the runway at the RAAF base when the second air raid – aimed at the airfield – occurred a couple of hours later: 'We were pretty close to the action, the strafing and bombing – the second raid was all high level stuff from 20,000 feet. We were quite prepared, we'd all dug slit trenches, and had rifles and machine-guns set up. But they just pleased themselves with what they did.' He remembers a couple of Zeros coming in after the bombing to strafe the runway, then heading over their position, so low that the Japanese pilot 'gave us a wave. We were very lucky.'

Ron 'Nick' Carter was a stoker on the ocean-going tug HMAS *Wato* and was on the midnight shift, in his bunk, when the raid commenced. He woke up when the *Neptuna* was hit: 'I noticed a sailor signalling with flags astern the USS *Peary* when I saw a dive bomber, which I thought was coming straight at us, veer at the last moment and attack the USS *Peary*. I actually saw the bomb leave the plane and hit the *Peary*, which split in two, the after part sinking with all hands. We went alongside the floating bow to take off the few sailors left, but they would not come off while their gun was still firing ...

'Regarding the first raid, the public down south were told that only the post office was hit and nine people killed. This was the belief for some time, even the official figure of dead and wounded was not ever believed by anybody up in Darwin. Most of us would say it was over the 1000 mark. Many bodies, assumed thrown overboard by ships, floated around the harbour for weeks ... back and forth with the tide ...' The Japanese were air raiding daily. At night, Carter worked on salvaging the sunken ships, unloading guns and jeeps.

Douglas Lockwood, for many years the Melbourne *Herald*'s correspondent in Darwin, titled his eyewitness account of these events *Australia's Pearl Harbor*.

Rex Ruwoldt of the 19th Light Horse Machine-gun Regiment

remembers what it was like under one of the 60 raids that came later: 'Sometimes you could see the bombs fall away from the bomb bays. If they were going to hit a mile or more away, you could also hear the pitch of the motors increase by about two half-tones as their load suddenly lightened, and you might hear the tearing shredding sound a bomb makes as it falls through the air. However, you don't hear a bomb or shell if you are sitting near the point of impact, because a bomb or shell travels faster than the speed of sound, and it explodes before the lesser sounds are heard.'

About half of Darwin's civilian population fled south after the raids, in what was called the 'Adelaide River Handicap'. There was looting by those who stayed behind, and a failure of leadership at the RAAF base; 278 personnel were still missing three days after the raids.

The Curtin government minimised information released about the raids, saying there were only seventeen casualties, which has allowed rumours to continue to run for 60 years about what actually happened.

Darko Hudson's Feat

Notable amongst the many gallant actions on the day the Japanese attacked Darwin was that of Gunner Wilbert Thomas 'Darko' Hudson. Gunner Hudson was stationed at what is now one of HMAS *Coonawarra*'s sports ovals in one of the posts manned by the 2nd Heavy Anti-Aircraft Battery. Each post consisted of a 3.7-inch gun surrounded by sandbags and machine-guns. Gunner Hudson ran from the shower and, when he couldn't get a good angle on the raiders from the emplacement, rested his machine-gun on a 44-gallon oil drum. But this wasn't high enough either, and he had to use a mate's shoulder. Hudson achieved a number of firsts: he shot down the first Japanese aircraft over Australia, and he was awarded the Military Medal for 'gallant and distinguished service' – the first award for bravery on Australian soil.

Hudson was badly burned in another air raid, on 16 June, when the oil tanks at Stokes Hill were bombed. On this raid Gunner Ray Fogarty, 23, from Cronulla, was killed and a number of others aside from Hudson were wounded. Sergeant Tom Fraser and Bombardier Fred Wombere were awarded the Military Medal, and Lieutenant Don Brown was awarded the MBE for courage and devotion to duty during the air raid.

A Life for Every Sleeper: The Thai–Burma Railway, 1942–1945

Work on the Burmese end of the Thai–Burma Railway began on 1 October 1942. Some of the men had already spent months labouring elsewhere in Burma, others were brought up packed in 'hellships' from Singapore, Sumatra and Java. They were concentrated at Thanbyuzayat on the coast of southern Burma, which became a POW administration headquarters and base camp in September 1942, with a base hospital organised in January 1943. By that time there were 5000 Australians in Burma, with many more thousands of British, Dutch and some Americans.

The Thanbyuzayat camp was deliberately located by the Japanese near the rail yards and marshalling area, and was bombed three times by Allied aeroplanes between March and June 1943, killing a number of POWs, and leading to the evacuation of the camp. Prisoners were then marched to a number of smaller camps along the line, although Thanbyuzayat continued to be used as a reception centre for the groups of prisoners arriving at frequent intervals to reinforce the parties working on the line. It seems that there was a certain amount of deliberate carelessness, perhaps sabotage, in the building of the track.

Journalist Rohan Rivett, author of *Behind Bamboo*, rode the railway in 1943, on his way from Thanbyuzayat to the infamous 105 kilo camp, just short of Three Pagodas Pass. By the end of the trip, most of his group had decided they would prefer to walk: 'The ballast had been laid only at intervals, and the sleepers were all over the place. The train seemed to bounce from rail to rail, and at corners there was a lurching and a groaning which was ominous in the extreme. But

Cholera Camp, Konyu, Thai–Burma Railway, 1943. (Ray Wheeler, 1943)

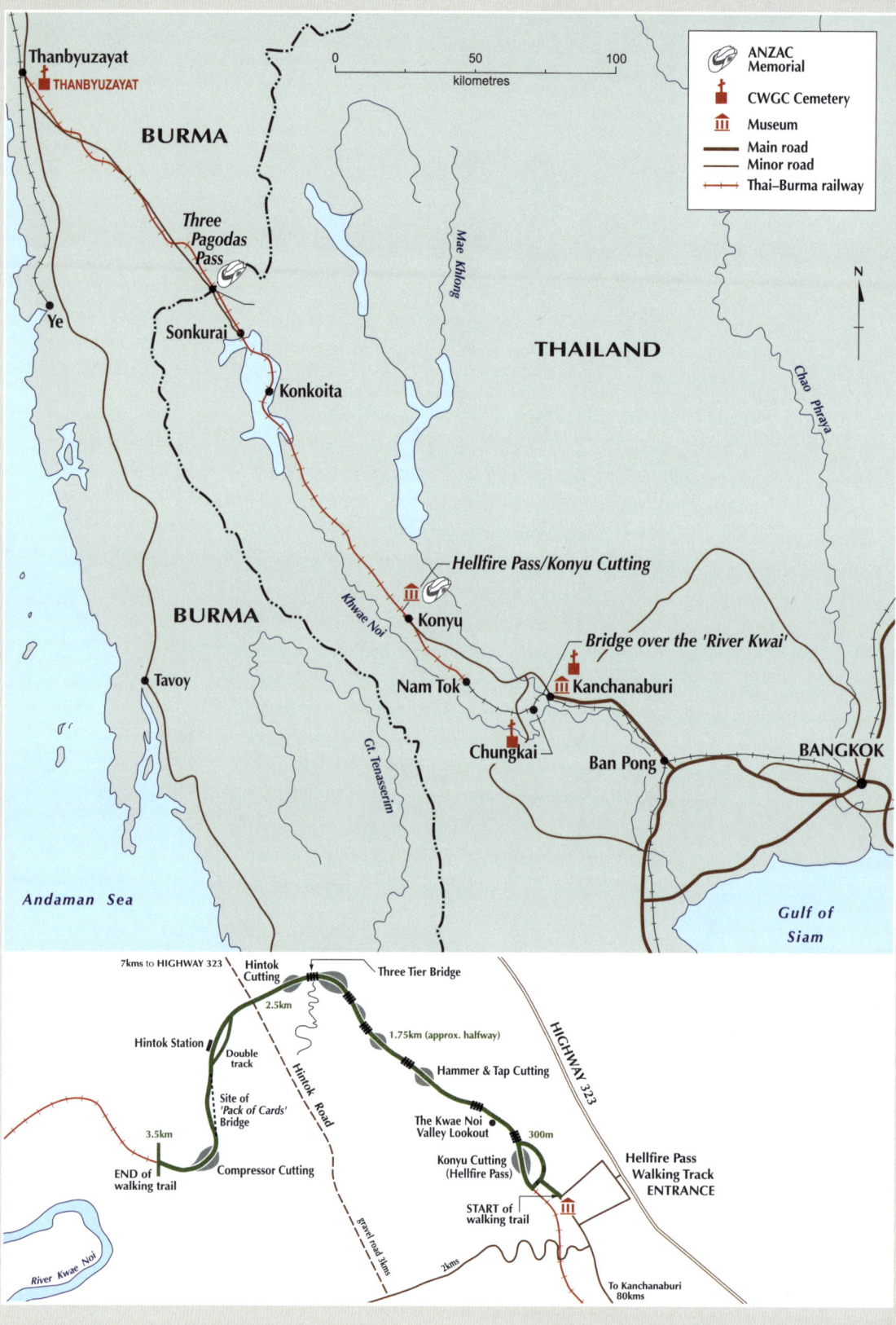

Opposite: Map of Thai–Burma Railway and Hellfire Pass Walking Track.

the real fun came at the bridges, 40 to 60 feet above the swollen rivers swirling through the shaky piles below ... There was much evidence of the haste and the carelessness with which the buttresses and embankments leading from the bridges had been constructed.'

On the Thai side, several groups of prisoners were sent from Singapore and Java to Ban Pong between January and June 1943. Weary Dunlop led 1788 men from Java to Changi and then on to the section of the railway around Konyu, or Hellfire Pass, as it was to become known. They went up by rail crammed into enclosed rice wagons, and then had to march, sometimes hundreds of kilometres, to start work. The 7000-strong F Force, which included over 3500 Australians, marched 300 kilometres to the Burmese border in sixteen nights. Many died on the way.

Work began immediately from the jungle camps – only rarely was there time allowed to build shelter or latrines. Illness, disease, including cholera, and malnutrition were compounded by the savagery of the guards – mostly Korean. Everyone was beaten, even doctors such as Weary Dunlop.

Australian camps were better organised and more hygienic than other camps, partly because of the leadership of officers like Weary Dunlop, and partly because of the adaptability, ingenuity and mateship of the Australian soldiers. They realised they had to stick together and support one another if any of them were to survive.

By mid-1943 there were about 8000 Australians working on the Thai section of the railway. They were working in dozens of camps on different sections of the railway, clearing trees, building embankments and bridges, trying to survive.

Some of the most impressive work was achieved around Hellfire Pass, where men from the Hintok camp, including writer Ray Parkin, dug cuttings and made the seven-metre embankment that is still impressive today.

The work was arduous, with few tools. Compressor Cutting, so called because of the more-frequent use of mechanical drills, is just past the site of the wooden 'Pack of Cards' bridge, so named because it fell down six times, killing 31 men. Twenty-nine men were also beaten to death during its construction in June 1943. It was built while the dry stone embankment was being built, itself a marvel of stone construction. The Pack of Cards is often pictured – a tall assemblage of three tiers of wood, propped up by long poles. All that remains today is a bundle of wire, and a rotting scrap of wood from one of the props.

The holes for the explosive charges were made by the rock drills by the method called 'hammer and tap'. One man had a long drill, his mate had an eight-pound hammer, which was banged directly into the rock. As the hole was deepened the man holding the drill lifted and turned it, and every so often the dust at the bottom had to be scooped out. Some of these holes had to be a metre or a metre-and-a-half deep. The hammer whistled close to the head of the man as well as the head of the drill. This was arduous and dangerous work for men on starvation rations, often sick with dysentery or coming down with something worse. Tropical ulcers were very bad, growing from cuts and gashes caused by the rock or from being slashed on bare feet (hardly anyone had boots) by spiky bamboo.

Not everyone shared Ray Parkin's philosophical attitude, but it was one that kept him alive. He wrote in his diary at the Hintok camp: 'We were hot, weak and hungry, and feeling a little sorry for ourselves. So, it was easy to fall into a mood of homesick loneliness – here in this inhospitable city of ants, millipedes, centipedes, scorpions, bees, wasps, butterflies, dinning cicadas and grasshoppers, in

which man is completely dispensable. At times like that you get a feeling in complete contrast to that of singleness with nature, and to the feeling of beauty that comes with it: the feeling that this life of the bush is in everyone and everything, which seems to be a guarantee that this life of arduous stumbling, of harassed thinking and inevitable doubting, of honest trying, is something worthwhile.'

Above left: 'A fine view over the Kwae Noi'.
Above: 'This life of the bush is in everything.' – Ray Parkin.

During the infamous 'speedo' period, July to October 1943, the desperation of the Japanese engineers to finish construction on time meant that many men were forced to do grinding manual labour around the clock – 62 hours work out of 72 appears to be the record.

At Hellfire Pass alone, 63 men were beaten to death and hundreds

'Out with the surveyors again over the rugged rock slides where we drove the last peg at the 156 kilometre 320 metre mark. From this peg we had a fine view of the Kwai Noi winding away in the distance below ... the top of the jungle was a sea of new leaf-green and the mauve-pink of bare branches. The near hills showed vertical rock slashes and jagged ridges: in the distance the blue mountains rolled away to the horizon.'
—Ray Parkin, *Into the Smother*

died from disease, including a first outbreak of cholera. The death rate on the railway reached its peak during this time.

As an example of the Japanese attitude to POWs, which allowed them to be harshly neglected and worked to death, Dr Roy Mills, a survivor of F Force on the railway, noted that medical officers who had to attend different parts of the camp were made to wear an armband which stated: 'One who has been captured in battle and is to be beheaded or castrated at the Emperor's will.'

After the railway was completed, with the line joined near Konkoita, the majority of the Asian labourers remained in the jungle camps to operate and maintain the railway under Japanese command, and from time to time POW work parties were taken back onto the line to carry out maintenance work and cut wood to fuel the locomotives. An average of six trains per day operated for the life of the line, well below original Japanese expectations but still a major contribution to their strength on the Burmese front.

Among the POWs who worked on maintenance after the railway was completed was Private John Durkin, who was still there in 1945. A mate, Tom Morris, told his story: 'One day he went out to work and collapsed. The next day he was sent out again, assisted by his mates. On the third day he lagged behind the work party, and when they arrived at the line he was missing. The next day the Japanese told the group that Durkin must be wandering somewhere in the jungle, and that they wanted to find him so he could be helped. Several days later Durkin was brought back – with a rope around his neck held by a Japanese guard, who was hitting him with a rifle butt.' Durkin was then kept for three weeks tied to a post, fed only rice and water, and often beaten, after which he was taken away by a few Japanese, armed with rifles and bayonets, who returned without him.

'A burial party of prisoners found a newly dug grave shortly afterwards. The Japanese returned his clothes saying they were no longer needed.'

The date of death on Private Durkin's headstone in Thanbyuzayat War Cemetery is 14 August 1945, the day Japan agreed to surrender.

Weary Dunlop

Lieutenant Colonel Edward 'Weary' Dunlop, a surgeon who had served in Greece, Crete and the Middle East before landing in Java in early 1942, where he commanded No. 1 General Hospital, was made a prisoner in April. He was just one of the determined, inventive and compassionate doctors on the Thai–Burma Railway, but came to embody, like Simpson and the donkey in the First World War, all the selflessness, sacrifice, endurance and mateship of his fellows.

After the war, Weary fought hard for the rights of the ex-POWs, and was a leader in the slow-healing relationship with the Japanese people. He made friends with Laurens Van Der Post in the POW camp in Java, and like him was an advocate of forgiveness. Without forgiveness, in Van Der Post's words, one 'became once again a member of the chain-gang of mere cause and effect from which life has laboured so long and painfully to escape'.

Weary Dunlop by Peter Corlett, King's Domain, Melbourne.

Opposite: Map of Borneo.

'The unnecessary war': Borneo, 1945

In July 1942 the first of 2434 POWs (including 1787 Australians, 641 British) were transported from Singapore to Sandakan, Borneo, to build an airfield.

For the next two years, conditions were comparable to working for the Japanese elsewhere in the region: brutality, illness, starvation. Punishment was worst for those such as Captain Lionel Matthews, who was betrayed from outside the camp in July 1943, and local people who helped with preparations for an uprising for when the Allies eventually landed. Matthews had been organising a clandestine radio, medical supplies, and an escape network. He was tortured but revealed nothing, and he was executed on 2 March 1944. (Matthews was posthumously awarded the George Cross, as well as a posthumous MC for his bravery at Gemas, before the fall of Singapore.)

In mid-1944, however, rations at Sandakan were further cut and particularly vicious guards arrived from Formosa; conditions

South-East Asia

The last prisoners at the Sandakan prisoner of war camp were too sick to be sent on the 260-kilometre marches to Ranau. After the camp was burned down at the end of May 1945, they were left to starve to death. The few who survived until August were murdered some two weeks after the Japanese surrender in 1945. Today their remains, known and unknown, are remembered at Labuan War Cemetery on the other side of Borneo. At Sandakan there is the Australian Memorial Park, and memories.

Above: Sepinggang Airstrip, Balikpapan. (Mick Sheehan, 1945)
Right: Balikpapan landing beach. (Mick Sheehan, 1945)

deteriorated rapidly. Torture became normal, with starving and ill men crammed into an open-air cage without food or water for days at a time.

General Douglas MacArthur, in charge of Allied operations in the region, had begun planning operations on Borneo aimed at removing Japanese control and access to oil, as well as freeing the POWs. These, at least, were the stated aims – many people from Prime Minister John Curtin and General Thomas Blamey downwards had misgivings about the strategy and its necessity when elsewhere in the region the Japanese were contained and isolated, and allowed to wither on the vine.

The operations were code-named OBOE: OBOE 1 at Tarakan; OBOE 6 at Brunei Bay/Labuan and OBOE 2 at Balikpapan. (Other OBOE operations, including OBOE 4 in Java, were not carried out.)

The Australian 9th Division's 26th Brigade was a vastly experienced formation, having fought at El Alamein and in New Guinea, commanded throughout by Brigadier David Whitehead. For the amphibious landing at Tarakan the 26th Brigade was expanded with additional services, in particular engineers and artillery. The landing on 1 May by the 2/23rd and 2/48th battalions was not opposed – the 2100 Japanese were holed up in bunkers in the low hills behind the town. At the end of the first day a two-kilometre-wide front had been established.

The Japanese fought with their usual suicidal tenacity, and had to be winkled out by bombing with napalm, artillery fire and assault with infantry using flame throwers. The airfield was captured on 5 May, but the last major objective was not secured until 20 June. Australian hero Tom 'Diver' Derrick VC was mortally wounded in the capture of a small knoll known as Freda, and died on 24 May. The airfield, which had been intended for use in support of the other OBOE operations, was found to be unusable. Australian casualties were 225 killed, and 669 wounded.

Next operation was codenamed OBOE 6 and involved the 9th Division, commanded by Major General Wootten with 20th Brigade (Brigadier Victor Windeyer) initially capturing the Brunei township area, and the 24th Brigade (commanded by Kokoda veteran Brigadier Selwyn 'Bill' Porter) captured the island of Labuan. Large naval and air forces were also involved. The landings occurred on 10 June, while the rest of the 9th Division was still mopping up on Tarakan. Brunei was in Australian hands on 13 June, as was Labuan, after some stiff resistance, a few days later. Australian casualties were 114 killed and 221 wounded.

Balikpapan, OBOE 2, saw the Australian 7th Division, expanded with additional arms and totalling some 33,000 men, perform the last major Allied land action of the Second World War. The landing on 1 July 1945 was widely regarded as even more unnecessary than the other Borneo operations. After a massive bombardment, and work clearing the beach defences, the 18th and 21st brigades landed, and by nightfall, a two-kilometre front had been gained. A week later, despite the Japanese use of booby traps and the necessity to clear over 100 tunnels, the airstrips were in Australian hands, and progress towards capturing the oil installations was proceeding. Skirmishing in the scrub continued until the final Japanese surrender in August, though most was completed by the end of July. It was victory at a cost: 229 Australians were killed or died of wounds and 634 were wounded; 1783 Japanese bodies were counted.

At Sandakan, work on the Japanese airfield had stopped by January 1945, mainly as a result of Allied air raids. In January the rice ration ceased, and prisoners were only allowed 70 grams per day from whatever had been accumulated.

The first of the death marches began on 28 January when 455 prisoners in wretched condition were forced to walk from Sandakan to Ranau, 260 kilometres up a barely scratched track. Anyone who fell behind was killed and left on the side of the track. By mid-February, 114 had died along the way, and the last of the survivors arrived at Paginatan, a day's walk from Ranau. At Paginatan, those who could walk were forced to carry sacks of rice to Ranau – rice not for the prisoners but for their guards. Some, incredibly, made six trips.

While a rescue plan involving trained Australian paratroops had been devised, it relied on intelligence supplied by Australian Z Special forces secretly in Borneo. It seems that faulty intelligence was supplied in April 1945 that all prisoners had been moved from Sandakan, and the plan to rescue them, codenamed Operation Kingfisher, was never undertaken. But even after the first march, hundreds of prisoners were still alive at Sandakan. This was a failure of intelligence and will that had horrendous consequences; after the war everyone from General MacArthur and General Blamey down was blamed.

Gunner Albert Cleary, a survivor of the first march to Ranau, escaped, but was recaptured after four days in the jungle. He was forced to kneel with a log tied behind his knees, while being beaten, and had his tormentors jump on the log. This went on for at least two days, witnessed by Keith Botterill, one of only six escapees from these camps who survived the war. Poor Cleary was then tied to a tree by the neck, and left for more than ten days. After this, he was allowed to die with his mates, on 20 March 1945.

Allied air raids on Sandakan in late May 1945 seem to have prompted the Japanese to move out of reach of rescue any remaining prisoners who could still walk. On 29 May they sent 536 prisoners on the second forced march to Ranau and burned the camp buildings. The 288 POWs who were too sick to walk were left behind in the ruins. On 15 June, a further 75 were sent up the track; all perished. At the end of June, the 183 survivors of the second march arrived at Ranau to find just six men alive from those who had walked in January.

At the end of July there were just 40 men, barely alive, at Ranau and ten at Sandakan. The last man at Sandakan was murdered on 15 August. We don't know his name, but he was an Australian. This was the day that Emperor Hirohito conceded that the war was 'not necessarily going in Japan's favour', and offered unconditional surrender. The Australian was beheaded and kicked into a ditch.

At Ranau, the fifteen men still alive were not executed until 27 August.

Just six men, all Australian, had escaped the death marches and bore witness – Keith Botterill, Richard Braithwaite, Owen Campbell, Bill Moxham, Nelson Short and Bill Sticpewich. Fifteen of the Japanese officers were tried after the war; four were found guilty of murder and were hanged at Rabaul.

The Tragedy of 'Diver' Derrick

At Tarakan nothing remains of the action its historian Peter Stanley describes as 'an Australian tragedy': 'Tarakan today is no evocative battlefield, like Gallipoli or Flanders. It has no war cemetery, no battlefield markers or plaques; only the [Ross Bastiaan] memorial in the military commandant's compound reminds visitors of its Australian past. Not that many Australians visit ...'

When Stanley visited in 1995 he found 'faint signs of the battle', including an eroded Snag's Track, which led towards Freda, where my own personal Second World War hero, 'Diver' Derrick, had been mortally wounded. (He is now buried in the Labuan cemetery on the other side of Borneo.)

Tom 'Diver' Derrick was born in Adelaide in 1914, left school at fourteen, and before the war worked as an orchardist near Berri. No one knows why he was 'Diver' – to his oldest friends he was always

Tarakan airstrip was never much good. (Mick Sheehan, 1945)

Stiffy (as in the 1920s comedian Mo McCackie's offsider) – but he did like swimming and mucking about in the water at Port Adelaide as a kid. Diver, his friends said, was 'born educated' and had a profound impact on just about everyone he met, especially after he found his true vocation as a fighting soldier. He had charisma, intelligence and leadership qualities; he was the epitome of the Second World War Digger.

Derrick joined up on 5 July 1940, and was posted to the 2/48th Battalion; his father-in-law had served in the 48th in the First World War. The 2/48th served six months at Tobruk in 1941, where Derrick was promoted to Sergeant. After a time in Syria, the 2/48th, with the rest of the 9th Division, was thrown into the Battle of El Alamein, where three members were awarded the Victoria Cross; Diver was awarded the Distinguished Conduct Medal and was wounded.

In 1943, the 9th Division, including the 26th Brigade and Diver's 2/48th Battalion, was ordered to clear the Huon Peninsula in New Guinea. On 22 September 1943 they landed on Scarlet Beach near Finschhafen, north of Lae, forcing the Japanese into the forbidding mountains between the coast and the valley of the Ramu River. After a Japanese counter-attack had been beaten off, their job was to winkle the Japanese out of their deep defences and capture Sattelberg in the extraordinary razor-backed mountains above Finschhafen.

This is how Derrick described the action in which he won the VC: 'Owing to the ground and slope and dense jungle I used only one section forward. We had to lift each other up, giving men a lift up with hands under boots. Then wormed our way forward to locate positions. About 30 yards forward of company position it was flatter – say 40 degrees. We were fired on by machine-guns – fifteen yards away. Position looked desperate. I sent runner to company to say I didn't think we had much chance. Meantime a Jap approached four yards from me and I downed him. Private Don Spencer, using a Jap LMG captured four days before on Coconut Ridge cleared a bunker in front of him containing a machine-gun. Runner came back with orders to withdraw. I thought we were going well so decided against the order and carried on ...'

They cleared the position. Unable to be reinforced, and out of ammunition Diver 'did not like giving up the ground'. They propped in Japanese holes for the night, and in the morning moved into Sattelberg: 'First task was to hoist flag. I hoisted it on to a tree – the red Australian flag – tied to tree with Japanese signal wire.'

Diver then went to officer training, graduating on 26 November 1944, and against practices of the AIF was appointed to his old battalion – to the great enthusiasm of all concerned. A few months later, the 2/48th were involved with the rest of the 9th Division in the vicious action in the ridges of Tarakan.

Frank Legg, an ABC reporter and former member of the 2/48th who had gone ashore with Diver Derrick and the first wave of the landing at Tarakan, spoke to Diver's mates after his death. Derrick said, 'I've been hit. I think it's curtains.' His mate Curly asked him where he had copped it. Diver, a notorious rhyming slanger, replied 'I've copped it in the fruit and nuts.'

'The bullet had gone right through his stomach,' according to Legg. 'Curly leapt up and pulled him into the weapon pit, flung two grenades over the crest, fired his Owen gun at a shadow, and called out to Blue Fernihough. Together they carried the wounded man to the shelter of a fallen log close by. While Blue felt for his wounds in the dark, and put on a field dressing, Curly gave Diver the last few drops of water from his own bottle. Then he dived back to his weapon pit to help beat off the enemy.' It was like Lone Pine up there on the razor ridges of Tarakan ... some two and a half thousand grenades were thrown by each side.

Diver: 'I've got a season ticket from the Richmond Football Club ... They sent it to me. Write and thank 'em Curly.' When the stretcher-bearers were carrying him down, Diver's last words were, 'If you find yourselves slipping, let go the stretcher and save yourself.'

Diver's death was felt widely throughout the army, and contributed to the feeling that the Borneo operations in 1945 were a waste of heroes.

Right: Diver Derrick raises the flag, Sattelberg. (1944, AWM 16246)
Far right: Derrick's funeral service, Tarakan, 1945; he is now buried at Labuan War Cemetery.

South-East Asia Today

Borneo

Today three separate nations occupy the island of Borneo – Brunei, Malaysia and Indonesia. The former British protectorates of Sarawak in the north-east and Sabah in the north make up East Malaysia; the Sultanate of Brunei lies between the two Malaysian states; the remainder of Borneo is the former Dutch East Indies and is now the Indonesian province of Kalimantan. Balikpapan and Tarakan are in Kalimantan; Sandakan, Ranau and Labuan are in Sabah.

1945 might have been the first time Australian military forces landed in Borneo on what was to become Indonesian sovereign territory in 1949, and Malaysian, in 1962, but it wasn't the last. During the *konfrontasi* or confrontation period, when Indonesia staged small-scale operations against the Malaysian mainland, as well as on Borneo, Australian troops were involved. Third Battalion, Royal Australian Regiment (3RAR), as part of the 28th Commonwealth Infantry Brigade, was involved in 1964 on peninsular Malaysia before being committed to Sarawak in Borneo in March–July 1965; 4RAR served between April and August, along with other units including the SAS and artillery. Australians were engaged in several clashes with Indonesian forces, including offensive action across the border. Twenty-three Australians were killed in Borneo; with seven Australians killed and eight wounded on operations. *Konfrontasi* ended with a peace treaty signed in August 1966.

In 1999, Australia was involved in military operations in another part of Indonesia, leading the UN peacekeeping force in East Timor. Australians were unpopular and riots fomented in various places, not least Balikpapan, resulting in the Australian consulate being closed, businesses departing and the 1945 memorials being destroyed and defaced.

Since 1999, the memorials in Balikpapan have been restored, but there has been trouble in different areas of Kalimantan. Civil unrest has occurred in many other parts of Indonesia, such as West Papua and Ambon, as well as the terrorist bombings in Bali and Jakarta. While peace has broken out in Aceh after the tsunami, parts of Indonesia are still problematic.

Balikpapan: A Debt Repaid

Balikpapan today is the major access point for the extensive mining and logging operations inland, some of them run by Australian companies. Today, as during the war, there is a very large oil refinery complex; off-shore drilling platforms glow at night, burning gas. Balikpapan is for most purposes just a stop on the way to Samarinda, the starting point for tours up the mighty Mahakam River to the remaining Dayak villages and the Borneo interior.

One day in Balikpapan in 1999 I hopped on a bemo, looking for the place where the Australians had landed in 1945, and where Lieutenant Mick Sheehan, whose wartime map I was using, had landed with the 2/5th commandos.

I stood on the beach, and looked inland at the town spreading across the hills so artfully codenamed on Mick's map: Record, Owen, Oxley, Newsreel, Naught, Parramatta ... That must be it, I thought – a big ridge, about 500 metres inland, across the Jalan Sudiman road, which the Australians had renamed Vasey Highway after General George Vasey, the 7th's former popular commanding officer, who had been killed in a flying accident off Cairns in early 1945. A note on the map says code names are for army use only and will not be used for inter-service communications, and I can see why. The bumps and topographical wrinkles they nominate must have been near impossible to discern on the ground, and now even those are covered by houses.

Sheehan described how he was sent along this track to make contact with the Japanese, somewhere out near Oxygen: 'We got to the end of the track as shown on the map and swung left along the spur shown there. After some time, it seemed that the ridge was not running in the right direction. In fact it was turning back towards the beach. By studying the map I concluded that the track actually went further than shown. It went to the next ridge. I concluded that we must be behind enemy lines and going to approach them from the rear. My little section had the Japanese army cut off!'

Sheehan led his section back under fire and, in the curious perspective of different units, found that the regimental intelligence officer decided it must have been 'friendly fire'; he preferred to believe the map, and decided that Mick's section 'had not gone far enough'. All this happened in what is now a suburb of red tin rooves and giggling children.

Captain Ray Allsopp, Labuan War Cemetery.

That day in 1945, another section of the 2/5th was operating near the feature code-named Sparrow, to the north-east of Balikpapan town, towards the airstrip. Here the Squadron Medical Officer, Captain Ray Allsopp, was killed while tending the wounded under fire. Allsopp saved the lives of at least three badly wounded men and was recommended for a posthumous Victoria Cross, which was not awarded.

I spent a frustrating hour being driven up and down streets in the general vicinity of Sparrow searching for map reference 612608 on Mick's Enemy Defences Balikpapan 1:10000 map but couldn't find the exact spot in the maze of streets and houses.

Between the landing beach and the road is a block of flats and, in the centre of the road, a roundabout where the Australian war memorials have been erected. In the centre of the roundabout surrounded by low, flowering shrubs was supposed to be the 7th Division memorial, a brick and white rendered cement plinth about three metres tall, with a bronze sword at the top and, on a smaller plinth to one side, a new Ross Bastiaan explanatory bronze unveiled in October 1998 by Bruce Ruxton and the mayor.

I was carrying a copy of a poem Mick Sheehan called 'War Graves Balikpapan', written by Flying Officer T O Latham, and printed and circulated in 1945 (after an earlier version had been written for Tarakan):

*Will you walk with me in the heat of the
  day
Till we come to the crossroads on the way
To a hill on war torn Balikpapan
The scene in the scheme of the World's
  mad plan.
There are soldiers there in a little square,
Who will breathe no more of the dust filled
  air,
On the trails they died, on the hill they rest,
With the foreign soil on each manly chest.*

Here was the spot to pay my respects to Mick's mates, and the 229 Australians who were killed at Balikpapan. I wanted to stand in front of the memorial and read the poem. But the monument had been defaced, wrapped in black plastic, daubed

Left: Defaced Australian memorials, Balikpapan. (1999)
Below: Japanese surrender on the Samarinda Road near Balikpapan. (Mick Sheehan, 1945)

with obscenities in English and Bahasa, and topped with an Indonesian flag. The new bronze had been ripped from its plinth. It was a terrible insult, 1999 politics spitting on the graves of the Australians who died here, in the cause of ending Japanese rule in Borneo. The anti-Australian mob had been organised, I was later told, by specially sent Indonesian special forces, Kompassus, who had marched down Vasey Highway to the most obvious sign of Australian military presence to protest what their own President Habibie had brought about in East Timor.

> You may gaze at the flags; that hang from
>   the mast
> To honour the men who were staunch to
>   the last,
> And fancy you hear a quiet voice say –
> 'Australia – my country – will you repay
> Will you warm my heart, give daily bread
> To the hungry mouths which once were fed
> Through the sweat and toil of the fallen
>   man,
> Who sleeps on the hill at Balikpapan.'

Cemeteries, Memorials, Museums: Kalimantan (Indonesia)

Balikpapan

The **7th Division Memorials** in Jalan Suduriman are opposite the landing beaches. The memorials were desecrated and the plaques stolen during the anti-Australian troubles of 1999, but were restored and re-dedicated on Anzac Day 2000 upon the initiative of then Australian ambassador John McCarthy. The local police chief is said to have found the plaque under his desk.

Desecrated Australian memorials, Balikpapan 1999. The memorials have since been restored.

Cemeteries, Memorials, Museums: Sabah (Malaysia)

Kota Kinabalu

The **Petagas War Memorial** in Kota Kinabalu is dedicated to the 146 Chinese executed on 21 January 1944 by the Japanese after the failure of the 'Double Tenth' uprising led by Albert Kwok (so called because it occurred on 10 October 1943). They are buried here.

Kundasang

Kundasang Memorial Garden.

The **Memorial Garden at Kundasang**, near Ranau, has a kind of non-national war memorial composed of connected garden terraces, the last of which has a wonderful and contemplative view of Mt Kinabalu. Locals say that the whole Mt Kinabalu National Park is a memorial to the suffering of the POWs and the people of Sabah who helped them because its clouded peak harbours the souls of the dead. The only national reference is to Australia, in the form of a plaque by Ross Bastiaan set in a wall just inside the entrance. This reads:

'This memorial garden is dedicated to the memory of the 1800 Australian and 600 British servicemen who perished in the POW camps in Sandakan and in the 3 forced marches from Sandakan to Ranau, and of the many Sabahans who suffered death in trying to assist them ... "Let them not depart from thine eyes, keep them in the midst of thine heart". (Prov. Iv.21) The memory of them shall live for evermore.'

Labuan

Labuan War Cemetery lies on the right side of the Jalan Tanjong Batu road, which leads from the airport to the town. The cemetery is only 500 metres from the airport, the only town on Labuan, Victoria. There are 1788 identified casualties.

There had been a cemetery at Sandakan, dedicated on Anzac Day 1947 and built around the original camp cemeteries; it included those found who had died along the track to Ranau. Unfortunately, the ground was swampy and the remains had to be disinterred and transferred to Labuan.

The **Labuan Memorial to the Missing** within the cemetery records the names of Australian POWs from Sandakan whose graves are unidentified or whose bodies have never been found, as well as others who died in the liberation of the island in 1945 who have no known grave. (British missing are recorded on the Kranji Memorial in Singapore.) Subsequently, it was found that a number of men belonging to the local forces of North Borneo, Sarawak and Brunei who were killed on war service also have no known grave, and they, too, are honoured here.

Work has continued to be done, particularly by Lynette Harvey Silver, to identify those now in the cemetery at Labuan under the headstone 'An Australian soldier of the 1939–1945 War. Known Unto God.'

Not far from the cemetery on the beach at Layang Layangan is an **Australian Battle Exploit Memorial** marking the spot where the 9th Division landed on 10 June 1945. A separate plaque marks the 'surrender point' where, on 9 September 1945, Major General George Wootten received the unconditional surrender of the 32nd Japanese Southern Army in Borneo. Close by is a Japanese 'peace park' with a stone bearing the words 'peace is the best'.

In front of the district office in the town of Victoria is a **Japanese memorial stone**, with a bronze translation reading: 'This memorial commemorates General Maida, Commander-in-Chief of the wartime Japanese forces in British Borneo who was killed in an air crash at Bintalu (Sarawak) on the 6th September 1942 when en-route to Labuan to open the airfield here.' On 9 December 1942 Labuan Island (Victoria) was named Maida Island by the Japanese government. The memorial was made by order of General Tojo, who passed through Labuan Island in July 1945.

Above: Labuan landing beach.
Below: Japanese memorial stone, Labuan.

Ranau

Gunner Cleary Memorial, Ranau.

The **Ranau Memorial**, also known as the Gunner Cleary Memorial, is situated at the place where Gunner Albert Cleary of the 2/15th Field Regiment had been horribly tortured and left to die after attempting an escape from the camp on 20 March 1945. The memorial was dedicated in 1985. It may have been moved from the spot that survivor Owen Campbell pointed out to the RSL's Bruce Ruxton in 1981. On my visit in 1999 it was to be found in front of a school building on the main road, two kilometres east of the river, in the direction of Sandakan. There is also a memorial to the 1821 uprising.

Sandakan

Sandakan Memorial Park is on the site of the POW camp, about twelve kilometres out of town, near the airport, and now almost in the suburbs, in what was a Sabah State Forestry Reserve. There is a polished black obelisk, originally dedicated in 1995, inscribed with the words 'In remembrance of all those who suffered and died here, on the death marches and at Ranau'. Within the park a commemorative pavilion holds educational material and includes a scale model of the original POW camp and a beautiful stained-glass window. A path winds through the park past preserved wartime relics. Signs and seats around the pathways provide rest points, and at points of significance there are numbered posts linked to the park brochure providing information on the former POW camp.

Lynette Silver rediscovered the route of the Sandakan Track. A section leading to Ranau was opened for trekking in mid-2006.

Australian Memorial Sandakan.

Darwin

Darwin has been through a lot since the war – especially Cyclone Tracy in 1974 – but has become a lively and cosmopolitan city quite unlike any in Australia. It has a strong military connection, with Tindal RAAF base nearby, and as a base for the peacekeeping operations in East Timor from 1999. The East Point Military Museum is well worth a visit, and the Adelaide River War Cemetery is an easy drive south from Darwin.

Sandakan: Australia's Auschwitz

Of all the sites I visited for this book, the worst place of all had the least impact. The remnants of the Sandakan death camp are today in a pleasant garden. Children scamper about, fishing in the pond. There are some bits of machinery and a small museum with a bright stained-glass window and wrought-iron gates with texts in two languages: *Lest We Forget, Tangan Sampalkita Tupakan*. The dark form of the memorial obelisk is lonely and striking – the physical remains of Australia's Auschwitz. A small, personal Auschwitz where neglect, torture and death are measured in the thousands rather than in the hundreds of thousands.

Sandakan doesn't have the symbols or cues that bring about an outbreak of tears in a cemetery, or finding an Australian headstone apparently unvisited for years, in the Libyan desert or Burmese jungle, after a long journey. Ian Buruma, writing about Auschwitz in *The Wages of Guilt,* states, 'To visit the site of suffering, any description of which cannot adequately express the horror, is upsetting not because one gets closer to knowing what it was actually like to be a victim, but because such visits stir up emotions one cannot trust.' He was writing of kitsch feelings, such as the 'warm moral glow of identification – so easily done and so presumptuous – with the victims: there but for the grace of God go I, and so on.'

Primo Levi – who was of course a longer-suffering victim of Auschwitz because he was among the 'saved' – felt on a return visit that it was like going to a museum. This was the central block of the vast Auschwitz complex, which is a museum, a shrine to martyrs. Levi felt more connected at Birkenau nearby where the ruins had been left, to a greater extent, unrestored, the bunks slatted to the ceiling, the rafters with their horrifyingly kitsch painted homilies. (Buruma on a later visit found the homilies had been repainted – for Birkenau had become a movie set.)

Battlefields, however much they change over time, however little remains, can still be recreated and remembered. This happened here – in a way it can be re-imagined. However tragic the result, there's a degree of choice and a sense of personal responsibility about going into action. Events that still bring tears, such as the charge at the Nek at Gallipoli, where the men of the Light Horse faced certain death, are about a positive kind of courage and heroism and selflessness.

But in Borneo, at the end, there was no redemption, just degradation, helplessness, brutality and murder – the stripping away of everything human from the prisoners by their captors.

Nothing brings that to mind at Sandakan. It's even different to the Thai–Burma Railway, and the suffering and death of the tens of thousands on that piece of evil engineering. Despite terrible disease, illness, beatings and executions, the railway workers were engaged in building something, and some even managed to stay alive by finding positive aspects to the work. The railway was finished in 1943, and the surviving POWs were mostly either sent to Japan to work in the coal mines or returned to Changi.

No such luck at Sandakan or Ranau, where in 1945, with the war clearly lost, the Japanese and Formosan guards murdered the few poor souls who were still alive. Sandakan, and Ranau, had become an extermination camp.

Cemeteries, Memorials, Museums: Northern Territory

Adelaide River

Above: Adelaide River War Cemetery.
Below: Northern Territory Memorial to the Missing.

Adelaide River War Cemetery is 113 kilometres south of Darwin on the Stuart Highway. The cemetery is located one kilometre east of the highway. It is cared for by the Office of Australian War Graves on behalf of the Commonwealth War Graves Commission.

The Adelaide River War Cemetery was established during the Second World War for the burial of servicemen and women who died in northern Australia. After the war, graves were moved from civil cemeteries and temporary burial grounds to Adelaide River. There are 434 burials – 181 soldiers and 201 airmen of Australia, seven from the Australian Merchant Navy, fourteen airmen from the RAF, twelve from the British Merchant Navy, and one Canadian soldier.

The **Northern Territory Memorial to the Missing** is located within the cemetery, and commemorates 293 Australians lost in the South-West Pacific who have no known grave: 103 from the Australian army, 164 from the RAAF and 26 from the Australian Merchant Navy. One of the army dead is a sister of the Australian Army Nursing Service. Ten panels bear their names. Other Australians who died in Timor in 1942 and who have no known grave are commemorated here.

Adelaide River Civil Cemetery is located immediately next to the war cemetery, and seems to be part of it. Among the 63 civilians buried here are the nine post office workers killed in the air raid of 19 February 1942, who were initially buried on a nearby beach in Darwin but were reburied here in 1947.

Darwin

Bicentennial Park on the Esplanade is on the western side of the city centre. In the park is the **Cenotaph,** the official Darwin memorial, and dozens of memorial plaques to the army, navy, airforce and Merchant Navy units that served in Darwin are set around it. Some 57 plaques commemorate the Australian and US units that served during the war, as well as some postwar units such as United Nations peacekeeping forces. The cenotaph was originally erected in 1921 as

Darwin Cenotaph in Bicentennial Park.

a memorial to the First World War, outside Government House in Liberty Square, which no longer exists. In 1970 it was relocated to the Civic Centre and in 1992 to its present location. Both moves were made because building development reduced the space available for ceremonies.

Bicentennial Park was once the Darwin Oval and the location for the 14th Anti-Aircraft Battery, which fired some of the first shots against Japanese aircraft raiding Darwin. As well as bombing raids, the monument has withstood major cyclones in 1937 and 1974, and earth tremors.

Among the other memorials in the park is **Site of No. 1 Gun 14th Heavy Artillery Battery,** and the **USS Peary and USAAF Memorial**. This is a 4-inch gun salvaged from the *Peary* in the 1950s by local diver Carl Atkinson. It was restored by the RAN for the Northern Territory's 1992 War Service Memorial Year and now points towards the *Peary*'s grave.

USS Peary memorial – a 4-inch gun salvaged in the 1950s.

Northern Territory Garden of Remembrance is located within the Thorak Regional Cemetery, Deloraine Road, Berrimah. Opened in 2002, the garden is a place of reflection which commemorates the veterans in the company of those with whom they served, where next of kin may have chosen to erect a private memorial or scatter ashes elsewhere rather than have an official memorial. There is provision for 200 plaques.

Northern Territory Parliament House is located on the site of the pre-war post office, which was destroyed in the bombing on 19 February 1942. The Postmaster Hurtle Bald lost his life, as did his wife, Alice, their daughter, Iris; and employees Archibald Halls, Arthur Wellington, Jennie Stasinowsky, sisters Eileen and Jean Mullen, and Emily Young. They are buried at Adelaide River.

A remnant of an original wall of the post office was relocated to the Parliament House lobby, near the entry to the Northern Territory Library. A piece of shrapnel that was recovered from the ruins and a commemorative plaque were placed in the Main Reception Hall, which is thought to be the exact location where the bomb fell.

On 18 February 2000 a permanent display of photographs and biographical information of the ten people who were killed in the first raid and photographs and information relating to the former Darwin post office was opened.

East Point Military Museum – the gun emplacement.

East Point Military Museum was established in 1965 by the Royal Australian Artillery Association and was officially opened on 16 August 1969. Located in an old bunker that served as a command post for artillery fire control, it was Darwin's first museum. Collection and conservation of a great variety of gear has continued since that time, including removing the earth around the No. 2 9.2-inch gun emplacement. In 1991 the committee of the Royal Australian Artillery Association appointed a full-time manager, and in 1995 the museum was refitted with new exhibits, mainly weapons on loan from the museums and art galleries of the Northern Territory.

A video documentary is shown continuously. There is also an excellent collection of artillery and transport, a highlight being the 9.2-inch coastal artillery emplacement – a facsimile gun barrel gives some idea of the size of the weapon – which was not used in anger in 1942 as the Japanese aircraft carriers stayed out of range.

East Point Military Museum
Address: East Point Rd, Fannie Bay 0820

The **oil storage tunnels** built into the cliff-face at Darwin Harbour below Kitchener Drive were constructed by the RAN in mid-1943 at a cost of £1,109,500. The above-ground tanks, which were capable of holding 75,000 tons of oil and were built in 1941 at Stokes Hill, are highly visible today, as they were to the Japanese. One of the eleven was hit in the 19 February air raid and seven more in subsequent raids.

They look small from the outside, but are huge inside. Access to Tunnel 5 is down steps from Kitchener Drive. Check hours of opening.

Stuart Highway, Northern Territory

Wartime airstrips around Darwin are marked by signs erected by the NT government for the 1992 War Service Memorial Year. On the Stuart Highway towards Adelaide River, are signs for the following airstrips, with kilometres south of Darwin.

Sattler (32 km) was used extensively in 1944, but military sites have disappeared.

Strauss (44 km) or 27 Mile Airstrip, was used by USAAF 49th Pursuit Group's 8 Squadron, which shot down 64 Japanese aircraft in all. 549 Squadron RAF flew Spitfires from here in mid-1944.

Hughes (46 km) was named for D D Hughes, Director of Mines in Darwin. 13 Squadron flew Hudsons and later Mitchells from here from May 1942 until early 1945. 76 Squadron, under squadron leader Bluey Truscott, flew from here briefly in late 1942 after the squadron's heroics at Milne Bay. Hughes experienced three Japanese air raids.

Livingstone (54 km) was the first of the roadside fighter airstrips to be constructed. Occupied by USAAF 49th Pursuit Group's 9 Squadron from March 1942, it was named for Lieutenant John D Livingstone, 9 Squadron, who crashed on landing on 4 April 1942 in a P40 Warhawk. 457 Squadron RAAF equipped with Spitfires arrived here in February 1943. Flying Officer J H Smithson of 457 was awarded the Distinguished Flying Cross for shooting down two Japanese bombers in the last raid on Darwin, 12 November 1943.

Livingstone: First of the fighter airstrips to be constructed in 1942.

Coomalie (86 km) was constructed in late 1942 and initially occupied by 31 Squadron RAAF with Beaufighters and later by No. 1 Photographic Reconnaissance Unit (which became 87 Squadron) flying Mosquitoes. Now privately owned, the original emplacements have been retained.

Batchelor (88 km), located in the township of Batchelor, 13 kilometres west of the Stuart Highway, is still in use. A highlight for Batchelor (named for E L Batchelor, a South Australian MP) was the flying visit of General Douglas MacArthur on 17 March 1942. It was used by 49th Pursuit Group 7 Squadron in 1942, and then by a variety of units including 2 Squadron (Hudsons), 77 and 76 Squadrons (Kittyhawks), 12 Squadron (Vengeance), 18 Squadron (Mitchells) and 6 Communication Unit – 'Fenton's Flying Freighters'.

The **Batchelor Battle of Australia Memorial** on Rum Jungle Road commemorates the people of the Coomalie area, RAAF wireless units and General Douglas MacArthur who, the plaque says, 'acting on instructions from President Roosevelt, left the Philippines on 12 March 1942 for Australia. After a perilous 4000 km journey by boat and aircraft through enemy controlled territory, MacArthur's party landed at Batchelor airstrip on 17 March 1942. MacArthur continued his journey to the southern capitals and established his headquarters in Brisbane.'

Cemeteries, Memorials, Museums: Australia

Canberra

The **Australian War Memorial** in Canberra includes the names of Australian servicemen (and one servicewoman) killed in Darwin on 19 February 1942. The four members of the army, one ordnance corps corporal and three members of the hospital ship *Manunda* (including a sister of the Australian Army Nursing Service) appear on panels 86 and 91. The six sailors, three from HMAS *Swan* and three from the shore establishment HMAS *Melville*, appear on panels 3, 4 and 7. The seven airmen, most of them members of the RAAF station headquarters, are commemorated on panel 97.

Malaya and Singapore

Wartime Malaya is now part of Malaysia, which consists of the Malayan peninsula and the provinces of Sarawak and Sabah on the island of Borneo (detailed in the Borneo section). Malaysia had a somewhat prickly relationship with Australia in the years when Mahathir Mohammed was prime minister, but this has improved since Mahathir retired in 2003. Malaysia is of course a predominantly Muslim country, and has been for hundreds of years. Some states adopt a more rigorous approach to Islamic law than others – banning alcohol, for instance – and this tension between secular and religious views, overlaid with the pro-Malay ethnic economic policies to the disadvantage of the substantial Indian and Chinese minorities, is still being played out. The Second World War forms a very small part of the Malaysian story.

In modern Singapore, however, there is a kind of overlay that has not quite covered over its wartime experience. When you fly into the world's best airport, you also fly into Changi, with the prison and the beach where so many POWs and Chinese were executed just up the road. Step out of the supercooled atria of Orchard Road shops, and you find things like an information panel saying that the Japanese *Kempetai*, the feared military police headquarters, was the old YMCA building, or that beneath Fort Canning park was the Battle Box, General Percival's headquarters during the battle of Singapore.

The cover-up is especially true of casualties suffered by civilian Singapore in the *Sook Ching* period in early 1942 when an unknown number of mostly Chinese civilians were executed. Estimates range between 5000 and 50,000. At this time all Chinese civilians were ordered to attend 'mass screening centres' and explain what job they did in Singapore. Many young men, especially teachers and students

Location of Kempetai East District Branch headquarters in the old YMCA building, Singapore.

were taken away for execution at a number of sites, including Changi, Bedok, Punggol and Sentosa beaches.

Down on the *padang* is the memorial to the civilian dead during the Japanese occupation – the 'chopsticks' memorial.

All the Singapore sites are easy to find. You can take a bus to the Changi Museum, but a taxi is easier, as it is to the Kranji War Cemetery. Older drivers, once they know of your destination, are quite likely to tell stories of their boyhood survival in Singapore – the location of 'secret tunnels' on Bukit Timah, and close calls with the Japanese. Equally, you might get an earful about the younger generation of Singaporese who know little and remember less.

Cemeteries, Memorials, Museums: Malaysia

Gemenceh River

Gemenceh River Memorial, Malaysia.

There is a **Malaysian memorial** beside the Gemenceh River bridge to the ambush of January 1942. Lynette Harvey Silver in her book, *Massacre at Parit Sulong*, matched up nearly all the places mentioned by Ben Hackney, a survivor of the Parit Sulong massacre.

Kota Bharu

Kelantan War Museum is on Jalan Sultan, on the north side of Padang Merdeka Freedom Square, near a **memorial to the victims of the Second World War**. The museum is in the mustard-coloured Bank Kerapu building, and offers a bedraggled history of the Japanese invasion and occupation. Some local heroes are commemorated, and one of the bicycles used by the Japanese after they landed fifteen kilometres north of Kota Bharu on 8 December 1941. Built in 1912, the former bank became the headquarters of the *Kempetai* – the feared occupation military police.

The museum exhibits include a clandestine radio from the war, a bent machine-gun, a rusty mine, and pictures of Japanese being hanged after the war, including General Shimpei Fukuyei, Yamamoto and Hamada. There are also details of some local heroes, such as Tengku Mahmood Mahyiddeen, a prince of the Royal House of Patani. He fought with the clandestine operation in the Malayan jungle, known as Force 136, but was living in Kota Bharu at the time of the invasion working as Kelantan Inspector of Schools. He was a member of the Kelantan Volunteers, retreated to Singapore, then escaped to India aboard the SS *Kuala* until it sank, swam to Sumatra, and finally made it to India, where he worked in All India Radio in the Propaganda Section.

In the museum is a **Japanese memorial stone**. Kota Bharu was defended mainly by Indian troops in the British army – a Punjabi battalion who held up the Japanese at 'Kemuning Bridge' to the north of the city, where they killed a Japanese commander and a number of troops. During the occupation their ashes were placed in a memorial, at the site. In Japanese characters (translation round the back) on a brooding black stone it says: 'A memorial stone in commemoration of the war dead a unit of NASU soldiers attack [indecipherable] 12 day of 12 month Year 6 Showa. It was captured at 11 am'.

The memorial was broken open in the 1960s and the urn containing the ashes of the Japanese dead taken back to Japan – it wasn't a gravesite but a place for the keeping of ashes. The base of the memorial is still at the bridge over the river.

Above: Kota Bharu War Memorial.
Below: Japanese memorial stone, Kota Bharu War Museum.

Kelantan War Museum
Address: Pengarah, Perbadanan Muzium Negeri Kelantan, Jalan Hospital, 15000 Kota Bharu

Cemeteries, Memorials, Museums: Singapore

Kranji War Cemetery includes 64 First World War burials and 4458 Second World War burials, 850 of which are unidentified.

Known locally as the **Kranji Memorial**, it is 22 kilometres north of the city of Singapore, on the north side of Singapore Island overlooking the Straits of Johore. It is just off Woodlands Road in the direction of Johore and the Causeway.

Before 1939, Kranji was a military camp, and at the time of the Japanese invasion it was the site of a large ammunition magazine, and then a POW camp. After the war, the small cemetery started by the prisoners at Kranji was developed into a permanent war cemetery by the Army Graves Service when it became evident that a larger cemetery at Changi could not remain undisturbed. In 1946, the graves from Changi were moved to Kranji. Many other graves from all parts of the island and elsewhere were then transferred to Kranji, including all Second World War burials from Saigon Military Cemetery in Vietnam.

The **Chinese Memorial** in Plot 44 marks a collective grave for 69 Chinese servicemen, all members of the Commonwealth forces, who were killed during the occupation in February 1942.

The **Singapore Memorial** stands within Kranji War Cemetery. It bears the names of over 24,000 Second World War casualties of the Commonwealth land and air forces who have no known grave. The land forces commemorated by the memorial died during the campaigns in Malaya and Indonesia or in subsequent captivity, many of them during the construction of the Thai–Burma Railway, or at sea while being transported to imprisonment elsewhere. The memorial also commemorates airmen who died during operations over the whole of southern and eastern Asia and the surrounding seas and oceans.

The **Singapore Cremation Memorial**, which stands immediately behind the Singapore Memorial, commemorates almost 800 casualties, mostly of the Indian forces, whose remains were cremated in accordance with their religious beliefs.

The **Singapore Civil Hospital Grave Memorial** stands at the eastern end of the Singapore Memorial. During the last hours of the Battle of Singapore, wounded civilians and servicemen taken prisoner by the Japanese were brought to the hospital. More than 400 died and were buried in a mass grave at the hospital. The 107 Commonwealth casualties buried in the grave are commemorated on this memorial.

Above: Singapore Memorial.
Below: Kranji War Cemetery.

Kranji Military Cemetery adjoins Kranji War Cemetery and is a substantial non-world war site of 1378 burials, created in 1975 when it was found necessary to remove the graves of servicemen and their families from Pasir Panjang and Ulu Pandan cemeteries.

The **Singapore Cenotaph**, the four-pronged 'chopsticks' memorial near Raffles Hotel, in the Memorial Park at Beach Road, was erected in 1966. It is a short walk from City Hall MRT Station. The memorial commemorates civilian deaths of all races in the Second World War, but especially the Chinese killed during *Sook Ching*. The remains of many of the victims of *Sook Ching* are buried beneath the memorial.

Singapore writer Pan Shou wrote that, 'The four towering columns of this memorial symbolise loyalty, bravery, virtue and righteousness, traits of which are reflected in the traditional harmony and solidarity of the multi-racial, multi-cultural and multi-religious society of Singapore.

'This memorial stands to prove that the people of Singapore were able to hold their own together in adversity and it also signifies their ever-readiness to share the common prosperity of the country in future ...'

His words were intended to be carved on the memorial, but in the end they were not used.

Johore Battery is a gun emplacement site consisting of a labyrinth of tunnels that were used to store ammunition to support three monster guns that could fire 15-inch shells. Built by the British in 1939 for the defence of Singapore, the guns were the largest installed outside Britain during the Second World War. The guns were destroyed before the surrender of the British army and the tunnels were sealed up after the war. Their location remained a secret until the Singapore Prisons Department rediscovered them in April 1991. Today a replica of a gun and a 15-inch shell are on view.

Singapore Cenotaph.

Johore Battery
Address: Cosford Road, off Upper Changi Road North

The **Battle Box** is a 26-room complex beneath Canning Hill that is now presented as it was between 0600 and 1115 hours on the morning of 15 February, when the bad news continued to pour in to the telephone exchange. Eerily lifelike, accurately uniformed figures actually operate some pieces of equipment accompanied by appropriate sound effects and recreated dialogue.

Visitors to the Battle Box today see several of the rooms set up as they were in the Second World War – the telephone exchange room with a working operator, the cipher office, the signal office, the signal control room, the fortress command office, the gun operations room where enemy aircraft were plotted, the office of the commander fixed defences and a small museum telling the Fort Canning Story.

The surrender conference is the most effective display. You can see General Percival and Gordon Bennett as they made up their minds.

Battle Box.

Battle Box
Address: 51 Canning Rise, Singapore 179872
Website: www.visitsingapore.com

Changi Museum and Chapel was relocated and reopened on 15 February 2001, replacing the old souvenir shop. The chapel is a replica of the sort erected at Changi camp during the war. The chapel has an *atap* back wall, a pitched roof of tin and *atap*-thatch protecting the altar at one end, flowers in vases, paintings and crosses. It is used for services – outside a dozen rows of bench seats on both sides of a central aisle. Stuck in the *atap* at the back are messages from the living: many red poppies, and dried flowers.

One of the original chapels was located near Selarang Barracks and was transported back to Australia after the war, and is now at Duntroon in the ACT. The altar cross, made from a shell casing, was returned to the Singapore chapel in 1992.

The new air-conditioned museum shows reproductions of the famous and previously difficult to see Changi Murals, painted by British artilleryman Stanley Warren in the chapel created in Block 151. Warren survived the war, but the murals were forgotten until the 1960s, when the artist was invited to restore the four remaining paintings. He worked on them in 1968, 1982 and 1988 in their original location.

There is an excellent display of photographs, drawings and personal items donated by former POWs and their families in the museum, and a Ross Bastiaan plaque outside.

Section of the Changi Mural.

Changi Museum
Address: 1000 Upper Changi Road North, Singapore 507707
Website: www.changimuseum.com

Reflections at Bukit Chandu is a museum that commemorates the 1400 soldiers of the Malay Regiment killed in the defence of Singapore at the Battle of Pasir Panjang. The museum displays photographs, maps, dates and information detailing the defence of Malaya and life in the Malay Regiment. Set amidst the lush greenery of Bukit Chandu (Opium Hill), this interpretive centre is a memorial to the last moments of these brave soldiers of the Second World War.

Reflections at Bukit Chandu
Address: 31-K Pepys Road, Singapore 118458
Website: www.s1942.org.sg

Sentosa

Images of Singapore features Singapore's history, from the 14th century to the Second World War, with life-sized figures, dioramas and archival materials, presented with the latest exhibition techniques.

Among the exhibits, Surrender Chambers depicts the Singapore war years through rare archival photographs and footage, with waxworks capturing the British and Japanese surrenders in Singapore.

The actual surrender-ceremony site at the old Ford Factory is inaccessible, but the room has been recreated here in wax, showing the main characters at the moment of surrender. General Percival looks wanly across the table at the unbending General Yamashita, leaning on his stick. The Surrender Chamber is part of a larger set of tableaux, some moving, some noisy, which in their variety and sheer interest make Madame Tussaud's look a bit like, well, a wax works.

The Surrender Chamber, Images of Singapore, Sentosa.

Images of Singapore
Address: 33 Allanbrooke Road, Sentosa, Singapore 099981

Fort Siloso is the only preserved British coastal fortification in Singapore. It was built in the 1880s on Sentosa's western end, and protected the western entrance to the Singapore harbour. During the Second World War, the guns of Fort Siloso engaged Japanese forces in the Battle for Singapore, even firing landwards in support of the British troops.

A walk through the fort today animates sounds and occasional movement from model figures who tell the story of the place up to 1942 and provide a unique chance to look into Singapore's colonial past. There are plenty of artillery pieces, including some of the guns famously guarding Singapore from the seaborne invasion which never came. Here in a little theatre, twenty or 30 Singaporeans, with children, and one Australian, paid attention to a ten-minute audio-video presentation of the Japanese invasion of Malaya and Singapore. Outside the kids enjoyed a programmed bang and puff of smoke from an artillery piece – still pointed out to sea.

The Thai–Burma Railway today

Siam became Thailand in 1939, as a formal indication of a more assertive nationalism by the pro-fascist government of the day. After the fall of France in 1940, Thailand invaded Laos and Cambodia, and acquiesced in the Japanese use of southern Thailand in the invasion of Malaya in December 1941. Thailand became an ally of Japan in January 1942, and formally declared war on Britain and the United States. Japan rewarded Thailand with provinces in Cambodia and Malaya. The Thai ambassador in Washington, Seri Pramoj, refused to deliver the ultimatum, and set up a resistance movement called Seri (Free) Thai. After the war, Seri Thai won the election, and the foreign provinces returned. Since then a series of short-lived governments have been formed in Thailand's individual style. Elected governments alternated with military rule through the 1970s. The present king of Thailand, Bhumibol Adyulyadej, has been a vital force in ensuring that stability and a kind of democracy have prevailed in Thailand. Compared to neighbouring Burma, Thailand is a paradise.

Burma was invaded by Japan from Thailand in January 1942 and the Japanese defeated the British-led Indian forces by June. Rangoon was taken on 8 March and the British retreat to India was completed by May 1942. Burma was granted a form of independence in August 1943 – which briefly involved Aung San Suu Kyi's father, Aung San,

End of the line: Thai–Burma Railway. (2003)

among others. Aung San soon became disillusioned with the Japanese and formed the Anti-Fascist People's Freedom League. Japanese forces surrendered in Rangoon on 28 August 1945, after a long and costly campaign by the British. Aung San was effectively prime minister and led Burma to independence in 1947, but was assassinated in the same year.

Burma was officially renamed Myanmar by the military dictatorship which has run, and run down, the country since taking over in 1962. Aung San Suu Kyi's democratic movement, which announced its presence in massive demonstrations on 8 August 1988, led the National League for Democracy to an election win in 1990 from house arrest, where she has been kept since 1989. Once South-East Asia's richest country, Burma is now one of the world's poorest and most oppressed. Aung San Suu Kyi feels that travel to Burma only supports the regime, however travellers can bring welcome news and dollars to non-government sections of the country.

Most of the Thai–Burma Railway track was recycled elsewhere in Thailand and Burma after the war – the only section that can be travelled is from Kanchanaburi to Nam Tok across the Bridge over the River Kwai. It is not even possible to walk the length of the railway – a section where the two ends met in 1943 at Konkoita is under a post-war reservoir. Time and the jungle have obliterated traces of it in most of Thailand, and nearly all of Burma. A section has been cleared and can be walked at Hellfire Pass, but looking for signs of the old line, even when you know exactly where it is, even when it is pointed out to you by an expert guide, is often impossible.

Since the Australian government opened the Hellfire Pass Memorial in 2000, it has become a popular place for commemoration and remembrance.

Salween River, Martaban, Burma, 1999.

Riding the Railway

The 18-hour train journey from Rangoon to Martaban on the north bank of the Salween was terrifying, the train seemingly leaving the track as it sped over places where the rails were not connected to the sleepers. This was entirely appropriate when looking for the Death Railway. The trip across the wide Salween River to Moulmein in the dark in a small boat was nearly as bad. Fairy lights from the pagoda of Kipling's poem winked on the dark ridge across the water – something Rudyard never actually saw. After being turned away from a couple of guest houses, one curiously reserved for Japanese, I found a bed, food, and next day a cousin of the proprietor to drive three hours further south to Thanbyuzayat.

We slipped quietly away, past solid but weedy red brick churches, and the gateways to nine or ten army camps – including the headquarters of South-East Area Command. This was the headquarters of the battle against the Mon and Karen insurgents. The refugee camp of Mae Sot was only 50 or 60 kilometres due east in Thailand, as the helicopter flew.

The road to Thanbyuzayat was kept in reasonable order, for military purposes. While the train line from Moulmein to Ye was still running, the old spur from Thanbyuzayat to Three Pagodas had been taken up after the war. A road now followed the same route to Three Pagodas – however it was 'not permitted' to travel on it.

We found the cemetery, a haven of green, on the dusty outskirts of Thanbyuzayat, 800 metres from the roundabout at the centre of town. It was a smaller, flatter version of Moulmein, but with a Victorian clock tower. A Burmese general from the independence year of 1948 is commemorated over the road by a monastery and memorial stone. Buffalo grazed peaceably at the back.

According to the head gardener, who was dressed in a blue and white checked longyi and a khaki shirt, there had been two visitors in the month of my 1997 visit, including me.

'Too young, and too many,' I said to the gardener.

'Yassir,' he replied as he walked with me, around his immaculate cemetery, treading as softly as he could.

The white magnolias were in bloom, the dead and their stories rest among a million butterflies here. The only sound is from the temple across the road, bells and a hum of chanting. Butterflies everywhere: small darting yellows, white and yellow flappers, brown-speckled types, fat fast black-bodied brown and tans. Low neat hedges make a perimeter around the sections of the cemetery. Buffalo munch across the lane. The messages on the headstones seem more personal, more Australian, even more political, here:

> *A true Australian who gave all for freedom.*
> *In sunshine and perfect peace a silent*
>   *thought brings many a tear.*
> *He gave his life that we might be free –*
>   *Proudly remembered.*
> *His spirit lives in the land he loved.*
> *He heard the call and answered. He died*
>   *open eyed and unafraid.*
> *To live in the hearts of those who love is*
>   *not to die.*
> *He loved life laughter and his fellow men.*
>   *For these he died.*
> *Pax.*

Finding the Thai track

Rod Beattie, long-time Australian manager of the Commonwealth War Graves Commission in Thailand, has spent more time on the railway than anyone. He physically cleared a big stretch of line near Hellfire Pass, and has walked as much of it as is possible. He has located the sites of most of the camps, and is also a director of the Thailand–Burma Railway Centre in Kanchanaburi, and is still researching at various sites. When I dropped in in 2003 he was digging at the spot behind the Chungkai cemetery where the kitchen for the camp had been.

On an earlier visit Rod put me on the right track. We began at the site of the Hintok River Camp, on the river north of Hellfire Pass. There was a freshwater spring into the pond below. Rod had brought a copy of Ray Parkin's *Into the Smother*, and he opened the book at a drawing of the Hintok River Camp, a perspective from the river showing the drinking water 'elevator', the mountains behind, and the railway running in from the left – and the camp on the cliff top. I looked back from the cliff top towards the railway – and there were the characteristic mountains, and behind the trees was the railway. This was the camp.

Parkin had made an illustration of the 'water chain' men sending tins and buckets up from the river, with a small boat which brought the meagre supplies for the camps up river from Kanchanaburi nearby. He wrote that in the awful monsoon floods of July 1943 the spring was covered by water, but now, at the beginning of the dry season, it was as idyllic as peace itself. In the banana grove nearby was the site of the Hintok cholera camp. Rod said he might plant macadamias there.

We walked up from the river to the railway. It took about twenty minutes to hack through straggly jungle vegetation and abandoned banana groves, and then another fif-

teen minutes climbing up the side of the hill; the railway was built along the 100-foot gradient, where possible, above the river plain. It wasn't raining, and no one was standing by us with a gun or a bayonet. We walked two or three kilometres through the stone of the rail bed.

It is not a difficult walk, even if the sun is hot and the humidity high, but you have to take care not to turn your ankle on the stones and rotting sleepers. Building this track, making the embankments and digging the cuttings was another matter altogether. Rod found me a dog spike, one of the collectibles of the railway, and I found the hard white shells of local snails, and myriad iridescent green beetles.

We came to the 156-kilometre peg marked by a red 44-gallon drum. Rod had cleared all this of its thick re-growth of bamboo and scrub, and he had also cleared the track for nearly four kilometres further to where the rail bed has fallen away in rock and mudslides. You can see it emerge again further up the valley.

Of the 156-kilometre peg, Ray Parkin wrote: 'From this peg we had a fine view of the Kwai Noi winding away in the distance below. The thin coiling of its green-blue, unreflecting surface could easily have been smoke curling through the trees. The tree tops seemed soft and feathery. Some leaves were bursting out in reds and greens: here and there a splash of blossom or fruit; red fruit in trefoil bunches; pale lilac blossom, like acacias. But in the main, the top of the jungle was a sea of new leaf green and the mauve pink of bare branches. The near hills showed vertical rock slashes and jagged ridges: in the distance the blue mountains rolled away to the horizon.' That day in 1943 a man in Parkin's group at 156 killed a cobra. 'In fifteen minutes, enemy and allies were sharing the modest five feet of the unfortunate snake. It was like strong rabbit ... '

In the November afternoon, 54 years later, the trees were feathery still, but the blossom and fruit were long gone. I wondered again at the capacity of the men who built the railway under such terrible conditions to revel in the environment.

Rod and I walked up the track through narrow Compressor Cutting, so named because of the frequent use of mechanical drills, past the site of the wooden 'Pack of Cards' bridge, built on the dry stone embankment on which we were walking, itself a marvel of stone construction. All that remains of the bridge today is a bundle of wire, and a rotting scrap of wood from one of the props.

A kilometre further on, we reached Hintok Station, where a siding was constructed enabling trains to pass. Now there are twin tracks marking where the line once ran. There is little ballast and hardly any sleepers in this area. Further on is the three-tier bridge, with concrete steps to climb down to the collapsed track, and the remains of a series of low trestle bridges. In the bamboo jungle below, Rod barged off but we couldn't find the bomb crater he was searching for in the green mist of the bamboo.

Reaching Hellfire Pass means confronting the enormity of the task undertaken by the men who built the railway. Towards dusk it was an eerie place, a silent narrow defile, rather like the wadi leading to Petra, or King's Canyon in the Northern Territory – except that Hellfire Pass was dug, scraped and hammered out in two months, whereas the others were created by nature in tens of thousands of years.

It is a lonely and inspirited place. There's a section of rail laid down the middle of the cutting, and above on the embankment a section of narrow-gauge light rail that was used to carry the spoil from the cutting to be dumped. One tree has been left in the centre of the cutting, and one drill left in the stone like Excalibur, waiting for a good man who will end all wars to come and pull it out. I imagine that 'Weary' Dunlop, some of whose ashes were scattered here, might have been able to get it out if he had had a go.

A couple of hundred metres from Hellfire Pass is a lookout, the Kwae Noi Valley Lookout, where I sat and contemplated the mauve and lilac sky and the blue hills across the valley. It was utterly peaceful. Even the bats in the cave behind had not yet barged out. For all the suffering and savagery here, it wasn't hard to feel some of the magic of this beautiful place, and to feel that the jungle was just waiting to reclaim the railway.

The Australian and British dead are back in Kanchanaburi, the Asian labourers, such as those who lashed together the Pack of Cards and died in the process – they're down in the valley somewhere. Rod told me he had found the remains of one or two, almost certainly *romusha*, in his jungle-bashing walks in the area, and left them in peace.

Contemplation: Hellfire Pass Memorial.

Cemeteries, Memorial, Museums: Burma

Rangoon (Yangon)

Rangoon War Cemetery is five kilometres from the centre of the city. It was first used as a burial ground immediately following the recapture of Rangoon in May 1945. Later, the Army Graves Service moved in graves from several burial sites in and around Rangoon, including those of the men who died in Rangoon Jail as prisoners of war. There are now 1381 Commonwealth servicemen of the Second World War buried or commemorated in this cemetery.

The **Rangoon Memorial** is situated in **Taukkyan War Cemetery**, which is outside Rangoon, near the airport about 35 kilometres north of the city. The Rangoon Memorial bears the names of almost 27,000 men of the Commonwealth land forces who died during the campaigns in Burma and who have no known grave. The Taukkyan War Cemetery is the largest of the three war cemeteries in Burma. It was begun in 1951 for the reception of graves from four battlefield cemeteries at Akyab, Mandalay, Meiktila, Sahmaw and elsewhere which could not be maintained. The cemetery now contains 6374 Commonwealth burials of the Second World War, 867 of them unidentified.

Thanbyuzayat

Thanbyuzayat War Cemetery, Burma. (1999)

Thanbyuzayat War Cemetery contains all the graves from the northern section of the railway, between Moulmein and Nieke. There are now 3149 Commonwealth and 621 Dutch burials of the Second World War in the cemetery.

Nearby a bit of track has been re-laid with an apparently authentic Second World War locomotive sitting on it, and some pathetic half life-sized cement statues of prisoners with picks, watched by a Japanese guard, and a sign 'Myanmar Thailand Japanese Death Railway line starts here 1942 1943', in English and Burmese.

Cemeteries, Memorials, Museums: Thailand

Hellfire Pass

Hellfire Pass Memorial includes a museum and four kilometres of cleared railway track. Its construction was financed by the Australian government, and it opened in 1998. The museum itself is informative and accurate, and has a very beautiful meditation place overlooking the valley of the river.

The walk (see map) goes from Konyu Cutting (Hellfire Pass) past the Kwae Noi lookout, Hammer and Tap Cutting, the Seven Metre Embankment, Hintok Cutting, Hintok Station (a length of double track) the site of the Pack of Cards Bridge, to Compressor Cutting.

Some of Weary Dunlop's ashes were scattered at the western end of Hellfire Pass, where there is some track, a plaque and memorial. The site was disturbed in building a new memorial in 2005. Look for the section of broken-off drill and the marks made by the drills on the walls of the cutting. There is a small section of narrow-gauge track above the cutting again at the western end and a truck used to carry away the spoil.

Hellfire Pass. (2003)

Beyond Hellfire Pass is the **Kwae Noi lookout**, a meditative spot during the war, and today. Look at the drystone craftsmanship of the **Seven Metre Embankment**. There is a tangle of wood and wire on the river side of the **Pack of Cards Bridge** site – all that remains of this tragic construction.

Hellfire Pass is perhaps the most evocative Second World War site for Australians, because, like Gallipoli, the site where the men worked and died is so well preserved, and so beautiful. You can really appreciate the sublime truthfulness of what Ray Parkin experienced here – the evil done to men by other men, the peculiar redemptive quality of work, and the beauty of the place itself.

A day spent walking up and back the track is not easy, but one of the more worthwhile things to do. Carry water, wear walking shoes and a hat, and tell the staff at the museum what you're doing. The walk from the museum to Compressor Cutting and back to Hintok Road is about two and a half hours. All the way back to the museum will take four hours or more. If you have come up from Kanchanaburi, 80 kilometres away, with your own transport, arrange to be picked up at the Hintok Road.

A map of the walking trail and other information is available at **www.dva.gov.au**

Kanchanaburi

Chungkai War Cemetery was one of the base camps on the railway and contained a hospital and church built by Allied POWs. The war

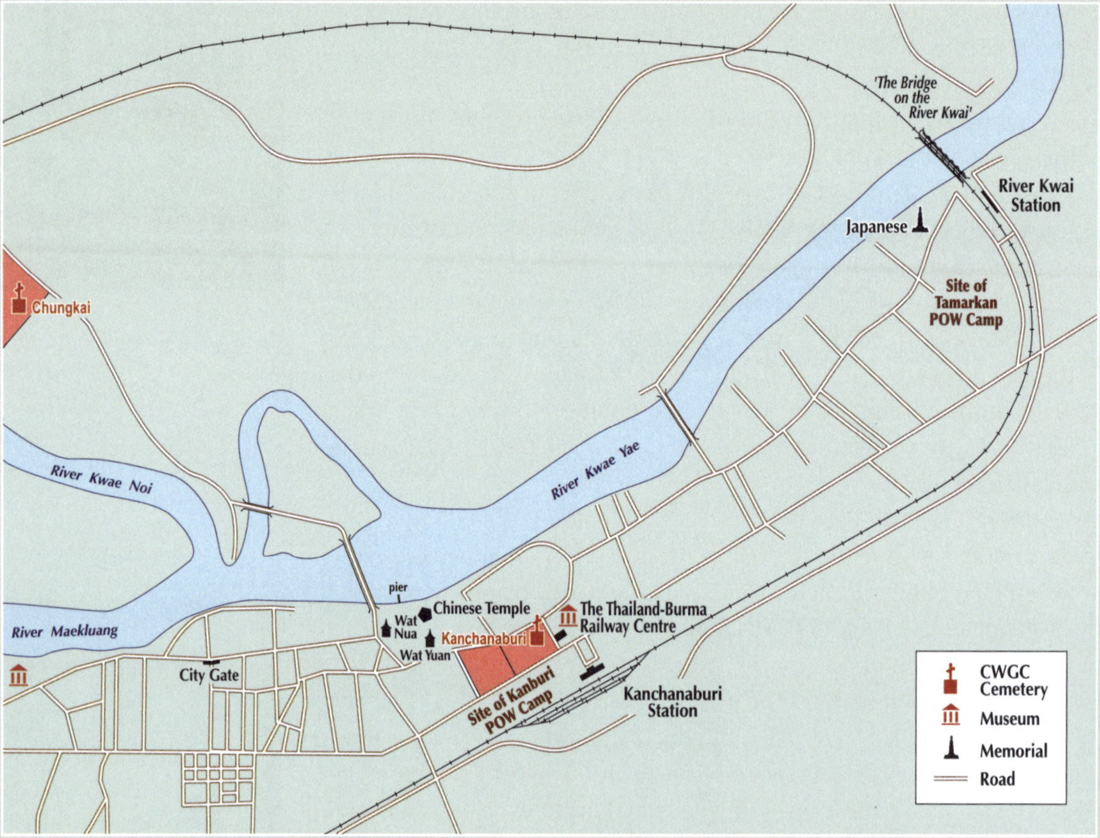

PILGRIMAGE

Kanchanaburi is the best place to stay for a day or two visiting the Thailand–Burma Railway Centre for history and orientation before visiting the two cemeteries, and the bridge. Hellfire Pass Memorial and walking track are an easy drive from Kanchanaburi, and you can take the train up the railway as far as Nam Tok.

Top: Map of Kanchanaburi.
Above: Kanchanaburi War Cemetery.
Left: A monk inspects the Australian bronze plaque at the bridge.

cemetery is the original burial ground started by the prisoners themselves, and the burials are mostly of men who died at the hospital. There are now 1427 Commonwealth and 314 Dutch burials of the Second World War in this cemetery. The cemetery was designed by Colin St Clair Oakes.

Kanchanaburi War Cemetery is 50 metres from Kanchanaburi station and only a short distance from the site of 'Kanburi', the prisoner of war base camp.

There are now 5084 Commonwealth casualties of the Second World War buried or commemorated in this cemetery. There are also 1896 Dutch war graves.

Chungkai War Cemetery, Kanchanaburi. (2003)

It contains all the graves from along the southern section of railway, from Bangkok to Nieke. Some 300 men who died during a cholera epidemic at Nieke camp were cremated and their ashes now lie in two graves in the cemetery. The names of these men are inscribed on panels in the shelter pavilion.

The **Thailand–Burma Railway Centre** is located across the road from the Kanchanaburi War Cemetery. This is the best museum about the history of the Thai–Burma Railway in Kanchanaburi – or anywhere else. Its comprehensive displays tell the history of the railway from the beginning through its brief period of use to its destruction and postwar demolition. The story is told very effectively through display panels about medical aspects, living conditions and deaths; maps; artefacts, including most of a guided Azon bomb of the type used to destroy the railway; re-creations of construction techniques; and interactive displays. A 3D electronic map of the route is particularly effective.

Thailand–Burma Railway Centre. (2003)

The centre publishes the best map of the railway route and camps. See **www.tbrconline.com**

The **Bridge over the River Kwai** [Kwae Noi] at Tamarkan in Kanchanaburi includes several curved spans that were imported from Java and put there during the war, and trains travelled across them for the time that the railway began running.

Of course the bridge is nothing like the one constructed in Sri Lanka for David Lean's film of Pierre Boulle's novel of mad leadership, *The Bridge over the River Kwai*, and American bombing – not an intrepid bunch of misfits accompanied by beautiful Thai women – blew up a span in 1945. The movie is obscenely distant from the suffering of the men who died building the railway. Yet the current bridge and the track to Nam Tok do serve as a memorial to what happened. There is one of Ross Bastiaan's Australian plaques at the Kanchanaburi end of the bridge near a wartime locomotive.

War Museum at the Bridge is a very strange museum which included, on my last visit, a glass case purporting to display human skeletal remains of railway workers. Presumably these are the remains of *romusha*, rather than Europeans, but that doesn't make the display less offensive. There are peculiar murals of Thai history, including military figures from the Second World War and some vehicles.

JEATH museum. (1999)

JEATH Museum is an acronym for the primary nations which participated in local action. These nations are: Japan, England, Australia, Thailand and Holland. The museum inside Wat Chai Chumphon has been constructed as an *atap* hut supposedly similar to that used by prisoners. It contains some nondescript memorabilia and tropically affected pictures.

Nam Tok

There is a **Second World War locomotive** on the roadside at Nam Tok, where the train line now ends. During the war this was the Tha Sao camp and hospital, where more than 1000 men died. The train from Bangkok and Kanchanaburi still comes across the bridge and this far up the Second World War track.

Three Pagodas Pass

At the border crossing between Thailand and Burma there is a Ross Bastiaan plaque. Sometimes the border opens so that visitors can, on payment of a few dollars of hard currency, step into Burma. It is definitely not an access point for travel more than a few metres inside.

Three Pagodas Pass. (1999)

Timor

After the Second World War, Timor drifted from Australian view for 30 years – Indonesia fought for independence from the Dutch, with sympathetic Australian support, and West Timor became an Indonesian province in 1949. East Timor did not become independent until after a coup deposed the ruling regime in Portugal in April 1974.

Several political parties quickly formed, including Fretilin, which had a radical vision for an independent East Timor. Indonesia, however, under the Suharto regime, wanted to incorporate East Timor. With the seeming acquiescence of the Australian government, it proceeded to bring about the conditions in which this could occur, undermining the pro-independence coalition government, which collapsed into civil war in May 1975. Indonesian forces invaded East Timor on 16 October 1975, and five Australia-based newsmen – Australians Greg Shackleton and Tony Stewart, Britons Malcolm Rennie and Brian Peters, and New Zealander Gary Cunningham – were killed, or murdered, at Balibo, near the border with Indonesian West Timor, while a sixth journalist, Briton Roger East, was executed by Indonesian forces while reporting on their deaths.

Indonesia declared East Timor its 27th province on 17 December 1975, and this was accepted by the Australian government in January 1978, though not by the United Nations. Led by Xanana Gusmao in Timor and Jose Ramos Horta in exile abroad, Fretilin maintained resistance for the next 25 years, despite international indifference and

The house in Balibo where the five journalists were killed. (Tony Clifton)

Indonesian attempts to eliminate the party. By the end of the 1980s, it seemed to the Indonesians that Timor had been 'pacified', but at a cost of 180,000 Timorese lives. But on 12 November 1991, as people marched to Santa Cruz cemetery in Dili to commemorate an independence supporter killed a fortnight earlier, Indonesian troops opened fire, killing at least 271. Film of the massacre, and the imprisonment of Xanana Gusmao a year later, stirred international interest again.

In 1999, in a startling about-face, Indonesia's new president, Habibie, agreed to allow the East Timorese to vote on their future. A UN operation (the United Nations Mission in East Timor, or UNAMET) oversaw the vote, held in August, which resulted in an overwhelming vote for independence. Xanana Gusmao, who had been transferred to house arrest, was freed on 4 September. But once the result of the vote was announced, pro-Indonesian militias, sometimes supported by elements of the Indonesian security forces, launched a campaign of terror, violence, looting and arson throughout the territory. Many East Timorese were killed, as many as 500,000 were displaced, and most of the infrastructure was destroyed – schools were burnt and wells poisoned with the bodies of murdered villagers.

Above: UNTAET headquarters, Dili.

With the violence uncontrolled, Indonesia agreed on 12 September to the deployment of a multinational peace-keeping force. Australia, which had contributed police to UNAMET, led the resulting International Force for East Timor (INTERFET), whose role was to restore peace and security, protect and support UNAMET, and facilitate humanitarian assistance operations. INTERFET began arriving on 19 September 1999; Australia contributed over 5500 personnel and the force commander, Major General Peter Cosgrove.

On 19 October 1999, Indonesia formally recognised the result of the referendum, and shortly thereafter, the United Nations Transitional Administration in East Timor (UNTAET) was established for the administration of East Timor during its transition to independence. Command of military operations was handed over from INTERFET to UNTAET by 28 February 2000. Australia has continued to support the UN peacekeeping operation.

East Timor officially became independent with the inauguration of Xanana Gusmao as president, and Mari Alkatiri as prime minister of the Democratic Republic of Timor-Leste on 20 May 2002.

On the Timor–Indonesia Border with 5/7th RAR, April 2000

Months after the handover of INTERFET to the UN in September 1999, thousands of Australian and New Zealand troops were still in Timor, helping stabilise the security situation on the border with Indonesian West Timor and creating as normal an environment as possible for the people of the Bobinaro District where Australians were stationed. Balibo is the major town there. I wanted to see for myself and write about Anzac Day in Dili and what the Australian soldiers were doing because on a personal level, this worthwhile peacekeeping operation had reconnected me to the Anzac tradition.

In April 2000, rebuilding in devastated Dili was in full swing. Blue plastic tarps covered the roofless houses. Dark, intense coffee beans were roasting in the market. Petrol was for sale at roadside pumping stations – Dickensian outfits where oil-soaked children hand-pumped dubious fuel from 44-gallon drums into the white utes and 4WDs readily available for hire. No smoking – hell – no electric glances, either, or the whole place would have gone up in an explosion.

5/7th Royal Australian Regiment, a mechanised unit, was based in the old Portuguese fort at Balibo, about 120 kilometres west of Dili, with forward patrol bases, checkpoints and observation posts closer to the border. The Balibo fort was a hive of activity, with rooms of 'geeks' tracking each Armoured Personnel Carrier (APC) and other vehicles via satellite navigation and other black arts – a first at battalion level for the Australians.

I spent a night at the Tonabibi patrol base, 24 kilometres west of Balibo, in the entertaining and informative company of A Platoon C Company and others – Sarge, Brett, Trav, Corporal Hovington, Snowy, Lieutenant Stew and Major Mick. I learned a lot about what it had been like repaying the debt owed to the Timorese since the Second World War, and what conditions were like for the Australians who fought in Timor in 1942.

In 1942 the 2/2nd Independent Company operated in the twisted hill country above Bobinaro and along the river flats that now marks the border with Indonesia, looking for opportunities to ambush the enemy. The job of the 5/7th was different – they were not looking for trouble, they were there to provide security on the border for the refugees that might want to come back, and in the words of the major, to 'tread lightly'.

They were camped in the ruin of an old Indonesian barracks, the troop of old but useful APCs parked out the front. The guest room had a tarpaulin roof, a stretcher. I was offered an olive-green 'rat pack' and made myself popular by giving away the 'gumpy bars'.

These young men were extremely modest about being in harm's way. While there might not have been bullets flying around down there on the border, there were strange moments in the early days in Dili spent clearing buildings in the dark, using night vision gear that turned night into a weird green day. They encountered drug-influenced Indonesian soldiers with weapons close at hand, a tense situation that might have turned bloody, except for their own calmness and professionalism and the residual common sense of the Indonesians. On a number of occasions weapons were pointed but not used; a soldier's sign of respect for the moment. Even the untrained and stirred-up militia could recognise a no-win situation when confronted with one. 5/7th RAR only fired three rounds in earnest in the whole time they were in Timor, a proud boast which demonstrates just how well they did their job.

We swapped yarns, watching the sun go down behind the APCs, and the moon come up. At 10 p.m., a few guys got their boots on, picked up their weapons, and clambered in the back of the APC for a very public two-hour moonlight patrol, just to let anyone interested know that the Australians were still about. Another patrol rumbled off at 4 a.m., and later that morning a two-day

patrol and observation headed for the hills behind. The routine of patrolling and standing piquet just seemed to happen, without a lot of shouting and parading.

Except in the matter of shaving, the contemporary Diggers were just like the legendary men of the 2/2nd in Timor (the 2/2nd were renowned for their piratical and flourishing beards; A Platoon was clean-shaven and short-haired, as befits the hot and humid climate). Otherwise they were the grandsons of the 2nd AIF – as was one member, literally, whose grandfather was a member of the ill-fated 2/40th captured and imprisoned by the Japanese on West Timor in 1942. They had the same ready humour, easy camaraderie, mutual dependence and the traditional concerns over beer (there is none), cigarettes (called 'dhurries'), and getting a brew. They were relaxed with officers, disciplined, and completely professional about their task and how to achieve it.

I went back to Dili in a convoy of army trucks, and was cheered all the way up Timor's magnificent version of the Great Ocean Road. At every village and hamlet, the kids and their parents, but especially the kids, came and cheered the waving soldiers. It was like a parade by a World Cup-winning team for 124 kilometres, through devastated buildings, past congregations singing in open churches, recently planted rice fields, fish hanging from trees, and UN workers lounging outside the big white buildings they inhabited.

This was Timor on the eve of Anzac Day, 2000. Debt repaid.

Cemeteries, Memorials, Museums: Ambon

Ambon War Cemetery is at the eastern end of what was the Dutch East Indies when it was invaded by the Japanese on 30–31 January 1942. The cemetery is built on the site of the Second World War POW camp.

Gull Force, mainly comprised of the 2/21st Battalion, defended Ambon heroically but were overrun by superior Japanese numbers. Except for 36 men who escaped and made their way to Australia, the surviving defenders became POWs. They suffered a death rate of 74 per cent.

Ambon War Cemetery. (CWGC)

Some members of the 2/2nd Independent Company are also buried at the Ambon Military Cemetery. Some were killed on the day of the Japanese landing, including Harry Cotsworth, one of the 'boys on the ration truck'.

Several of the commandos served under false names: Robert Ewan Oliver, who served as Robert Ewan, was killed in August and is buried at Ambon. William Patrick Cotter, who served as Pat Knight and was mentioned in despatches, was killed in March 1942 and is buried, as Cotter, also at Ambon. He is also recorded, as Pat Knight, at the Australian War Memorial. Three of the other twelve members of the 2/2nd killed in action are also buried at Ambon.

There are 644 identified and 317 unidentified Australians buried here.

Cemeteries, Memorials, Museums: Timor

Balibo

Balibo Flag House. (Tony Clifton, 2005)

Balibo Flag House is where journalist Greg Shackleton painted the Australian flag on the wall in the hope that this would offer some protection from the Indonesian invasion in 1975. It did not. Shackleton and four colleagues were killed nearby as they filmed invading Indonesian forces attacking Balibo on 16 October 1975. The five had spent their final days at the house before being shot dead.

The Flag House has been renovated as a community centre, financed by the Victorian government and opened on 31 October 2001. It is a permanent memorial to the journalists killed in Timor. Remarkably, as workmen removed layers of burnt and peeling paint, they discovered the faded outline of the flag painted by Greg Shackleton, and the single word above it – Australia.

South-East Asia

The Royal Australian Regiment memorial below the old Portuguese fort in Balibo, that was its headquarters 1999–2002. 'This memorial, dedicated to the peace and prosperity of the people of Timor Leste, commemorates the contribution of the Royal Australian Regiment to the creation of a secure, free and democratic nation.' Dedicated in 2004. (Tony Clifton)

The community centre provides essential services such as literacy classes, vocational training in trades and other skills, and childcare facilities for the Balibo community and surrounding region.

There is a new Australian memorial below the old fort that was the Australian headquarters in Balibo.

Betano

The **wreck of the HMAS *Voyager*** is still visible on the beach at Betano. RAN clearance divers were at Betano in March 2000 when HMAS *Betano*, a 'landing ship – heavy' (LHS), visited the place after which she was named. The divers surveyed the wreck, and disposed of some of the hazardous material there – a torpedo, depth charges, fuses and shell. They located an anchor, three four-inch guns and the ship's two propellers.

Dili

Fatunaba Memorial Pool is the main memorial to Australian involvement in 1942, and is located a few kilometres up the switchbacked road from Dili, near the village of Dare.

Above HMAS *Voyager* wreckage, 1990s.
Below Fatunaba Memorial Pool. (Tony Clifton, 2005)

Dili is hot and humid, but higher up, heading south up this mountainside, it is often wet, with cool mists lurking in the twisted terrain. The view between the clouds is misleadingly beautiful, but like the jungle reclaiming a killing ground, the greenery is mere camouflage.

Fatunaba is a little way up the hill, with its memorial to the Australians who fought and died here in 1942. The memorial includes a plaque, garden and wading pool at a resting place for the people who walk from the market in the lee of the steep hill. It's dug into

the downward slope of the mountain, as the road south zags back and up.

The track to Dare and the Jesuit seminary where over 30,000 refugees sought shelter from recent horrific events in Dili continues along the ridge.

The memorial was opened on 13 April 1969, with money raised by the 2/2nd Commando Association, and matched by the Australian government.

The plaque, in Portuguese, reads: 'To the Portuguese people everywhere, from Minho to Timor. This memorial has been given for your use by the people of Australia in gratitude for the help you gave our soldiers during the years 1939–1945 and particularly to the people of Timor. From the men of the 2/2nd Commando Independent Company who served here in 1942.'

Some time after the Indonesian invasion of 1975, the plaque disappeared. Restoration of the memorial commenced in December 1999, with work by volunteer Australian personnel from the Headquarters Force Logistic Support Group and 17 Construction Squadron. It was completed for a re-dedication ceremony on 13 April 2000, in the presence of members of the 2/2nd Commando Association. They felt that since the Timorese people had won their independence, new wording for the plaque was appropriate. It now reads, in Tetum and English, 'To all the peoples of East Timor. This memorial and resting place is given to them for their use by the Australian people in grateful recognition of their assistance to Australian soldiers especially members of the 2/2 and 2/4 Independent Companies during the Second World War.'

The ceremony had taken place just before my visit before Anzac Day in 2000. A few fading wreaths marked the spot on the roadside. The reflective pool and the flat-roofed shelters had been rescued from the jungle, the pool had been cleaned and sealed, the cement painted beige. Children from the nearby village of Dare were busy cleaning and weeding the pool area – it doesn't take long for the vegetation to grow and regrow – but the new plaque wasn't there. The security situation had not settled sufficiently for Australian evidence to be left in plain view. The situation had improved by 2005 when the plaque had been restored.

Travel Tool Kits

Borneo

Getting to and around Kalimantan in Indonesian Borneo is not easy, but it is possible. Sabah, part of Malaysia, is better set up for travellers, and the Australia-related sites are not difficult to get to.

The Australian government still warns against travel to Indonesia, a warning widely ignored in Bali even after two terrorist bombings but one which should be taken seriously in Kalimantan and Ambon. Australians were in physical danger during the 1999 anti-Australian riots against our role in Timor, shortly before I arrived there. That was political, and especially since the Boxing Day 2004 tsunami, relationships have improved immeasurably. However, religious and ethnic violence is an ever-present possibility, particularly in Kalimantan, Ambon and West Papua. Transport – ferries and aircraft – are unreliable and sometimes dangerous. Individuals will have to make their own risk assessment about where they go and how they get there.

Above: General Douglas MacArthur lords it over Jayapura, West Papua.
Below: Ranau, Sabah, Malaysia.

In 1999 I flew to Balikpapan from Jayapura in West Papua, via Solo (Surakata). There were no direct flights, and the Pelni ferry to Makassar (Ujung Pandang) was not running on my timetable. This took two days and was quite expensive. Balikpapan is an oil town, with few of Borneo's charms. There is little to recommend it except as a way of getting into the interior – Samarinda and the Mahakam River. On my visit the Australian memorials had been desecrated, wrapped in black plastic and the plaques stolen. They were restored in 2000. Balikpapan's battle sites have also been taken over by the growth of the town, although it is easy enough to follow the broad outline of the campaign from beach-head to the airport, and into the hills along the Samarinda road.

I flew from Balikpapan to Tarakan on a dodgy turboprop aircraft with crates of raucous chickens. This was adventurous, even dangerous, but flying over the places about which Joseph Conrad wrote his early novels was a consolation – as was actually landing.

Tarakan has little to offer, it's an oil-producing backwater as it was in 1942. Many of the little hills so hard fought over are now covered in modern developments. It was one of the least friendly places I have ever been to, and I couldn't wait to get out. But that took some time before I discovered and boarded a ferry to Tawau in southern Sabah,

Malaysia. This was quite fast; the 100-kilometre journey took about four hours, during which I had the dubious pleasure of watching a Jackie Chan movie set in Melbourne on the onboard video. The locals thought it very exotic.

Ferry and airline timetables don't often mesh. I had to stay overnight in Tawau, before flying to Sandakan. At that time just getting to Malaysia made me feel safer. Sandakan is a pretty town, and the base for a good deal of tourist activity and handy to the wonderful Sepilok orang-utan sanctuary. The Sandakan Memorial Park is on the site of the Second World War prisoner of war camp, a short taxi ride from the centre of town. Drivers will take you there and wait. They will also jump at the chance to drive you to Ranau, or Kota Kinabalu along the route of the death marches. There are also buses and regular flights to 'KK'.

Kota Kinabalu, the former Jesselton, is a pleasant place (I can recommend the small hotel of that name) and the base to get to the Labuan War Cemetery. There's a ferry, which takes about three hours or you can fly – which takes about twenty minutes. Taxi drivers in Labuan will know where to find the cemetery, the Australian memorials, and the Japanese Peace Park.

Darwin

Darwin has suffered more calamities than any other city in Australia – from the Japanese air raids to Cyclone Tracy – but has survived everything to become a unique Australian place. You don't need an excuse to go, but the wartime sites can help structure a couple of days in and around Darwin before heading off to the Tiwi Islands or Kakadu, or beyond. (Timor is just a short flight from Darwin.) Driving is easy, but walking, even in Centennial Park is hot.

I found Billy Can Tours (**www.billycan.com.au**) excellent for organising a camping trip into Kakadu, where meeting a few of the more-celebrated crocodiles, or crocodile yarns, is great. You can also have a tremendous amount of fun in Darwin going to the football, either the Northern Territory Football League games or the extraordinary game played on the Tiwi Islands of Bathurst and Melville. The Mindil markets are fun, the seafood is wonderful, and there are spectacular crimes (mostly at Uluru and down the Stuart Highway) to talk about. And now you can of course catch the train.

Malaysia

The Japanese landing point at Kota Bharu in the north-east corner of peninsular Malaysia is easily accessible by car on the motorway, and the train from Singapore to Bangkok stops nearby at Pasir Mas. Catching the train is a cheap and fun way to get from Singapore to Kanchanaburi and the Thai–Burma Railway, literally in the tracks of the men who went this way in 1942. But the mainly Islamic states of southern Thailand are experiencing periodic bouts of unrest. It's not worth getting off the train.

Kota Bharu is in Kelantan, an alcohol-free Malaysian state, but aside from that is quite a pleasant town. The main attractions are six intimate palaces and museums within walking distance of each other near the wide, muddy and shallow Kelantan River.

Finding and getting to the key war sites in Malaysia near Singapore – Gemas, Muar and Parit Sulong – can be difficult. It looks easy on a modern map, and the distances are not great, but when I hired a car in 2003 and went looking for the ambush site at Gemas, I found it more by accident than good navigation. But it is certainly possible to spend two or three fruitful days in the area, using Singapore or Malacca as a base, and finding what is left there.

Singapore

One of the ways Singapore has refocused itself as a destination with other things to offer besides shopping has been to recognise and

Singapore harbour – the guns are still pointing out to sea.

remember its history. The Second World War is plainly a big part of this. The museums and memorials are now well organised, and tours are easy to plan. For Australians, the main places – Kranji War Cemetery and the Changi Museum and Chapel – can be visited in a day, and most easily by taxi.

The 60th anniversary of the end of the Second World War saw the tourist authority detail three self-guided tour itineraries, with maps, details on how to get there at **www.visitsingapore.com**. Alternatively, guided tours are available.

If you have a spare Wednesday afternoon, the easiest way to see the major Singapore battlefield sites is on the entertaining Singapore Walks Battlefield coach tours. These tours were created by the Changi Museum. The itinerary includes Labrador Battery, the site of Fort Pasir Panjang and the old WW2 6-inch gun battery; Alexandra Hospital; Mount Faber; Faber Fire Command; and Kranji War Cemetery. Meet at Little India MRT Station Exit E (Buffalo Road) or take a cab to the junction between Race Course Road and Buffalo Road. The tour commences at 2 p.m. and lasts for three hours. You are dropped off at City Hall MRT at the end of the tour.

Alternatively, the Saturday morning Changi WW2 Tour includes the Changi Museum and Chapel; Changi Beach, the site of the *Sook Ching* massacre; Changi Village; Johore Battery, a replica of a WW2 15-inch gun battery; and the exterior of Selarang Barracks, part of Changi POW camp. Meet at Pasir Ris MRT, outside Exit B at 10 a.m. You will be dropped off at Pasir Ris MRT at the end of the tour.

Bookings are via email (**fun@singaporewalks.com**) otherwise, availability is on a first-come-first-served basis. Brochures and timetables available at **www.singaporewalks.com**

Thai–Burma Railway

Since the Australian government opened the Hellfire Pass Memorial in 2000, it has become a popular place for commemoration and remembrance. It is easily accessible from Bangkok, via the cemeteries at Kanchanaburi, and the place itself – Konyu Cutting, or 'Hellfire Pass' – is extraordinarily evocative. You can see the individual marks made by the drills in the rock, and walk a couple of kilometres down the track and try to square the circle of the beauty of the river valley with the bestiality of what happened here in 1943. Until 2005 there was a section of reconstructed track, near the plaques at the northern

The macabre memorial to the 'Myanmar–Thailand Death Railway,' Thanbyuzayat.

Above: A Buddhist park between Moulmein and Thanbyuzayat in Burma.
Above right: Hellfire Pass.

end of the cutting where some of Weary Dunlop's ashes had been scattered. The area was renovated and a new memorial put in place, to the astonishment of many veterans and historians.

The joining point of the two parts of the railway is under the water of the Khao Lam Dam, close to the Thailand–Burma border. You can see where the track emerged from the water from the road to Three Pagodas Pass. The town of Sanklaburi on the Khao Lam Dam is most extraordinary, and a boat trip on the reservoir offers a different view of the railway.

For Kanchanaburi and Hellfire Pass in Thailand, it is possible to hire a car and driver and do a big day from Bangkok – but this leaves little time to walk the railway at Hellfire Pass. However, it would be possible to visit the Kanchanaburi War Cemetery and the Thailand–Burma Railway Centre in the morning, drive 80 kilometres to the Hellfire Pass Memorial and walk the 300 metres to the cutting, and still get back to Bangkok that night. But it is a long day.

One-day minibus tours from **www.hotelthailand.com** depart Bangkok hotels at 6.30 a.m., and return at 6 p.m. These tours, and most hotel-based tours, do not go to the two best sites for Australians: Hellfire Pass (with the Hellfire Pass Museum) and the Thai–Burma Railway Centre in Kanchanaburi. However, it is easy enough to organise this yourself.

Trains in Thailand are safe, cheap and if slow, also one of the best ways to meet and talk to the locals. The train to Kanchanaburi leaves from Thonburi station several times a day, and costs less than a dollar – third class. The trip takes about three hours. Some trains go across the bridge along the old railway track as far as Nam Tok.
www.kanchanaburi-info.com

PILGRIMAGE

A car and driver transfer from Bangkok airport or hotel to Kanchanaburi can be arranged. The services at **www.hotelthailand.com** are recommended. There is plenty of accommodation, ranging from guest houses on the river to more luxurious resorts. See **www.kanchanaburi-info.com**

Visiting the Burmese side of the railway and getting to the cemetery at Thanbyuzayat is not easy. You can't cross from Three Pagodas Pass, and must fly to Rangoon (Yangon) from Bangkok and with permission take the train to Moulmein, and find Thanbyuzayat by car or train 50 kilometres further south. That's where the main POW camp was situated and where the Commonwealth War Graves cemetery is now.

Details of current visa and foreign exchange requirements for Burma can be obtained from their embassy in Australia.

Embassy of the Union of Myanmar
Address: 22 Arkana Street
Yarralumla ACT 2600

The Commonwealth War Graves Commission entry for Thanbyuzayat cemetery warns that special permission is needed to travel there and that three days should be allowed for the journey, south from Rangoon on the train. I visited the cemetery in 1997, and didn't know that I needed permission. I just bought a ticket on the train, and headed for Moulmein.

Timor

Travel to Timor-Leste is more than possible today. The country is beautiful and varied, poor but on its feet, and it is as safe and friendly as anywhere in the world. The coffee is universally splendid, the cooking in Dili inventive, and the climate and geography diverse. And after the decline of the UNTAET bubble economy, they need visitors.

I don't suppose anyone would travel to Timor-Leste merely to look at Australia's military associations, there are not many memorials, but there is a lot of shared history which makes it a better bet for a meaningful visit than virtually anywhere else in South-East Asia.

The best way into Timor from Australia is on one of the Airnorth twice-daily flights from Darwin. Merpati fly from Bali, and buses are available from Kupang in West Timor to the border, where you can

Descendants of the *creados* who helped the Australians in 1942, and a sturdy Timorese pony whose forebears also did their bit.

cross and pick up an East Timorese bus. Visas are available at the Presidente Nicolau Lobato International Airport in Dili for 30 days.

Once in Timor, many places are within a day's drive of Dili. The memorial at Fatunaba is an hour's drive up the hill outside Dili, and Balibo takes a few hours. Getting to Betano is also possible, provided the road has not been washed away.

Getting around is easy on buses, or by hiring a car, or 4WD. Drive on the left.

Accommodation in Dili is improving – there is the famous beach-front Turismo hotel, East Timor Backpackers, or the classier, newer Esplanada. You can stay at the 'container hotel' (now called the Timor Lodge Hotel) that I enjoyed in 2000, five kilometres from Dili on the way to the airport. Accommodation outside of Dili is more difficult to find.

Intrepid Travel have begun running 15-day small-group tours from Dili, which are interesting and reliable: **www.intrepidtravel.com**

Further Information

Frank Alcorta, *Australia's Frontline: The Northern Territory's War*, Allen & Unwin, Sydney, 1991.
Stan Arneil, *Black Jack*, Macmillan, Melbourne, 1983.
Stan Arneil, *One Man's War*, Sun Books, Melbourne, 1982.
Aviation Historical Society of the Northern Territory, *Darwin's Air War*, Darwin, 1991.

Bridge over the River 'Kwai'.

Des Ball and Hamish McDonald, *Death in Balibo, Lies in Canberra*, Allen & Unwin, Crows Nest, 2000.
Bob Breen, *Mission Accomplished*, Allen & Unwin, Crows Nest, 2000.
Tim Bowden, *Changi Photographer*, Times Editions, Singapore, 1997.
Micool Brooks, *Captive of the River Kwae*, Merman Books, Bangkok, 1995.
Ian Buruma, *The Wages of Guilt*, Oxford, London, 1999.
Bernard Callinan, *Independent Company*, Heinemann, Melbourne, 1953.
Archie Campbell, *The Double Reds of Timor*, John Burridge, Swanbourne, 1995.
Luis Cardoso, *The Crossing: A Story of East Timor*, Granta, London, 2000.
Peter Charlton, *The Unnecessary War*, Macmillan, Melbourne, 1983.
Discover Dili **www.discoverdili.com**
E E Dunlop, *The War Diaries of Weary Dunlop*, Nelson, Melbourne, 1986.
James Dunn, *Timor: A People Betrayed*, ABC Books, Sydney, 1996.
East Timor Action Network **www.etan.org**
Murray Farquhar, *Derrick VC*, Rigby, Adelaide, 1982.
Cameron Forbes, *Hellfire*, Pan Macmillan, Sydney, 2005.
Don Greenlees & Robert Garran, *Deliverance: The Inside Story of East Timor's Fight for Freedom*, Allen & Unwin, Crows Nest, 2002.
G Hermon Hill, *Royal Australian Navy 1942–45*, Australian War Memorial, Canberra, 1968.
Betty Jeffrey, *White Coolies*, Angus & Robertson, (1954) 1997.

Jill Joliffe, *Cover-Up: The Inside Story of the Balibo Five*, Scribe, Melbourne, 2000.

Clifford Kinvig, *River Kwai Railway*, Brassey's, London, 1992.

Tom Lewis, *A War at Home: Tall Stories*, Darwin, 2003.

Douglas Lockwood, *Australia's Pearl Harbour*, Penguin, Ringwood, (1966) 1992.

Gavin Long, *The Final Campaigns*, Australian War Memorial, Canberra, 1963.

Dudley McCarthy, *South West Pacific Area, First Year Kokoda to Wau*, Australian War Memorial, Canberra, 1959.

Gavan McCormack & Hank Nelson, *The Burma–Thailand Railway*, Allen & Unwin, Sydney, 1993.

Gilbert Mant, *You'll Be Sorry*, Frank Johnson, Sydney, 1944.

Gilbert Mant, *Massacre at Parit Sulong*, Kangaroo Press, Kenshurst, 1995.

John Martinkus, *A Dirty Little War*, Random House, Milsons Point, 2001.

Ministry of Foreign Affairs and Cooperation Timor-Leste **www.mfac.gov.tp**

Athol Moffitt, *Project Kingfisher*, Angus & Robertson, Sydney, 1989.

John Moreman, *Australians on the Burma–Thailand Railway*, Department of Veterans' Affairs, Canberra, 2003.

John Moreman and Richard Reid, *A Bitter Fate: Australians in Malaya and Singapore*, Department of Veterans' Affairs, Canberra, 2002.

Ray Parkin, *Into the Smother*, Hogarth Press, London, 1962.

Ian Denys Peek, *One Fourteenth Part of an Elephant*, Macmillan, Sydney, 2003.

Bob Reece, *Masa Jepun: Sarawak Under the Japanese 1941–1945*, Sarawak Literary Society, Kuching, 1998.

Richard Reid, *Laden, Fevered, Starved: The POWs of Sandakan North Borneo 1945*, Department of Veterans' Affairs, Canberra, 1999.

Rohan Rivett, *Behind Bamboo*, Penguin, Ringwood, (1946) 1991.

Lynette Ramsay Silver, *Sandakan: A Conspiracy of Silence*, Sally Milner, Burra Creek, 1997.

Lynette Ramsay Silver, *The Bridge at Parit Sulong*, Watermark Press, Sydney, 2004.

Peter Stanley, *Tarakan: An Australian Tragedy*, Allen & Unwin, Sydney, 1997.

John G Taylor, *East Timor: The Price of Freedom*, Pluto Press, Annandale, 1999.

Michele Turner, *Telling East Timor: Personal Testimonies 1942–1992*, UNSW Press, Sydney, 1992.

Turismo de Timor-Leste **www.turismotimorleste.com**

Janet Uhr, *Against the Sun: The AIF in Malaya 1941–41*, Allen & Unwin, Sydney, 1998.

Laurens Van Der Post, *The Night of the New Moon*, Chatto & Windus, London, 1985.

Don Wall, *Sandakan: The Last March*, Mona Vale, 1997.

Tony Wheeler, *East Timor*, Lonely Planet, Melbourne, 2004.

Lionel Wigmore, *The Japanese Thrust*, Australian War Memorial, Canberra, 1957.

Christopher C H Wray, *Timor 1942*, Hutchinson Australia, Hawthorn, 1987.

6.

NEW GUINEA 1942
THE BATTLE FOR AUSTRALIA

Japan may not have set out to physically invade Australia in 1942, but we didn't know that at the time. The bombing of Darwin and other north Australian towns, the landings in New Guinea – first at Rabaul, then at Lae – and the fighting on the Kokoda Track certainly appeared to be preparation for a serious attack.

The Japanese definitely intended to defend the enormous territories in South-East Asia and the Pacific that they had gained in their extraordinarily quick and successful campaigns through Malaya and Singapore, Burma, and the islands of the Dutch East Indies and the Pacific.

p.305: Steven Wanire inspects the tip of Kokoda Plateau, 1999.

To defend all this they needed to destroy the American Pacific fleet and gain secure bases at strategic points. Australia was an option to be looked at, perhaps, after Rabaul, Port Moresby, Fiji, and New Caledonia had been captured, the sea-lanes between Australia and the rest of the world had been cut, and the American fleet which had survived the attack on Pearl Harbor had been drawn into battle after the capture of Midway Island.

Rabaul was the main centre in the former German territory of New Guinea, administered by Australia under a mandate from the League of Nations after the First World War; Papua, the southern part of the island, was an Australian territory. On Rabaul, Lark Force, consisting in the main of the 2/22nd Battalion, had been sent as a garrison in April 1941. Rabaul was captured in one day, 23 January 1942, by a much larger Japanese force. Some 400 survivors escaped, but another 160 were massacred.

Port Moresby, Darwin, Broome and Rockhampton were bombed in February 1942, and Salamaua and Lae, on the north coast of New Guinea, were captured unopposed on 8 March.

While the Japanese prepared to attack Midway, in the mid-Pacific Ocean, General Douglas MacArthur (appointed commander-in-chief of the South-West Pacific Area on 18 April, after his escape from the Philippines) began to make defensive preparations in Papua and New Guinea. Airstrips were surveyed at Milne Bay, Port Moresby began to

Below: Map of New Guinea and Northern Australia.

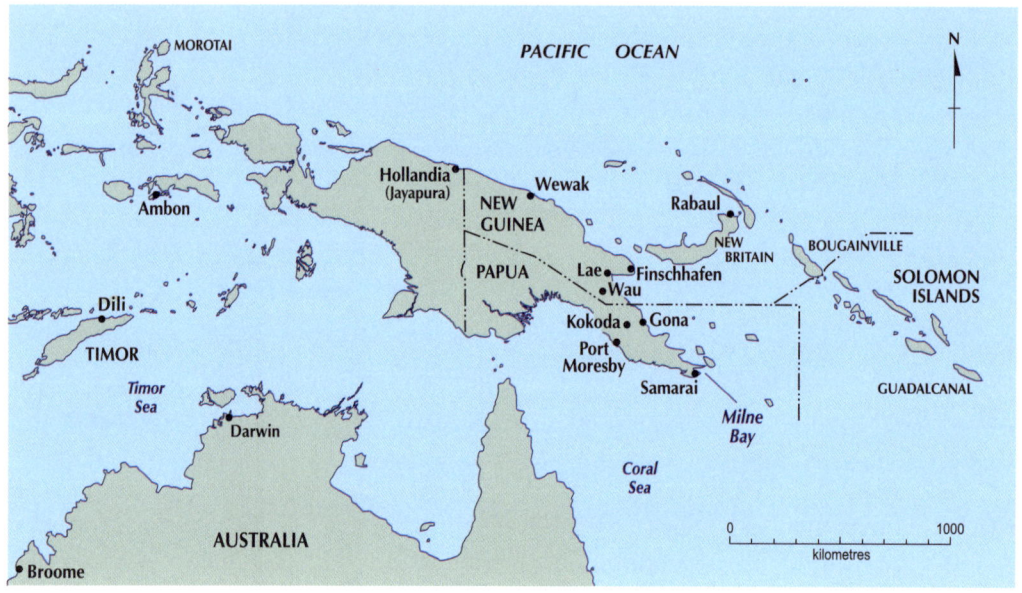

be reinforced, and Kanga Force commandos were sent to the Wau/Lae/Salamaua area to keep an eye on the Japanese.

Two naval battles were decisive in changing the course of the war against Japan: the Battle of the Coral Sea, 4–8 May 1942; and the Battle of Midway, 4–7 June. The first significant defeats were inflicted on Japan by the United States; these, with the Australian victories on land in New Guinea, turned the tide of the war.

The Battle of the Coral Sea was fought between aircraft-carrier-based planes – it was the first naval battle fought between ships that never sighted each other. The Japanese force had been sent from their base at Rabaul to cover the invasion of Port Moresby. This convoy was delayed after being found by the Americans, and failed to continue to Port Moresby while the battle was engaged. One Japanese aircraft carrier was sunk, substantial damage was done to two others, and the Americans lost two. The major impact of the battle was that the Japanese abandoned the idea of a seaborne invasion of Port Moresby, and were forced to try across the mountains from the north coast. (The Japanese plan to take Midway as a base from which to attack Hawaii and force the United States to negotiate a peace deal was decisively defeated a month later.)

New Guinea was to be defended by two Australian militia brigades, which had arrived in May 1942. These were of varying quality, as the subsequent fighting was to find out, but the 39th Battalion was a first-class unit. A company of the 39th – about 110 men – had been sent up the Kokoda Track, and was stationed thinly around the area in July. With a handful of local volunteers, they stood between Port Moresby and the Japanese invasion.

The Japanese landed at Buna and Gona on the north coast of New Guinea on 21 July 1942. They landed about 2000 men, to be reinforced to over 14,000 if the reconnaissance on the track beyond

Bulolo River Valley, near Wau: Kanga Force was based near Wau from August 1942. (1999)

Kokoda was feasible. Commanded by Colonel Yosuke Yokoyama, they comprised an engineering regiment, a battalion of 144 Regiment, some of the 55th Mountain Artillery, a company of the 5th Sasebo Naval Landing Force – who were six-foot-tall tough marines.

The 39th harassed the Japanese effectively, but were outnumbered, and withdrew down the track. Reinforcements from the Australian 7th Division, now returned from the Middle East, were not due until mid-August.

Meanwhile, the Americans had landed in force on Japanese-held Guadalcanal in the Solomon Islands, east of New Guinea, on 7 August. This demanded a response from the Japanese, and diverted resources away from New Guinea for a considerable time. After terrible casualties (1752 Americans died) and seven major naval battles, the last Japanese were evacuated in January 1943.

The Japanese resumed the offensive in New Guinea on 25–26 August. On the Kokoda Track they attacked the Australians (the 7th Division's 21st Brigade and the 39th Battalion) at the village of Isurava. This desperate battle, and subsequent actions at Brigade Hill, delayed the Japanese advance for crucial weeks, eventually stretching their supply lines to breaking point.

The commandos of Kanga Force, after some successful raids, had pulled back to a base in the gold-mining town of Wau, inland from Lae and Salamaua, following Japanese attacks in August 1942. Reinforced in September, their presence prevented the Japanese moving further inland. A big Japanese attack was defeated from the airfield at Wau in January 1943. The Japanese were finally defeated in Lae and Salamaua in September 1943.

Milne Bay at the eastern end of New Guinea was also attacked on 25 August. Unknown to the enemy, the garrison had been reinforced just a few days before by the 7th Division's 18th Brigade, and

Above: Kokoda airstrip: one of the objectives of the Japanese on the north coast of New Guinea. (1999)
Above left: The last ridge: Hombrum's Bluff above the Laloki River, near Port Moresby, was never reached by the Japanese in 1942. Second World War Marsden matting fences the road. (2000)

New Guinea 1942

Battle for Australia: On 19 November 1941, a few weeks before the Japanese invaded Malaya, HMAS *Sydney* was lost with all 645 crew in a battle with the German raider HSK *Kormoran* in the Indian Ocean off Carnarvon. The rare picture of the *Sydney* in Albany Harbour in 1941 was taken by 19-year-old Bombardier Jack Hutchinson, serving in the Albany coastal battery. Hutchinson joined the AIF and served with E Battery, Australian Heavy Artillery at Milne Bay in 1942. (Jack Hutchinson, 1941)

by Kittyhawk fighter aircraft. After stiff fighting, and numerous Japanese atrocities, the landing was defeated, and the Japanese evacuated back to Rabaul by 5 September. The crucial battle was at Three Strip, which would be the furthest south and east the Japanese advanced in the war. After the battle, Milne Bay became a large base for Australian and American forces in later campaigns in the South-West Pacific.

The Japanese advance down the Kokoda Track was finally halted on 24 September, at Ioribaiwa, just 60 kilometres from Port Moresby.

Kanga Force flies in: American DC3 (Dakota) transports 2/5th Commandos to Wau. (Mick Sheehan, 1942)

The starving and diseased Japanese could not be reinforced or resupplied, and were ordered back up the track when almost in sight of their objective. They withdrew down the track; it was now their turn to fight delaying battles, while building their defences at the beachheads of Buna, Gona and Sanananda.

The Australians re-entered Kokoda on 2 November 1942. There was no resistance. Local plantation owner Bert Kienzle, who had become a legend by reconnoitring the track, and organising the local carriers – the 'fuzzy-wuzzy angels' – arrived the next day and saw that all the buildings had been demolished. The locals turned up 'bedecked with flowers and shrubs and all smiles' as he noted in his diary. On 6 November, there was a ceremony to mark the event.

But at Buna and Gona the Japanese preparations had been well made. Only after suicidal resistance, and heavy Australian casualties, was the battle for Australia concluded – 22 January 1943.

New Guinea 1942

The defeat of the Japanese on the beach-heads in January 1943 after the Kokoda Track campaign, and at Guadalcanal, was the end of the battle for Australia. But the war was not won, and Japan did not surrender in New Guinea until 15 August 1945.

In 1943 it was decided that rather than trying to capture the Japanese fortress of Rabaul, it should be neutralised and bypassed. From June 1943, American forces recaptured New Georgia in the Solomons and destroyed much of the Japanese airforce at Wewak. Australian and some American forces recaptured Salamaua on 11 September, Lae on 16 September, and Finschafen on the Huon Peninsula north of Lae on 2 October. After four months of hard fighting by the 7th and 9th divisions in the extraordinary country of the Finisterre Range – Sattelberg, Shaggy Ridge, Ramu Valley – the Japanese were finally in retreat in this area. The Americans took Hollandia (Jayapura) on 22 April, Biak on 27 May, and by September 1944 were ready to return to the Philippines.

Jayapura in today's West Papua was named Hollandia in the Second World War. It was captured by the Americans on 22 April 1944. (1999)

The Australians had the task of mopping up the Japanese in New Guinea. General Blamey, commander in chief of the Australian forces, was determined not to simply bypass Japanese positions near Rabaul, on Bougainville and around Wewak but to destroy them where this was possible with few casualties.

At the time, no one knew when the war would end. It was presumed the fighting would continue until the mainland of Japan itself was invaded. However, the 1945 campaigns on Bougainville cost 615

Mambare River: Bert Kienzle's plantation was located here. (1999)

Australian lives and some 23,500 Japanese were still there at the surrender. On New Britain, five divisions of Japanese were still bottled up in Rabaul at war's end, nearly 100,000 men. Wewak was captured on 11 May 1945 and the remainder of the Japanese forces in the area surrendered on 15 August. Australian losses were 454 killed.

Gili Gili, 2000.

On 6 November 1942 at four o'clock, the SS *Tasman*, a 4492-ton transport, arrived in Gili Gili, carrying six officers and about a hundred men of other ranks (including my father), two 155 mm guns weighing 10,500 kg each, two Sperry searchlights, and assorted plotting equipment. This was E Battery Australian Heavy Artillery which had been ordered to guard Milne Bay from a malarial position at Dawa Dawa.

Finding the war at Gili Gili today isn't impossible, but there's nothing left here to remind anyone of the tens of thousands of men, the hundreds of thousands of tons of material, which had been unloaded here.

After the war virtually everything useful was destroyed, but concrete foundations of buildings survive all over the place, as well as rusting landing craft, old engines and bits of Marsden matting.

Mubo July 1942: 2/5th Independent Company patrol leaves Mubo, between Wau and Salamaua. (Damien Parer, AWM 127957)

The Australians in New Guinea

Australia on the Offensive: Wau & Salamaua, March 1942–September 1943

The sloping airfield at Wau, a gold-mining centre five days' walk inland from Salamaua, was a prime objective for both invader and defender. Salamaua itself was the district headquarters of the area.

After the Japanese came ashore unopposed at Lae and Salamaua on 8 March 1942, initial resistance was provided by Kanga Force, composed of elements of the local New Guinea Volunteer Rifles, but mainly by one of Australia's commando units, the 2/5th Independent Company. The 2/5th arrived by air in May 1942 with the job of harassing the Japanese, and discouraging them from moving inland towards Wau. The 2/5th undertook the first aggressive action by Australia against the enemy in June 1942 when they hit the Japanese camp at Salamaua, inflicting over 100 casualties at the cost of three wounded.

War correspondent Osmar White and photographer Damien Parer drove the last kilometre into Wau and the headquarters of Kanga Force late in June 1942. They deserved a lift, having completed an extremely arduous journey, by boat, canoe and on foot over the Bulldog Track. They brought supplies for the commandos, and were to take back stories and pictures of the early Australian action against the Japanese.

White, the correspondent for a swag of Australian, English and American newspapers, was working for the Melbourne *Sun News-Pictorial* when he joined up in 1941 and was 'manpowered' out by Sir Keith Murdoch who told him, 'Oh, we don't want you rushing around with a pack on your back, you'll fight the war with your pen, dear boy.' Unlike virtually everyone else in New Guinea, White had some experience of working in the tropics as a journalist before the war. White's classic book *Green Armour* was mostly the result of walking the Bulldog and Kokoda tracks with Damien Parer, who was also good at looking for action. As a photographer for the Department of Information, Parer had already been in North Africa, Greece and Syria. This walk into Wau was his first adventure in New Guinea, although, extraordinarily, he had a family connection because his errant father had opened the Wau Hotel in 1934.

Parer's first film from the journey to Wau was called *The Strangest Supply Route of the War* and shows the journey by tramp steamer to the Lakekamu River and by canoe up that river to the camp called Bulldog, which gave the track its name. From there, it was seven days' trek to Wau. After filming the journey to Wau, and re-enacting the

Opposite: Map of the area of operations around Wau and Salamaua, where Mick Sheehan and the 2/5th Commandos fought in 1942.

Osmar White called the Bulldog Track the 'spilled loads of Heaven.' Bulldog was wilder than the Kokoda Track: incredibly, Australian engineers did forge a jeep road through in 1943.

Wau 1942: An aerial view of Wau airstrip. (Mick Sheehan)

raid on Salamaua, Parer filmed the retreat from Kokoda, narrating and starring in the film *Kokoda Frontline*, which won the 1943 documentary Oscar.

The country around Wau was even higher and wilder than along the Kokoda Track. Here is White overlooking the Eloa River in June 1942: 'Just after midday I poked off the trail and found a spur about two miles down. It ran on to a great bluff overlooking the Eloa valley and I looked up to the crest of a great unnamed mountain ... Deep through this tilted eternal savagery of growth was cut the cleft of the river. Three thousand feet below, it wound like a white snake in leafy canyons – a mighty roaring stream glutted with the clouds' burden. Rapid upon rapid, fall upon fall, whirlpool upon whirlpool ... since life began the forest has been growing and decaying, growing and decaying. Until all forests end, it will still grow and decay, and the white river groan under the spilled loads of heaven.'

Unbelievably, a road was eventually built over Bulldog Track, started in February 1943 and opened for trucks by September: a great engineering feat made redundant by the course of war and quickly taken back by those 'spilled loads of heaven'.

White and Parer had a couple of days' recuperation wandering around Wau. Parer 'walked into the home where Dor and Jock were living and picked up some cloth animals – now sorely battered – they were some I had sent them from Palestine last year – also the big leather cushion affair I had sent mother from the Mussky bazaar in Cairo! ... What a strange war it seemed to me. From the far sands of Egypt – I had come home to see my own people's homes struck by the enemy.'

White described the walk back to Wau as the worst he ever did. He was in the middle of an attack of malaria, and by the time he struggled into the airstrip was grateful for a lift back to Port Moresby.

Damien Parer and Sergeant J B McAdam of the New Guinea Volunteer Rifles observing the Japanese at Salamaua in August 1942. The tree was called Parer's OP (Observation Post) by the 2/5th commandos. (Mick Sheehan, 1942)

Above: Big Wau Creek: Big Wau Creek was the scene of desperate fighting in the Japanese attack on Wau in January 1943. (1999)

Above right: Wau Airfield: In January 1943 Australians arrived and fought straight out of the plane. It was so close that some wounded were evacuated on the same aircraft in which they had arrived. (1999)

The Japanese staged their major effort to defeat the Australians by attacking Wau at the end of January 1943, but were defeated by the 17th Brigade and were forced back to Mubo, halfway between Wau and Salamaua.

At the end of June an American regiment landed at Nassau Bay nearby and fought to join the Australians. The Japanese, as usual, did not give up easily, and hard fighting was needed to retake Mubo in July. It took three brigades and many air raids by the RAAF and help from the Americans on the ground and in the air to finally defeat the Japanese at Salamaua.

Salamaua – which had boasted government offices, the Salamaua Hotel Bar Room and Freezer, AWA wireless station banks, trading houses, tennis courts, the Guinea Airlines office, two practice cricket pitches, sea baths, a quarantine hospital, a European hospital, Holes motion picture theatre, Burns Philp store and customs sheds old and new – was bombed flat.

When the Japanese abandoned the devastated place on 11 September 1943, the enemy survivors withdrew north-west towards Madang and met their fate at Shaggy Ridge and Sattelberg into 1944, long after Kokoda had been won.

The defence of Wau in late January 1943 cost about 100 dead and 250 wounded. Taking Salamaua took another 350 killed and 750 wounded. The battles at Wau and Salamaua might be less well remembered than other campaigns in New Guinea, overshadowed by Kokoda. But Australians first took the offensive there in May 1942 with a successful commando raid on Salamaua, and prevented the Japanese from seizing the strategically important airstrip at Wau. The continuing presence of the Australians in the area tied up over 10,000 Japanese troops, keeping them uncomfortable while their comrades were being cleaned out of Milne Bay and the Kokoda Track.

The Weeping Cross of Gona: July 1942

Before 1942, Gona was one of the most ordered, cheerful, beautiful spots on the north coast, with a clean black-sand beach, a mission station of park-like proportions with lawns and flourishing gardens, a hospital across the creek, a large sago-thatched church, a two-storey timber Mission House, and a flourishing school.

In other parts of New Guinea, Europeans, especially women and children, had already been evacuated, but at the All Souls' Mission Station the Anglican missionary James Benson, teacher Mavis Parkinson from Ipswich, and nurse May Hayman from Adelaide resolved to stay.

War came first in early June 1942, when an American single-seat fighter flew low over the mission, heading east attacking a Japanese aircraft, but was itself attacked by two more Japanese and turned

The Gona cross: The graveyard at the Gona Mission. (1999)

back. The pilot tried to bail out but his parachute failed to open, and he fell into the ground by a tulip tree shading the church. Mavis Parkinson went to his aid, but Lieutenant Howard Winkler had been killed by the impact. He was buried in the mission cemetery.

Then on the afternoon of 21 July, a boy came running up from the beach, saying, 'Father, father great ships are here!' The ships were Japanese, and soon began shelling Buna, and then Gona. Boats were lowered, and men clambered into them. Shells from the Japanese cruiser whizzed overhead. Bullets soon swept the beach. It was now too dangerous to stay.

Benson, Mavis and May packed a few items and took the road to Kokoda, heading for the inland mission station of Sangara. Dodging Japanese and Allied air raids, the trio spent almost three weeks in hiding, having met the friendly villagers from Siai, who built a bush shelter for them.

On 8 August, two Australian soldiers walked into the village, part of a group of five Australians and five American airmen, who were intending to walk to Port Moresby. Benson eventually agreed to go with them. Four days later they reached the Japanese lines near Popondetta, but when one of their guides hurriedly left, probably to betray them, they headed back the way they had come. Later in the day, they were attacked by Japanese rifle fire. When a Japanese patrol caught up with them, the Australian soldiers with the group returned fire until they were all dead or injured. A villager offered to take the women to a friendly place, but led them directly to the Japanese at Popondetta. Next morning, the women were taken by Japanese soldiers to a freshly dug open grave. One tried to embrace Mavis, but she resisted, and he bayoneted her in the side. May covered her face with a cloth, and was herself bayoneted. They were thrown on top of one another in the grave.

The missionaries and others from Sangara Mission, including one child and May's fiancé, Father Vivian Redlich, had been betrayed and captured a couple of weeks earlier. They were beheaded on the beach at Buna on 13 or 14 August 1942.

May's and Mavis's burials were noted by locals, and their bodies exhumed in February 1943 and reburied at Sangara Mission Station – which was obliterated in the Mt Lamington eruption of 1951.

Meanwhile Father Benson, separated from the others, decided that the best thing he could do was to give himself up, and spent five days without food and with little water trying to do that. On the sixth day he found the Gona Road and wearing his old white cassock was met by several hundred Japanese soldiers.

Benson told them he was the priest from Gona. The Japanese shouted that he was a spy and administered a short beating and knocked off his spectacles. He was set free, but was blind and was given a lift by friendly Japanese soldiers singing, 'It's a Long Way to Tipperary'. Eventually he was taken back to Gona and searched the ruins for some spectacles. He was given a pair of one-eared, scratched specs. Still there in January, he used them to watch the Japanese evacuate. He was taken with them to spend the war as a prisoner on Rabaul. He re-established the mission at Gona after the war.

Bishop Philip Strong, who visited Gona in May 1943, five months after the Japanese were defeated, was moved by the fact that the only physical material to survive the occupation and the awful battleground were the cross, the stump of the font, and the platform of the altar. He was told that the cross wept blood, and saw the reason why – bullets hitting the metal beneath the white paint marked it with dark red blotches 'giving a most amazing effect of blood, so realistic and symbolic'.

'I heard there was some action up here': Kokoda, July 1942

In 1942, Kokoda was an unremarkable New Guinea village, at the northern edge of the forbidding Owen Stanley mountain range, about 75 kilometres south-west of the Solomon Sea. The Mambare River to the north and the Kumusi about 25 kilometres to the west form a formidable barrier when in flood.

A path ran south from Kokoda, through the Owen Stanleys, towards Port Moresby. A more usable track led north-west to the government station on the coast at Buna, to the nearby coastal villages of Sanananda and Gona (where there was an Anglican mission), and to the mouth of the Giruwa River, where trading vessels dropped anchor off shore.

Alluvial gold was discovered in the tangle of creeks such as the Eora and Yodda that flowed from the mountains into the Mambare and Kumusi rivers. Prospecting began in the area in the 1890s, and a government station was established in the healthier upland climate of Kokoda in 1904. The earliest official European use of what came to be called the Kokoda Track was as a mail route, pioneered in December 1904. The track was also used for unofficial village-to-village mail, expeditions and patrols. With the decline of the goldfield and the shift of the area's administration to Buna – which was in regular steamship communication with Port Moresby – mail runs ceased.

By 1942, Australian rubber and oil-palm planters, such as Bert Kienzle (who came to the area in the 1920s), were running well-established plantations in the area. As part of the belated defence preparations in June 1942, Kienzle was asked to reconnoitre and then construct a road from Port Moresby to Kokoda through the Owen Stanleys – in just three months. He thought it would be a colossal undertaking and impossible in the time, if at all. He was already involved in recruiting local carriers – the fuzzy-wuzzy angels – when on 3 July when he was told the first elements of Australia's defence, B Company of the 39th Battalion, were looking for a guide and

New Guinea 1942

Kokoda: a view of the village from the Kokoda plateau. The Japanese attacked up this slope.

porters to get them to Kokoda. Soon after, on 21 July 1942, the Japanese landed – unopposed – between Gona and Buna.

The 39th Militia Battalion had been patched together to serve as a garrison unit in Port Moresby. It was mainly eighteen- and nineteen-year-old boys, many from Victoria, led by First World War veterans. Among them were some of the most remarkable soldiers to have served Australia – 'Uncle Sam' Templeton, and 'Doc' Vernon. The 39th had little training and not much equipment, but was nevertheless sent to meet a battle-hardened and far larger Japanese force. What the 39th did at Kokoda – and at Isurava, after they were joined by Middle East AIF veterans in the fighting withdrawal towards Port Moresby – was vital to the ultimate victory. They also had the grim satisfaction of being there at the end, suffering further grievous casualties prising the Japanese out of their last beach-head bunkers.

Under the command of Captain Sam Templeton, guided by Bert Kienzle and with most of their gear carried by porters, B Company made it to Kokoda on 15 July. Warrant Officer Jack Wilkinson, the medic, recorded many of the things that have plagued walkers of the track ever since –

ANZAC Memorial
Memorial
CWGC Cemetery
Museum
Road
Track
Kokoda Track
OWEN
STANLEY
RANGES
Solomon Sea
Gona
Basabua
Sananda
Buna
Popondetta
Kumusi River
Girua River
Mambare River
Kokoda
Hoi
Oivi
Wairopi
Isurava
Alolo
Eora Creek
Templeton's Crossing
Mt Bellamy
The "Gap"
Efogi
Myola
Menari
Brigade Hill
Mt Nisbet
Nauro River
River
Nauro
Ioribaiwa
Hombrom Bluff
Imita Ridge
Laloki
Goldie River
Uberi
McDonald's Corner
Owers' Corner
Bomana
Sogeri
River
Port Moresby
Bootless Inlet
Coral Sea
0
10
kilometres
Bismarck Sea
New Ireland
New Britain
PAPUA NEW GUINEA
Solomon Sea
Gulf of Papua
Port Moresby
AUSTRALIA
Coral Sea

1 Sogeri
2 Uberi
3 Ioribaiwa
4 Menari
5 Efogi
6 The 'Gap'
7 Isurava
8 Kokoda
9 Oivi
10 Wairopi
11 Popondetta
metres
4000
3000
2000
1000
0
Owen Stanley Ranges
KOKODA TRACK
Port Moresby
Buna
0 kilometres
50
100
150
200
237

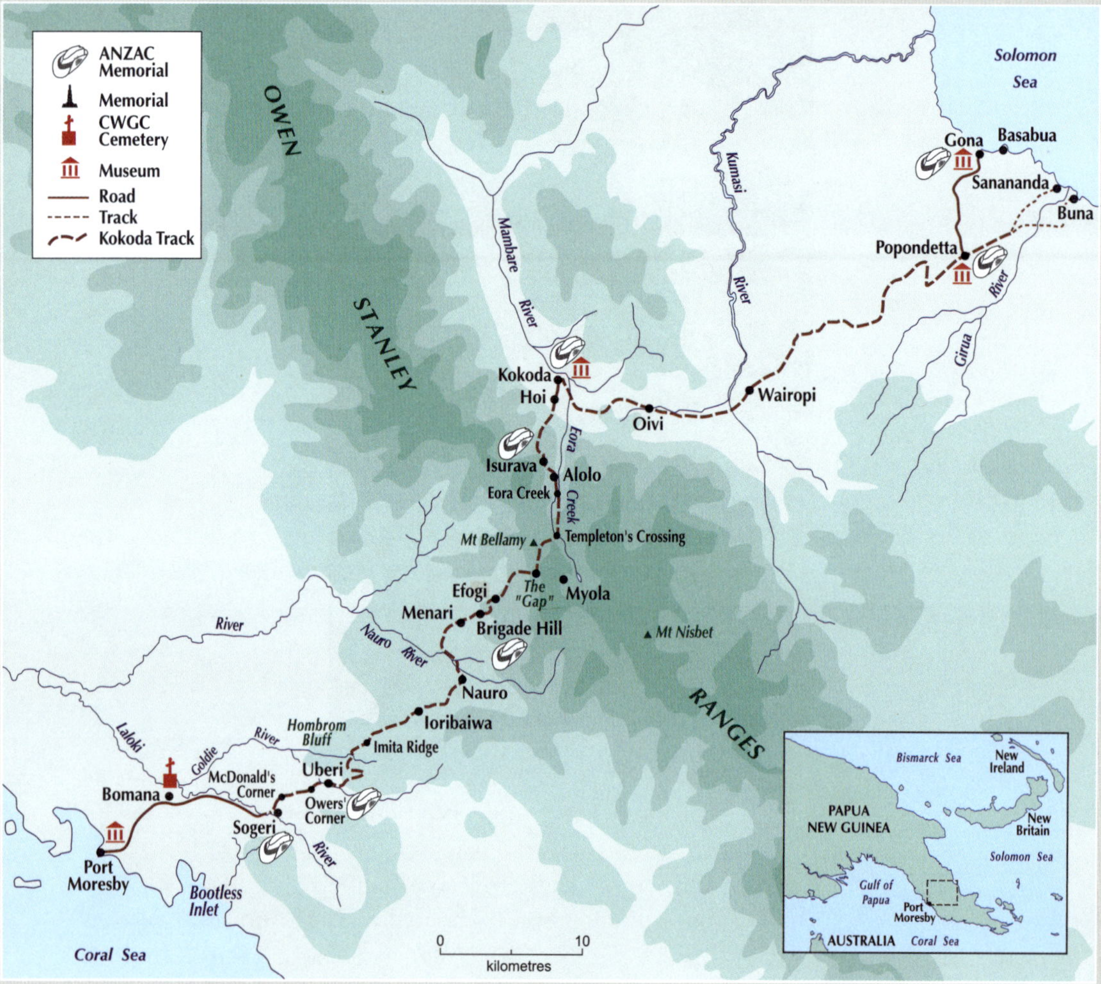

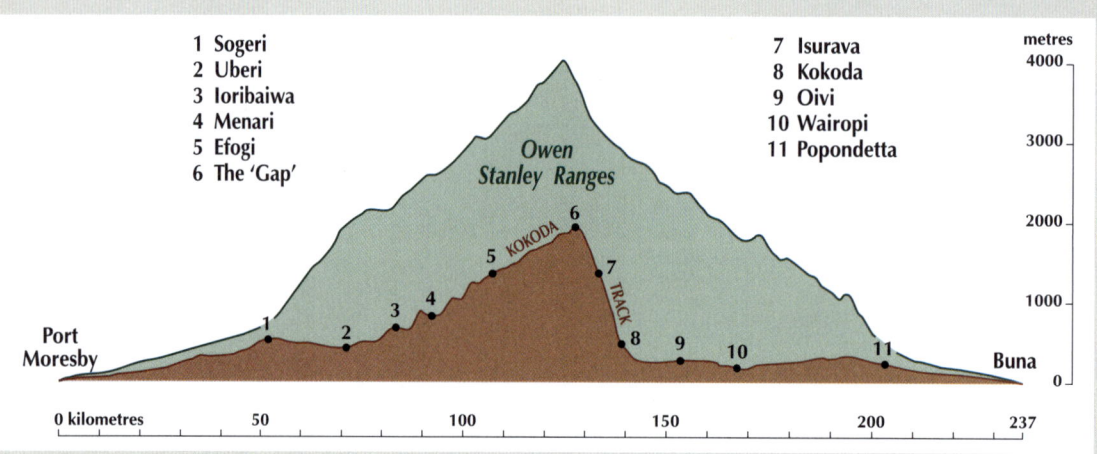

New Guinea 1942

Opposite: Maps of the Kokoda Track. The cross section indicates why it is twice as long to walk than as the crow flies.

7 July Several chaps sent back here with fever and bad knees. Hell of a strain on knees on down grades.

9 July Bothered by native bees en route crawling all over us after salt in sweat.

13 July To Eora Crossing No 2. Long day over range. Rain forest and lawyer vines. Deep moss and slippery track. Rain and mist. Cold and dreary. Camp not too good. Creek roaring loudly. To bed in wet clothes.

Weapon pit, Kokoda. (1999)

Sam Templeton was much admired. Aloof and hyper-energetic, he was always on the move, and taking risks. On arrival at Kokoda he had ordered two platoon-strength patrols forward towards the coast, and a third to defend the Kokoda airstrip. That was the strength of the defenders of Kokoda as the Japanese landed.

Templeton, who was at Buna making sure all supplies sent by sea for his company had been cleared, headed back to Awala. Colonel W T 'Bill' Owen had been ordered to concentrate the 39th at Kokoda and take charge of Maroubra Force – which was the 39th plus a handful of men from the Papuan Infantry Brigade (PIB) and the (civilian) Australian New Guinea Administration Unit (ANGAU). Owen arrived at Kokoda by air on 24 July, and he and Templeton joined the forward platoons.

Lieutenant Chalk of ANGAU was the first to engage the Japanese, near Awala. The Japanese responded vigorously to Chalk's small-arms fire with mortars, machine-guns and an artillery piece. Chalk withdrew and lost most of his PIB men, who 'melted' into the bush. On the morning of 24 July, the forward platoon was on the inland side of the Kumusi and had destroyed the bridge over the river.

Templeton now knew that between 1500 and 2000 Japanese had landed, and sent a message: 'In view of the numbers, I recommend that your action be contact and rearguard only – no do-or-die stunts. Close back on Kokoda.' On the following days, the Japanese advance on Kokoda was delayed by an ambush at Gorari, and by fighting Australians at Oivi.

Templeton headed to Kokoda to meet the reinforcements – one solitary platoon – who had arrived by plane. Ten minutes after he set off, some rifle fire was heard; Templeton was never seen again. The Official Historian notes evidence that suggests he was wounded, given first aid and later killed by the local Orakaivas. Raymond Paull, 39th

Battalion historian, says Templeton was wounded by the Japanese and later killed by them.

Meanwhile, at Kokoda, Owen prepared to evacuate, burned some stores, and left for Deniki, where he met the survivors from Oivi. The next day, he learned that the Japanese had not taken Kokoda. He had a decision to make: there might be time for reinforcement if they could hold the airstrip.

The little force returned to Kokoda. There, another of the great characters of Kokoda turned up: Dr Geoffrey Vernon. Born in 1882, 'Doc' Vernon had been a captain in the 4th Light Horse Field Ambulance, served in the Middle East as Regimental Medical Officer for the 11th Light Horse, was awarded the Military Cross in 1916, and lowered his age by eight years to join the Army Medical Corps in 1942.

Jack Wilkinson of the 39th noted: 'Captain Vernon arrived out of fog. Very pleased to see him. He had some instruments and dressings in two triangular bandages. He nearly got shot when first seen, owing to his unregimental dress ... He saw me and spoke, "Jack, I heard there was some action up here and thought you may need some assistance. Where do I start?" What a man.'

Midday on 28 July, the 39th was established around the prow of the little Kokoda plateau. There were no Japanese to be seen, and Colonel Owen thought there was time for reinforcements. He radioed

Far left: The Kokoda memorials in the early morning mist, 1999. **Left:** The road to Kokoda. (1999)

Moresby that the airstrip was open. Two DC3s, with two platoons of D company of the 39th aboard were sent north but the pilots felt it was too dangerous to land.

At around 7.30 p.m., there were cat calls heard and a mortar or two. By midnight, there was much shooting. At around 2 a.m., the Japanese attacked up the steep slope.

Lieutenant Garland, whose platoon was dug in around this perimeter of the plateau, said of Owen, 'He was another one similar to Sam Templeton, that wanted to show his leadership, and he walked around the top of the perimeter where we were all lying down; naturally you would because you could see the Japs a couple of hundred yards away forming up. And I said, "Sir, I think you're taking an unnecessary risk walking around amongst the troops like that." "Well," he said, "I've got to do it." I suppose half an hour later he got shot right through the forehead.' Owen was in the act of throwing a grenade at the advancing Japanese.

Jack Wilkinson, Major Watson and Doc Vernon dragged Owen back up the slope, under fire. Vernon described him 'struggling violently yet more than semi conscious, quite unable to realise where he was, or to help us get him out.'

At 2.30 a.m. the Japanese attacked up the slope at the northern end of the plateau. A melee of confused close-order fighting ensued – the Japanese uncaring of casualties, the Australians out-gunned and out-numbered.

Then an order came for all to retreat. They made Colonel Owen as comfortable as possible. Vernon noted that: 'At the time of our withdrawal he had become quite still ... He probably did not survive another fifteen minutes.'

Hiding in the rubber trees, Vernon watched parties making for the hills in dense mist, by moonlight. Finally, Major Watson, Lieutenant Brewer and a couple of officers came past and told him 'we are the last out,' and they all headed up the track to Deniki.

'It was an experience I would not have cared to miss,' wrote Vernon, who described 'the thick white mist dimming the moonlight, the mysterious veiling of trees, houses and men, the drip of moisture from the foliage, and at the last, the almost complete silence, as if the rubber groves of Kokoda were sleeping as usual in the depths of the night, and men had not brought disturbance.'

'Paying for every yard': Isurava and Brigade Hill, August–September 1942

The battle for Isurava was the key delaying battle fought on the Kokoda Track. The Japanese had set out with barely sufficient supplies to simply walk the track; every battle consumed time and casualties that they could not afford. Every day's delay was another nail in

Brigade Hill: the view north to Isurava. (1999)

the coffin. This wasn't understood by high command back in Australia, but it was by the leader on the ground, Brigadier Arnold Potts. Potts is another of Australia's under-acknowledged heroes. He commanded 21st Brigade (2/14th, 2/16th and 2/27th Battalions) on the Kokoda Track and was sacked for his work, as part of the blame-game played by Blamey over the Papua campaign.

A Gallipoli veteran, Potts was made a sergeant at nineteen, at Anzac, and by 1918 he was a captain in charge of a battery of trench mortars, and was awarded the Military Cross for bravery at Pozières. Promoted to brigadier in July 1942, he arrived in Port Moresby on 8 August 1942. His orders were simple: the 21st Brigade was to recapture Kokoda. The 39th and 53rd battalions were still forward. Supplies were promised.

The 2/14th and the 2/16th started up the track on 16 and 17 August, and Potts took over the combined Maroubra Force on 23 August. The 2/14th arrived at Isurava on 28 August, where the exhausted and depleted 39th was defending the position against the Japanese swarming up the track. Brigade HQ was a short distance away at Alola.

The Japanese attacks around Isurava had begun on 26 August and by 29 August were intense. Here Bruce Kingsbury, a 24-year-old real estate agent from Preston, Victoria, won the only VC awarded on the Kokoda Track, and was killed here by a Japanese sniper. He had charged down the track firing a Bren gun from his hip through the terrific machine-gun fire and succeeded in clearing a path through the enemy, gaining 100 yards. The intense fire from both sides devastated the jungle.

But the situation at Isurava was deteriorating rapidly, despite the heroics of the 2/14th, 2/16th and the 39th (but not the 53rd, which did not perform well). Next day, Potts realised the whole force was in danger of being cut off and enveloped. Brigade HQ was in danger. Despite being ordered to hold the position, Potts decided he had to withdraw. If they stayed, they would be killed, sooner rather than later, and the track would still be open. It was better to withdraw to Eora Creek.

Chester Wilmot, legendary war correspondent, was with Brigade headquarters after the battle, on the withdrawal to Eora Creek: 'We go on ... looking for a place for Brigade HQ but there's nowhere you can get off the track and it's raining now and the six o'clock cricket which makes a noise like an air raid siren warns us how late it is.'

Osmar White wrote in *Green Armour*: 'None wanted to talk about the Kokoda fighting. They merely said that the Japs were hard to see in the bush, but that the 39th had got amongst them in the rubber plantation and inflicted high casualties. What impressed me most deeply about these wounded was their apparent desensitisation. They were completely inured to suffering. They accepted it as an integral part of living ...'

Although the Japanese had the upper hand, as Wilmot wrote 'he's still paying for every yard he advances, he's still being fought all the way by men who hate withdrawing and refuse to admit defeat ... Nothing tests troops as much as withdrawal and they're standing this test.'

Colonel Ralph Honner, another hero, commanding the 39th Battalion, said of the action there: 'The decisive action was not some valiant, fruitless venture at Kokoda but the grinding four-day battle of Isurava. If Isurava's defenders had wavered in the face of the first

Brigade Hill: at ease after a stiff climb. (1999)

Eora Creek: beauty belies the savage fighting in 1942. (1999)

onslaughts, or had fought less tigerously through the succeeding days and nights, the ensuing course of the campaign must inevitably have been radically changed.'

A week later, the 2/27th was dug in on the forward slope of Brigade Hill in the narrow, precipitous, forested area, two days' walk from Isurava. Back from the front of the ridge was a 20-metre step up to the then densely covered top of the ridge. Astride the track at the front was the battered 2/14th, and in the centre the decimated 2/16th. The distance between the 2/27th forward position closest to Efogi, and the rear at Brigade HQ, was about four kilometres. Brigade HQ 'lay across a narrow saddle farther back, in a decrepit, roofless shack in a small kunai patch ... the ground dropped away precipitously on both sides, a dense growth of jungle clinging to its face,' noted Kokoda historian Raymond Paull.

The Australians held the high ground, and could wait astride the track; on the other hand, the Japanese could work their way around the creeks at the base of the ridge, cut off the Australians at the rear, and let them try to walk out. The best Potts and the 21st Brigade could hope to achieve was to again delay the Japanese advance, wearing out their resources of health, food and ammunition and waiting for reinforcements.

On the night of 6 September Lieutenants McGavin and Clements of the 2/27th 'derived endless amusement from the spectacle of lights flying wildly through the night from the hands of Japanese slithering on the greasy track or stumbling on protruding roots and boulders.' All night 'the procession of lights went on unceasingly, descending the main track, winding down the zigzag through the garden area above the creek crowding below the knoll on which Efogi village stood.'

During the next afternoon the 2/27th consolidated the Australian position by withdrawing up the hill and, without entrenching tools, digging in with tin hats, bayonets and hands. Private Mannion, 2/27th remembered, 'We could dig a six foot face and still have only a conspicuous platform to sit on, with a nice slide of dirt but no cover in front.' There were about 28 officers and 560 men.

It was a hot, stifling day. There was no water, and little or no food. The water bottles sent off with patrols in the morning never came back. Mortar rounds and mountain gun shells were whistling in sporadically and occasionally fatally. Australian 3-inch mortars, gruellingly man-packed from Myola, replied. The Japanese had penetrated around Brigade Hill and attacked Potts' headquarters company, aiming to cut the track between HQ and the 2/16th. Bert Ward of the 2/27th admitted to 'some degree of amazement as to how active they were, to be able to keep going ... Well you'd have to be a qualified mountain goat to be able to do physically what they did – to be able to get right around the battalion, around Brigade Hill.' That night the Australian dead were buried somewhere on the ridge-top, and big fires, thought to be Japanese funeral pyres, were reported in the hills beyond Efogi.

The Japanese attack, almost 6000-strong, came on 8 September. At dawn, the forward company of the 2/27th was ferociously mortared and strafed with machine-gun fire, and assaulted by eight waves of Japanese troops. A Company, while taking casualties, used all their 1200 grenades and 100 rounds of ammunition per man in repelling the Japanese.

By mid-morning the 2/27th, the 2/16th and Brigade HQ were under heavy attack. The Japanese had cut the track and the telephone line between Potts' HQ and the 2/16th commanded by Colonel Albert Caro. Communications by radio were intermittent, but Potts told Caro that if the brigade was wiped out, or his position became untenable, Caro was to regroup down the track at Menari.

Brigadier Potts called for an attack back down the track to try and relieve the situation at HQ and 2/14th companies responded. Captain

Claude Nye and a couple of platoons of B Company attacked, despite tremendous opposition from the well-concealed Japanese. Eight got through, seventeen – including Nye and Charlie McCallum, one of the heroes of Isurava a week earlier – died.

The 2/16th needed help, and asked Brigade HQ to attack from their end. Captain 'Lefty' Langridge took up the challenge with two platoons. In one of the many occasions of self-sacrifice that day, he handed his pay book and dog tags to a mate and set off. He and twenty men perished. The pressure on Potts' HQ was somewhat relieved by Langridge's heroic effort, and by the arrival of Major Challen and 40 men. But the situation was untenable.

Countless deeds of bravery had taken place on this day, a day that gave Brigade Hill its other name: Butcher's Hill. As night fell, Brigadier Potts and the men from the 2/14th and 2/16th who had fought their way back to his position at the end of the ridge trudged carefully back to Menari. Kokoda historian Peter Brune comments that 'Potts had once again eluded Horii's net of encirclement and annihilation. Although he had lost half his force at Mission Ridge and Brigade Hill, he had once again delayed his enemy ... fighting a magnificent, copybook withdrawal.' Potts and his men had suffered dreadful casualties, killed a thousand or so of the enemy, and held up the Japanese for another three days.

On 17 September the Japanese reached Ioribaiwa Ridge, just 60 kilometres from Port Moresby. They had optimistically set off in July with ten days of food, and were after four months of fighting and living off nonexistent local resources, literally at the end of the road. The delaying battles fought by the Australians were crucial in winning the campaign. On 23 September Australian patrols started to probe the Japanese positions. On 28 September they attacked, to find no enemy there. Now it was the turn of the Japanese to fight delaying actions, while others were digging in and making coconut log fortresses at the original beach-heads on the north coast. They intended to fight until reinforced, or they were killed.

The End of the Beginning: Milne Bay, August–September 1942

Early in 1942, General MacArthur, American overseer of the Allied fight-back in the South-West Pacific, had decided that an airfield was needed at the eastern end of New Guinea, both to harass the Japanese

New Guinea 1942

Above: Map of Milne Bay. Gurney is today's airport for the provincial capital, Alotau.

Above: The Goilani river was running high on 4 September 1942, when Corporal John French, 2/9th Battalion, attacked Japanese machine-gun posts on the east bank (left bank, below) and lost his life. He was awarded a posthumous VC.
Left: Looking back at the Goilani from French's memorial.

to the north, and to prevent them using the area as a base to attack Port Moresby and Australia. The plan, code-named Fall River, saw various locations surveyed, and settled on the coconut plantation owned by soap kings the Lever Brothers near the village of Gili Gili.

The first airstrip – One Strip – was constructed using American dynamite and labour organised by the remaining Australian New Guinea Administrative Unit, and took just 22 days. The coconut trees were chopped and the stumps blown up, and the ground flattened and covered with interlocking steel mesh called Marsden matting, making it capable of taking P40 Kittyhawks with which the RAAF was being equipped. These aircraft, competitive with the Japanese, would be crucial in winning the battle of Milne Bay. The airfield was ready on 21 July, the day the Japanese landed at Buna and Gona on the north coast. One strip, later named Gurney Airfield, is today the Milne Bay airport. A second airstrip, Two Strip, was built five or six kilometres to the west, but was too boggy for use during the war. Three Strip, the most easterly, was under construction when the Japanese landed in August.

Milne Bay was a swampy malarial place, where there were more casualties from sickness than from battle. The official Australian war correspondent, Ken Slessor, was at Milne Bay after the battle, in early June 1943. He noted, 'Insects everywhere – earwigs in the washbasin, a scorpion under the tent board, and a large black tarantula on top of the box in which I keep my clothes ... Mould and mildew put their soft, spongy fingers over everything. Even cigarettes mottle with brown spots and droop limply. Matches have to be wax, kept in a tin, or better still a glass bottle or jar, sealed up ... Airstrips seem tiny grooves in an infinity of jungle; bruised indigo mountain-tops, swimming out of clouds, apparently without base on earth – uprooted peaks, floating like an aerial continent.'

Gili Gili, at the western end of the bay, was the main port. There's deep water metres from shore where relatively large ships could berth. Milne Bay later became a huge fortress, repair-station and storage camp, and hundreds of thousands of men passed through on their way to the campaigns to liberate the rest of New Guinea, the Dutch East Indies and the Philippines. In 1942, most of the Australian forces were concentrated there in defence of the airstrips.

The Japanese initially landed about 2700 men in Milne Bay, on 25 August 1942, believing that only a small number of troops were guarding the airstrips (as had been their experience at the start of the

New Guinea 1942

Japanese landing barge at Ahioma, Milne Bay. (1999)

Kokoda campaign, the month before), but there were some 9000 men, mostly Australian, but including some American engineers, and two squadrons of P40 Kittyhawks.

Villagers along the northern shore heard the ominous dull throb of big ships passing. The Japanese landing was unchallenged. The barges came ashore on the stony beaches a kilometre east of Ahioma, about fifteen kilometres west of Gili Gili, just before midnight. It had been stormy all day, but the moon was up that night, fitfully glimmering through the clouds. The Japanese cruisers began shelling Gili Gili headquarters area and the airstrips an hour later, at around 1 a.m. on 26 August. But amphibious landing in the tropical dark is difficult – one dark ridge outlined against the dark sky, one beach dropping coconuts and rain, looks much like another; the Japanese had not landed as close to the airstrips as they had intended. They were ten kilometres to the east, and would have to find their way forward against a much larger force than they had anticipated. This was not a handful of men but thousands of troops, well-led and well-enough equipped – especially in the air.

The most forward unit of 61 Battalion was D Company, which had been patrolling at Ahioma. HQ had sent two luggers to pick them up, and return to Gili Gili. One was the *Elevala*, and the other the *Bronzewing*, a two-masted ketch that had once been owned by Errol Flynn, who sailed it to Milne Bay before the war.

The *Bronzewing*, with 22 men aboard, had the great misfortune to run into the Japanese barges ferrying men ashore. Under heavy fire, the survivors abandoned ship and struggled to the beach. George Thurlow was the first Australian casualty at Milne Bay when he was killed in this attack, one of eleven to die on the *Bronzewing*.

One who made it overboard was Sergeant Jim McKenzie, who survived machine-gun fire by swimming under water, getting ashore and finding his way through the mangroves to higher ground, and eventually making his way back to the Australian lines.

The action was watched with dismay by the sick aboard the second boat, the *Elevala*. Private Albert Ramsden beached it at the mouth of a creek, and the eight or nine sick men tried to make it back to their lines, some delirious with malaria. Most eventually made it.

Villagers in Ahioma and Waga Waga unfortunate enough to be at home when the Japanese landed were interrogated. Some were tortured by being tied to trees and bayoneted. One boy aboard the *Bronzewing* was captured and killed, as was one of the Australians from the

Elevala. In the next few days Australians unlucky enough to be wounded and captured were also killed.

In all, 59 local people were tortured and mutilated in disgusting fashion and 36 Australians were captured, tied up, tortured, and used for bayonet practice.

A Japanese soldier described the Australian soldier from the *Elevala* tied to a palm tree: 'I looked at an enemy face for the first time. He was a young man of about twenty with blonde hair and a pale face ... when a nearby soldier tried to take a fountain pen from his breast pocket, he shook his head saying "No, no." This gave me a peculiar feeling. He showed none of the solemn realisation that having been captured, he could not return alive. I thought his attitude to be very different from ours.'

Koeabule – or KB – Mission, the largest outstation of the Kwato Mission founded in 1891, was the scene of some desperate fighting on 27 August, as the Japanese advanced towards Three Strip, where Australians and some Americans were waiting.

There, a soldier remembered: 'Red flare at midnight, 31 August 1942, a gauzy tropical sky, no report of the moon. The Japanese across the cleared strip in the jungle, formed up in ranks, clanking gear and making bugle calls, advancing. The Australians calm under pandanus leaves, waiting. This was like the Nek or Krithia at Gallipoli, except it was the Australians (and some Americans) who were pre-

KB stands for Koeabule Mission. From the 1890s to the war it was the plantation outstation of the Kwato Mission, and was the scene of desperate fighting on 27 August 1942.

pared, ready. Both edges of the airstrip piled with palm logs and debris from the clearing. The grass lands became a sea of fire, a rainbow of tracer bullets, which burned through the Japanese marines walking and screaming across the bare, bullet ripping, kunai strip. A killing field. Three times they came, three times they were scythed. The Australians mowers stood inches deep in hot empty cartridges. You could have read the paper from the glow of the tracers. Next morning one soldier remarked that the jungle across from the strip now looked 'like a field of tomato stakes'.

That was as far south and east as the Japanese were allowed to go in New Guinea, or anywhere else in the Second World War. The Australians began to force them back up the coast. On the afternoon of 4 September 1942, the 2/9th Battalion pushed the Japanese back from the Goilanai river.

The Goilani then was a jungle-shrouded torrent – the water running shoulder-high twenty metres wide, with head-high kunai grass covering its bank. Japanese with three machine-guns were hidden in the scrub on the far side. The guns sounded to some men like woodpeckers, their rifles had a sharp whip-cracking sound. The Australians put up a terrific barrage of automatic weapons fire, lobbed mortars across the river and got to the other side, pinned down in the kunai by the machine-guns.

Two companies of the 2/9th crossed the river, A Company to attack across the river a little downstream of the present-day bridge; B Company to cross upstream. Corporal John French told the men in his section to take cover, and, with Corporal Merv Ball, he went after the machine-guns. Arthur Hinz, from French's section, recalled: 'Johnny French ordered us down, and he went in and got the first two posts. And for the next one, he came back and got a grenade off us and finished the other one off. And that was the finish, when we advanced he was dead.'

French was awarded a VC for these actions. His citation noted that, 'It was found that all members of the three enemy gun crews had been killed and that Corporal French had died in front of the third gun pit. By his cool courage and disregard of his personal safety this non-commissioned officer saved members of his section from heavy casualties and was responsible for the successful conclusion of the attack.'

This was the final decisive defeat on the Japanese force that had attempted to seize Milne Bay. The Goilani River carried bodies down the river to where some of the 2/12th rested, while the battle raged on. Japanese bodies and Australians were pulled from the sea from the jaws of hungry sharks.

September 1942 was, in the Churchillian phrase, the end of the beginning for Japan in New Guinea. Milne Bay had been the left claw of the pincer on Port Moresby, the right claw still ripping across the Kokoda Track. But it was downhill and out to sea from now on.

Cecil Abel to the Rescue

Cecil Abel commanded the support vessel *Osiri* during the battle for Milne Bay. One of the sons of Charles Abel, founder of the Kwato Mission, Cecil had led the mission since his father's death in 1930.

Osiri was one of the five vessels used to ferry troops and supplies around Milne Bay. On the night of the Japanese landing, all five boats were at Gili Gili. The *Elevala* and the *Bronzewing* were sent to Ahioma, to bring back the elements of 61 Battalion who were isolated there.

Later he recalled his actions with the *Osiri*: 'We cast off and moved away from Gili Gili jetty. Sila, the skipper of the *Osiri*, knew of the urgency of our stores predicament. As a matter of routine, however, he came down from the bridge or the helmsman's cabin and asked "Where to, Taubada?" It was then it happened, as clearly as if someone had been standing behind me, something, someone said quite simply, "Spend the night at Wagawaga." ... I repeated what I had heard and told Sila "We'll spend the night at Wagawaga." Sila looked at me hard and repeated "Wagawaga?" "Yes," I said, "Wagawaga. And we'll go for our stores tomorrow morning."'

This was not an unusual occurrence; Cecil had heard many such messages over the years and had learned not to treat them lightly. Later that night came the sound of a heavy bombardment across the bay – the Japanese naval bombardment. The next morning Cecil took the *Osiri* back to Gili Gili and commenced four days and nights of ferrying men up the coast and bringing the wounded back.

Ric Throssell, the son of Hugo Throssell VC, who was in Milne Bay at the time, remembers having to take two badly wounded men back on one of the luggers: 'You had to put some distance between yourself and those sickening torn bodies ... There was no place for compassion. This was what war was. All the rest had been playing games, Poor bastards ... No one could imagine the way war turned men into lumps of meat, the scrag ends of flesh and offal of a butcher's rubbish bin; scraps for the dog.'

On the afternoon of 4 September 1942, the day John French won the VC, Cecil Abel was moored at KB Mission and was asked to sail down to the mouth of the Gama River, to evacuate a badly wounded Australian soldier. The 2/9th was still under fire, the battle was still being won. No one knew that the retreating Japanese were keeping the Australians busy to cover a major withdrawal the next day.

Cecil wrote later, 'The wounded soldier had been brought out on

New Guinea 1942

Cecil Abel was the son of Charles Abel, who founded the Kwato Mission on that island near Samarai in 1891. Kwato Mission was famous for its boat-building before the war. Here one lies on the cricket field on Kwato in 2000.

the upraised arms of his mates and some of the *Osiri* crew who had waded out into the sea to get his stretcher on board. He was unconscious but he had come to just before being carried on board. We chugged back to Gili Gili on one cylinder and he was taken to the 2/5th Field Ambulance near the wharf at Gil Gili.' Cecil never heard more of him, whether he had survived or not.

In 1992, Cecil Abel, then aged 90, told this story at a ceremony at French's memorial on the 50th anniversary of the Milne Bay battle. John French's sister was there, with some Australian veterans. At the end of the service one of the men stood up and to the astonishment of all said that he, Harry Triffit, was the man Cecil and the *Osiri* had saved that day.

Harry said, 'If you had not come for me that afternoon I could not have survived the night.' Life is full of meaningful coincidences and meetings; this one was of the more extraordinary.

Football and Flying

Milne Bay was the first time the Japanese were beaten on land; it was also the first time the Japanese were defeated from the air. Apparently

Far left: Left to right; Wing Commander Sam Balmer (100 Squadron Beauforts), Squadron Leader Bluey Truscott (76 Squadron – Kittyhawks), Squadron Leader Les Jackson (75 Squadron – Kittyhawks), Milne Bay, 1942.

Left: One Strip or Gurney is now Milne Bay's airport, Three or Turnbull Strip shown here in 1999 is overgrown, and Two Strip was never used.

unknown to the Japanese, 75 and 76 RAAF squadrons, flying Kittyhawks, were at Milne Bay before the landing. They were led by some of the most famous flyers Australia has produced, including the redheaded Keith 'Bluey' Truscott DFC. Even more important in establishing legendary status, Bluey had played 50 games for the Melbourne football club, including two winning grand finals.

A genuine ace, Truscott shot down sixteen German aircraft flying Spitfires for 452 Squadron, returning to Australia in May 1942. He played a last game for Melbourne (against Richmond) while on leave on 16 May, before heading north.

Truscott landed or skidded to a halt at One Strip at Milne Bay on 25 July 1942. He was lucky to have made it, having wrecked one Kittyhawk trying to take off from Townsville. He was a notoriously indifferent lander of aircraft – his mates accused him of usually trying to put the aircraft down twenty feet above the ground. The Kittyhawk was heavy, well-armoured and flew like a bull elephant run amok. Coming into land, you couldn't see – the nose stood up in front like a brick wall.

The RAAF Kittyhawks, flying from One Strip (Gurney) were crucial to the outcome of the battle. Squadron leader Peter Turnbull, commanding officer of 76 Squadron was shot down while strafing the advancing Japanese below Cameron Plateau. Three Strip was named for him and he is remembered with a tree and plaque laid by his sisters in 1988.

Truscott took over 76 Squadron after Peter Turnbull was killed on 27 August, and was mentioned in despatches. His squadron was posted to Darwin in early 1943, where Truscott shot down another Japanese aircraft. He died in an accident off Exmouth in Western Australia on 28 March 1943.

'A war of attrition': Gona, Sanananda, Buna, November 1942–January 1943

By the end of November 1942, it was clear that finishing off the Japanese who had retreated back up the Kokoda Track was going to be costly. Similar problems of supply applied to the Australian forces at the north end of the Kokoda as had hindered the Japanese at the southern end. Attacks wasteful of life on well-prepared Japanese defensive positions, often carried out without adequate planning or reconnaissance, were another difficulty. General George Vasey, commander of the 7th Division charged with the task of winkling out the enemy, said it would be 'a war of attrition' and noted that 'the Jap won't go till he is killed and in the process he is inflicting many casualties on us.'

Sanananda Creek. (1999)

Sergeant Jack Scott of the 2/16th likened the actions at Gona to the First World War: 'It was open ground against fixed positions. We knew the Japs had been preparing for months. That was the part we couldn't understand, it was beyond comprehension. And even if we got through we had no idea what we'd find when we got there.' What they got was days of killing. By 3 December, the 21st Brigade had lost a third of the 1000 men who had struggled into Gona, and the 25th Brigade had suffered 200 casualties. The Japanese waited in their camouflaged strong points, hoping that the Australians would use what historian Peter Brune calls 'this almost perfectly prepared killing ground'. The Australians accommodated them over and over again, as casualties mounted.

The 39th Battalion joined with the remnants of the 21st Battalion for a more considered attack on the Japanese on 8 December – not over the killing fields from the east, but through the jungle east of the track into Gona. The Japanese tried to escape that night down the coast to Sanananda, and many were killed in the sea, but Colonel Ralph Honner of the 39th was eventually able to send a message back to Brigade HQ – 'Gona's gone.'

The 2/16th Battalion War Diary notes: 'The village and beach were in a shambles, with dead Japs and Australians everywhere.

Sanananda: scene of the Japanese last stand. (1999)

Below: Map of the Gona Buna area. The Japanese landed on the beach at Gona on 21 July 1942.

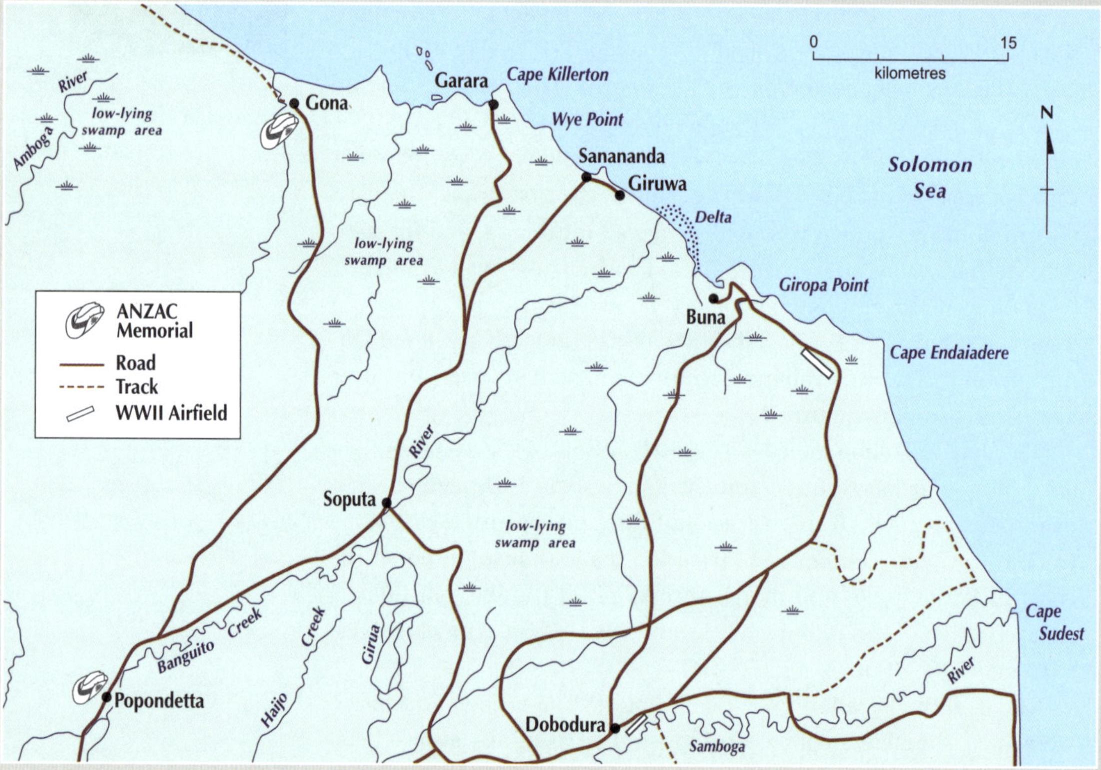

The black volcanic sand still lends an eerie feeling to the beaches around Sanananda, where the last Japanese were evacuated or killed by 23 January 1943. Corporal Bill Neate, 2/10th Battalion told historian Peter Brune that he remembered 'The moon. A beautiful moon used to come up each night and shine down. It looked lovely. And in the morning ... ghastly, bloody battlefields, dead bodies floating everywhere ...'

Taking a drink in the new Sanananda village. (1999)

Apparently the enemy had made no attempt to bury the dead, some of whom had obviously been lying out for days. The stench was terrific. The Japs had put up a very stubborn resistance. They still had plenty of ammunition, medical stores and rice ... In one dug-out rice had been stacked on enemy dead. More Japs had died lying on the rice and ammunition had been stacked on them again.'

Sanananda was the most defensible of the three Japanese beachhead redoubts, and the most bitterly fought over. Before war came, it was a trading post, the end point of a rough corduroy road where small amounts of goods from inland could be canoed to trading ships waiting off shore. At the end of 1942 there were more bomb craters than coconut trees. The guest house, the Resident Magistrate's house, the Station Office were all gone, bombed flat.

Efforts by under-trained Australian and inexperienced American units had failed and by the end of December 1942, Official Historian Dudley McCarthy says that Sanananda had become 'a ghastly nightmare ... the primeval swamps, the dank and silent bush, the heavy loss of life, the fixity of purpose of the Japanese for most of whom death could be the only ending, all combined to make this struggle so appalling that most of the hardened soldiers who were to emerge from it remember it unwillingly and as their most exacting experience of the whole war ...'

An attack with tanks failed with heavy casualties on 12 January, but that was also the day that the Japanese had their last serving of rice. A decision was taken to evacuate. Those who could were to find their way to the west of Gona, where they might be picked up by boat, or to head overland for Lae and Salamaua. At the beginning there were more than 5000 Japanese in the area, including 1800 in hospital. During the defence they were reinforced by sea, and by survivors coming down the Kokoda Track, swelling their numbers to about 7000. Of these, 1600 were buried after the battle, 1200 sick and wounded were evacuated, and 1000 escaped. While the Japanese evacuation was taking place, thousands still in the area had to be extracted. This nightmare continued until 22 January.

Meanwhile, at Buna, the most easterly of the Japanese positions, the Americans had made an initial attack on 16 November, and under a new commander, Lieutenant General Robert Eichelberger, were now ordered to 'take Buna or don't come back alive'. While the Americans were involved in one part of Buna, Australians, always energetic, were dying in another part. An Australian attack on 5 December was a catastrophe – five lightly armoured Bren-carriers were shot to bits in a frontal attack on the entrenched Japanese positions.

On 18 December, the 2/9th Battalion with the 2/6th Armoured Regiment with 2/10th in reserve, and some American support, was ordered to capture the Duropa Plantation Cape Endaiadere section of Buna. Once again under pressure from higher command, they had arrived after a twenty-mile forced march through swamp only the day before, with no reconnaissance.

As Peter Brune wrote: 'Think of it. Battalions of Americans who had made no ground. No reconnaissance, no measured planning, questionable support consisting of reconnaissance tanks. Not infantry tanks. And above all else, a movement into an enemy position brilliantly fortified with numerous bunkers and snipers and an enemy who will not withdraw when the pressure mounts, but will carry on the war with a terrible resolve. The Queenslanders of the 2/9th Battalion had the odds of war stacked inexorably against them.'

The courage and determination of the 2/9th cost five officers and 49 killed on that day, with 111 wounded. On 22 December the first phase was over, but the battle for Buna was not concluded until 2 January. By then the 2/9th casualties amounted to 23 officers and 351 others.

The 2/10th arrived at Buna on 21 December and had the task of clearing the Japanese from around the old airstrip, a killing field for the Japanese defenders. Once again men were sacrificed in the interest of expediency. The attack up the airstrip on 23 December cost 21 dead and 91 wounded. Hard and desperate fighting left only 138 men standing. By the end of the Buna operation, 91 had been killed in action, 21 had died of wounds, and 219 were wounded – 331 casualties sacrificed in a series of ineptly planned if bravely carried out operations.

The lessons of the first two phases of the Buna operation were learned in the roll-up of the Japanese in their smaller, last redoubt. The 2/12th had the job, beginning on 1 January 1943, of clearing the Japanese from Giropa Point. The Japanese here did not surrender – each one had to be killed. It cost the 2/12th 66 killed and 126 wounded.

This was the end of the Kokoda Track. Australian casualties were 5698 including 2165 dead. The Americans, committed to action from mid-November, had 2848 casualties and 854 dead. Some 12,000 Japanese died in the Kokoda campaign alone.

Papua New Guinea Today

Papua and New Guinea were administered as one territory – Australian New Guinea – by the Australian army's Australian New Guinea Administrative Unit (ANGAU) from early 1942 until mid-1946. The UN trusteeship for New Guinea replaced the former mandate in 1946, and the Australian government decided to administer the two territories as one unit, Papua New Guinea, from Port Moresby.

There had been a Legislative Council in place, but with an official appointed majority and no elected local members. In 1960, six locals were allowed as members. An elected House of Assembly was set up in 1962. A timetable for independence was detailed in 1971, and was declared on 16 September 1975. Sir Michael Somare, PNG's first prime minister, pledged to govern in the 'Melanesian way'.

While the country is blessed with great natural resources, they have not provided PNG with wealth or stability. Secessionist movements, particularly in Bougainville, and environmental damage have seen mines close down. Urban violence by raskol gangs affects visitors and locals alike.

PNG can be a dangerous place to travel in, especially in towns such as Port Moresby, Mount Hagen and Lae. It is inadvisable to wander around Port Moresby by yourself, even in a car. Hotels are safe enough, but if you go out at night, go with someone else, with transport from your hotel – even if it is only a few hundred metres.

To the first-time visitor, Lae, PNG's second-largest city, seems just about as dangerous today as it was in 1942. Walking around in the daytime is safe enough, though there is the risk of stumbling into one of the numerous scams pulled by some devious individuals. I was escorted off the street one evening by an observant security guard.

Bou, a village on the north arm of Milne Bay, also housed a battery of Australian artillery in late 1942, according to the great grandfather of these children. (2002)

The Black Cat Track connected Wau and Salamaua in 1999 as it did in 1942. The trek takes a few arduous days. I walked a couple of hours in from both ends in 1999, taking this picture near Wau, and catching dengue fever in the Francisco River near Salamaua.

'Too danger here for you,' he said, and rang a friend to drive me the 50 metres to the hotel. That, in a nutshell, is travel in the towns, a combination of great friendliness and potential danger.

Milne Bay is different – it's quiet and relaxed, remote enough from the rest of PNG to have fewer of the country's troubles, and with a tremendous potential for sustainable tourism. The islands – Samarai and Kwato around the eastern end of Milne Bay in China Strait – are beautiful. Milne Bay seems to be as much part of the Pacific as of PNG.

All that said, organised travel here is as safe as anywhere else in the developing world, and PNG has some of the most spectacular natural and human attractions anywhere. There has been trouble on the Kokoda Track from time to time, but organising your walk using experienced local people as guides and porters will see most villages put out the welcome mat.

New Guinea 1942

Kokoda, the Trek

It's only 25 minutes or so flying time from Port Moresby to Kokoda, across a mountainous rough green sea of jungle. In the Second World War it might have taken 45 minutes to fly. It's a deceptive introduction to what lies ahead for anyone who walks back, days of mind and body breaking.

Kokoda is like the prow of a boat pointing north, 50 metres above the valley of the Mambare River. Standing on the prow in the misty morning, where Colonel Owen of the 39th Battalion was killed on 29 July 1942, it's hushed and quiet; then it was noisy and very dangerous. Owen was walking the perimeter here on the eastern side where the Japanese memorial now stands. He was told he was taking an unnecessary risk. 'Well I've got to do it,' he replied, and half an hour later was shot.

It's a pilgrimage, coming here, testing yourself on the walk back over the ridges and Owen Stanleys. You can walk in the shadow of those ordinary men, Australia's extraordinary heroes.

Early in the morning, the mist wraps around the memorials. There are weapons pits on the edge of the cliff, a coconut tree with a bullet hole in it, said to have happened in 1942. Kokoda village is below to the east, the airstrip to the west. The Owen Stanleys loom behind, and the Mambare River runs not far away to the north. There is a small museum named for Bert Kienzle, whose Mamba plantation is a short drive away, down the Mambare.

John, the hospital's caretaker, is the keeper of the museum key and lives across the road from the Kokoda Guest House. 'The key? Yes surely – when this place was opened – two

prime ministers! – think of it – all Kokoda was alarms and excitement.' John could not remember his father speaking of the war time. He wishes he had asked.

The guest house is in the hospital grounds. Perhaps like me, you've spent a night there in preparation for the trek, and have had a final bed, chair and solar-warmed shower before setting off. Time for a last walk around this place which has become a key to understanding bravery, sacrifice and the incompetence of higher command. You can't help wondering: Could Kokoda have been defended? Could it have been reinforced? Could the Japanese landing on the coast have been opposed?

Day One: Kokoda to Hoi

In 1999, I drove up the rough road to Kokoda, across the Kumusi and Mambare rivers, and met my travelling companions – guide Jessie Eloda and porters Steven Wanire and Iana Leva – at the Kokoda Guest House. Jessie, 35, was from Menari, a village up the track. An expert bushman, he could light a fire, put up a shelter and cook a pot of rice in no time flat in any conditions. This was his eleventh trip. Steven, on his eighth trip, was 31, tall and strong, and liked a chat. Iana, like Steven, was

from Owers Corner, at the Moresby end of the track. On his third crossing, he was in his 40s, smaller than the others, wore a rastafarian woollen cap and old shorts, and walked in bare feet. When he wasn't walking he was a subsistence farmer.

The first day, Jessie said, was 'warm up day'. The track is relatively flat for the two-hour stroll to Hoi. The first day was sweaty, hot and humid, passing by overgrown gardens and an old rubber plantation where Doc Vernon stood and waited in 1942 for the last of the men to leave. After the build-up, I was a little disappointed that it finished so soon – but was extremely grateful by the end of the following day.

A creaking atap hut high off the ground, a stream nearby, a little garden seat overlooking it amid swarms of wild butterflies: if this is what the campsites will be like, give me more, I thought. Kids were swimming, cows came on down for a drink. I sat reading about the suffering on the track. An iridescent blue and black butterfly came to rest on my book. At 3.30 it rained, the garden quickly flooded, and you couldn't see bank or track from ten metres away.

Day Two: Hoi to Isurava and Alola

The track from Hoi passed through a hymn-singing village (it was Sunday) and a hillside of choko vines, escapees from a Japanese wartime garden, according to Jessie.

On the track at 6.30 a.m., a relentless grind, most of it uphill, for six hours before emerging into the deserted and clean-swept village of new Isurava.

It was deserted. Everyone was away at a Seventh Day Adventist jamboree in Port Moresby. The old Isurava village, the battle site, the new memorial and the place where Bruce Kingsbury won a VC are further up the hill. Osmar White, the great war correspondent and New Guinea hand, walked towards this place in 1942, just after the battle for Isurava: 'Just after eight o'clock there was a sudden chatter of machine-gun fire that echoed from rolling miles of tree tops. Boom of mortars again. Four bombs.

'Down there behind the white cloud bank is Kokoda. One can see the blue smear of the coastal plain.

'More walking wounded. Then the remnants of a post cleaned out by a heavy Jap attack – faces pallid under a four days' stubble, grinning tightly ... If I dared I'd go off the track and slip through the bush. But a man couldn't, not with the wounded coming up the track so slowly and calmly.'

White's article, published in the *Daily Telegraph* on 14 September 1942, was copied and stencilled and passed around as the truth of Kokoda. It puts the self-inflicted pain of the volunteer trekker into perspective.

To Alola, in the afternoon gloom. On the cross-section map it looked pretty flat, even with a downward slant – but hidden in the wrinkles of the map were some 50-metre straight-down descents, a greasy creek gorge and 50 metres up a slippery bank. Iana skipped straight across the creek like a barefoot Blondin, but I had to use my hands and a stick. Anything to avoid wet boots. The track was not ankle- or knee-deep in mud, as much of it was during the Second World War, but it was nearly as treacherous.

Alola, where Brigadier Potts of the 21st Brigade had his headquarters during the Isurava battle, was four more exhausting hours away, the last of it like walking in a

black fog. At Alola I celebrated my 50th birthday in Mr Suga Sega's thatched guest house feeling like I'd just been hit by a tank, and figured that Potts had four years advantage on me. After an hour, some bananas, Gastrolite, sultanas, chocolate and water, I could sit up and admire the afternoon rain storm, miraculously restored. When I could talk, I found that that one of Mr Sega's children had been to the Royal Children's Hospital in Melbourne to have some orthopaedic surgery. Small world.

Day Three: To Templeton's Crossing

Next day, not for the first or last time on the track, I understood that in Papua New Guinea what goes down must go up. We were off to Templeton's Crossing.

It's not hot up there, but the highest elevation 1910 metres (6300 feet) in this section made me feel short of breath, and I had to work hard to suck in adequate oxygen to walk uphill. Clearly I hadn't done enough training for this altitude, nor for the relentless downhill sections of the track, where it feels like kneebone rubs on kneebone, all connected to aching foot bones and tortured thigh bones.

Five hours later we stopped for lunch on the bank of the swift-flowing and glorious-tasting Eora Creek. The creek (more like a little river) wasn't running very high, and we could scramble across on the boulders, boots and pants off, rather than use the bundle of poles that made the bridge. Osmar White and photographer Damien Parer were here in 1942: 'Lines of exhausted carriers were squatting on the fringes of this congregation eating muddy rice off muddy banana leaves. Their woolly hair was plastered with rain and muck. Their eyes were rolling and bloodshot with the strain of long carrying. Some of them were still panting.'

It started raining, so I was wet for the four hours to the campsite at Templeton's 2, one of the two crossings of Eora Creek that Bert Kienzle named for Captain Sam Templeton. Some poles held up a tin roof, which was at least dry-ish underneath. There was a memorial plaque in front. Just as we were settling in, a dozen Adventists arrived, and Jessie thought it better if we walked five minutes further up the bank.

Jessie and Steven wordlessly built a shelter from a blue plastic tarp and fresh-cut poles, and had a fire going within five minutes. I slept, or steamed, in a one-person tent watching fire flies and listening to an extraordinary orchestra of clicking, squeaking and screaming insects.

Days Four and Five: At Myola

With boots that hadn't dried out by the fire overnight, I felt blisters breaking out and tiredness enveloping me. I concentrated on putting one foot in front of the other, on a non-slippery spot, but sometimes failed. I day-dreamed of fried eggs, and fell over. Steven, beating the path ahead, said that if he slipped (he never did) he would be thinking of fried chicken.

We were heading to the top of Mt Bellamy, some 2190 metres high and the highest point on the track. A shrug on the shoulder of Mt Bellamy is the famed Kokoda 'Gap'. A few hours past the ridge, after a very steep descent, there's a propeller marking the left turn to the dry uplands of the two so-called dry lakes at Myola. The walk there is through an undulating forest with soft leaf-fall covering the track and the sun filtering through – Steven said it was an air-conditioned track with carpet. Along the track is a hole in the jungle where a wartime aircraft had recently been excavated.

Myola, named after the wife of Kienzle's ANGAU comrade Syd Elliott-Smith, means 'dawn of day'. After the intense interior of the jungle, a first sight of Myola is breathtaking: open space and sky, a wide expanse of grass, low forested hills on the other side, a wild pig staring and galloping off in the middle distance. Bert Kienzle remembered this swampy grassland valley as a good place to air drop supplies for the defenders on the track.

There was no one home at Myola. There was a collection of huts, some ruined and falling over, but I had a good one all to myself to sleep in. There was birdsong, the sound of rattling pandanus, spectacular flowers, black bird of paradise, and not far away the wreck of an American Kittyhawk. A rest that night,

New Guinea 1942

and next day quiet exploration of the fringing forest, looking for birds of paradise, and finding the Kittyhawk.

Brigadier Potts arrived at Myola on 18 August 1942 looking for the promised supplies for the 39th. When, later, the biscuit bombers did drop things, they were hard to find, sunk in the swamp or lost in the jungle.

Osmar White tells of a young officer going in search of a load of mortar bombs which had landed in the jungle away from the drop zone, and who wandered lost for about four days before finding his way back. 'No one could blame the man for lack of bushcraft,' says Osmar, something I thought about as I went back along the track from the rest house, over the dry wooden fence, across the sodden flood of the little creek, where a pipe carried water to the tap in the compound. At the head of the pipe, the clear water gurgled from a bamboo spout into the black plastic. This was the wrong direction, I knew within five minutes. Where was I? Just for a moment, lost. But then I was back on the track, on the garden track.

Day Six: To Kagi and Efogi

Two nights here in the cold upland air made the rest of the trek possible to finish. After walking out of Myola for an hour and a half, we met a man and a boy coming the other way. We stopped for a chat, and were introduced to Jessie's brother-in-law. After a few minutes we parted, but an hour after that, the brother-in-law passed us on his way back from Myola – proof that locals walk, skip and bound along the track.

After the carpetted forest, the track descends in a knee-killing descent, first to Naduli where we drank water next to a deserted school and set of rugby goal posts. The walk into Kagi was hard. Kagi, as Osmar White said, was 'a russet round-thatched vil-

lage clinging to its jungle crag'. It is perched on the bend of a 1000-metre ridge, perhaps twenty houses on stilts, around hard red earth swept meticulously clean, with a church. Jessie, Steven and Iana are greeted as long-lost brothers by a group of village men and boys headed off for a couple of days' hunting and fishing before flying to Moresby to take up another guiding job along the track.

Leaving Kagi next morning, we passed a new health clinic, and slid down a 350-metre descent, almost vertical, hand over hand, foot on root, down to a dark creek where we crept for a time as if in a tunnel. Then a tedious hot climb out of the creek through kunai and a stand of 'eucalyptus generalis' at the top of the ridge to Launumu village, also known as Efogi 2. The only things out in the street were butterflies and burbling chooks.

In Launumu is a memorial to a Japanese soldier, a rough stone and cement plinth with an artillery-shell-shaped object on top,

inscribed in Japanese. Jessie told me that this was a memorial by one Japanese soldier to his brother. Both of them fought at Brigade Hill, one was killed, one saved himself by hiding in a tree and escaped through the jungle to Buna, where he was one of the few to escape that particular killing field. The survivor had returned to make this memorial 50 years later. There is a small business, especially around Buna and Gona, in touring Japanese veterans around the sites.

Efogi, in the afternoon. Efogi is a big village of about twenty huts, some with tin rooves, built around a black hard-packed square, glinting with mica in the sun. It's hot and dry. Walking the square is like crossing a hot Australian beach, the heat reflects into your face. The houses are settled among trees, and have flower gardens, low-growing grass, and locals sitting around chatting and apparently telling funny stories. In 1942 it was wet, the square was mud, the trees splintered by mortars and automatic weapons fire, white men pale with exhaustion, wounds, shock, hunger. It had only taken us four hours to walk here from Kagi. The walk hadn't been that hard – in fact, more-diligent walkers did Kagi–Menari in a day, stopping at Efogi for lunch.

We had collected a package of supplies dropped at the airstrip. Without more carriers, it is impossible to carry enough food for the journey. Unlike the hungry men of 1942,

our resupply worked. We had more dehydrated pasta, more rice, more tooth-loosening Navy Biskit, and more bully beef. In 1942 they had nothing much.

The guest house at Efogi had a kitchen room, where Jessie and Steven and Iana soon had the fire going on the floor. The whole structure, up on stilts, had a pleasant swaying and creaking character as people moved around. There was even a separate little room to lay a sleeping mat and bag, with a glassless window looking out onto some pink bougainvillea and a little shelf with scraps of a hymn book.

Efogi was another Seventh Day Adventist village. Many villagers had left to walk the track to Bautama outside Port Moresby for a ten-day jamboree. The church has a membership of more than 300,000, growing, according to the Port Moresby *Post-Courier*, at 8 per cent a year. The Central Papuan Mission, of which the villages along the Kokoda Track are part, has between 20,000 and 30,000 faithful, and began its work in 1908. It is the smallest of the Adventist missions in PNG, but what it lacks in numbers it makes up for in enthusiasm.

The best thing about the Efogi rest house was that it had a chair with a back. It was the only chair I came across between Kokoda and Port Moresby, and to the amusement of my comrades, after a walk to the water pipe and a wash I sat straightening my back for a couple of hours, watching the Efogian afternoon pass by outside, asking questions of Steven and Jessie, who had gone to sit in the circle of locals under the shady tree. I liked the way everyone talked at the same time, but burst into laughter individually when they overheard something funny. Questions interjected. No, there was no one who remembered the war. Old people dead. Yes, village in same place. That's it.

Huge claps of thunder announced the end of the afternoon at about four o'clock. Later, over the rice and pasta, Jessie let slip that his 'grandfadder' had been a carrier on the track. Walking it was something of a family tradition.

Torch-lit mutterings outside when I went to clean my teeth, escorted by big Steven with his bush knife. Strangers had been seen. Keep they-selves in bushes. Might be bad men. A few determined souls gathered with torches for a look around.

In my sleeping bag later, I was awoken first by Steven's screams in his sleep, some nightmare which he wouldn't talk about. Later I became half aware of a snuffling and a scratching nearby, in the kitchen where Jessie, Steven and Iana were sleeping. Then the noises came nearer, in the little corridor outside, then at the door, then in my room. Pigs? Djinns? Bats? Nats? The bad men? Then the unmistakable smell of dog. In the morning, the bad men manifested as half a dozen Adventists who didn't want to bother anyone and had camped off the track.

Day Seven: To Brigade Hill

The track from Efogi to Brigade Hill climbs up a hill past one of the airstrips for which Papua New Guinea is famous, short and steep. No wonder they don't play much cricket in this part of PNG – anything long and flat enough to be a cricket pitch is an airstrip.

There are some steep and scary sections on the climb up to Brigade Hill. One section requires inching around a slippery foot-wide track on the ridge above a precipice. It's an open forest with grassy undergrowth at about 1400 metres. There's a view back from Mission Ridge to Efogi, where the 2/27th watched the Japanese advance on the night of 6 September 1942.

Just about here Jessie pointed out a tree, 'Jap brother tree,' he said. It was a splintered and rotting stump, a metre wide, between two offspring saplings. It might have served as a hiding place, but maybe it was a convenient prop for a story.

The top of Brigade Hill is cleared and tended by the Koiari people. Incredibly, there is a memorial here, one of Ross Bastiaan's bronze plaques describing the battle, set on a cement plinth, with a little shelter built over it, a little garden, and a garland of flowers. The view from up here is very special. Although not the highest point of the track, it is about half way, and the ridges and razorbacks already walked offer some satisfaction given that there are the same still to be overcome.

Only 30 per cent of the track is exactly where it was in 1942, and there has been tremendous regrowth of forest, and movement of villages. But Brigade Hill is where it was in 1942, and it is all too easy to understand the awful events that happened there. There was where valiant defence was infiltrated by the Japanese coming up these precipitous sides of the ridge, and there was where Brigadier Potts nearly copped it, and there was where the 2/27th survivors had to scramble down to escape. You can see for miles and over years, you can feel in the clean air and the clear sky a sense of peace. You can't drive to Brigade Hill, you have to struggle in.

In the clearing behind the memorial about twenty sticks set in the ground mark the original location of graves. As everywhere on Australian battlefields (except Vietnam), the remains were re-interred after the war in the country where the men had

Kokoda Track panorama: villages are, from left: Efogi, Naduli, Kagi. Brigade Hill is the ridge in the middle distance above Naduli.

died, in this case at Bomana cemetery at the end of the track outside Port Moresby.

Day Eight: To Menari

Walking off Brigade Hill in the daylight without anyone shooting at you is hard enough, a stiff descent of about 700 metres or so, the first part along a ridge that is barely a metre wide, falling away steeply to the Enili Creek to the west of the track, or down to Vabuiagi River on the east.

Walked through gardens, track slippery, along the airfield to Menari, Jessie's home town. A biggish village with rugby league posts at the ends of the muddy square. The tops of the goal posts were sprouting new growth.

We arrived at the two-room guest house, built next to one of Jessie's relative's kitchen

house, stripped the wet gear and looked for a fire to dry boots. Heaven on the track is a boot-drying fire. Evil is getting into wet gear after a sleepless night, and walking again.

This rugby field was where Colonel Honner and the remnant 39th Battalion had paraded on 6 September, after being relieved by the 2/27th, three days before the Brigade Hill battle. Damien Parer was there, and shot some film, of 'those ragged bloody heroes'.

Parer's picture shows Lieutenant Johnson at attention with his Kokoda stick under his right arm. Johnson seems to have cut off his long pants and rolled up the remains into shorts. The boys, for all the world like bushmen in a thunderstorm, at attention too, with sticks and rifles, a tin hat, unslouched hats, shorts.

That afternoon and night at Menari it rained, on and off. When it wasn't raining, kids came out to play with a village puppy, cutting grass, collecting green bananas, singing. An old man looked up at me from splitting cane to make a basket, women hidden in the smoke-swarmed cooking hut. War remnants – a Japanese helmet, some rusty long things. We were given the hospitality of relatives, kaukau, hot water, boot-warming.

Day Nine: To Nauro

By 8 September 1942 the Japanese had caught up to the withdrawing Australians and mortars began to fall in the area around Menari. The withdrawal to the next village, Nauro, was ordered. The 2/14th and 2/16th harassed the Japanese on the track.

Potts withdrew to Nauro on the 9th. Along the track to Nauro, Potts came across some men of the 2/14th. He had a single escort, and carried a fair bit of gear. He said, 'Come on you men, keep moving, the Japs aren't far behind.' They started to move, a bit unwillingly. They were tired and hungry so he said, 'Give me your Bren, I'll carry it up the hill for you.' Which he did. In the way of the heroes of Kokoda, Potts had been sacked and was to meet his replacement, Brigadier Porter, south of Nauro on 10 September, the next day, and report back in Moresby a day after that.

Luckily, it was, as Jessie said, 'Just a one-mountain day', but this hill outside Menari felt like 400 metres straight up, then 500 metres straight down. Potts thought he was pretty sprightly for a 46-year-old, but he must have felt something carting that bloke's Bren gun up that bloody mountain.

An hour and a half through this bog and slop, boots on, boots off, doesn't matter any

more. This is a foetid part of the track. There are stinging bugs which I can't see, and a lot of weird fruit. Osmar White came across some of these as well, in 1942, things that looked just like a Golden Delicious apple, or a cherry, or some bright blue plum – assuredly poisonous. White commented: 'How typical of this country! Never could imagination conceive a clime where beauty and death, plenty and poverty, action and decay are such close bedfellows.'

White reckoned he could live off the land more easily here than he could in the Australian bush. This fibrous fruit, big as a bowling ball with peach yellow flesh and big black seeds, for example – White saw cassowaries eating it and gave it a try, with no ill effect. I wasn't that game.

Eventually, wet but surprisingly cheerful, we trudged past the overgrown and soggy airstrip at Nauro to find the guesthouse, an L-shaped open-sided thatched affair, with a sleeping platform, on one side of a grassy village square. Five kina a night, each, said the sign. Strip off, clothes hung on a wire, boots in front of a fire.

A loud rushing and roaring in the trees, in tomorrow's mountains, was the afternoon rain. The storm was advancing, like a precision water-soaking outfit. A few drops, then an advance of rain steady as a marching team. It roared across Nauro compound. As it came, chooks hid under houses; the dog looked up in mid-scratch and did the same. A girl in a bright red skirt and a long green t-shirt picked her way from one hut to another.

Jessie and Steven covered themselves in olive-green ground sheets and went to sleep. Half an hour later, the rain eased to a tropical drenching and half the chooks tip-toed out to get the insects driven to the surface. A bloke with a baby on his shoulder under a lopsided broken black umbrella called on Iana for a chin-wag. We gave him some biskits, and later he came back with some bananas and kaukau, and collected his twenty kina.

The rain stopped, the fire needed wood, boots needed drying, more desiccated pasta, lay down on the mat. This is a pestilential place at night. Huge rhythmic flaps of bats or flying foxes mixed with the mozzies, all bloodsuckers after my blood.

Day Ten: A Two Mountain Day to Ua-Ule Creek

We had to wade through the creek at Nauro, cross some swamp, into the creek again, before a climb through the mist to an abandoned Nauro village, and then an even stiffer and longer climb to the top of the Maguli Range, 1350 metres up. Along the way, evi-

dence of the 1942 fighting was not hard to find. Ammunition, grenades, a mortar bomb that stuck in a tree. Maguli is advertised as having eleven false crests, like mirages. From ground level, it seemed there were many more than eleven. Then the most excruciating descent of all – it seemed almost vertical, with knees howling – to Ofi Creek. I knew doing this that there was another climb up the Ioribaiwa Ridge and another descent down to the Ua-Ule Creek, where we would camp for the last time.

Ioribaiwa is as far as the hungry and exhausted Japanese got in 1942; the equally depleted and battle-weary Australians in their strategic withdrawal had snapped the Japanese supply line, picked off hundreds of lives, drained them of food, so much that there seemed little will or interest by the Japanese commanders to reinforce and resupply the few who had made it this far. The Australians had withdrawn to Imita, across the trackless meander of Ua-Ule Creek. Skirmishing, artillery shelling and ambushing went on for ten days, before on 26 September 1942 the Japanese themselves withdrew back down the track.

Tired or not, I wouldn't attempt walking this part of the track without an experienced guide. This is where an English walker was lost in early 1999, and had to be plucked out by helicopter.

On one of the crossings, I slipped on a greasy boulder and fell into the water, my only major mistake in footwork. It didn't help my mood, thinking about ambushes. Camp always seemed just another little way off, but in sympathy, Jessie pitched the blue tarp in a gloomy glade by the cold creek. 'Last campfire,' said Steven.

Day Eleven: Last Day

The last day is a haze. I was wet, exhausted, concentration was hard to maintain. There's an extremely tiring climb up to Imita, and a steep descent along the ridge from where the infamous Golden Stairs formed in 1942

as an introduction to the pains of the Kokoda Track.

There's a notch, a cleared patch at the top of Imita Ridge, a grassy spot perhaps four metres wide and a couple of metres across, with a rock to rest on after the last of the big hill climbs. You can see the notch from north and south of the ridge – it marks the last big ridge, the last defensive position before Port Moresby.

Below lies the swift and often high-flowing Goldie River, and beyond that the stiff and sticky little 1000-foot mud hill climb to Owers Corner. For the Japanese, attacking razor-backed Imita across Ua-Ule Creek would have been very problematical, even in strength, and outflanking high points do not exist.

Sitting on that impregnable rock, it was possible to see the Australian strategy – to stretch and harry and bleed the Japanese to defeat – as it developed, and to appreciate the finality of the geography of the Owen Stanleys. The mountains, the creeks and the ridges were the enduring winners.

We descended to the Goldie River, which luckily was low and wade-able. I kept my boots on; they were still sodden from the day before, and it was easier not to slip and to walk on the stones on the river bottom. I squelched up the last green hill on the other side to Owers Corner, feeling more tired than I had ever been while still awake and walking. There are monuments here, the road to McDonald's Corner and Port Moresby, and a sign: Kokoda Trail.

Bugger that, I thought, I've just walked the Kokoda *Track*.

New Guinea 1942

Cemeteries, Memorials, Museums

Cape Wom

The **Surrender Memorial** is located in the Cape Wom Memorial Park. The cairn bears a central plaque, which commemorates the surrender of the Japanese army on 13 September 1945. It stands on the site of the surrender by Lieutenant General Hutazo Adachi, commander of the Japanese XVIII Imperial Army, to Major General H C H Robertson of the 6th Division. Other plaques in the park commemorate the acts of valour by Lieutenant Albert Chowne on 25 March 1945 and Private Edward Kenna on 15 May 1945, each of whom was awarded the Victoria Cross.

Australian Memorial, Gona. (1999)

Gona

The **Australia Remembers Memorial** is on the site of the Anglican Gona Mission and there is a **Ross Bastiaan bronze plaque** at the centre of Gona village. The rusting hulk of a Japanese transport ship lies aground a couple of kilometres up the beach, marking the spot where the Japanese landing took place. Japanese pilgrims sometimes come, when the tide is out.

Kokoda

The **Kokoda Memorial and Museum**, named for Bert Kienzle, was opened in 1995, with the nearby guest house by then prime ministers Paul Keating and Sir Julius Chan. There is a small explanatory display with pictures. Entrance is obtained from the caretaker – ask at the guest house.

Above: Bert Kienzle Memorial Museum, Kokoda. (1999)
Below: Kokoda memorials. (1999)

Nearby on the Kokoda plateau are a number of other memorials, including a **memorial to the Papuan carriers**, a **Japanese memorial to all war dead**, and the **39th Battalion Memorial**, as well as a **Ross Bastiaan plaque**.

Kokoda Track: Kokoda to Sogeri

There are a number of memorials along the Kokoda Track.

At **Isurava** the **Isurava Memorial** was opened in 2002 on the site of

The Isurava Memorial, dedicated in 2002, stands near the spot where Bruce Kingsbury won the only VC awarded on the Kokoda Track. (DVA 2002, Mick Stone, 2003)

the battle. The memorial features four Australian black granite pillars that are each inscribed with a single word – 'courage', 'endurance', 'mateship' and 'sacrifice' – representing the values and qualities of those Australian soldiers who fought along the Kokoda Track. There is a small Ross Bastiaan plaque in the main clearing of the new village.

A big boulder – Kingsbury's rock – marks the spot where a Japanese sniper killed VC winner Bruce Kingsbury. A plaque was placed there in 2002.

At **Alola** there is a small plaque to the west side of the trail at the north end of village.

At **Eora Creek** there is a small plaque at Eora Creek in the clearing.

At **Templeton's Crossing** the plaque is on the east side of Eora Creek.

At **Efogi** the plaque is to the west side of the trail 200 metres south of the village.

There is a small Ross Bastiaan plaque beneath a shelter on top of **Brigade Hill**.

Brigade Hill. (1999)

At **Owers Corner** is the Kokoda Memorial Arch, erected in 1999. It is a six-metre by fifteen-metre, eleven-tonne steel sculpture with ten attached bronze plaques listing all units that fought in the Kokoda Campaign, with campaign details. There is also an Australian memorial cairn.

Lae

Lae War Cemetery was commenced in 1944 by the Australian Army Graves Service and handed over to the Commonwealth War Graves Commission in 1947. It contains the graves of men who lost their lives during the New Guinea campaigns – including at Wau, Mubo, Salamaua, Lae, Finschhafen, Sattelberg and Shaggy Ridge – and whose graves were brought here from the temporary military cemeteries in those areas.

The immaculately kept cemetery contains 2818 Commonwealth Second World War burials, including 2337 Australians. There are 444 unidentified burials.

Walking to the war cemetery, next to the pretty but unkempt Lae Botanic Gardens, takes half an hour or so from either of Lae's better hotels, through Top Town, up Huon Street, from 3rd Street to 13th Street to Memorial Avenue.

The **Lae Memorial**, which stands in the cemetery, commemorates more than 300 officers and men of the Australian army, the Australian Merchant Navy and the Royal Australian Air Force who lost their lives during operations in the area and have no known grave.

The **AIF Memorial** in Lae is the result of a decision taken in 1945 by Australian Commander General Thomas Blamey. He ordered that 43 memorials be erected at various battle sites throughout New Guinea. All the bronze panels were to be cast in the army workshops. Most, but not all, were erected, but by 1961 it became apparent that proper maintenance of such widely dispersed memorials would present considerable difficulty.

The Lae Memorial.

The (then) Battle Exploit Memorials Committee, comprising representatives of the Papua New Guinea administration, the Commonwealth War Graves Commission, Returned Services League, Apex and Rotary Clubs, decided to reposition these memorials at a more central location.

Memorials from Salamaua and the Lae areas as far as Nadzab, but not Wau, were incorporated on a memorial cairn positioned at the entrance to the Lae War Cemetery as the AIF Memorial. It is a circular arrangement of ten bronze divisional and battle exploit memorials brought in from the battlefields in the vicinity – including for the 3rd Division, Salamaua, Nadzab and Sattelberg.

AIF Memorial, outside Lae War Cemetery. (1999)

The **Lae Victory Plaque** is on a plinth beneath a flagpole in a small park near the Lae International Hotel, on the spot where Brigadier Ken Eather of the 25th Brigade raised the flag on 16 September 1943 on the recapture of Lae. On the other side of the plinth is a 1914–1918 plaque.

Milne Bay

After the battles of August–September 1942, the war moved on. Air raids continued through 1943 and there were hot spots of Japanese not far away in Rabaul, Bougainville and Wewak until the end of the war.

Milne Bay became a substantial hospital, supply and engineering base as the Allied forces built up through 1943 and 1944. Hundreds of thousands of servicemen passed through the port, protected by batteries of heavy artillery. My father served on E Battery Australian Heavy Artillery at Dawa Dawa on the south arm of Milne Bay, and later at Sideia Island at the head of the bay. In 2000 we made a pilgrimage looking for evidence that it had actually happened.

And found, 200 metres from the mouth of the Dawa Dawa River, a twenty-metre ellipse of cement, with a rusting rail in it – the Panama mount of Number One Gun. The emplacement is a rail enabling the gun to traverse through 200 degrees or more. A coconut log bisects the circle, pointing like a gun barrel straight across the bay. A knowledgeable local must have put it there, remembering what the shape was. Number Two Gun was a further 50 metres along the beach, but

Camouflaged E Battery guns, Dawa Dawa, 1942. (AWM 069947)

was in the water. The whole beach had been washed from under the emplacements.

The camp was between the palms and the water, behind the tents on the old picture. Now it made a bit of sense. The camp site is washed away, like memory and mates. There is nothing left but these two semicircles, a rune, a standing stone, a monument to this corner of the war.

Above: Dawa Dawa artillery emplacement with coconut log gun. **Below:** Memorial to Bob Gurney at the airport bearing his name. (2000)

One Strip – now Gurney Airport, where flights from Port Moresby arrive today – was constructed in July 1942 by local villagers and American engineers.

Gurney was named during the war for Bob Gurney, a pioneer Australian flyer, who commanded 11 Squadron and then 33 Squadron. He was killed in 1942 in the Trobriand islands to the north while on a raid from Townsville via Port Moresby to Rabaul. A **stone cairn** with a propeller on top commemorates Bob Gurney. A green-painted anti-aircraft gun sits next to it. There is also a small Ross Bastiaan plaque outside the terminal.

Three (Turnbull) Strip, on the rough road from Gurney Airport to Alotau, was the furthest south and east that the Japanese advanced on land, and where the Australians turned them back – the first time they were beaten on land.

There's a 1942 plaque, the first victory plaque put up in New Guinea, now set in a white-painted plinth; it commemorates the Australians who gave their lives defending this place, and the 83 unknown Japanese marines buried there.

The **Milne Bay Memorial** was installed in 2002.

The **John French VC memorial** is at Alotau near the bridge over the Goilani, down a turnoff on the eastern side of the road. Two black-bronze plaques in a poinciana garden marked by white painted river stones mark where he died winning his VC.

French VC and 18 Brigade Memorial. (1999)

Popondetta

The **AIF Memorial** at Popondetta bears seven battle exploit plaques which commemorate the campaigns at Buna, Dobodura, Giropa Point, Gona, Sanananda Point and Wye Point.

Port Moresby

Above: Bomana War Cemetery, Port Moresby. (2000)
Below: John French VC, Bomana War Cemetery, Port Moresby. (2000)

Port Moresby (Bomana) War Cemetery is nineteen kilometres north of Port Moresby on the road to Sogeri and the start of the Kokoda Track. It is approached from the main road by a short side road called Pilgrims Way.

Most of those who died in the fighting in the Papuan campaigns – on the Kokoda Track and at Milne Bay – and on Bougainville are buried here, their graves brought in by the Australian Army Graves Service from burial grounds in the areas where the fighting had taken place. The cemetery contains 3819 Commonwealth Second World War burials, including 3030 identified Australian burials. Of the 702 unidentified burials, 690 are Australian.

The **Port Moresby Memorial** behind the cemetery commemorates almost 750 men of the Australian army – including Papua and New Guinea local forces, the Australian Merchant Navy and the Royal Australian Air Force – who lost their lives in the operations in Papua and who have no known graves.

The **Port Moresby War Museum** is a collection of aircraft and other equipment first established in 1978 by Bruce Hoy, who brought in many of the exhibits. It is now housed in an extension of the National Museum in a separate small building and yard. The items are important, but poorly conserved. Some items are on permanent loan – including pieces of the bomber in which Japanese Admiral Yamamoto was shot down in 1943 – to the Yamamoto Museum in Tokyo. The museum is open irregularly and is located in Ahuia Street, Port Moresby.

Bren carrier among the relics in the yard of the Port Moresby War Museum. (2000)

Rabaul

Rabaul (Bita Paka) War Cemetery was established in 1945 and contains the graves of those who lost their lives during the operations in New Britain and New Ireland, or who died in the area while prisoners of war. The graves were brought into the cemetery from isolated sites, from temporary military cemeteries and from camp burial grounds. The cemetery contains 206 identified, and 190 unidentified Australian burials. It is located 50 kilometres south of Rabaul.

Rabaul (Bita Paka) War Cemetery.

It appears to have been the Japanese plan to remove Europeans taken prisoner on these islands to areas from which it would have been harder to escape and to replace them with labour forces of Indian and other Asiatic troops captured in Malaya and elsewhere. This explains the large number of Indian remains recovered by the Australians during the 1945 campaign in New Britain and New Ireland, and the preponderance of Indian army casualties buried here. The cemetery contains 1114 Commonwealth burials of the Second World War, 495 of them unidentified.

There is also a plaque telling the story of the capture of the German radio station, the first battle in which Australians fought in the First World War. The plaque is in the cemetery near the graves of Captain Pockley and Able Seaman Williams killed in that action. In all, 32 First World War servicemen are now buried or commemorated in the cemetery.

The **Rabaul Memorial**, which stands within the cemetery, commemorates more than 1200 members of the Royal Australian Army (including personnel of the New Guinea and Papuan local forces and constabulary) and Royal Australian Air Force who lost their lives in the area in January and February 1942 and from November 1944 to August 1945, and who have no known graves.

The **Rabaul 1942–45 Memorial** on the foreshore of Simpson Harbour honours all those who lost their lives in the air, on land and at sea in the defence of New Britain and in the course of the Japanese occupation during 1942–1945. The memorial also features a cairn in remembrance of the *Montevideo Maru*, which sailed from Rabaul in June 1942 carrying 845 Allied prisoners of war and 208 civilian internees who had been captured by Japanese forces on New Britain and New Ireland during the Second World War. The ship was torpedoed off the

Philippines on 1 July 1942 and sank with the loss of all lives. Due to the memorials being buried by the 1994 volcanic eruptions they were relocated to a raised platform in 2002.

Sanananda

Japanese Memorial, Huggins Roadblock.

At Huggins Road Block, at the junction of the road to Cape Killerton and Sanananda, there is an **American memorial**. The brown and gold painted metal plaque reads:

> Capt Meredith M Huggins USA
> 3rd Battalion 126th Infantry Regiment
> 32nd Division 'Huggins Road Block'
>
> After his commanding officer was killed Captain Huggins assumed command of companies of the 126th Infantry, 32nd Division. Tasked with securing a tactical choke point to thwart a rapid Japanese advance across the Kokoda Trail, Huggins' bravery under fire and his ability to hold a numerically superior Japanese force at bay, laid the groundwork for an American victory in New Guinea. The place where he fought and was wounded on 5 December 1942 now bears the name 'Huggins Road Block', in honour of his valour.
>
> With grateful appreciation
> The American Legion remembers
> Capt. Meredith M Huggins.

Across the road is a Japanese monument.

American Memorial, Huggins Roadblock. (1999)

New Guinea 1942

Ten kilometres east of Wau, at Kaisenik, is the wreck of an American B17 Flying Fortress, which crash-landed after being damaged by anti-aircraft fire bombing Lae on 8 January 1943. See Justin Taylan's excellent website www.pacificwrecks.com for more information on this and other sites in the South-West Pacific.

Sogeri

The **Sogeri Memorial** was designed and built in 1943 by the Australian 7th Infantry Brigade in conjunction with the Australian 2nd Watercraft Workshop. It stands at the road junction where the Kokoda Track to McDonald's and Owers Corners intersects the Sogeri Road. There is a Ross Bastiaan plaque.

Wau

The **Wau Battle Exploit Memorial** stands next to the airfield where the battle of January 1943 was fought – soldiers going into the fight directly from aircraft as they landed.

Left: McDonald's Corner.
Far left: Wau War Memorial. (1999)

Travel Tool Kit

For independent travel through Papua New Guinea generally, the Papua New Guinea Tourism and Business Directory is a highly recommended first stop for all kinds of travel and tourism information: **www.pngbd.com**. The forums are especially useful.

Qantas and Air Niugini fly daily to Port Moresby's Jackson Airport (named after squadron leader John Jackson, killed above Port Moresby in 1942). The relatively new terminal is efficient (and cool) enough by Pacific standards. You can get a 30-day tourist visa at the airport, though as always you should check on current visa and travel conditions before you go: **www.dfat.gov.au**

If you plan to do any form of research or work, for example travel writing, you will need a research visa. Your specialist PNG or Kokoda Track travel agent will be able to help.

PNG runs on aircraft. Air Niugini flies to just about everywhere there's an airstrip, including regularly to Nadzab Airport in Lae (for access to Wau and Salamaua), Gurney Airport in Alotau (for Milne Bay) and Popondetta (for Kokoda). Service is cheerful, safe, but occasionally erratic due to weather or some such.

Air Niugini have a downloadable timetable at **www.airniugini.com.pg/main.htm**. Links to tours and accommodation and other material are very good, and there are discounted mid-week airfares.

To get to Wau from Lae it is possible to catch a PMV (Public Motor Vehicle) in 8th Street. Scams may be experienced at the bus stop, and robberies of the actual vehicle are frequent. The few 'tourists' aren't actually targeted but the poor locals are. If you can afford to, it might be better to hire a 4WD or car and driver, or contact the guest house you choose in Wau for transport.

Salamaua is an hour or so's ride in a banana boat or tinnie from

Voca Point, Lae. (1999)

Voca Point in Lae. Some of the boats available for hire are dangerous, and you put your life into their hands getting to Salamaua, and more especially getting back; transport may be safely arranged through the Haus Kibang guest house.

The best place to start for tourism information and accommodation information for Lae and Wau is the tourist office for the province, Morobe Tourism:

Morobe Tourism
Address: P.O. Box 475, Lae, Morobe Province, Papua New Guinea, 411
Website: www.tourismmorobe.org.pg

It is possible to walk the Kokoda Track by yourself, without help, but I strongly advise against it. Except for the super-fit, it is very hard work. While you do need to have a high level of aerobic fitness, there is no training your knees, as I found to my cost. You will be grateful for

Villages along the track, and the track itself, have moved since 1942. This is 'old' Nauro, on the ridge above 'new' Nauro.

well-loved boots and socks. You will be wet, either from the rain, or from slipping into a creek, and you will have to endure a certain amount of mental pain.

You don't have to carry your own gear all the way. Carrying ten kilos of personal stuff – water, cameras and so on – is sufficiently difficult. My 'solo' trip involved a guide, and two porters, who were happy for the work. And I was extremely grateful for their company, wisdom and concern for my safety on the track.

Most guided walks recommend eight days on the track, but my experience is that unless you simply want to look at your feet day after day and collapse into a sleep at the end of the day, you should take more time to do the walk. I took twelve days in 1999, Kokoda to Port Moresby, including two nights at Myola, and walked north to south from Kokoda to Owers Corner: said to be the 'easier' direction. (The world record for Kokoda to Owers Corner is less than 24 hours walking/running time, established in 2005.)

Every centimetre of the track is owned by someone, and you should pay a few kina for the privilege of walking on their land. This will be organised by your guide, which is another good reason to travel with one. With my experienced local guide, I was welcomed as a long lost friend in virtually every guest house.

October–November seems to be a slightly drier time to walk, though dryness is relative. Above about 300 metres, the temperature is cooler, and less humid. It has been known to drop to freezing point at Myola.

Accommodation at Kokoda is on the plateau in a basic modern guest house next to the hospital, opened in 1995. On the Kokoda Track you'll mostly be in local accommodation, which varies from a steel-roofed shelter or open-sided hut made from pandanus, to more elaborate thatched huts. Otherwise you're in a tent. There are occasional bush showers (Myola, Kagi).

Japanese gun, Salamaua. (1999)

In Milne Bay I recommend staying at Masurina Lodge in Milne Bay. There are more modern (and expensive) places, but the guest-house-style lodge was the first and is the best. It is owned by Masurina Ltd, a company owned by local people including Chris Abel, whose family has been in the area since his grandfather Charles started the mission on nearby Kwato in 1891.

Meals, transfers from Gurney Airport, tours, transport by road or sea in the area can all be arranged. There's a live-aboard research and dive boat run by Wayne and Lee Thomson, *Marlin 1*, associated with Masurina. I am still dreaming of cruising on the *Marlin 1* to the Trobriand Islands. See **www.masurina.com**. There are two comfortable modern hotels in Lae, the Melanesian, a Flag-branded hotel, and the Lae International, where I stayed. Both are safe and comfortable.

In Salamaua the guest house Haus Kibang has reopened, and is worth staying at. In Wau I stayed at the Harvey-Hall's Valley View Guest House and couldn't imagine a better or friendlier place.

Valley View Guest House
Address: P.O. Box 51, Wau, Morobe Province

Masurina Lodge
Address: P.O. Box Alotau
Email: masurinalodge@masurina.com.pg

New Guinea 1942

The Masurina wharf at Alotau, principal town of Milne Bay.

Tours and Guides

I organised my Kokoda trek through Kokoda Expeditions at Niugini Holidays. See **info@ngholidays.com**. I would recommend their Essential Kokoda tour, a 10-night/11-day trek with a porter (he will carry 18 kg). Their Battlefields Trek is of the same duration, but is harder, using much of the 1942 track. The company also offers other treks and extensions to Buna and other places in PNG.

Frank Taylor's Kokoda Treks & Tours is a highly experienced tour organiser and leader, highly recommended. See **kokoda@arach.net.au**. He has also organised treks of the Bulldog Track and the Finschafen area.

Kokoda Trekking Adventures also have a good reputation. See **www.kokodatrail.com.au**. The website has excellent information and pictures on Kokoda and travel in New Guinea.

Further Information

Victor Austin, *To Kokoda and Beyond: The Story of the 39th Battalion*, Melbourne University Press, Melbourne, 1988.

Clive Baker & Greg Knight, *Milne Bay 1942*, Australian Military History Publications, Loftus, 2nd ed., 2000.

James Benson, *Prisoner's Base and Home Again: The Story of a Missionary POW*, Robert Hale, London, 1957.

Peter Brune, *A Bastard of a Place*, Allen & Unwin, Sydney, 2003.

Peter Brune, *We Band of Brothers: A Biography of Ralph Honner*, Allen & Unwin, Sydney, 2000.

David Dexter, *The New Guinea Offensives*, Australian War Memorial, Canberra, 1961.

Peter Dornan, *The Silent Men*, Allen & Unwin, Sydney, 1999.

Bill Edgar, *Warrior of Kokoda: A Biography of Brig. Arnold Potts*, Allen & Unwin, Sydney, 1999.

Paul Ham, *Kokoda*, HarperCollins, Sydney, 2004.

Stuart Hawthorne, *The Kokoda Trail: A History*, Central Queensland University Press, Rockhampton, 2003.

Reg Kidd & Ray Neill, *The 'Letter' Batteries: The History of the 'Letter' Batteries in World War Two*, published by the authors, Castlecrag, 1998.

Neil McDonald, *War Cameraman: The Story of Damien Parer*, Lothian, Melbourne, 1994.

Neil McDonald & Peter Brune, *Two Hundred Shots: Damien Parer, George Silk and the Australians at War in New Guinea*, Allen & Unwin, Sydney, 1998.

Lida Mayo, *Bloody Buna*, Australian National University Press, Canberra, 1975.

John Moreman, *Wau Salamaua*, Department of Veterans' Affairs, Canberra, 2003.

Raymond Paull, *Retreat from Kokoda*, Heinemann Australia, Richmond, 1958.

Andy Pirie, *Commando Double Black: 2/5th Independent Company*, Australian Military History Publications, Loftus, 2nd ed., 1996.

Alan Powell, *The Third Force: ANGAU's New Guinea War*, Oxford University Press, South Melbourne, 2003.

Ivan Southall, *Bluey Truscott*, Angus & Robertson, Sydney, 1958.

Osmar White, *Green Armour*, Angus & Robertson, Sydney, 1945.

7.

KOREA

The Korean War, sandwiched between the Second World War and Vietnam, was for many years a war forgotten by many Australians, though not by men and women from all the three services, who endured conditions as unforgiving as any Australian forces before or since.

Korea was an independent, united nation for a thousand years, though influenced and occasionally subject to China. In the latter part of the 19th century the 'Hermit Kingdom', as it was known, was of great interest to Russia and Japan. Japan's defeat of Russia in a war in 1905 resulted in Korea becoming a Japanese colony in 1910. Korean communist guerrillas led by Kim Il Sung operated against Japanese occupation in the 1930s and through the Second World War. Forty years after its defeat in 1905, Russia, now the Soviet Union, belatedly entered the

p.371: Korean guards allowed the author 125th of a second alone to snap this 'illegal' picture of Maryang San, now in North Korea from the Taepung Observatory. **Right:** South Korea plans to explode the sides of this cutting should any North Korean forces use this road as an invasion route.

Second World War against Japan – on 8 August 1945, two days after the atomic bomb was dropped on Hiroshima, and seven days before Emperor Hirohito announced Japan's unconditional surrender. On this day, 15 August, the United States accepted the Japanese surrender south of the 38th Parallel, and the Soviet Union took over in the north.

Both countries had substantial numbers of troops in Korea. After elections in 1948, the Republic of Korea was proclaimed in the south on 15 August, and the communists proclaimed the Democratic People's Republic of Korea on 9 September. Soviet and American forces left both countries in 1949, but there was sporadic fighting across the border, and guerrilla warfare in the south.

Then, at 4 a.m. on 25 June 1950, South Korea was invaded by North Korea. The United Nations Security Council called upon its members to support the Republic of Korea, and American forces were sent to the country, later to be joined by forces from 22 other nations, including Australia. By the end of July, RAAF 77 Squadron and two ships of the RAN – HMAS *Shoalhaven*, a frigate, and HMAS *Bataan*, a destroyer – were involved. By October, the third battalion of the Royal Australian Regiment – 3RAR – which had been on occupation duty in Japan, was also heavily committed in Korea.

At first the North Koreans made rapid progress, taking the South Korean capital of Seoul on 28 June 1950 and driving back the South

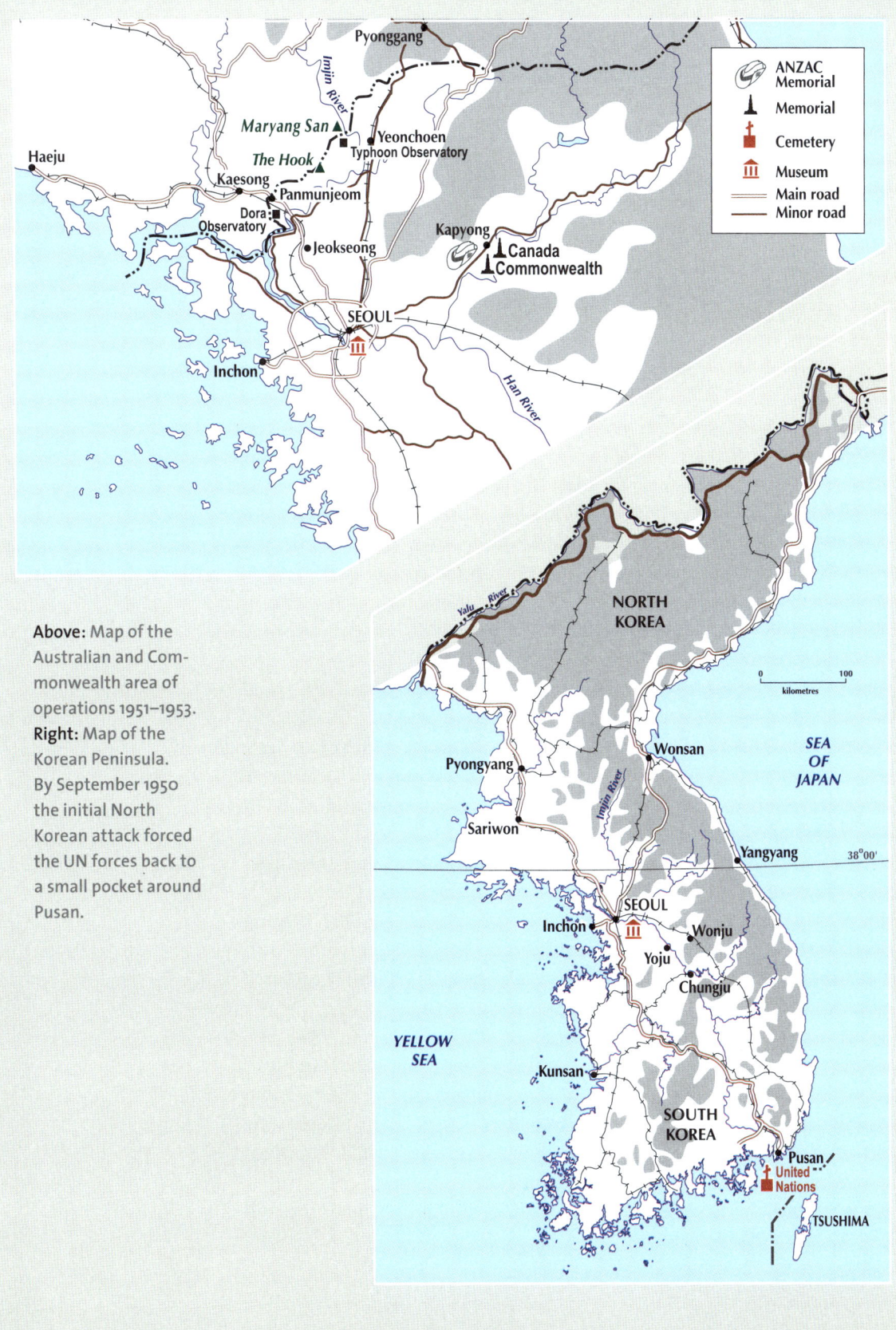

Above: Map of the Australian and Commonwealth area of operations 1951–1953.
Right: Map of the Korean Peninsula. By September 1950 the initial North Korean attack forced the UN forces back to a small pocket around Pusan.

Above left: Landscape in which the Commonwealth forces, including Australians, fought, near the Imjin river. The blue field is ginseng.

Above: Korean memorial at the 38th Parallel marking the 50th anniversary of the armistice.

Korean and American troops to a bridgehead around the southern port of Busan (formerly Pusan).

General MacArthur, commanding the predominantly American UN forces, had his moment of tactical triumph with the amphibious landing at Inchon (near Seoul) on 15 September that outflanked the North Koreans; the UN forces broke out of the Busan bridgehead and rapidly advanced north. With British units, 3RAR formed the 27th Commonwealth Brigade and took part in the pursuit of the enemy into North Korea. Pyongyang, the North Korean capital, was captured on 19 October and by late November 1950, UN forces were only 40 miles from the Chinese border.

The Chinese felt that an invasion by the UN was on the cards, and told intermediary nations that it would not tolerate American or South Korean forces on the Yalu River, their border with Korea. Their intentions were unknown to American intelligence, and the Chinese decision to intervene on 2 October 1950, and the major attacks on 27 November came as a surprise.

The 27th Commonwealth Brigade held them off from their positions on the Chongchen River, but the Chinese broke through elsewhere. In freezing conditions, the UN forces carried out a fighting retreat across extremely difficult terrain, but on 25 December 1950 the Chinese entered South Korea, and in early January they captured Seoul.

The 27th Commonwealth and 29th British brigades acted as a rearguard until a defensive line was re-established on the Han River. In March 1951, a UN counter-offensive pushed the Chinese back and recaptured Seoul. As winter cleared, the UN forces dug in close to the 38th Parallel and in early spring they advanced a few miles north in order to create a buffer north of Seoul.

On 22 April the Chinese counter-attacked, aiming to break through to the capital. They were held up for a crucial amount of time by two significant operations, one by the 27th Brigade, including 3RAR, near Kapyong, and the other by the 29th Brigade on the Imjin River by the British Gloucestershire Regiment. The heroism of the Glosters' last stand, near Castle Hill, helped to break the Chinese advance but resulted in heavy casualties.

In April 1951, President Truman sacked the insubordinate MacArthur who had wanted to use atomic weapons on China, threatening a third world war. Armistice negotiations began at Kaesong in July 1951, and there followed two years of largely static fighting, often in conditions of extreme cold. 3RAR served for the duration, although individual soldiers were rotated out, while the other RAR battalions also served – 1RAR from March 1952 to September 1953, and 2RAR from March 1953 to September 1954.

From July 1951, Australian forces were designated part of the 1st Commonwealth Division. In October 1951 the division took part in Operation Commando, a limited attack designed to disrupt the Chinese potential for attack, and dominate the routes across the 38th Parallel. For Australians, this operation included the Battle of Maryang San, which is part of a ridge overlooking the Imjin River. 2RAR fought the last Chinese attack at a position called the Hook on the Somichon River on 25 July 1953, two days before the Armistice was signed on 27 July 1953 at Panmunjeom.

Between June 1950 and July 1953, 17,000 Australians served in Korea, 3RAR served for the duration 1950–1953, and 1RAR and 2RAR served on rotation 1952–1953. The Royal Australian Navy deployed two aircraft carriers, two destroyers and thirteen frigates. The RAAF supplied three squadrons. All were volunteers. Korea was the last time Australians enlisted in the traditional way, three years or the duration. It was, as one of them put it, 'the last and final call of the bugle'.

Australian casualties in Korea were 339 killed, 1216 wounded and 29 POWs. Korea remains divided.

Maryang San is the highest hill in this contemporary photograph. It was captured by the Australians in October 1951.

The Australians in Korea

Saving Seoul: Kapyong, April 1951

Kapyong is just 67 kilometres from Seoul. A day after the major Chinese offensive which began on 22 April 1951, South Korean soldiers and civilians were in full retreat down the Kapyong Valley. Unless the Chinese were delayed, Seoul would fall, with catastrophic consequences for the war. The 3rd Battalion, Royal Australian Regiment (3RAR), with the 2nd battalion, Princess Patricia's Canadian Light Infantry (2PPCLI) and tanks from the US 72nd Heavy Tank Battalion were ordered to slow down or stop the Chinese advance.

The Australians of 3RAR had planned a big Anzac Day party with the UN forces' Turkish contingent, but instead found themselves positioned on four hills to the east of the Kapyong Valley on 23 April, with the Canadians to the west, and down the middle the flow of thousands of refugees, mingled with South Korean troops and Chinese infiltrators. That night the Chinese attacked in the moonlight in wave after wave, over their own dead and wounded, cutting the Australians off but unable to dislodge them. Next day it started again, but supported by the 25-pounder guns of the New Zealand 16th Field Regiment, the Australians stayed put, holding up the Chinese. But it was an unten-

able position – on the night of 24 April, the Australians staged a fighting withdrawal down the ridge from Hill 504. At Kapyong, 3RAR lost 32 killed, 59 wounded and three captured.

The river and the hills around Kapyong, scene of the epic battle involving Australians, New Zealanders and Canadians in April 1951.

Hill 677, defended by the Canadians, was attacked on Anzac Day morning, and helped by the New Zealand artillery, the Canadians also beat off the Chinese assault. The Kiwis methodically lobbed their 1500 25-pounder shells on the enemy over 35 minutes, and with supplies parachuted in, the Canadians held on until the Chinese withdrew.

In this operation three UN battalions had held up and defeated a full Chinese division, and substantially contributed to the defeat of the Chinese offensive. The Chinese began to withdraw at the end of the month. Seoul was saved.

A US Presidential Citation – the highest available award for a unit – noted that the Australians, Canadians and Americans had 'displayed such gallantry, determination and *esprit de corps* in accomplishing their missions as to set them apart and above other units participating in the campaign'.

Captain Reg Saunders, the first Aboriginal soldier to be commissioned in the Australian army, said after Kapyong: 'At last I felt like an

Anzac, and I imagine there were 600 others like me.' That's saying something: Saunders, who commanded C Company of 3RAR on Hill 504, was a veteran of the Second World War who had fought with the 2/7th on Crete, escaping to Egypt twelve months after the rest were evacuated. He returned to the 2/7th for the tough Salamaua campaign, and was serving as an officer at Wewak at the war's end. Saunders rejoined for the Korean War.

Opposite: Australians in 2RAR being resupplied, Imjin River, near the position known as the Hook.

A Storming Display: Maryang San, 3–5 October 1951

As part of Operation Commando, an advance across the 38th Parallel by the Commonwealth Division was ordered in late September 1951, and 3RAR was given the task of attacking a number of features, including Little Gibraltar, Kowang San, the Hinge and Maryang San. Maryang San was a highpoint on a ridge above the Imjin River, occupied by the Chinese. The idea was not to attack frontally up the slopes against a well-entrenched and numerically superior enemy, but to take him by surprise, coming along the ridge line, a tactic the Australians had developed through cruel necessity in New Guinea during the Second World War.

Fog obscured the movement of the Australians in the valley of the Imjin. C Company were to assist some British colleagues, the Kings Own Scottish Borderers (the 'KOSBY'S'), in the capture of Hill 355, known as Little Gibraltar, on 4 October. But they did more than assist: they captured the position in a storming display. The Chinese fought hard for a while, but were unprepared for such a determined assault. As one participant, Private Jim McFadzean, later put it, the Kosby's 'were able to occupy their objective unmolested, by courtesy C Company 3RAR'.

Loudspeaker array at the Taepung Observatory used to broadcast from the civilised South to the seemingly uninhabited wilds of North Korea.

Picture taken from the theatre at the Taepung (Typhoon) Observatory. The diorama used for illustrating the course of battle is in the foreground of the photograph, seats are reflected in the glass.

The next objective was Hill 317, Maryang San, on 5 October. Once again, morning fog covered the Australian advance. After hard work by D Company clearing the Chinese from the lower slopes, C Company passed quickly through and attacked the peak, Maryang San. Only a few men at a time could get up the steep sides of the hill, but 7 Platoon scrambled up with little opposition from the enemy. The Chinese, who had been prepared for a frontal assault, couldn't cope with the flanking attack and had given in.

Major Jack Gerke, commanding C Company, thought that 'if a company of Australians had been holding the feature and had the supplies, it would have held the position indefinitely'. Gerke was awarded a DSO for his bravery in this and other actions. Others among the many recognised for actions here were Lieutenant Laurie Pears, who despite being wounded was awarded the Military Cross for outstanding courage and leadership; and Arthur Stanley, the Company Sergeant Major, who won the Military Medal for outstanding service in bravely organising resupply and evacuation of casualties. Theirs are just a few of the individual acts singled out in a collective effort.

3RAR held Maryang San against fierce enemy shelling. On 6 October, C Company, on a hill west of Maryang San, was hit with 262 shells and 70 mortar bombs. During this bombing, two badly wounded members of C Company were being carried to the rear when a Chinese shell killed two stretcher-bearers and wounded two others. Jim McFadzean was mentioned in despatches for his selfless action that day, when he ran from his weapons pit, carried them to safety while under constant artillery, mortar and machine-gun fire.

B Company captured the final objective, a ridge called the Hinge west of Maryang San, after a fierce fight on 7 October in which two Australians were killed and twelve were wounded. The Hinge had been taken, but that night the Chinese unleashed a tremendous artillery barrage, followed by three waves of attacks. The Chinese who survived the Australian machine-guns crept up within a few metres and threw grenades into the Australian trenches – they were promptly thrown back.

3RAR had been fighting and carrying and digging and not sleeping for five days, yet so mauled the Chinese division that it was withdrawn. Casualties were significant: twenty Australians killed and 89 wounded, of whom fifteen remained on duty. 900,000 rounds of small arms ammunition were used, as well as around 5000 grenades and 7000 mortar bombs – all of which had to be carried in by Korean Service Corps porters. Two Distinguished Service Orders, nine Military Crosses, two Distinguished Conduct Medals, nine Military Medals and one MBE were eventually awarded for the Maryang San action, and fifteen men were mentioned in despatches.

The battalion was relieved on 8 October by the KOSBYs, who lost it, bravely, on 4 November. Maryang San then remained in Chinese hands until the end of the war – no unit except 3RAR managed to capture it.

The 3RAR Memorial at Kapyong.

Charles Yacopetti POW

After Maryang San, the war in the Australian (Commonwealth Division) sector was a kind of trench warfare, with traditional Aussie aggressive patrolling of no man's land, a tactic perfected at Tobruk just ten years before. Costly and often fruitless raids to capture prisoners were also ordered.

On 25 May 1953, a 3RAR patrol, led by Lieutenant Charles Yacopetti ambushed 40 Chinese north of the battalion's position at Hill 355, inflicting many casualties. Yacopetti, wounded, ordered a withdrawal, carrying other wounded. The Chinese attacked the Australians, who were slowed by carrying wounded, and Yacopetti was hit again. He continued to control the patrol, and the Chinese dispersed. He then insisted that all the other wounded be carried out before him – which required all the able-bodied men. As they left, they saw

Yacopetti, in the words of the Official Historian Robert O'Neill, 'sitting upright in a small hole, with a loaded Owen gun and bayonet fixed, ready to fight it out with the remaining Chinese, some of whom were just 30 metres away'.

In the event, Yacopetti was not killed, but was taken prisoner after falling unconscious. He was interrogated and tortured for a month by his captors opposite Hill 355, as the Chinese believed officers were repositories of vast amounts of military information. After a month he was sent north to the notorious camp known as the 'caves'. Here, he received his first medical attention.

The prisoners were exposed to bombing and strafing by UN aircraft, and many were killed or wounded. Yacopetti on one occasion left the safety of his cave to rescue the wounded, for which he was mentioned in despatches for outstanding bravery as a POW. Repatriated in August 1953, Yacopetti was awarded the Military Cross for his action on the patrol at Hill 355.

Yacopetti was one of 29 Australians listed as POWs in the Korean War, one of whom, Private Horace 'Slim' Madden died while a prisoner. Madden, a 3RAR signaller and Second World War veteran, had been captured at Kapyong on 24 April 1951 and after a time at the caves was sent on the forced march to the Yalu River, 300 kilometres further north, in winter November 1951. Too ill to walk, he was on a cart, where five of the eight died. He died on 6 November 1951 and was awarded the posthumous George Cross, the equivalent of a VC, in 1956.

Many POWs – and, of course, not only Australians – were tortured, starved, kept in solitary confinement and denied medical treatment. What happened to individuals seems to have depended largely on when they were captured (the earlier the capture, the worse the treatment), as well as on individual actions such as trying to escape.

Private Horace 'Slim' Madden, 3RAR, was awarded the George Cross, the equivalent of the Victoria Cross for his bravery as a POW.

Korea Today

Seoul and South Korea are quite extraordinary places. I thought Tokyo was the model for Ridley Scott's *BladeRunner* film metropolis, but now I think it has to be Seoul. It felt like the biggest city in the world, and despite, or perhaps because of, having been destroyed by war, has that mixture of the blatantly modern and the secretly ancient that is the essence of *BladeRunner*.

The Han River that flows through the city is enormous, with twenty bridges across it. The subway system is gigantic – but easy to navigate. There is a giant market of all things digital, streets of tea shops and antique shops, and a tremendous variety of food, as long as you like *kimchi* with it. I loved it.

Even to an outsider it's pretty clear that although the armistice was signed over 50 years ago, the war is still very much present. It's not so much the history or the memorials, but the presence of North Korea, barely 100 kilometres north of Seoul. The 'Two Brothers' sculpture outside the War Memorial of Korea symbolises this very well.

The two soldiers are reunited over a fracture in a sphere representing the Korean world. The elder brother looks down on the little brother – whose arms clutch pathetically from below. It is a sentimental, teary image, that mirrors the somewhat hysterical relationship between south and north, who love and hate each other, and where family reunions are extraordinarily difficult.

The Korean War is still not over, and threatens to break out again at any time, which makes visits to battlefields and memorials contemporary rather than purely historic occasions.

The 'Two Brothers' are reunited outside the War Memorial of Korea in Seoul.

Cemeteries, Memorials, Museums

Busan (formerly Pusan)

The **United Nations Memorial Cemetery Busan** is the only cemetery maintained under the auspices of the UN anywhere in the world. Established by United Nations Command in 1951, the land was granted to the UN in perpetuity by the Republic of Korea in 1959. Since 1974 the cemetery has been administered by a UN Commission of representatives of the eleven countries whose fallen lie here.

There are 281 Australians in this plot at the UN Cemetery, Pusan.

It has a different emotional impact to the Commonwealth War Graves Commission cemeteries and memorials where other Australians lie or are commemorated; the familiar symbols such as the Cross of Remembrance and the Stone of Sacrifice and the words 'Their Name Liveth for Evermore' are not found in Busan. The CWGC cemeteries are about remembrance and contemplation, their symbols conceived after the First World War by a generation smashed by the slaughter of that war. The UN cemetery is less sentimental. The memorial is soberly modernist, the gardening is Korean style, the UN flag and the flags of the nations who lost men fly there. On my visit, a dozen Koreans came to walk solemnly around, inspecting each gravestone in turn. In the small museum, a father and daughter of five or six years looked closely at the photographic display, and shook my hand vigorously when I pointed to the Australians.

The United Nations Memorial, Pusan.

Twenty-two nations are represented with plots in the Symbolic Area, with twenty plots dedicated to the Republic of Korea. There are 2300 burials in all. The 281 Australians lie next to 462 Turks, and 34 New Zealanders are not far away. The togetherness is a striking reminder of the changed world of war in the decades after Gallipoli. There's an Australian flag marking our spot; small Turkish flags on each of their graves. On the Turkish memorial are these words:

All us martyrs utterly awake
Our hands united and stretched to the skies;
In common we are through the throbbing soil,
Which by a sense of belonging has become our own.

The Turks in Korea were famously brave, and adepts of the bayonet. According to Australian war correspondent Harry Gordon, after one affair in 1951 which put the Chinese to flight, the American supply depot received this message: 'Enemy attacked, we attacked, send more bread.'

The **Australian Memorial**, within the Australian plot, was dedicated in 1998. The **Commonwealth Memorial** remembers the 386 Commonwealth soldiers who died in Korea but whose burial places are unknown. The inscription says they died 'with men of other countries, fighting to uphold the ideals of the United Nations'.

UN forces suffered 37,895 dead in the Korean War, and nearly four million Koreans and Chinese died, half of them civilians.

During the war, remains of about 11,000 men of the United Nations Command forces were gathered here. After that, most of the remains of the soldiers from Belgium, Colombia, Ethiopia, Greece, India, the Philippines, Thailand and United States, and some of the remains of the soldiers from France and Norway, were repatriated to their home countries.

The **Memorial Service Hall** was built in 1964, and the **Exhibition Hall** in 1968. There is a display of historic photographs. The **Main Gate**, designed by Kim Chungup, was dedicated on 30 November 1966, 'to honour the fallen UN Forces in the Korean War by the citizens of Busan'.

Private James Daunt 3RAR volunteered for Korea, putting his age up. After he was killed in action, and his plaque made, it was discovered that he was not 21, but only seventeen.

DMZ

A number of Korean war memorials and museums are found at various places along the DMZ – the demilitarised zone – which has been untouched and untilled for 50 years. It is now a haven for all kinds of rare plants and animals, and is being marketed by the Koreans for its

Telescopes at the Dora Observatory peer into North Korea.

ecotourism potential. As the war is not actually over, some places are still used by the military especially at Panmunjeom. Other locations are more like tourist attractions than solemn memorials but that is the Korean way. A number of observatories have been built along the DMZ. The closest to Seoul is the Dora observatory, where visitors are invited to look into North Korea.

Nearby is the **Dorasan Station,** an empty modern expression of divided Korea – which people visit in the hope that the train will one day run between the two parts of Korea again. Also nearby, and part of most DMZ tours is the **3rd Infiltration Tunnel** discovered in 1978. This was apparently dug by North Koreans in order to access South Korea without being seen. There were two others that you cannot visit. There's a display of infamous North Korean conduct in a small museum, and you take a little train down the 73-metre deep slope, for an eerie walk under the DMZ – it's built for smallish visitors, and tall people risk knocking off their hard hats.

Jeokseong

This memorial commemorates the valiant deeds of the Gloucestershire Regiment 'surrrounded and outnumbered' at the battle of Solma-ri 22–25 April 1951.

The **Gloucester Valley Monument** marks the site of the battle of the Imjin River around the town and the hills of Solma-ri, including what came to be known as Castle Hill, in April 1951, and the heroic action of the Gloucestershire Regiment.

Castle Hill is not an Australian site: it marks the site of the battle of the Imjin River around the town Jeokseong (formerly Choksong)and the hills of Solma-ri, including what came to be known as Castle Hill in April 1951 fought by the 29th Brigade, and in particular the heroic action of the Gloucestershire Regiment. These battles were occurring at the same time as 3RAR and the 27th Brigade were heavily involved at Kapyong.

On 22 April 1951 three divisions of the Chinese 63rd Army began an attack on Seoul across the Imjin River. This part of the front was defended by the Gloucestershire Regiment and a mortar battery of the Royal Artillery now known as the Imjin Battery, all part of 29th Brigade. Through the night of the 22nd the Glosters held their positions on the river, but were forced back by the overwhelming numbers to the hills around Choksong, including Castle Hill and Hill 235 (later called Gloucester Hill), where the Glosters' last stand took place on 25 April. (This is the hill above the Gloucester Valley Monument.) Only 67 of the 586 men who went into the battle managed to escape. There were 59 dead, and 526 were captured, including 180 wounded. Thirty-four died in captivity. Two Victoria Crosses were awarded, and the battalion was awarded a Distinguished Unit Citation by the President of the United States. Lieutenant Phillip Curtis was killed during his VC action and is buried in the UN cemetery at Pusan. Colonel Phillip Carne VC DSO died in England at the age of 80 in 1986.

At Castle Hill some of the trenches and bunkers have been preserved and are well worth visiting.

Coming from Seoul on Route 1, turn right at Muksan on route 34 for seventeen kilometres to Jeokseong. Turn left at the T junction up the hill past the camouflaged tank trap. The track is on the left, near a Confucian school. To find the Gloucester Valley Monument turn right at the T Junction for 1.5 kilometres. There is a carpark and picnic spot marked by flag poles. The memorial is a short distance away.

Restored trenches at Castle Hill. The hills are in North Korea.

Kapyong (Gapyeong)

The Kapyong battlefield is in the hills above the river, twelve kilometres out of Kapyong. In modern Korean transliteration, Kapyong is 'Gapyeong', but in this case we have stuck with the name familiar to the Commonwealth servicemen who fought there.

The Commonwealth Memorial is in the town of Kapyong, and is dedicated to those from Australia, Canada, Great Britain and New Zealand who fought to defend freedom and democracy in the Korean War.

Australia's main memorial in South Korea is at Kapyong. The battle of Kapyong cost Australia and 3RAR 32 killed, three captured, and 59 wounded. The dead from that battle which occurred around Anzac Day 1951 are buried at the United Nations Memorial Cemetery hundreds of kilometres south at Busan. Among them are (above left) Private H Bolitho, (below left) Sergeant S K L Lenoy, (below) Private D J D Lee.

The **Australian Memorial, New Zealand Memorial** and **3RAR Memorial**, as well as a **Ross Bastiaan bronze plaque** are in a small park, beneath Hill 504, on the right twelve kilometres north on the road out of Kapyong. The **Princess Patricia Canadian Light Infantry Memorial** is on the same road, on the left, six kilometres from Kapyong town. The **Kapyong Commonwealth Memorial** is in the town.

Panmunjeom

Panmunjeom is where the armistice negotiations were held, and is the only place actually within the DMZ that you can visit, but only as part of a tour group. The Panmunjeom/Joint Security Area tours include a visit to Camp Bonifas for a lecture, and then to the conference room which straddles the demarcation line, except when it is in use. North and south have villages here – the southern Freedom Village is a farming community that has curfews and a tax-free status. The village in the north doesn't have any people living in it. The Korea Travel Bureau organises Panmunjeom tours. **www.ktbonline.com**

Above: The New Zealand Memorial at Kapyong.
Below: The Canadian Princess Patricia Light Infantry Memorial at Kapyong.

Seoul

The **War Memorial of Korea**, opened in 1994, is a huge assemblage of materials concerning the 5000 years of war and invasion that the people of the Korean Peninsula have endured.

Australia is represented in the Korean War Room as one of the proudly acknowledged sixteen 'combat support nations' with a Digger in uniform, one of the sixteen comrades standing under the dome of the UN. There are lots of dioramas and equipment, and a loud and atmospheric 'combat experience room'. Outside there is patriotic

War Memorial of Korea, Seoul.

PILGRIMAGE

Soldiers of all nations defend South Korea outside the War Memorial of Korea.

statuary and a collection of large objects, including a B52. It is worth half a day, or more.

The War Memorial of Korea
Address: No. 8, 1-ka, Yongsan-dong, Yongsan-ku, Seoul
Website: www.warmemo.co.kr

Yoncheon-gun

Shrines at the Taepung Observatory.

Taepung (Typhoon) Observatory provides a view of the site of the battle of Maryang San, which lies just to the north of the DMZ, in North Korea. You can't go there, but you see it from this most spectacular of all the observation towers along the DMZ, the Taepung (Typhoon) Observatory, in the National Security and Eco Tourism Zone of Gyeonggi Do province, which was opened in December 1991.

Like everything along the DMZ, the observatory is accessible as a day trip from Seoul or in a car from the nearest town, Yoncheon. A tour company will be able to organise it. From Seoul, take Road 3 for Uijongbu and Yoncheon, then take a left at Jeong town and take Road 324 for about twenty minutes. The observatory is on the Gyeonggi province tourist map.

There are all kinds of war-related items on the road to Taepung – including tank-traps (Lego-like constructions of cement designed to be blown up, blocking the road), minefields and a checkpoint at Sang-gun-ri where you will have to hand over your passport so that you'll come back from the DMZ.

The observatory is high on a ridge above the Imjin River and the DMZ. It has a Buddhist shrine, and a huge array of loudspeakers used to broadcast the good news from the South to the seemingly depopulated North. The place is manned by young South Korean soldiers who are posted here for up to two years, which has given them the opportunity to perfect their American-inflected English, and obey their prime directive, which is to stop people taking photographs with their cameras pointed north. There's a lecture theatre and diorama of the area, and a fantastic view across the bend of the Imjin, the low hills and, in the afternoon light, the steep sides of Maryang; it's easy

The Korean War is not officially over, and defensive preparations such as minefields are still in evidence around the DMZ.

to trace the route of the Australians in 1951 through the hazy light.

A long conversation with the guards about the great deeds of the Australians at Maryang San failed to convince them to allow an official photograph pointing north, but they were sufficiently circumspect to allow an unofficial snap while they were otherwise occupied.

About 200 metres from the observatory, in P'ilsung-kyo, there is a room displaying 'daily necessaries of the North Korean army that were floated along the Imjin River from the north, and devices and other stuffs that were used by North Korean spies who tried to infiltrate into the south for 34 times', as the guide says.

Information is available from Yoncheon County Bureau of Public Cultural Information or from Gyeonggi Province at **www.kg21.net** or from **www.paju.cyberct.net**. These sites are slow to open, but full of useful information when you drill down. Both are in English as well as Korean.

Travel Tool Kit

Getting around the Korean countryside is in general terms pretty easy – trains, buses and internal flights are reliable, safe and frequent. However, touring the DMZ can only be done as part of a group tour, and looking for and getting to some out-of-the-way Australian-related places is more easily done with a car and driver. I wouldn't recommend driving yourself – just getting out of Seoul on its intricate knot of twelve-lane freeways is a test, even for locals.

Most visitors to Korea will organise a battlefield tour around other sites and sights; all the relevant battlefields – Kapyong, Maryang San, Somichon River – plus the DMZ can be visited in a day trip from Seoul. Most of the time spent visiting anywhere out of Seoul seems to be taken up with getting in and out of that gigantic metropolis.

The easiest way to visit the sights near Seoul is to hire a car, driver and guide. This way you can spend time where you want, and also enjoy the tastes of authentic Korean food along the way. On my visit the driver was a Korean War veteran, and *kimchi* connoisseur, who became a fast friend as soon as he found out I liked that fragrant pickled vegetable dish.

To visit the UN Memorial Cemetery in Busan, on the south-east coast of Korea, requires an hour's flight (or a train) from Seoul, and twenty minutes in a taxi. Busan could, of course, be on the itinerary of a wider tour of South Korea.

Tours and Guides

For Australians, my recommendation is to use the Plaza 21 tour company, which has experience of the Australian-specific sites, and now knows that Maryang San is visible from the Typhoon Observatory. They also organise tours of Panmunjeom and the Third Tunnel.

Plaza 21 Travel Service
Address: 208, SK Richemble, 28-5, Hap-dong, Seodaemun-gu, Seoul, 120-030
Email: nplaza21@yahoo.com
Website: www.koreatourplaza.com

The 'Freedom' bridge at Dorasan, ready for reopening when the Korean War is finally ended.

One tour operator is the Panmunjeom Travel Centre. They pick you up from your hotel, take you to a central point, in this case the Lotte Hotel, load up the bus and take the hour and a half drive to Panmunjeom.

You can do a regular one-day tour of Panmunjeom daily except Sundays or tour with a North Korean defector on Saturdays, or take a VIP tour for a group of ten or less. A combined tour of Panmunjeom and Third Tunnel operates on Fridays, which is the best option if you are in town for the day.

Panmunjeom Travel Centre
Address: Seoul City, Chung-Gu, Sogong-dong, Lotte Hotel 2nd floor (Main Bldg)
Website: www.koreadmztour.com
www.Panmunjeomtour.com

Gyeonggi Tourism Information Centre operates a convenient transit tour to the DMZ for those with half a day in transit at Incheon Airport. It's on a first-come first-served basis until ten minutes before the tour departure at the Gyeonggi Tourism Information Centre in front of Arrival Terminal Gate B2 on the first floor of the Incheon International Airport. The tour takes 4 hours 30 minutes (8 a.m. – 12.30 p.m.). There is no tour on Mondays.

Gyeonggi Tourism Information Center
Address: 208, SK Richemble, 28-5, Hap-dong, Seodaemun-gu, Seoul, 120-030

Further Information

Norman Bartlett, *With the Australians in Korea*, Australian War Memorial, Canberra, 1954.

Bob Breen, *The Battle of Kapyong*, Doctrine Wing – Combined Arms Training and Development Centre, Georges Heights, 1992.

Bob Breen, *The Battle of Maryang San*, Headquarters Training Command, Sydney, 1994.

Ben Evans, *Out in the Cold*, Department of Veterans' Affairs, Canberra, 2001 (a terrific online exhibition based on this book is at the Australian War Memorial website – **www.awm.gov.au/korea**)

Jon Halliday & Bruce Cumings, *Korea: The Unknown War*, Viking, London, 1988.

Robert O'Neill, *Official History of Australia's Involvement in the Korean War 1950–1953*, Volume I, 'Strategy and Diplomacy', Volume II, 'Combat Operations', Australian War Memorial, Canberra, 1985.

Maurie Pears & Fred Kirkland, *Korea Remembered*, Doctrine Wing – Combined Arms Training and Development Centre, Georges Heights, 2002.

8.

VIETNAM

THE WAR IN VIETNAM – AND CONSCRIPTION – divided Australian opinion and split families. It left a lasting wound in the relationship between many Australians, the Australian military and the Anzac tradition that has only recently healed through Australia's role in peacekeeping around the world.

The Second World War came to French Indochina, as Vietnam, Cambodia and Laos were then known, in June 1940 when Japan pressured the colonial administration to cut off the railway to China, where Japan had been fighting for over a decade. After some negotiation and a little fighting, Japan made French Indochina part of the 'Greater East Asian Co-Prosperity Sphere' and occupied Saigon in July 1941 and gained access to its considerable resources of

p.395: Australia's major area of operations, the Long Hai Hills, taken from the Horseshoe.
Right: The Horseshoe.

rice, coal and rubber. About 35,000 troops were stationed in the area. The French administration was still nominally in charge, but the Japanese took everything they could, especially after Allied successes elsewhere in the Asia-Pacific cut them off from Japan.

The only organised opposition to Japan was the communist-nationalist guerrilla organisation the Viet Minh, established by Ho Chi Minh in May 1941. With American help – from the Office of Strategic Services (OSS), precursor to the Central Intelligence Agency (CIA) – the Viet Minh had by late 1944 established its own administration in the north of the country.

With the imminent defeat of Germany in 1945, the Free French under Charles de Gaulle decided to fight the Japanese in Indochina. The Japanese killed or massacred some 1700 French troops, and arrested the administration. They declared the Indochinese territories independent, and installed Bao Dai, Emperor of Annam (southern Vietnam) as puppet emperor in Vietnam on 11 March 1945. This 'independence' was worse than ineffective. Nearly two million people died of starvation in Vietnam in 1945.

Ho Chi Minh formed the Viet Minh-dominated National Liberation Committee on 13 August, entered Hanoi on 20 August, five days after the Japanese surrender, and declared the Democratic Republic of Vietnam on 2 September. Bao Dai abdicated and became the 'supreme adviser' to the new government, before going into exile in 1946.

Meanwhile an international agreement at Potsdam in 1945 between the soon-to-be victorious Allies divided up the postwar world. American policy during the war had not been to return Indochina to the French after the war was won, and the northern part of Vietnam was to be occupied temporarily by the Nationalist China of Chiang Kai Shek, and the southern part was to surrender to the British. However the French colonial government soon returned, after an interregnum where some of the Japanese were re-armed to control the local independence movement.

After negotiations between Ho Chi Minh and France broke down in 1946, the Viet Minh withdrew from Hanoi and the first Indochina War commenced. Bao Dai returned from exile in 1949, and was installed as head of state of a pseudo-independent Vietnam. Ho Chi Minh maintained that the Democratic Republic of Vietnam was the only legitimate government, and substantial fighting took place in the north.

Major international events in the region formed the political background to the French Indochina war, particularly the victory of Mao Zedong and the Chinese communists in 1949, and the breakout of the Korean War in 1950, where the non-communist forces were backed by the United Nations. This war ended in an armistice in 1953 which divided Korea, as Germany had also been divided after the Second World War.

These events somewhat overshadowed the military difficulties faced by the French. Despite being underwritten to the sum of $3.5 billion by the Americans, the French were not in a position to defeat Ho Chi Minh's commander, General Vo Nguyen Giap, in the north.

The climactic battle of the war took place at Dien Bien Phu, in wild country 300 kilometres west of Hanoi. It commenced on 13 March 1954 and after tremendous casualties and hard fighting by both sides, the North Vietnamese defeated the French on 7 May. An international conference to discuss settlement of the wars in Vietnam and Korea had commenced in Geneva in April. Korea was first, Vietnam commenced on 8 May, the day after Dien Bien Phu. Vietnam was divided between north and south at the 17th Parallel in July, pending nationwide elections in 1955. This decision was not accepted by the prime minister in the south, Ngo Dinh Diem, who had been installed by Bao Dai on 16 June, or by the United States.

Soviet Union aid flowed to the north, and American to the south. Positions hardened after Diem refused to participate in the elections in July 1955, a decision supported by the Americans. However Diem defeated Bao Dai in a referendum, declared himself president, and proclaimed the Republic of Vietnam.

The insurgency in the south recommenced in 1957, with many local units from the French war reactivating, and support flowing down the many tracks of the Ho Chi Minh trail from the north after 1959. In 1960 the North Vietnamese organised the insurgent forces in the south as the National Liberation Front (NLF) which Diem dubbed the Vietcong – Vietnamese communists – which not all of the NLF were.

The United States began to provide increased aid and advisers after Vice-President Lyndon Johnson visited in May 1961. The American Military Assistance Command was formed in February 1962. At this time the NLF already controlled many of the villages in the countryside, as well as being strong in cities such as Saigon and Hué.

Ngo Dinh Diem was ousted and later killed in a coup on 2 November 1962. The coup, if not the assassination, had the approval of the United States. By the end of 1962 there were 15,000 American military advisers in Vietnam.

Australia's involvement in Vietnam began with the arrival of the Australian Army Training Team Vietnam (AATTV) in May 1962. This 36-strong force commanded by Colonel Ted Serong was invited by the United States, and was tasked to train the South Vietnamese army in jungle warfare techniques. By 1964 the AATTV had a strength of 100 and operated throughout South Vietnam.

War escalated on 2 August 1964. North Vietnamese patrol boats attacked the USS *Maddox* in the Tonkin Gulf, and US aircraft bombed North Vietnam for the first time. Various unstable governments were formed in South Vietnam, and Vietcong attacks increased in frequency. Sustained bombing of North Vietnam began in February 1965, and the first ground forces arrived to protect the airfield at Da Nang on 8 March 1965. By December there were 200,000 American troops in South Vietnam, and the first clashes with non-guerrilla North Vietnamese forces had occurred.

In Australia, the commitment of the AATTV to Vietnam had been uncontroversial. But there was pressure from the South Vietnamese government and the Americans to commit regular troops to the con-

Members of the Australian Army Training Team Vietnam won four Victoria Crosses – posthumously to Warrant Officer II Kevin Wheatley, 13 November 1965; Major Peter Badcoe for actions between 23 February and 7 April 1967; Warrant Officer II Ray Stewart, 6 and 11 May 1969; and Warrant Officer II Keith Payne, 24 May 1969. AATTV remained in Vietnam in an advisory role until December 1972.

flict. The Australian prime minister, Robert Menzies, was enthusiastic, but for domestic political reasons demanded and eventually received a formal invitation from South Vietnam.

The issue became more controversial with the announcement on 10 November 1964 that a birthday lottery system of conscription was to be introduced. The first ballot took place on 10 March 1965, and on 29 April 1965 Menzies committed the first battalion of Australian troops.

First Battalion, Royal Australian Regiment (1RAR) left for Vietnam on 27 May 1965 aboard HMAS *Sydney*. There would be a rotation of thousands of Australians, including conscripts, in combat in Vietnam. This unit served with American regular forces in Bien Hoa, and saw considerable action, suffering 23 killed in action. However there were differences in the tactics and training of Australian and American forces, which made this way of operation unsatisfactory. It was decided that 1RAR would be replaced by a larger Australian Task Force, consisting of two battalions, with supporting services, some 4500 servicemen, to operate in its own area. This was to be Phuoc Tuy province, east of Saigon, based on the seaside town of Vung Tau.

In 1966 most of Phuoc Tuy was out of South Vietnamese government control, and there were no large American or South Vietnamese forces there. It seemed possible that Australia could pursue limited military objectives in its own style, with some chance of success.

The Australians set up a staging camp on the sand dunes of the back beach at Vung Tau in April 1966 in preparation for the increased commitment. It was an awful spot for a camp, waterless and hot. The main base was set up at Nui Dat in May–June 1966. *Nui* means hill; *dat* means mud or dirt: the countryside is mostly flat, except for these mud hills, and some limestone formations. There are several *nui dats* in the area, all less than 150 metres high. The Australian base was set up at Nui Dat 1. Nui Dat 2 was a kilometre away, and overshadowed the rubber plantation at Long Tan. The limestone outcrops, 70 or 80 metres high, were used as artillery emplacements, and one known as the Horseshoe, for example, controlled these heights and gave some measure of control over the lower areas.

The local resistance, Vietcong guerrillas, were in the established Minh Dam Secret Zone in the Long Hai hills in an extensive series of caves.

The first task of the Australians in 1966 was to clear the area around Nui Dat inside what was called the Alpha Line, which meant flattening the villages of Long Phuoc and Long Tan. It was during this action that the RAR suffered its first casualty, a mix-up between two companies of 5RAR. One had established a listening post. At 6.25 p.m., on 24 May 1966, Private Erroll Noack – a conscript – happened to stand up there, and the other company fired on what it thought was the enemy and he was seriously wounded. He died in hospital at Vung Tau that night. It is estimated that half the Australian casualties in Vietnam from 1968 to 1970 were from our own mines.

Major Australian actions included the battle of Long Tan where on 18 August 1966, 6RAR defeated a much larger enemy force, but lost eighteen killed and 24 wounded. This and other actions, while small compared to other wars and other actions in Vietnam, asserted Australian influence in the area which was not challenged for the duration of the Australian commitment.

Australians also fought in nearby provinces, and during and after the Vietcong's Tet offensive in early 1968 fought major engagements at Fire Bases Coral and Balmoral in May 1968.

During the Tet offensive in 1968, the National Liberation Front staged simultaneous attacks all over South Vietnam, including on the American Embassy in Saigon and the Citadel in Hué. While this was unsuccessful in the strict military sense and resulted in the destruction of a substantial proportion of the local strength of the NLF, it was a political victory, demonstrating that the Americans, Australians and South Vietnamese did not control the country. It brought the North Vietnamese more strongly into the conflict.

In Hué the fighting was particularly savage. The NLF took the city on 31 January, and were not defeated until 24 February. There were substantial civilian casualties from both the bombing and the execution of anti-communist locals. The city was destroyed, including the

Above left: The Imperial Palace, Hue, scene of ferocious fighting during the 1968 Tet offensive. The Flag can be seen from all over the city.
Above: The Horseshoe was a forward patrol position, extending surveillance beyond Nui Dat. Graffiti scratched in the old cement.

citadel, the palace built in the early 19th century by the emperor along the lines of Beijing's Forbidden City. Some 5000 Vietnamese died as US marines recaptured the citadel, at a cost to the Americans of 600 killed.

Prime Minister John Gorton announced on 22 April 1970 that one of the three battalions in Vietnam would not be replaced, and in February 1971 operational responsibility for large areas of Phuoc Tuy was handed over to the South Vietnamese government army. The last Australian action was fought at Nui Le by 4RAR in October 1971. The last Australians returned home in December 1972.

In mid-1968 there were 540,000 Americans in Vietnam. President Lyndon Johnson announced a partial halt in the bombing in March, when he announced he was not running for re-election. Richard Nixon, newly elected president, withdrew the first American troops in 1969, and in 1970 secret peace talks began in Paris. The policy was to 'Vietnamise' the war by handing over responsibility to the government of South Vietnam. The last American troops left Vietnam on 29 March 1973. North Vietnamese troops captured Saigon on 31 March, 1975.

More than 500 Australians (and more than 50,000 Americans) were killed in action serving in Vietnam, 200 of them conscripts. Of 804,000 men who registered for national service when they turned twenty, 63,740 were conscripted in the birthday ballot, and 15,542 of them served in Vietnam. An unknown number of men, several thousand, did not register for 'national service', for political reasons. Hundreds of thousands were involved in the anti-war movement.

Many of the soldiers who fought felt let down not only by those in the anti-war movement but also by the public in general and the politicians in particular. They felt they were not welcomed as Anzacs who had served their country. They felt that when they returned they were unwanted and neglected. Many came home with significant physical and psychological problems. The Welcome Home Parade in October 1987 was a significant turning point in the reconciliation process, but it took nearly fifteen years to happen.

Ho Chi Minh Mausoleum, Hanoi.

Khe Sanh, which was held by the United States from 1966 to the end of the war despite tremendous North Vietnamese pressure – 205 Americans were killed and between 10,000 and 15,000 Vietnamese – was made musically famous after the war by Australian band Cold Chisel. The song, by Don Walker, told the story of a Vietnam vet who couldn't settle down:

I left my heart to the sappers round Khe Sanh
And my soul was sold with my cigarettes to the blackmarket man
I've had the Vietnam cold turkey
From the ocean to the Silver City
And it's only other vets could understand ...

In the end, Australia was on the losing side of the political argument in Vietnam, but unlike America, Australia came out of the conflict with its military reputation enhanced. Then as now it is difficult for people involved on the ground to understand that while we might vehemently oppose the politics of a conflict, especially the conscription of young men without a vote, we can still strongly support the men and women involved. As one who chose not to go in the 1960s, I still regret that we did not make that point strongly enough.

The Rockpile was a feature near Khe Sanh defended at cost by the Americans through the war. (Stephen Downes, 2005)

Australians on patrol 1966.

The Australians in Vietnam

'Clouded with euphemisms': Long Phuoc, June 1966

The Australians, newly arrived in Vietnam, had the task of clearing the area around Nui Dat. The area was characterised by an extensive tunnel system; the local explanation is that these were dug in 1948 in the fight against the French, and maintained after 1954.

The village of Long Phuoc was the headquarters of the NLF provincial committee, and was first cleared by South Vietnamese government and American troops in 1963, and defended by a company of D445 Battalion – the locally raised militia unit which since 1947 had drawn its fighters from Long Phuoc, Hoa Long, Long Tan and other nearby villages. D445 used the tunnel system to fight government

Left: The Vietnam War Memorial at Dandenong RSL, Melbourne, features the sculpture *Side by Side* (2005) and a Huey 'dust-off' helicopter.
Opposite: Map of Vietnam and the Australian area of operations in Phuoc Tuy province.

forces for four days: nineteen Americans were killed, and 90 wounded, and an estimated 45 Vietnamese were also killed. The 300 residents of Long Phuoc were evicted after the battle, half going to Hoa Long. The tunnel system had been damaged in 1963 by the South Vietnamese army but was held onto by the locals. The soldiers of D445, after an interval, returned to use it.

Vietnam is perfect tunnelling country; the red clay of the area sets like concrete when exposed to moisture and air. The system around Long Phuoc was extensive; one tunnel was said to have connected with Long Tan village, three kilometres away. Entrances were hidden under houses, with some exits across a road, near a tree. These could be used by snipers who could pop up around the village when it was raided by government forces. The 'long tunnel', as discovered later by the Australians, had gas-proof doors, firing posts, weapons and food storage areas, a first-aid section, water storage and many *panji* stake traps.

The Australians, in securing the perimeter of the Nui Dat base, decided at the end of June 1966 to destroy Long Phuoc village. This was called Operation Enoggera. According to the Official History, official reports are 'clouded with euphemisms'. Defence Department reports describe a 'slow meticulous clean up of the area'. Other materials describe how the tunnels and fortifications in Long Phuoc village, and all Vietcong installations above and below the ground, were destroyed and the village denied for later Vietcong use.

Bulldozers and TNT were used to demolish buildings, flame-throwers and TNT to blow up everything under them. The operation

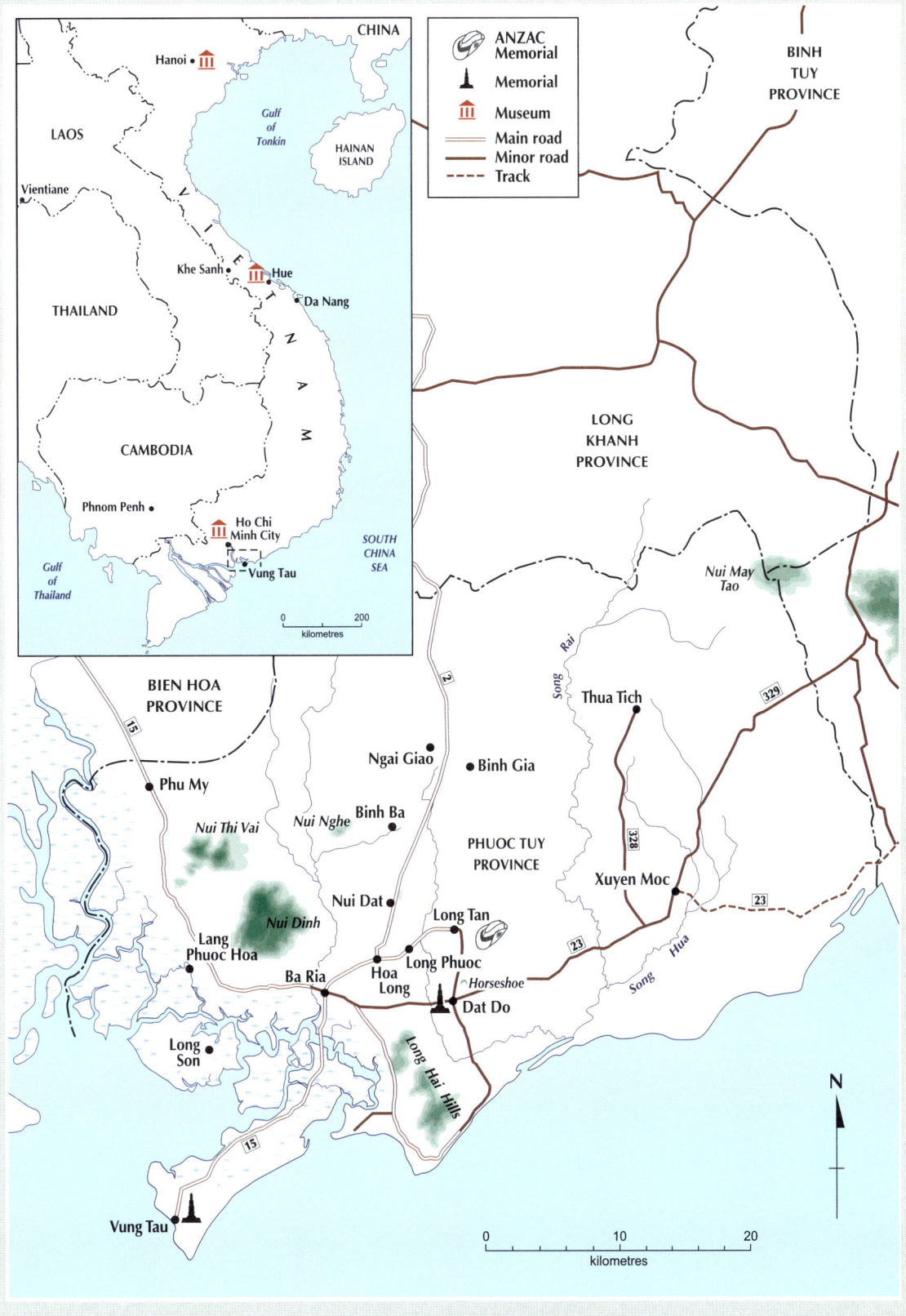

destroyed 537 houses and 1500 metres of tunnel – with more than 500 escape tunnels, bunkers, air raid shelters and firing bays – were blown up. The Australians captured 43 tons of rice, 3.5 tons of salt, *panji* stakes, clothing and medical supplies. The village was destroyed.

Battle in the Rubber: Long Tan, 18 August 1966

On the afternoon of 18 August 1966 it was overcast and foreboding as Delta company, 6RAR, left Nui Dat base on patrol. They were searching for traces of the enemy who had mortared the base for 22 minutes early the previous morning. They approached the village of Long Tan from the south. Through the rubber trees there was a hut, in the lee of Nui Dat 2, swathed in impenetrable bamboo jungle.

The Australians had been patrolling that day and the day before, and had not made contact with the enemy. They were surprised when a patrol of Vietnamese soldiers appeared, coming from the south at about 3.45 p.m. The local NLF unit, D445 Battalion, was thought to

The Long Tan rubber plantation in 1999. The trees were shredded in 1966, and replanted several times in following years.

have only bolt-action rifles, and its soldiers dressed in black pyjamas and other civilian gear. The Australians were therefore even more surprised to see that the Vietnamese carried automatic weapons, AK47s, and were in khaki uniforms – they were regular North Vietnamese troops.

The Australians resumed patrolling, and at 4.08 p.m. came under heavy machine-gun fire from a position on the hill. Just as the Australians came under fire, the clouds opened. A monsoon storm has to be experienced to be believed. Sheets of hard rain, large high-intensity drops. Almost immediately, the ground turned to red mud, visibility was down to 50 metres or less, the rubber trees were exploding as they were hit by explosive rounds.

Eleven platoon suffered immediate casualties, and were saved from completely being wiped out by some precise artillery fire. D Company was being attacked not only by the local militia but also, it seemed, by a main force North Vietnamese regiment. They were facing surprising and overwhelming odds, and an enemy with a better field position, on the slopes of Nui Dat 2. The Australians survived because of personal bravery, artillery support, a bit of luck, and the arrival of the APCs from Nui Dat base.

The Vietnamese filtered back into the bush, but left behind many dead and some wounded. The official body count was 245 enemy left dead on the battlefield and three captured, with estimates of another 250 killed. Hundreds were wounded. Seventeen Australians (eleven conscripts) were killed in action, one died of wounds, and nineteen were wounded. It is counted as a victory for Australia; as a costly skirmish by the Vietnamese.

Long Tan was a powerful initiation into battle, and although other actions were bigger, and just as fierce, Long Tan is the one that has come to represent the resourcefulness and mateship of the Vietnam Diggers. Delta Company, 6RAR was awarded a US Presidential Unit Citation for bravery.

An Australian APC (armoured personnel carrier) on patrol in 1966. APCs were decisive in winning the Battle of Long Tan.

Vietnam Today

Most Vietnamese are too young to remember the war, but the evidence is still visible. Flying into Vietnam you can see the round water-filled bomb craters, and flying into Ho Chi Minh City, still Saigon to most people who live in it, the American era hangars and bunkers are still to be seen.

Vietnam has resumed normal relations with its former enemies, and Australia and Australians are doing useful things large and small, especially in the former Phuoc Tuy province (now Baria-Vung Tau Province). The Vietnam Veterans Reconstruction Group is responsible for rebuilding schools and other projects, and other service clubs have been working in the health area. South of Saigon, the Australian government financed the building of the My Thuan bridge across the Mekong River.

War-related museums are to be found all over Vietnam, all telling the story of what the Vietnamese call the American and French wars, and the atrocious things done to the Vietnamese people. There is virtually no interest in being fairer or more balanced. Most of the museums have similar collections of tatty black and white photographs, National Liberation Front flags, and scraps of military equipment. Compared to Australian or European war museums, they are one-sided, and even offensive to those on the losing sides, whether Vietnamese, French, American or Australian.

While Australia shares with France the privilege of being allowed

The school at Hoa Long has been rebuilt by the Vietnam Veterans Reconstruction Group.

The old Saigon municipal offices, now the Ho Chi Minh City council headquarters.

a memorial at a ceremonial site – in Australia's case, at Long Tan; in France's, at Dien Bien Phu – there is very little Australian-related material in museums or elsewhere. There are no cemeteries as are to be found just about everywhere else in the world, and perhaps the hardest thing of all, so little memory of the fact that Australians were in Vietnam at all.

Australian Vietnam casualties were nearly all repatriated to Australia (there is no easy way to find out where they are buried, as the Commonwealth War Graves Commission only cares for the dead of the First and Second world wars); 330 are identified by the Office of Australian War Graves as buried or cremated in Australian cemeteries, and 165 named in Gardens of Remembrance. One soldier is buried in Kranji War Cemetery (Non War Plot) in Singapore. There are 24 Australians buried in the cemetery of the Terendak Garrison at Malacca, in Malaysia. They include Major Peter Badcoe.

Cemeteries, Memorials, Museums

Bien Hoa City

The **Dong Nai Museum** in Bien Hoa City is where the original Long Tan Cross is to be found. Entrance is free, but unless you are on a guided tour you will need to make an appointment. Bien Hoa is 35 kilometres from Saigon, and a suitable base to visit Fire Support Bases Coral and Balmoral. There is a Vietnamese monument at Coral.

Dat Do

The **Dat Do War Cemetery** has a cenotaph, a tower emerging from a Vietnamese portico on a high plinth, with red lettering on the side:

PILGRIMAGE

Above and above right: Vietnamese war cemetery and memorial near Dat Do. This is a symbolic cemetery, with graves representing local villages.

'They died for their country'. There are about 1000 names individually memorialised here in white cement blocks with a brass plaque, showing where each was born. They all seem to be from local villages such as Hoa Long, Ba Ria or Long Dat. None appear to have died at Long Tan on 18 August 1966.

Nearby is another memorial which is like a Vietnamese serviceman's club or shrine, with red flags with hammers and sickles inside, and portraits of dead heroes going back to the French time. Outside, a couple of vets played cards.

There are no memorials in Vietnam to the Vietnamese who died fighting the Vietcong and North Vietnamese, in the anti-communist army of the Republic of Vietnam.

Hanoi

The **Ho Chi Minh Mausoleum**, the **Ho Chi Minh Museum**, **House 54**, the **House on Stilts**, and the **Presidential Palace** are all in a park that fronts Ba Dinh Square, two kilometres west of Hoan Kiem Lake.

Here Ho Chi Minh declared independence on 2 September 1945: 'We, members of the People's Revolutionary Government of the Democratic Republic of Vietnam solemnly declare to the world that Vietnam has the right to be a free and independent country and in fact is so already. The entire Vietnamese people are determined to mobilise all their physical and mental strength, to sacrifice their lives and property in order to safeguard their independence and liberty.'

The Ho Chi Minh Mausoleum is generally only open in the morning, and is frequently closed in September to October, when Ho Chi Minh goes to Moscow for conservation. This is the only queue that forms in Vietnam, a silent and respectful crowd shuffling past the ramrod guards whose eyes are the only things that move. It is the coolest and quietest place in Hanoi. The only sounds are the shuffling

Queuing to enter the Ho Chi Minh Mausoleum, Hanoi.

of feet on the plastic protective covering on the carpet and the whisper of the air-conditioning. You must leave cameras and bags at the reception centre opposite.

After 1954 Ho did not live in the Presidential Palace but in **House 54**, former residence of the palace's electrician, and then in 1958 the even more modest **House on Stilts**, which visitors can see as they leave the Mausoleum.

The **Ho Chi Minh Museum** is a modern triangular structure in white cement embossed above the entrance with a hammer and sickle and a Vietnamese star. The museum tells the story of Ho Chi Minh's life and aliases – from birth to his time in France, to China and Vietnam – through assorted documents and objects: pictures of his father and his school, his commode from Paris, his letters and writings, beginning in 1919, his USSR visa from 1929, and so on. You wind around a circular track that combines such evidence of Ho's life with uplifting imagery of Vietnam's struggle.

Ho Chi Minh Museum, Hanoi.

There's Picasso in *Guernica* mode and Salvador Dali's soft clocks making a statement about the horror of war. There's a volcano and national totems symbolising the great power of the national liberation movements throughout the world. There's that flop of a car, the Ford Edsel, representing the failure of American capitalism. At the top of the perambulation is a broken chain, and a four-metre-high pyramid and some giant fruit representing, perhaps, the cornucopia to come after the successful revolution.

You won't find Ho Chi Minh here. There are pictures, there are letters, but in this big echoing exhibition there isn't much of his spirit, or the connection he had with the Vietnamese people.

Ho Chi Minh City (Saigon)

The **War Remnants Museum** was first named the War Crimes Museum, and then the War Relics Museum. The names give the flavour of the displays. Instead of a ticket, visitors are given a pamphlet with a quote from Robert McNamara, who was Secretary of Defense under Lyndon Johnson, from his *mea culpa* book published in 1995: 'Yet we were wrong, terribly wrong. We owe it to future generations to explain why.' Inside, there is a picture of General Vo Nguyen Giap meeting McNamara in November 1995. Everyone wants to get back to business, especially the tourism business.

American aircraft at the War Remnants Museum.

The pamphlet gives some of the facts and figures of disaster for the Vietnamese: the millions of young people 'who took turns in fighting'; millions of litres of defoliants, including dioxin; millions of tonnes of bombs that destroyed thousands of schools and hospitals.

The museum is a series of small white buildings with some topiary deer growing near a tank (supposedly one of the ones that broke through the gates of the Presidential Palace in 1975), a rather small camouflaged US jet (an A37), and a number of bombs. There is the last guillotine used to execute a Vietnamese patriot in 1960, and two souvenir sheds. Behind the main exhibition buildings is a replica of a couple of the 'Tiger Cages' where prisoners were held and tortured by a variety of governments in Vietnam, with a model prisoner inside.

One display shows the heroic struggle of the Vietnamese people that begins with Ho Chi Minh's 'historic truth' enunciated on 2 September 1945. The Royal Australian Regiment gets a mention, as does

Outside the War Remnants Museum in Ho Chi Minh City is a tank like the one that crashed through the gates of the Presidential Palace on 30 April 1975. The war officially finished during that flash of film by Australian cameraman Neil Davis.

HMAS *Hobart*, as forces against the revolution. There are plenty of pictures and models of alleged atrocities, and malformed Vietnamese babies sealed in jars.

Another room is devoted to the anti-war movements from around the world. Some weirdly random pictures from Australia are included.

One building is devoted to the 'anti-revolutionary' bodies which have apparently formed in Vietnam from time to time since 1975. These are for the edification of any local visitors.

In the end, the War Remnants Museum made me feel a bit sick. I couldn't bring myself to buy a souvenir of the war, a badge or a zippo lighter, whether real or not. The War Remnants Museum is at 28 Vo Van Tan.

Hué

The **Provincial Museum – Bao Tang Thuan Thien – Hué** is on Le Truc Street on the opposite side from the Museum of Antique Objects, with its dull objects in a beautiful building. This is a well-presented Vietnamese 'Museum of the Resistance against US invaders 1954–75'. In this museum I had an interesting conversation with a young woman curator, whose education had not included Australia's participation in the war.

On the south side of the Perfume River at 7 Le Loi Street, is a small **Ho Chi Minh museum**.

A lesson at the Provincial Museum in Hue.

Long Phuoc

On the site of the rebuilt Long Phuoc village is a small **museum**. On my visit the caretaker, a Long Tan veteran who had fought with D445 Battalion, was away, but his daughter opened the museum. The room, with its busts of Ho Chi Minh, a relief map of the area, battle flags, honour rolls, shell casings and weapons, was a shrine to the local tradition.

Outside, under a cement lid, is one of the **tunnels**. I asked the translator to ask whether this tunnel had been widened or restored. It had been 'cleaned-up' but was still too narrow for an Australian body to squeeze very far. The electricity failed, which made the whole thing extremely claustrophobic.

Except for some intermittent electric light in one section, the tunnels do not seem to have been widened or reconstructed for tourists, as they have been at the tourist tunnel site at Cu Chi outside Saigon. I couldn't go very far down the Long Phuoc tunnels, and cannot vouch for their extent. Some believe that they are postwar constructions designed to provide a war tourist attraction – if so, they represent a huge amount of work for very little return.

Above: The museum at Long Phuoc.
Below: A Vietnamese Long Tan veteran sits on the entrance to the Long Phuoc tunnels.

Long Tan

The **Long Tan Memorial** is on the site of the 1966 battle and is in the form of a replica of the cross first erected in 1969; the original cross is now in the Dong Nai Museum in Bien Hoa City. The original plaque is kept at a local police station to avoid it disappearing.

When I first saw it in 1997, the memorial at Long Tan was a cement

PILGRIMAGE

The Long Tan Cross. 'In memory of those members of D Coy and 3 Tp 1 Apc Sqn who gave their lives near this spot during the Battle of Long Tan on 18 August 1966. Erected by 6RAR/NZ (Anzac) Bn 18 Aug 69'.

cross in the red soil, surrounded by four concrete posts and a bit of wire enclosing some straggly succulent plants, a circle of red bricks surrounding a dying white bush, and a couple of cement posts indicating where a gate and a larger fence might once have been. After a $60,000 renovation of the site, which was re-opened in 2002, there is now a paved area with a low fence, and places for commemorative flowers.

The Horseshoe, the Australian fire support base on a hill not far from Long Tan is accessible by a stony track bulldozed in 1966 to the top. It's a breezy place, with banana trees and bits of cement, the remains of mortar positions, perhaps. There's a fine view to Nui Dat 1 across the flat plain.

At the bottom of the hill is a quarry. We were accosted by a running man, who came from behind a heap of stones and argued in rapid-fire Vietnamese. We should have asked permission to climb the hill because of land mines, some of which are used by the locals in the quarry.

Minh Dam Secret Zone

Entrance to one of the caves at Minh Dam.

Minh Dam Secret Zone is located in the tangle of boulders and granite outcrops of the 400-metre-high Long Hai hills, south-east of Vung Tau, known to the Australians and Americans as the 'Long Hais'. It is rather like a bigger version of Hanging Rock in Victoria. A Vietnamese stronghold had first been established here in the war against the French and the war in Phuoc Tuy was directed from the caves of Minh Dam throughout the war against America. In 1997, a road was opened to the visitors' centre near the top, where there's a tea house and a **small museum**. It's possible to explore **the series of deep caves,** where big meeting chambers, sleeping rooms, cooking places and a hospital once were.

414

Vietnam

There are four significant Vietnam War memorials in Australia: the Bowral Vietnam Memorial (begun in 1996 and rededicated by the Governor-General and former 8RAR veteran Major General Michael Jeffrey on 28 February 2004), which includes an avenue of 526 cherry trees, one for each Australian killed in Vietnam; the Dandenong RSL statue dedicated to the soldiers of the South Vietnamese Army; the Vietnam Memorial pavilion in King's Park, Perth, and the Australian Vietnam Forces National Memorial on Anzac Parade in Canberra (dedicated on 3 October 1992 and re-dedicated on 5 October 2002), which is the joint work of architect Peter Tonkin and sculptor Ken Unsworth and is designed to express 'the link between the Australian Vietnam Forces and the original ANZAC Force' and also to represent 'the controversy at home'.

Clockwise from above: Canberra (two details); Perth; Dandenong.

The northern stele has 34 quotations in stainless steel lettering fixed to it; these were selected from quotes provided by Vietnam veterans as typical of the language of the war. They include: 'What we did on the battlefield in the morning was on our living room TV screens that night', 'The enemy joined our command radio net, threw coloured smoke and almost sucked the co into a landing', 'Big contact tonight in the Binh Ba rubber. Troops hit with RPG's. Ready reaction force went out in APC's', 'Nobody's got 365 days and a wakey to go', 'I don't seem to have many friends since I came home. If you weren't there, you can't understand.'

In the landscaped area surrounding the central building there are three concrete memorial 'seats'. At each end of these memorials is the name of one of the six Australians recorded as Missing In Action: Robert Charles Carver, Michael Patrick John Herbert, Peter Raymond Gillson, Richard Harold John Parker, John Francis Gillespie and David John Elkington Fisher.

415

Travel Tool Kit

Paradoxically perhaps, Vietnam has become regarded as a safer destination than Indonesia for Australian tourists. War-related travel is the least of it. The food, beaches, scenery and ambience of Vietnam are attracting more and more people. It is easy to get around, not expensive, and maintains an exotic but friendly quality that is very attractive.

Vietnam is very accessible from Australia, and has a well-developed war-related tourism industry, for Vietnamese people as much as for visiting Americans; Australians will have no trouble finding Ho Chi Minh in Hanoi or the Cu Chi Tunnels near the former Saigon (Ho Chi Minh City) but you might encounter difficulties finding and getting to Long Tan.

It is not practical to hire a car and simply drive around. However, it is possible to travel on trains, buses or ferries to most places, such as HCMC to Vung Tau, but getting local transport is less easy.

Vietnam is still a Communist state, and permission is needed to visit sensitive sites in Phuoc Tuy outside the main towns. The plaque for the Long Tan cross is held by the local police, and they will want to sight your permission. You could make contact with the Vung Tau Ba Ria Tourist Corporation, but it is easier to arrange a two- or three-day side trip from Ho Chi Minh City through Haivenu Tours.

Hué is the best place to take a tour towards the Laotian border, and the American battlefields at Khe Sanh (now called Hoang Hoa) and Hamburger Hill. In Hué you can buy a seat on a minibus tour to the DMZ, Ho Chi Minh Trail, the Rock Pile, Khe Sanh (where there is a small but well-presented museum) and the tunnel complex at Vinh Moc.

Above and right: the Khe Sanh Museum. (Stephen Downes)

Tours and Guides

Getting to the Australian sites such as Long Tan can be difficult to organise yourself, as most tour operations in Vietnam are American-oriented. One Vietnam-based company that offers Australian-related tours is Haivenu Tours.

Based in Hanoi, Haivenu is the only company I know that can organise a relevant tour while you are visiting Vietnam for other reasons. The standard tour is three days and two nights from Ho Chi Minh City, driving to Vung Tau, visiting the Long Tan cross, the Horseshoe and the Long Phuoc Tunnels, Nui Dat and the Ba Ria Orphanage. Next day they will drive you to Long Hai town and the sites in the Long Hai area of operation, such as Phuoc Hai and Dat Do. The return to Ho Chi Minh City includes visits to Long Dien town and the War Museum in Dong Nai to see the original Long Tan cross.

Haivenu will also tailor individual tours, and arrange tours of American sites, the DMZ and the Cu Chi Tunnels.

Haivenu Tours
Address: 12 Nguyen Trung Truc St, Ba Binh District, Ha Noi
Email: haivenu@fpt.vn
Website: www.haivenu-vietnam.com/veteran-australian-theatre

Veterans might prefer the South Australian company Battle Tours' Veterans itinerary, which is eight days/seven nights and includes Saigon, Vung Tau, Long Tan, Nui Dat, Baria, Binh Ba and Cu Chi. Battle Tours also provide more extensive tours of Vietnam and other Australian battlefields.

Battle Tours
Address: Shop 8, 560 North East Road, Holden Hill, SA
Email: info@battletours.com.au
Website: www.battletours.com.au

Official Vietnamese tourist website:
Website: www.vietnamtourism-info.com/english

South Vietnamese and Australian soldiers side by side, Dandenong RSL, Melbourne.

Further Information

Terry Burstall, *The Soldiers' Story*, University of Queensland Press, St Lucia, 1986.
Peter Edwards, *A Nation at War*, Allen & Unwin, Sydney, 1997.
Peter Edwards, *Crises and Commitments*, Allen & Unwin, Sydney, 1992.
Garrie Hutchinson, *Not Going to Vietnam*, Sceptre, Sydney, 1999.
Stanley Karnow, *Vietnam: A History*, Viking, New York, 1983.
Greg Langley, *A Decade of Dissent*, Sydney, 1992.
Gary McKay, *Australia's Battlefields in Viet Nam*, Allen & Unwin, Sydney, 2003.
Gary McKay, *In Good Company*, Allen & Unwin, Sydney, 1987.
Ian McNeill, *To Long Tan: The Australian Army and the Vietnam War 1950–1966*, Allen & Unwin, Sydney, 1993.
Ian McNeill & Ashley Ekins, *On the Offensive: The Australian Army and the Vietnam War 1966–1968*, Allen & Unwin, Sydney, 2003.
Bao Ninh, *The Sorrow of War*, Hanoi 1991, London, 1998.
Stuart Rintoul, *Ashes of Vietnam: Australian Voices*, Melbourne, 1987.
Vietnam Veterans Association: **www.vvaa.org.au**

INDEX

A

Abel, Cecil 336-7
Abel, Chris 368
Achi Baba (Gallipoli Peninsula) 20, 28
Adachi, *Lieutenant General* Hutazo 357
Addison, *Lieutenant* 40
AE2 (submarine) 76
Ahioma (Milne Bay) 333
Albert (France) 137
Alcitepe *see* Krithia
Alexander, *Private* Peter 235
Alexandria 212
Alkatiri, Mari 288
Allenby, *General Lord* Edmund ('Bull') 84, 93, 95
Allsopp, *Captain* Ray 258
Almaro (Timor) 233
Alola (Kokoda Track) 346-7
Amann, *Sergeant Major* Max 118
Ambon 295
American Army
    72nd Heavy Tank Battalion 376
Amiens 106, 129
Amman 91, 92-3
Anderson, *Lieutenant Colonel* Charles 218, 227
anti-war movement (Australia) 401
Anzac Commemorative Site (North Beach) 49
Anzac Cove 21-2, 25, 42, 43-6
    map 50
Arab Army 93
Arab-Israeli War 88
Arblaster, *Captain* Charles 113
Ari Burnu (Gallipoli Peninsula) 25, 26, *27*, 44
armoured personnel carriers (APCs) 407
Armstrong, *Lieutenant* Francis Leofric 63-4
Askifou (Crete) 174, 192-3
Atatürk, Kemal *see* Kemal, Mustafa
Aung San 276-7
Aung San Suu Kyi 277
Australian Army
    Battalions
        7th 30, 37
        15th 146
        16th 146
        18th 39
        39th 320-1, 326-7, 339, 353
        40th 232-4

        45th *109*
        48th 183, 251
        51st 123-4
        58th 113
        60th 113
        61st 333
        2/7th 173
        2/9th 335, 336, 342
        2/10th 342
        2/11th 172
        2/12th 335, 342
        2/13th 163, *165*, 168
        2/14th 326-30, 353
        2/15th 225
        2/16th 158, 179, 326-30, 339, 353
        2/19th 227
        2/21st (Gull Force) 232, 292, 339
        2/22nd (Lark Force) 232, 306
        2/23rd 251
        2/27th 202-3, 328-9, 353
        2/30th 225
    Brigades
        2nd 28, 31
        3rd 32
        4th 122
        8th 112
        12th 122
        13th 123
        14th 112, 113
        15th 110, 112-13, 123, 124, 150
        16th 159
        17th 159, 178
        18th 166, 251
        20th 251
        21st 175, 177, 251, 326, 328, 339
        22nd 224
        24th 251
        25th 175, 177, 339
        26th 250-1
        27th 224
    Divisions 104
        1st 105, 119
        2nd 105, 119, 122-3
        3rd 106
        4th 105-6, 119

5th 115
6th 158, 159
7th 158, 175, 177, 221, 251
8th 158, 217, 219, 221, 228
9th 158, 166, 180, *211*, 251
Field regiments
2/4th *238*
2/6th Armoured *342*
Independent companies
2/2nd 232-6, *234, 235*, 289, 291, 292, 294
2/4th 236
2/5th 237, *313*
Light Horse regiments 32, 33, 83-4, 87
2nd 86
4th 88
5th 92
7th 92
9th 40
10th 40
12th 88, 89
Royal Australian Regiment
1st *375*, 399
2nd 375
3rd 372, 374-6, 377-8, *379*, 381
5th 400
5/7th 289-91
6th 400, 406
Australian Army Training Team Vietnam (AATTV) 398
Australian Corps 104, 106, 125-6
Australian Flying Corps No. 1 Squadron 92
Australian Historical Mission 41, 58
Australian New Guinea Administration Unit (ANGAU) 323, 343
Australian War Memorial (Canberra) 9-10
Hall of Memory *10*
Roll of Honour 9
website 10-11

B
B17 flying fortress *365*
Badcoe, *Major* Peter 398, 409
Bain, *Sergeant* Duncan 51
Baker, Bill 56
Baldwin, *Trooper* Alfred *61*
Balibo (East Timor) *287*, 289, *301*
Balikpapan (Borneo) 251, 256-60, 295
Ball, *Corporal* Merv *335*
Balmer, *Wing Commander* Sam *338*
Bao Dai, *Emperor of Annam* 396-7
Bao Ninh 8
Bapaume (France) *137*

Barclay, *Private* J. E. 66
Bardia (Libya) 158-9, 166
Bastiaan, Ross *14, 15*
Bataan (destroyer) *372*
Bean, Charles Edwin Woodrow 2, 3-4, 22, 30-1, 41, 58
Beatham, *Private* Robert 144
Beattie, Rod 279-81
Beazley, *Trooper* Jack 90-1, 97
Beersheba *83, 86*, 90, 96
map *85*
Beersheba War Cemetery *91*
Beirut 177, 178, 213-4
Bellenglise (France) *138*
Bennett, *General* Gordon 218-19, 224, 228, 273
Benson, *Father* James 318-19
Bertha (gun) *126*, 131
Betano (Timor) 236, *301*
Bethel, *Private* Robert 64
Bhumibol Adyulyadej, *King of Thailand* 276
Bien Hoa (Vietnam) 399
Big Wau Creek (New Guinea) *317*
Birdwood, *General* William 27, 35, *127*
Birkenau Concentration Camp (Poland) 263
Birks, *Second Lieutenant* Frederick 135
Black Cat Track (New Guinea) *344*
Blackburn, *Lieutenant* Arthur 121
Blamey, *Field Marshal Sir* Thomas 2, 158, 200, *201*, 250, 311, 326, 359
Bolitho, *Private* H. *388*
Bomford, Lance *231*
Borell, *Lieutenant* Albert 125
Borneo 223, 248-62
death marches 252-3
map *249*
travel 295
Botterill, Keith 252, 253
Bou (New Guinea) *343*
Bougainville 343
Bowles, Leslie *10*
Braddon, Russell 229
Brasell, *Lieutenant* J. S. 92
Braund, *Lieutenant Colonel* George 53, 67
Breavington, *Corporal* R. E. 6
Brewer, *Lieutenant* 325
Brigade Hill (Kokoda Track) *326, 327*, 328, 330, 351-2
Brill, *Private* John 206
British Army
7th Armoured Brigade 159
8th Army 180, 182, 183
42nd Division 31

420

60th Division 91
61st Division 110, 113
Gloucestershire Regiment ('Glosters') 375, 386, 387
Kings Ows Scottish Borderers ('KOSBY'S) 378, 381
Bronzewing (ketch) 333, 336
Brown, Dixon 237
Brown, *Lieutenant* Don 242
Brown, *Captain* Roy 125
Brown, *Corporal* Walter 125
Brune, Peter 330, 339, 342
Brunei 256
Bryant, *Private* Jim 25
Buie, *Private* Robert 127
Buissy (France) 139
Bulldog Track (New Guinea) 314, 316
Bullecourt (France) 106, 122-3, 138
Bulolo River Valley (New Guinea) 307
Buna (New Guinea) 318, 341-2
Burma 299
    map 244
    travel 300
Burma-Thai Railway *see* Thai-Burma Railway
Burnet, *Sir* John 42
Burns, *Corporal* James 66
Burton, *Corporal* Alexander 38, 60
Buruma, Ian 263
Busan (Korea) 374

C

Callinan, *Major* Bernard 234, 237
Campbell, *Colonel* 172-3
Campbell, Alexander 61
Campbell, *Lieutenant* Archie 235
Campbell, Owen 262
Canadian Army
    2nd Battalion Princess Patricia's Canadian Light Infantry 376-7
Canea (Crete) 173, 174, 192
Çanakkale 2, 20
Çanakkale campaign *see* Gallipoli campaign
Cape Helles (Gallipoli Peninsula) 20, 21, 28
    map 68
Carne, *Colonel* Phillip 387
Caro, *Colonel* Albert 329
Carter, Ron ('Nick') 241
Carver, Robert Charles 415
Castleton, *Sergeant* Claud 121-2
Cater, *Commander* Edward 53
cemeteries 8-9, 12
    see also Office of Australian War Graves

Australia
    Adelaide River Civil Cemetery (Northern Territory) 264
    Adelaide River War Cemetery (Northern Territory) 13, 262, 264
    Atherton War Cemetery 13
    Centennial Park War Cemetery and Cremation Memorial (South Australia) 13
    Cowra Australian War Cemetery 13
    German Military Cemetery (Tatura) 13
    Hobart War Cemetery and Tasmanian Cremation Memorial 13
    Japanese War Cemetery (Cowra) 13
    Perth War Cemetery 13
    Springvale War Cemetery (Melbourne) 13
    Sydney War Cemetery (Rookwood) 12-13
Gallipoli Peninsula 41, 43
    Ari Burnu Cemetery 42, 49, 51
    Azmak Cemetery 73, 74
    Baby 700 Cemetery 51, 53
    Beach Cemetery 53-4
    Canterbury Cemetery 54
    Chunuk Bair Cemetery 54-5
    Courtney's and Steel's Post Cemetery 55-6
    Embarkation Pier Cemetery 56
    Farm Cemetery 57
    4th Battalion Parade Ground Cemetery 5, 57
    French National Cemetery and Memorial 72
    Green Hill Cemetery 75
    Hill 60 Cemetery 75
    Johnston's Jolly Cemetery 59
    Lala Baba Cemetery 76
    Lancashire Landing Cemetery 69
    Lone Pine Cemetery 37, 59-60
    Nek Cemetery 60-1
    New Zealand No. 2 Outpost Cemetery 62
    No. 2 Outpost Cemetery 61-2
    Pink Farm Cemetery 69-70
    Plugge's Plateau Cemetery 62-3
    Quinn's Post Cemetery 63-4
    Redoubt Cemetery 70
    7th Field Ambulance Cemetery 64
    Shell Green Cemetery 64-5
    Shrapnel Valley Cemetery 22, 43, 65-6
    Skew Bridge Cemetery 70-1
    Twelve Tree Copse Cemetery 71
    V Beach Cemetery 72, 74
    Walker's Ridge Cemetery 66-7
Greece
    German Military Cemetery (Malame) 195
    Phaleron War Cemetery (Athens) 191, 193-4, 213

Suda Bay War Cemetery (Crete) 191, 196, 213
Korea
    United Nations Memorial Cemetery (Busan) 23, 384, *388*, 392
Lebanon
    Beirut War Cemetery 198-9
    Sidon War Cemetery 201-3
New Guinea
    Bomana Cemetery 353
    Port Moresby (Bomana) War Cemetery 362
North Africa
    Alexandria (Chatby) Military Cemetery 187
    Alexandria (Hadra) War Memorial Cemetery 187
    Benghazi War Cemetery 206
    Cairo War Memorial Cemetery 187
    El Alamein Italian Military Shrine 190-1
    El Alamein War Cemetery 187-8
    French Cemetery (Tobruk) 208
    German Memorial and Cemetery (Tobruk) 208
    Halfaya Sollum War Cemetery 191
    Knightsbridge War Cemetery (Acroma) *11*, 207-8
    New British Protestant Cemetery (Cairo) 187
    Tobruk War Cemetery 204, 207
    Tripoli Military Cemetery 210
    Tripoli War Cemetery 210
Palestine
    Beersheba War Cemetery 97
    Gaza War Cemetery 99
    Jerusalem War Cemetery 98
South-East Asia
    Ambon War Cemetery 292
    Chungkai War Cemetery (Kanchanaburi) 283-5
    Kanchanaburi War Cemetery (Thailand) *284*, 285
    Kranji Military Cemetery (Singapore) 272
    Kranji War Cemetery (Singapore) *228*, 271, 272, 298
    Labuan War Cemetery (Borneo) 11-12, 261, 296
    Lae War Cemetery 359
    Rabaul (Bita Paka) War Cemetery 363
    Rangoon War Cemetery 282
    Taukkyan War Cemetery (Burma) 282
    Thanbyuzayat War Cemetery 278, 282, 300
Syria
    Aleppo War Cemetery 99
    Damascus War Cemetery 100
Vietnam
    Dai Do War Cemetery 409-10
    Ho Chi Minh Mausoleum (Hanoi) *401*, 410
Western Front 108
    Adelaide Cemetery (Villers Bretonneux) 151-2
    AIF Burial Ground, Grass Lane (Flers) 139
    Bapaume Australian Cemetery 137
    Buttes New British Cemetery (Zonnebeke) 136
    Heath Cemetery (Harbonnières) 144
    Hem Farm Military Cemetery (Mont St Quentin) 144
    Hill 60 Cemetery (Belgium) *40*
    Le Trou Aid Post Cemetery (Fromelles) 143
    Polygon Wood Cemetery (Zonnebeke) 137
    Queant Road Cemetery (Buissy) 139
    Rue David Cemetery (Fleurbaix) 143
    Rue-du-Bois Military Cemetery (Fromelles) 142
    Rue Petillon Cemetery (Fromelles) 143
    Sailly-sur-la-Lys (France) 142
    Somme 1916 Museum (Albert) 137
    Tyne Cot Cemetery (Passchendaele) 134
    VC Corner Australian Cemetery (Fromelles) *108*, 141-2
    Villers Bretonneux Military Cemetery (France) *103*, 151
Chalk, *Lieutenant* 323
Challen, *Major* 330
Challis, *Sergeant* George 143
Chamberlain, Neville 157
Chanak kale *see* Çanakkale
Changi (Singapore) 228-9
    prison camp 5-6, 221, 229
Chapman, *Colonel* A. E. 39
Chauvel, *General Sir* Harry 32, 83, 84, 88-9, 93, 95, 199-200
Cherry, *Captain* Percy 139
Chinese in Korean War 374
Chowne, *Lieutenant* Albert 357
Chunuk Bair 21, 22, 33, 36, 47-8
Churchill, Winston 19
Clarke, *Lieutenant Colonel* Lancelot 53
Cleary, *Gunner* Albert 252, 262
Clements, *Lieutenant* 328-9
Coates, *General* John 178
Coley, *Private* Rex 90, 91, 97
Commonwealth War Graves Commission 6, 11-12, 409
    see also Imperial War Graves Commission
conscription 399, 401
Cooke, *Private* Thomas 121-2
Coral Sea Battle 307
Corlett, Peter 141
Cosgrove, *General* Peter 288
Cotter, *Trooper* Albert ('Tibby') 89, 90, 97

Index

Courtney, *Lieutenant Colonel* R. E. 56
Creforce 159-60
Crete 159-61, 192, 213
    map 172
Crocker, *Captain* Robert 70
Croker, *Private* James 37
Curtin, John 250
Curtis, *Lieutenant* Phillip 387
Cutler, *Lieutenant Sir* Roden 178-80
Cuttle, *Second Lieutenant* Robin 128
Cyrene (Libya) 204

D

Dadswell, Lyndon 200
Dalziel, *Private* Harry 143-4
Damascus 93-5, 96, 163, 177
Damour (Lebanon) 177
Darwin 262, 296
    bombing 238, 239-42
Daunt, *Private* James 385
Davidson, *Second Lieutenant* E. S. 151
Davidson, Frank Dalby 88
Dawa Dawa (Milne Bay) 360-1
DC3 (Dakota) aeroplanes 310
De Gaulle, *General* Charles 396
Delebarre, Martial 129, 140
Dentz, *General* 178
Department of Veterans' Affairs 13
Derrick, *Lieutenant* Thomas Currie ('Diver') 11, 12, 251, 253-5, 255
Desert Mounted Corps 84
Dicker, 'Snow' 240-1
Diem, Ngo Bien 397-8
Dien Bien Phu (Vietnam) 397
Dili (Timor) 289
    airfield 233-4
Dillon, *Corporal* Frank 183
Dimitrakis, Yorgo 174
Don Hotel (Darwin) 238
Donovan, *Lance Corporal* John 237
Dora Observatory (South Korea) 385
Doughty-Wylie, *Lieutenant Colonel* Charles 72
Doyle, *Lance Corporal* Cyril 234-5
Dunlop, *Lieutenant Colonel Sir* Edward ('Weary') 245, 248, 281, 283, 299
Dunstan, *Corporal* William 36, 38
Durack, *Private* Thomas 75
Durkin, *Private* John 247

E

East Timor 256
    travel 300-1
Eastern Mediterranean 23
Eastforce 224
Eather, *Brigadier* Ken 360
Edmondson, *Corporal* Jack 169-71, *170*, 205
Efogi (Kokoda Track) 350-1
Egypt 186-7
    travel 212
Egyptian Expeditionary Force 83-4
Eichelberger, *Lieutenant General* Robert 341
El Alamein 164, 180-3, 212
    map 181
Elevala (boat) 333-4, 336
Elliott, *Lieutenant Colonel* Harold ('Pompey') 35, 37, 110, 113-15
Eloda, Jessie 345, 347, 350, 351, 354, 356
Eora Creek (Kokoda Track) 328
Ewan, Robert (Robert Ewan Oliver) 292

F

F Force 245, 247
Fackerell, *Private* Les 13
Fearnside, Geoffrey 165
Fernihough, 'Blue' 255
Feronza, Ermino Cyrillo 189
Ferrier, *Corporal* Sutton Henry ('Syd') 40
Fisher, David John Elkington 415
Fisherman's Hut 27
Fitzgerald, *Brigadier* P. D. 88
Flers (France) 139
Fogarty, *Gunner* Ray 242
Fort Siloso (Singapore) 228
Foss, *Captain* Maitland 145
Founi, Hussein 214
Fraser, *Second Lieutenant* Simon 141
Fraser, *Sergeant* Tom 242
Free French Army 175, 178, 396
Freeman, *Lieutenant* Neil 115
French, *Corporal* John 331, 335, 362
French Indochina 395
Fretilin 287
Freyburg, *General* Bernard 160
Froissy 140
Fromelles (France) 109-18, *110*, *112*, *114*, 140-3
    map 111
Fukuyei, *General* Shimpei 270
fuzzy-wuzzy angels 320-1

G

Gabatepe (Gallipoli Peninsula), 20
Gaby, *Lieutenant* Alfred 125, 144
Gaddafi, *Colonel* Muammar 203
Gale, *Private* V. L. 6

Galleghan, *Colonel* Frederick Gallagher ('Black Jack') 6, 229
Gallipoli campaign (1915) 3, 19-82
  casualties 22
Gallipoli Peninsula 3-4, 41-8
  maps 24, 68
  travel 79-81
Garland, *Lieutenant* 325
Gartside, *Colonel* Robert 30, 70
Gaza, battles of 84, 89-90
Gemas (Malaya) 225
Gemenceh River (Malaya) 225, 227
Gerke, *Major* Jack 380
German Army
  Africa Corps 163, 180, 190
  6th Bavarian Reserve Division 110
Giap, *General* Vo Nguyen 397, 411
Gili Gili (Milne Bay) 312, 332
Gillespie, John Francis 415
Gillison, *Battalion Chaplain* Andrew 57
Gillson, Peter Raymond 415
Goilani River (New Guinea) 331, 335
Goldie River (Kokoda Track) 356
Gona (New Guinea) 318, 339
  All Souls' Mission Station 318
Gordon, Harry 384-5
Gorton, John 401
Grant, *Brigadier* William 88
Gratwick, *Private* Percy 183, 189
Grave Registration Unit 41
Greater East Asian Co-Prosperity Sphere 395-6
Greece 159, 161, 191, 213
  partisans 161
Guadalcanal (Solomon Islands) 308
Gullett, Henry Baynton Somer ('Harry') 84, 86
Gurney, *Squadron Leader* Bob 361
Gurney, *Private* Stan 180, 189
Gurney Airfield 332, 361
Gusmao, Xanana 287-8

H

Hackney, *Lieutenant* Ben 227, 270
Haking, *Lieutenant General* ('Butcher') 109
Halliday, *Private* Norm 100
Hamada, *General* 270
Hamann, *Corporal* Alfred 196
Hamel (France) 106, 143-4
Hamesh, Mohammed 11
Hamilton, *General Sir* Ian 20, 27, 30, 35
Harbonnières (France) 144-5
Hatzidakis, George 192
Hayes, *Private* Keith 235

Hayman, May 318-19
Hejaz railway 91-2
Helles *see* Cape Helles
Hellfire Pass (Thailand) 245, 246-7, 277, 281, 283, 299
  map 244
Heraklion (Crete) 160
Herbert, Michael Patrick John 415
Hewett, *Corporal* Frank 64
Hill 60 (Gallipoli Peninsula) 38-40, 135
Hill 3039 (Jebel Amman) 92
Hintok River Camp 245, 279, 280
Hinz, *Private* Arthur 335
Hirohito, *Emperor of Japan* 223, 253
Hitler, *Corporal* Adolf 118
Ho Chi Minh 396-7
Ho Chi Minh City 408
Ho Chi Minh Trail 397
Hoi (Kokoda Track) 346
Holton, *Private* C. L. 60
Hombrum's Bluff (New Guinea) 308
Honner, *Colonel* Ralph 327, 339, 353
Hore, *Captain* George 34
The Horseshoe (Vietnam) 400
Horta, Jose Ramos 287
Houston (cruiser) 239
Howell, *Corporal* George ('Snowy') 123
Howell, *Trooper* Ray 61
Hudson, *Gunner* Wilbert Thomas ('Darko') 242
Hué (Vietnam) 400-1
Huggins, *Captain* Meredith M. 364
Hughes, *Lieutenant* Cyril 41
Hunter Weston, *Lieutenant General* Aylmer *see* Weston, *Lieutenant General* Aylmer Hunter
Hutchinson, *Major* Arthur 113-4
Hutchinson, *Corporal* Bill 97
Hutchinson, *Private* C. 187
Hutchinson, *Private* G. A. 6-7
Hutchinson, *Bombadier* Jack 309

I

Idris, *King of Libya* 203
Ieper *see* Ypres
Imita Ridge (Kokoda Track) 355
Imjin River (Korea) 374
Imperial Palace (Hué) 400
Imperial War Graves Commission 41
  see also Commonwealth War Graves Commission
International Force for East Timor (INTERFET) 288
Israel 186-7
  travel 101-2
Isurava (Kokoda Track) 325-7, 346

J

Jacka, *Captain* Albert 12, 56, 119, 121, 122
Jackson, *Squadron Leader* Les 338
Jager, *Gunner* Charles 173-5, 193
Janissary Band 78
Jayapura (New Guinea) 311
Jeffrey, *Major General* Michael 415
Jeffries, *Captain* Clarence 134-5
Johnson, *Lieutenant* 353
Johnson, *Sergeant* Jack 178
Johnson, Lyndon 401
Johnston, *Brigadier General* George 59
Johore Strait 221
Jordan 97
Joynt, *Lieutenant* William Donovan 130
Judell, *Quartermaster Sergeant* Elias 67

K

Kacmaz, Huseyein 66
Kagi (Kokoda Track) 349
Kalimantan (Borneo) 256, 295
Kanchanaburi (Thailand) 281, 283
    map 284
Kanga Force 307, 308, 314
Kapyong Valley (Korea) 376-7
Kay, *Colonel* W. E. 193-4
Keiran, *Lieutenant* Richard 69
Kemal, Mustafa 4-5, 23, 26, 35-6, 47-8, 78, 86, 99
    statue (Chunuk Bair) 47, 55
Kempetai (Japanese occupation police) 269, 270
Kenna, *Private* Edward 357
Kenneally, John ('Paddy') 231
Keyser, *Lance Corporal* Leonard 37-8
Khallassa (Palestine) 90
Khe San (Vietnam) 401-2
Kibby, *Sergeant* William Henry ('Bill') 182-3, 189
Kienzle, Bert 310, 320-1, 347
Kingsbury, *Private* Bruce 326-7, 346, 358
Kirkpatrick, John Simpson 42, 52
Kittyhawks (aeroplanes) 338
Knight, Pat (William Patrick Cotter) 292
Knyvett, *Corporal* Hugh 114-15
Koeabule (KB) Mission (Milne Bay) 334
Kokoda (New Guinea) 320, *321*
    airfield *308*
Kokoda Track 307-8, 310-11, 320-30, 323, 324, 339, 342, 344-56
    map 322
    tourism 367, 369
Konyu (Thailand) 243
Korea 371-94
    demilitarised zone (DMZ) 385-6, 389, *391*, *392*
    maps 373
    partitioning 372
    see also South Korea
Kota Bharu (Malaysia) 297
Kota Kinabalu (Sabah) 296
Krac des Chevaliers (Syria) *197*
Krait (boat) 229-30
Kriloff, Herb 240
Krithia (Gallipoli Peninsula) 20, 22, 28-31, *28*, *30*
Kumkale (Turkey) 20
Kupang (Timor) 233-4
Kwae Noi Valley Lookout (Thailand) 281, 283
Kwae River (Thailand) *217*, *246*, *247*
Kwato Mission (New Guinea) 336-7
Kwok, Albert 260

L

Lady Be Good (aeroplane) 209
La France, *Private* Merv 201-3
La France, *Private* Ray 201-3
Lalor, *Captain* Joseph Peter 27, 53, 61
Lambert, George 33-4, 41, 89
Langridge, *Captain* 'Lefty' 330
Lataille, Jean 138
Latham, *Flying Officer* T. O. 258
Launumu (Kokoda Track) 350
Lavarack, *Major General* John D. 162, 175, 177
Lawrence, Thomas Edward 84, 89, 91, 95, 99, 199
Leak, *Private* John 121
Lebanon 161-2, 197-8
    travel 213-4
Leckie, *Lieutenant* George 128
Lee, *Private* D. J. D. 388
Leese, *Lieutenant General* Oliver 183
Legg, Frank 255
Leggatt, *Lieutenant Colonel* William 233-4
Lenoy, *Sergeant* S. K. L. 388
Lester, Lawrence 3
Letaille, Jean 129
Leva, Iana 345, 356
Levi, *Captain* Keith 71
Levi, Primo 263
Libya 203-4
    travel 214-5
Livanos, Dimitri 175
Livingstone, *Lieutenant* John D. 267
Lockwood, Douglas 241
Lone Pine (Gallipoli Peninsula) 21, 27, 35-8, *36*
Long Hai Hills (Vietnam) 396
Long Phuoc (Vietnam) 403-4
Long Tan (Vietnam) 7, 8, 400, 404, 406-7
Lord Haw Haw 163

Loveless, *Signaller* Joe 237
Ludendorff, *General* Erich 125

M
McAdam, *Sergeant* J. B. 316
McAllister, *Private* John 42
MacArthur, *General* Douglas 221, 222-3, 250, 268, 295, 306, 330, 374-5
Macarthur Onslow, *Major General* George 65
McCallum, Charlie 330
McCarthy, Dudley 341
McCarthy, John 260
McCay, *Lieutenant General* James Whiteside 30-1, 117
McCrae, *Major* Geoffrey 142
McCrae, John 132
McFadzean, *Private* Jim 378, 380-1
McGavin, *Lieutenant* 328-9
McGee, *Sergeant* Lewis 134-5
McGrath, *Father* John 239
Mackay, *General Sir* Iven 158
Mackell, *Lieutenant* Austin 169-71
McKenzie, *Sergeant* Jim 333
MacLaurin, *Colonel* Henry 58
McNamara, Robert 411
Mactier, *Private* Robert 144-5
Madden, *Private* Horace ('Slim') 382
Maguli Range (New Guinea) 355
Mahathir Mohammed 269
Mahyiddeen, *Tengku* Mahmood 270
Maida, *General* 261
Malame (Crete) 160, 173
  airfield 172, 195
Malaya 224, 269
  map 226
Malaysia 297
Mambare River (New Guinea) 311
Manders, *Colonel* Neville 62
Marshall, *Colonel* Norman 150
Martin, Bill 237
Martin, *Private* Tom 183
Maryang San (Korea) 371, 375, 376, 378, 380-1, 391
Matthews, *Captain* Lionel 248
Maubisse (Timor) 232
Maygar, *Lieutenant Colonel* Harry 97
Mehmet, *Sergeant* 61
memorials 14, 15, 129
  Australia
    Australian Vietnam Forces National Memorial (Canberra) 415
    Batchelor Battle of Australia Memorial (Northern Territory) 268
    Bicentennial Park (Darwin) 264-5
    Bowral Vietnam Memorial 415
    Cenotaph (Darwin) 264-5
    Darwin Harbour oil storage tunnels 266
    Light Horse Monument (Albany, Western Australia) 32
    Northern Territory Garden of Remembrance (Darwin) 265
    Northern Territory Memorial to the Missing (Adelaide River) 264
    Northern Territory Parliament House (Darwin) 265-6
    Rats of Tobruk Memorial (Canberra) 211
    USS Peary Memorial (Darwin) 265
    Vietnam Memorial Pavilion (Perth) 415
    Vietnam War Memorial (Dandenong) 404, 415, 417
    Wartime Airstrips (Northern Territory) 267-8
  Gallipoli Peninsula
    Anzac Cove Marker 54
    Çanakkale Martyrs Memorial 67, 68, 69
    Chunuk Bair Memorial 41, 42
    Dardanelles inscriptions 77-8
    Helles Memorial to the Missing 41, 72, 74
    Hill 60 (New Zealand) Memorial 75-6
    Hill 971 Marker 58
    Lone Pine Memorial 41, 43, 60
    Mustafa Kemal Monolith (Ari Burnu) 54
    New Zealand National Memorial (Chunuk Bair) 55
    Sergeant Mehmet Cavus Memorial Tomb 60-1
    Turkish 57th Infantry Regiment Memorial Park 66
    Turkish Monolith (Anzac Cove) 5-4
    Turkish Soldiers Memorial 55
    Twelve Tree Copse Memorial 41, 71-2
  Greece
    Athens Memorial to the Missing 194
    Hellenic-Australian Memorial Park (Rethymno) 195
    Monument of National Resistance (Heraklion) 194
    Priveli Memorial 195
    Stavromenos Memorial 195-6
  Korea
    3RAR Memorial (Kapyong) 381, 389
    3rd Infiltration Tunnel 386
    38th Parallel Memorial 374
    Australian Memorial (Busan) 385
    Australian Memorial (Kapyong) 388, 389
    Castle Hill (Jeokseong) 386, 387
    Commonwealth Memorial (Busan) 385
    Commonwealth Memorial (Kapyong) 387, 389

Dorasan Station (South Korea) 386, 393
Gloucester Valley Monument (Jeokseong) 386
Main Gate (Busan) 385
Memorial Service Hall (Busan) 385
New Zealand Memorial (Kapyong) 389
Princess Patricia Canadian Light Infantry Memorial (Kapyong) 389
Taepung Observatory (South Vietnam) 378, 380, 390-1
Two Brothers Memorial (Seoul) 383
United Nations Memorial (Busan) 384
War Memorial of Korea (Seoul) 389-90

Lebanon
Inscriptions at Dog River (Nahr al Kalb) 199-200

New Guinea
AIF Memorial (Lae) 359
AIF Memorial (Popondetta) 361
American Memorial (Sanananda) 364
Australia Rermembers Memorial (Gona) 357
Brigade Hill Memorial 358
Isurava Memorial 357-8
Japanese Monument (Sanananda) 364
Kokoda Memorial 357
Kokoda Memorial Arch (Owers' Corner) 358
Kokoda Track memorials 358
Lae Memorial 359
Lae Victory Plaque 359
Memorial to the Papuan Carriers (Kokoda) 357
Milne Bay Memorial 361
One Strip Cairn (Milne Bay) 361
Port Moresby Memorial 362
Rabaul Memorial 363
Rabaul 1942-45 Memorial 363
Sugeri Memorial 365
Surrender Memorial (Cape Wom) 357
39th Battalion Memorial (Kokoda) 357
Three (Turnbull) Strip Plaque (Milne Bay) 361
Wau Battle Exploit Memorial 365

North Africa
Australian Memorial (Tobruk) 207
Australian 9th Division Memorial (El Alamein) 188, 189
Bardia Murals 206
Cremation Memorial (El Alamein) 188
El Alamein German Memorial 189-90
El Alamein Memorial 188-9
Fig Tree (Tobruk) 209
South African Memorial (El Alamein) 188

Palestine
Abraham's Well (Beersheba) 98
Allenby Monument (Beersheba) 98
Anzac Memorial (Beersheba) 98
Turkish Memorial (Beersheba) 96

South-East Asia
Australian Battle Exploit Memorial (Labuan) 261
Balibo Flag House (East Timor) 292-3
Battle Box (Singapore) 273
Bridge over the River Kwai (Thailand) 284, 285-6, 302
Changi Murals (Singapore) 274
Chinese Memorial (Singapore) 272
Fatunaba Memorial Pool (Dili) 293-4
Hellfire Pass Memorial (Thailand) 277, 281, 282-3, 298
Japanese Memorial Stone (Kota Bharu) 271
Japanese Memorial Stone (Labuan) 261
Japanese Memorial to All War Dead (Kokoda) 357
John French VC Memorial (Milne Bay) 361
Johore Battery (Singapore) 273
Labuan Memorial to the Missing 261
Malaysian Memorial (Gemenceh River) 270
Memorial Garden (Kundasang) 260
Memorial to the Victims of the Second World War (Kota Bharu) 270, 271
Myanmar Thailand Japanese Death Railway Memorial (Thanbyuzayat) 282, 298
Pentagas War Memorial (Kota Kinabalu) 260
Presidential Palace (Hanoi) 410
Ranau Memorial (Sabah) 262
Rangoon Memorial 282
Royal Australian Regiment Memorial (Balibo) 293
Sandakan Memorial Park 262, 296
Second World War Locomotive (Nam Tok) 286
7th Division Memorials (Balikpapan) 259, 260
Singapore Cenotaph 272-3
Singapore Civil Hospital Grave Memorial 272
Singapore Cremation Memorial 272
Singapore Memorial 272
Three Pagodas Pass (Thailand) 286

Syria
Baron Hotel (Aleppo) 99-100
Cavalry Memorial (Aleppo) 99

Vietnam
Hoa Long School 408
The Horseshoe (Long Tan) 414
House 54 (Hanoi) 410, 411
House on Stilts (Hanoi) 410, 411
Long Phuoc tunnels 413
Long Tan Memorial 413-4
Minh Dam Secret Zone 414

Western Front
  Australian Corps Memorial Park (Hamel) 143
  Australian Memorial (Fromelles) 140-1
  Australian National Memorial (Bullecourt) 138
  Australian National Memorial (Villers Bretonneux) 148-51, *149*, *150*
  Australian Plaque (Amiens) *129*
  British Memorial to the Missing (Thiepval) 147
  Buttes New British Cemetery (New Zealand) Memorial (Zonnebeke) 136-7
  Canadian National Vimy Memorial 152
  5th Division Memorial (Zonnebeke) 136
  1st Division Memorial (Pozières) 146
  4th Division Memorial (Bellenglise) 138
  Great Cross (Fromelles) 142
  Hill 60 Memorial (Zillebeke) 135
  Menin Gate Memorial (Ypres) 132, 134
  Mouquet Farm Memorial (Pozières) 146
  2nd Division Memorial (Mont St Quentin) 144
  Slouch Hat Memorial (Bullecourt) 138
  Tank Corps Memorial (Pozières) 145-6
  Tyne Cot Memorial (Passchendaele) 135
  Villers Bretonneux marker *131*
  Windmill 2nd Division Memorial (Pozières) 145
Menari (Kokoda Track) 353
Menzies, *Sir* Robert 157-8, 399
Merdjayoun (Lebanon) 175, 177, 179
Mesudiye Gun 51, 53
Midway Battle 307
Miell, *Lieutenant Colonel* Albert 51
Miles, *Sergeant* William ('Billy') 115-17
Mills, *Major* John Brier 70
Mills, *Doctor* Roy 229, 247
Milne Bay 308, 310, 330, 332-5, 337-8, 344, 360, 368
  airstrips 338-9, *338*
  map 331
Monash, *General Sir* John 39, 103-4, 106, 125, *126*, 143
Monks, *Staff Sergeant* 31
Mont St Quentin (France) 144-5
Montevideo Maru (ship) 363-4
Montgomery, *Field Marshal Lord* Bernard 164
monuments *see* memorials
Moon, *Lieutenant* Rupert 123
Moorehead, Alan 159
Moorehead, Frank 65
Morris, *Private* Tom 247
Morshead, *General Sir* Leslie 25, 163, 166, 168
Mortimer, *Captain* Ken 116
Muar River (Thailand) *218*
Mubarak, Hosni 187

Mubo (New Guinea) 313, 317
Murdoch, *Major* Alex 117
Murdoch, *Sir* Keith 314
Murray, *Captain* 113
Murray, *General Sir* Archibald 84
museums
  Australia
    Australian Hellenic Memorial (Canberra) 196
    Australian War Memorial (Canberra) 152, 268
    East Cape Military Museum (Darwin) 240, 266
    East Point Military Museum (Darwin) 262, 266
  Gallipoli Peninsula
    Cemenlik/*Nusret* Museum 76
    Gabatepe Museum 67
    Istanbul Military Museum 78
  Greece
    George Hatzidakis War Museum (Askifou) 192, 194
  Korea
    Exhibition Hall (Busan) 385
  New Guinea
    Bert Kienzle Memorial Museum (Kokoda) 357
    Port Moresby War Museum 362
  North Africa
    Al Watany Museum (Tobruk) 208-9
    Derna Museum (Libya) 206
    El Alamein Military Museum 191
    International Military Museum (Tobruk) 209
  Palestine
    First World War Museum (Beersheba) 96, 98
  South-East Asia
    Changi Museum 225, 274, 298
    Fort Siloso (Singapore) 275
    Images of Singapore 275
    JEATH Museum (Kanchanaburi) 286
    Kelantan War Museum (Kota Bharu) 270
    Reflections at Bukit Chandu (Singapore) 274
    Thailand-Burma Railway Centre (Kanchanaburi) 279, 284, 285
    War Museum at the Bridge (Kanchanaburi) 286
  Vietnam
    Dong Nai Museum (Bien Hoa City) 409
    Ho Chi Minh Museum (Hanoi) 410-11
    Ho Chi Minh Museum (Ho Chi Minh City) 413
    Khe Sanh Museum 416
    Long Phuoc Museum 413
    Provincial Museum - Bao Tang Thuan (Hué) 413
    War Remnants Museum (Ho Chi Minh City) 411-2

Western Front
    Bullecourt Museum 138
    Fromelles Museum 140
    Historial de la Grande Guerre (Péronne) 146-7
    Hooge Crater Museum (Ypres) 135
    In Flanders Fields Museum (Ypres) 132
    Memorial Museum (Passchendaele) 136
    Museum of Military and Industrial Railways (Froissy) 140
    Thiepval Visitor Centre 147-8
Myanmar *see* Burma
Myola (Kokoda Track) 348-9

N
Nahr al Kalb (Lebanon) 2
Nasser, *Colonel* Gamal 186
National Liberation Front 400, 403
    see also Vietcong
national service 399, 401
Nauro (Kokoda Track) 353-5, 367
Neate, *Corporal* Bill 340
The Nek 21, 27-8, 31-5, 33
New Guinea 305-70
    maps 306, 315, 340
    see also Papua New Guinea
New Zealand Army
    16th Field Regiment 377
    28th Maori Battalion 173
    Auckland Infantry Battalion 51
    Infantry Brigade 28-9, 31
Nishimura, *General* 227
Nixon, Richard 401
Noack, *Private* Erroll 7, 400
Norman, *Lance Corporal* Herbert 59
North, *Major* John 4
North Africa 167
North Beach (Gallipoli Peninsula) 27
Nui Dat (Vietnam) 7-8, 399-400, 403, 404
Nui Dat 2 (Vietnam) 406, 407
Nusret (mine-layer) 76-7
Nye, *Captain* Claude 330

O
Oakes, Colin St Clair 285
OBOE operations 250-1
Ocean Beach *see* North Beach (Gallipoli Peninsula)
Office of Australian War Graves 12
Olden, *Lieutenant Colonel* 95
O'Meara, *Private* Martin 146
Onan, Necmettin Hahl 77-8
One Strip (Milne Bay) *see* Gurney Airfield
Operation Enoggera 404
Operation Jaywick 229-30
Osiri (boat) 336-7
Ottoman Empire 83
Owen, *Colonel* W. T. ('Bill') 323-5, 345
Owen Stanley Ranges 320, 322, 345, 356
Owers' Corner (Kokoda Track) 356

P
Pack of Cards bridge (Thailand) 245, 280, 281, 283
Palestine 83-102, 162
    cemeteries 42
    map 85
Panmunjeom 389, 393
Papua New Guinea 343-4
    travel 366-9
Parer, Damien 233, 236-7, 314, 316, 347, 353
    Men of Timor (film) 237
Parker, Richard Harold John 415
Parker, *Lance Corporal* Walter 56
Parkin, Ray 245-6, 279-80, 283
Parkinson, Mavis 318-19
Parramatta (destroyer) 168
Passchendaele 134-5
Paull, Raymond 323-4, 328
Payne, *Warrant Officer* Keith 398
Pearce, *Corporal* Arthur Mueller ('Joe') 62
Pears, *Lieutenant* Laurie 380
Peary (destroyer) 239-41
Penny, Ern 61
Percival, *General* Arthur 218-9, 224-5, 228, 269, 273, 275
Péronne 146-7
Perth (China Wall) Cemetery (Zillebeke) 135
Petain, *Marshal* Henri Philippe 161-2
Phuoc Tuy Province (Vietnam) 399, 408
    map 405
Pittendrigh, *Corporal* Ronald 57
Plugge, *Colonel* Arthur 63
Plugge's Plateau 4, 5, 44, 45-7
Pockley, *Captain* 363
Polygon Wood (Belgium) 136
Popkin, *Sergeant* Cedric 127
Port Moresby 306-7
Porter, *Brigadier* Selwyn ('Bill') 251, 353
Potts, *Brigadier* Arnold 326-30, 347, 349, 352-4
Pozières 105-6, 119-22, 145-6
Pramoj, Seri 276
Preston (destroyer) *see* William B. Preston (destroyer)
Pugsley, Christopher 29
Pusan *see* Busan
Pyongyang (North Korea) 374

Q

Quilter, *Colonel* Arnold 71
Quinn, *Major* Hugh 63, 65-6
Quinn's Post (Gallipoli Peninsula) 43

R

Rabaul 306
Ramsden, *Private* Albert 333
Ranau (Borneo) 252-3, 263, *295*
Ras el Medauur (Tobruk) *157*, 163, 168
Rashid Ali 162
'Rats of Tobruk' 163, *169*, *211*
Rayak (Lebanon) 94
Redford, *Major* Thomas 67
Reidel, Hans W. 189
Retimo (Crete) 160
    airfield 171
Reynell, *Colonel* Carew 40
Reynolds, Bill 230
Richards, *Signaller* K. 237
Richthofen, *Baron* Manfred von ('Red Baron') 125, 127
Rivett, Rohan 243
Roberts, *Captain* Peter 183
Robertson, Alex 65
Robertson, *Major General Sir* Horace Clement Hugh ('Red Robbie') 357
Robertson, *Major* Sydney 53
Robinson, *Captain* Adrian 178
Robinson, *Corporal* S. A. 234
Robinvale (Victoria) 128
The Rockpile (Vietnam) 402
Roisin, Jean-Marc 130-1
Rommel, *General* Erwin 163-4
Rosenthal, *Major General* Charles 123
Royal Australian Artillery Association 266
Rush, *Trooper* Harold 33, 34
Russell's Top 26
Ruwoldt, Rex 241-2
Ruxton, Bruce 262

S

Sabah 295
Sadat, Anwar 187
Sadlier, *Lieutenant* Clifford 124
Said, *Emir* 95
Saigon *see* Ho Chi Minh City
Salamaua 313, 317, *368*
The Salient (Libya) 168, *171*, *210*
Salween River (Burma) 277
Sanananda (New Guinea) *339*, *340*, 341
Sanctuary Wood Cemetery (Zillebeke) 136

Sandakan (Sabah) 223, 252, 296
    airfield 222, 248
    prison camp 248-50, 263
Sanders, *General* Liman von 35
Saunders, *Captain* Reg 377-8
Schmidt, *Sergeant* Ernst 118
Schorn, *Lieutenant* 168
Scott, *Sergeant* Jack 339
Searle, *Lieutenant* A. H. 92
Sega, Suga 347
Seoul 374
Sergeant, *Corporal* John 237
Serong, *Colonel* Ted 398
Seven Metre Embankment (Thailand) 283
Seventh Day Adventists 346, 347, 351
Sfakia (Crete) 172-4, *192*
Shackleton, Greg 287, 292
Sheehan, *Lieutenant* Mick 257-8
Shell Green Gallipoli Peninsula) *64*, 65
Sherman, *Private* Percy 61
Shoalhaven (frigate) 372
Shout, *Captain* Alfred 60
Shrine of Remembrance (Melbourne) 13-14, *14*
Shrapnel Valley (Gallipoli Peninsula) 46
Sila (New Guinea) 336
Silver, Lynette Harvey 261, 270
Simpson, John *see* Kirkpatrick, John Simpson
Simpson, *Warrant Officer* Ray 398
Sinai *101*
Singapore 269-70, 297-8
    invasion (1942) 218-20, *220*
    map 226
Slessor, Kenneth 2, *184*, 189, 200, 332
    'Beach Burial' (poem) 184-5
    'An Inscription for Dog River' 200
Smith, *Lieutenant* Alfred 71
Smith, *Corporal* Dale 69
Smithson, *Flying Officer* J. H. 267
Smyth, *Trooper* James 100
Somare, *Sir* Michael 343
Somme River, battles of 104, 106, 119
South-East Asia 217-304
    map 219
South Korea 383
    travel 392
Sparrow Force 230, 232-5
Spencer, *Private* Don 254
The Sphinx (Gallipoli Peninsula) *1*, 26, *47*
Stanley, *Sergeant Major* Arthur 380
Stanley, *Trooper* Herb 61
Stanley, Peter 253
Stavramenos (Crete) 171-2

Index

Steel, *Major* T. H. 56
Steele, *Lieutenant* N. L. 92
Stokes, *Sergeant* Charlie 124
Strong, *Bishop* Philip 319-20
Sugarloaf (Fromelles) 110, 113, 142
Suvla Bay (Gallipoli Peninsula) 20-1
   map 73
Sydney (cruiser) 309
Symons, *Lieutenant* William 38
Syria 96, 161-2
   travel 101-2

T

Tarakan (Borneo) 253, 295
   airfield 253
Taylor, *Lance Corporal* Edwin Hutchinson 59
Tell el Saba (Palestine) 88
Templeton, *Captain* Sam ('Uncle Sam') 321, 323-4
Templeton's Crossing (Kokoda Track) 3478
Thai-Burma Railway 221-2, *222*, 243-8, 263, 276-81, *276*, 297, 298-300
   map 244
Thailand
   map 244
Thanbyuzayat (Burma) 278
   prison camp 243
Thiepval (France) 147-8
Thompson, *Lieutenant Colonel* Astley Onslow 58
Throssell, *Second Lieutenant* Hugo Vivian 39
Throssell, Ric 336
Thurlow, George 333
Timor 232-6, *232*, 287-91, *301*
   map 231
   see also East Timor
Tobruk 159, 163-9, *170*, 180, 203-4
   map 167
   'Rats of Tobruk' 163, 169, *211*
   Red Line 166
Tojo, *General* 261
Tommies Trench (Gallipoli Peninsula) 31
Tonkin, *Flying Officer* A. E. H. *210*
travel risk 16-17
Treloar, John 10
Triffit, Harry 336-7
Truman, Harry S. 375
Trumper, Victor 89
Truscott, *Squadron Leader* Keith ('Bluey') 267, 338-9
Tubb, *Lieutenant* Frederick 38, 60
Turkey 79-81
Turkish army 87
Turnbull, *Squadron Leader* Peter 338-9

U

Ua-Ule Creek (Kokoda Track) 355, 356
United Nations Mission in East Timor (UNAMET) 288
United Nations Transitional Administration in East Timor (UNTAET) 288, 300

V

Van der Post, Laurens 248
Vasey, *General* George 257, 339
Veale, *Brigadier* William Charles Douglas 233-4
Vernon, *Captain* Geoffrey ('Doc') 321, 324-5
Victoria Cross 12
Viet Minh 396-7
Vietcong 398
Vietnam 397
   map 404
   travel 416-17
Vietnam Veterans Reconstruction Group 408
Vietnam War 7, 403
   Tet offensive 400
Villers Bretonneux 104, 106-7, 123-5, 127-31, *130*, 148-52, *153*
   map 149
Voca Point (Lae) 366
Vose, Dudley 240-1
Voyager (destroyer) 236, 293
Vung Tau (Vietnam) 399

W

Waldie, John 241
Walford, *Captain* Garth 72
Walker, *Brigadier General* 66
Walker's Ridge 26-7, 47, 67
Wanire, Steven 305, 345, 347, 350, 354, 356
war memorials 16
   plaques *14*, *15*
Ward, Bert 329
Warren, *Artilleryman* Stanley 274
Waterhen (destroyer) 168
Watson, *Major* 325
Watson, Don 150
Watt, Walter 67
Wau (New Guinea) 308, 313-17
   airfield *314*, *317*
Wavell, *General* Archibald 162, 177
Webb, *Corporal* Harry 60
Wells, *Major* Richard 69
Western Front 103-56
   map 105
   travel 153-5
Westforce 218, 224

Weston, *Lieutenant General* Aylmer Hunter 20, 29-30
Wewak (New Guinea) 311
Wheatley, *Warrant Officer* Kevin 398
White, *Sergeant* John 139
White, Osmar 314, 327, 347, 354
White Mountains (Crete) *164*
Whitehead, *Brigadier* David 251
Wiedemann, *Lieutenant* Friedrich 118
Wilkinson, *Warrant Officeer* Jack 321, 324-5
William B. Preston (destroyer) 239-40
Williams, *Able Seaman* 363
Wilmot, Chester 168, 207, 327
Wilson, *Brigadier* 94-5
Wilson, *General* Henry Maitland 162
Windeyer, *Brigadier* Victor 251
Winkler, *Lieutenant* Howard 318
Winnie the War Winner (radio) 237
Wombere, *Bombadier* Fred 242
Woods, *Rev.* Maitland 86
Wootten, *Major General Sir* George Frederick 251, 261
Woolley, *Sergeant* 41
Wright, *Corporal* Fred 60
Wyman, *Trooper* Leo 67

Y

Yacopetti, *Lieutenant* Charles 381-2
Yagumo, *Admiral* Chuichi 220
Yalu River (China) 374
Yamamoto *General* 270
Yamashita, *General* 218, 275
Yokoyama, *Colonel* Yosuke 308
Ypres (Belgium) 132-4
    map 133

Z

Z Special Unit 229-30
Zillebeke (Belgium) 135-6
Zonnebeke (Belgium) 136-7